THE COMPLETE Entrepreneur

THE ONLY BOOK YOU'LL EVER NEED to Manage Risk and Build Your Business Wealth

MARK A. PETERSON, CPA, CVA

DEDICATION

To my children,
Tiffany, Courtney, Brittany, and Parker,
without whose loving attention
this book would have been written
in half the time.

All inquiries should be addressed to:
Barron's Educational Series, Inc.
250 Wireless Boulevard
Hauppauge, New York 11788

Library of Congress Catalog Card Number 95-53341

International Standard Book No. 0-8120-9716-5
Library of Congress Cataloging in Publication Data

ISBN 0-8120-9716-5

PRINTED IN THE UNITED STATES OF AMERICA

9 8 7 6 5 4 3 2

BEFORE YOU GET STARTED

This book is a bible for many entrepreneurs. For some, it is a handbook that never leaves their side. For others, it is a tool that they readily use to fix things in their business. For all, it is the equivalent of a graduate business degree.

Whether you keep it at your office, in your library, or on your nightstand, *The Complete Entrepreneur* will have a profound impact on your business. The day you finish reading this book, the way you look at business risk will never be the same.

The speed at which you build business wealth will also never be the same. That is particularly true if you take the time to reread the lessons that I have summarized for you at the end of the book. Each time you consult them, you will discover something new about business. What you discover will usually save you money. You can reinvest the money in your business or take it to the bank. The normal course of business will reliably confirm your new awareness and the lessons you have learned.

The stories in this book may be familiar to you. However, any resemblance between the individuals described in this book and entrepreneurs whom you may know is purely coincidental.

Any similarity between the lessons provided in this book and the activities in your business must be intentional. It is the only way you can be certain you will ever make your business your best investment.

ACKNOWLEDGMENTS

I am indebted to William Robert Stone for encouragement, for suggesting changes in the manuscript, and for his help with the process of transforming an idea into a published book.

My wife, Wendy Peterson, was a great source of personal support and readily accepted the additional family responsibilities that allowed me to direct my attention to this book.

Chris Peterson taught me some incredible lessons about business risk. Elliott Cushman and Lawrence Cushman taught me some invaluable lessons about running a business.

Charlie Thompson taught me how to think out of the box before anyone even knew there was a box. Phil Kotler encouraged me to test the limits of generally accepted business theories by continually challenging them, his own included. Marc Noël provided me with memorable insight, confirming through the achievement of spectacular entrepreneurial results that only integrity can make you a real leader. Steve Mazda showed me how the right blend of fairness, persistence, and dedication will allow you to prevail under any business condition.

My editor, Warren Bratter, gave new meaning to the term "seamless interface" with the kid gloves, solid recommendations, and considerable editorial skills he brought to this project.

Ric Beach, Rick Cardwell, Barbara Champion, Craig Champion, Lee Champion, John Frazzini, Tony Fyock, Kevin Hoffberg, Christopher Kemp, Phillip Koeppel, Jeffrey Luce, Glenn Martin, Steve McKinney, Amy Peterson, Guy Peterson, Loretta Peterson, Joseph Sandoval, and Peter Zekauskas read the manuscript in various stages and provided helpful critical comments.

My dad realized a few years ago that an entrepreneurial tonic was probably the best elixir a young teenager could drink. That is equally true today. I fondly remember the lessons I learned those hot Cleveland summers under the scrutiny of a stern and loving mentor.

You can search for a lifetime and find just a few good investments. When you finish reading *The Complete Entrepreneur*, you will know exactly where to look in order to find your best investment.

TABLE OF CONTENTS

Part Three
Starting Your Business

Part Five
Running Your Business

PART SEVEN
Working with Professionals

INTRODUCTION

"What is my best investment?"

I have been asked that question by company presidents, their employees, gamblers, and armchair entrepreneurs. I have been asked that question by people who have just started their businesses and by people who have owned their businesses for the last twenty years.

I wrote *The Complete Entrepreneur* to answer that question.

There are many good investments, but only one investment can be the best. The best investment you can ever make is starting your own business. You must first learn some rules before you do, but they are worth the time. These rules will help you build wealth faster than you have ever built anything before.

There are many books available on how to start a business. Some of these books want you to believe that running a business is as simple as having an idea and a bank loan application. Other books often assume that the generic business is a $500-million publicly traded company with more vice presidents than you have fingers and toes. Most of them miss the point that nearly all of the businesses in the United States are privately held, entrepreneurial operations.

The ownership of these businesses and the reasons entrepreneurs start them are both broadly mixed.

Individuals with no formal business education routinely establish successful entrepreneurial businesses. Professionals with no relevant business experience but graduate degrees that read like alphabet soup also form these enterprises.

They are founded by individuals who know little more than the fact that job security means betting on yourself and managing your own business. These days, quite a few are also started by individuals with twenty years of corporate experience, a ten-page résumé, a recent severance package, and nowhere else to go.

All of these individuals have a vested interest in this book. So do you.

The Complete Entrepreneur shows you how to build business wealth. That is where it leaves previously written books on entrepreneurship and small businesses in the dust.

I organized *The Complete Entrepreneur* the way you build wealth, from the day you dream of starting a business to the day you retire. The book guides you step-by-step through all phases of your business. It alerts you to the opportunities in working with partners, banks, customers, and employees. It shows you how to create value for your customers. It reveals the tricks of buying a business, running a business, and selling a business. It tells you how to identify risk, assess risk, take reasonable risk, avoid major risks, and lay off excess risk. It keeps you from shooting yourself in the foot. It teaches you what you need to know about taxes, how to work with professional advisors, and how to retire in style.

I encourage you to apply the specific lessons you learn in this book to your business. The techniques in this book have all been time-tested. That means they work.

You will not need to sacrifice your business, your family, your career, or your bank account in exchange for learning these lessons. I have summarized them for you. Having *The Complete Entrepreneur* on your desk is like having a CPA firm at your fingertips:

- ❑ Do you know if you have what it takes to be a successful entrepreneur? Turn to Chapter 1: Some Basic Requirements for Entrepreneurs to see if you have what it takes.
- ❑ What do you know about business risk? Read Chapter 3: How to Assess Risk to take the mystery out of recognizing business risk.
- ❑ What do you do with a partner of yours who is causing you to lose sleep? Look at Chapter 8: Do You Really Need a Partner? to discover how to make your partner work effectively.
- ❑ Are you looking for a relationship with a bank? Turn to Chapter 9: The Challenge with Banks so you understand the bank's unique role as a vendor of investment capital and how to identify hidden agendas.
- ❑ Are some customers taking a great deal of your time and returning none of it to your business? Chapter 12: The Opportunities with Customers will show you a quick way to balance your customer portfolio.
- ❑ Do you want to avoid making those routine but costly mistakes that every entrepreneur makes? Look at Chapter 16: How to Avoid Shooting Yourself in the Foot.

- ❑ Do you think you know all of the basics about running a successful business? Turn to Chapter 21: Some Finer Points of Running Your Business.
- ❑ You just got sacked by your largest customer and have every right to stick your head in the sand for a month. See Chapter 25: Living with Your Losses to learn how to show up for work the next day.
- ❑ Want to learn a few things about business law that will help you avoid costly mistakes? Read Chapter 28: Living with Contracts and Documents.
- ❑ Oops! Is that an IRS Notice of Intent to Levy? Consult Chapter 29: The Taxman Cometh to see how to file an Offer in Compromise.
- ❑ Thinking of selling your business yourself? Chapter 30: Selling Out will alert you to the risks of converting your business to cash.

The Complete Entrepreneur shows you how to make your business your best investment, year, after year, after year.

When you know how to make your business your best investment, you know how to build equity. When you know how to build equity, you know the secret of business wealth. When you apply what you learn in *The Complete Entrepreneur*, you can build wealth in any business.

Get started reading *The Complete Entrepreneur*. It is time you got serious about managing your business.

PART ONE

Recognizing the Basic Requirements

SOME BASIC REQUIREMENTS FOR ENTREPRENEURS • SOME BASIC CONCEPTS ABOUT BUILDING WEALTH

1

SOME BASIC REQUIREMENTS FOR ENTREPRENEURS

- ➤ You Need a Feeling for Risk.
- ➤ You Need Total Commitment.
- ➤ You Need Stamina.
- ➤ You Need to Know How to Sell.
- ➤ You Need a Self-Employment Opportunity.

The failure rate of new businesses could be halved if prospective entrepreneurs had to pass an exam. I am not suggesting that local governments regulate business activities any more than they already do. I am suggesting that most entrepreneurs are not qualified to start *any* business.

There is simply no point in starting a business if it does not have a reasonable chance of success. A successful business is one that will build your wealth.

Some entrepreneurs have what it takes to make a business succeed. It takes a certain kind of entrepreneur to make a successful business your best investment.

YOU NEED A FEELING FOR RISK

LESSON

THERE IS NO SUCH THING AS WEALTH WITHOUT RISK.

It takes many different skills and talents to run a business. Some of these include initiative, independent thinking, and a flair for marketing.

Making a business your best investment also requires an entrepreneurial instinct for taking risks.

Successful entrepreneurs know that risk is inherent in any business. These entrepreneurs take reasonable risks. They make them reasonable by managing whatever risks they take.

When you are not effective managing the risks in your business, you start to gamble. Skillful entrepreneurs do not gamble. Neither should you.

Entrepreneurs who have successfully managed the risk in their businesses have usually found a series of small but repetitive investment opportunities. Each opportunity provides them with a chance to build business wealth.

There is a distinct advantage in working with small investments. The risk in small investments can also be small. Further, those risks are usually ones that entrepreneurs can identify, understand, and successfully manage.

I am sure that most entrepreneurs could not handle the situation of only a few large investments each year, even though they may be tempted to try.

Large investments bring with them significant financial risks. These risks can be difficult to identify. The capital requirements for these investments can also be burdensome and are almost certainly beyond your limited resources.

Yet there is also another reason to leave most large investments alone. No entrepreneur is infallible. When you have made an error in judgment in a large investment, there is the potential for considerable economic loss. Large losses are just not easily absorbed by any small business.

YOU NEED TOTAL COMMITMENT

LESSON

DO NOT WASTE YOUR TIME STARTING A BUSINESS UNLESS YOU ARE TOTALLY COMMITTED TO IT.

It is clear to me that some entrepreneurs have a better feel than others do for running a business. Perhaps it is their intuitive feel for risk and return. That intuition can sometimes be lifesaving.

Running a business has many of the same risks as picking up $100 bills scattered through a minefield. If you want to walk through the field, you should know what you are doing.

It may be their strong grasp of business fundamentals that allows some entrepreneurs to step confidently from theory to practical application without missing a beat or a bet.

And then again, it could be just plain dumb luck.

I am certain you have witnessed this. An entrepreneur who more closely resembles a bumbling fool just muddles through, oblivious to dangers. Yet, like Rumpelstiltskin, he spins straw into gold.

What are the qualifiers that put a guardian angel in one entrepreneur's hip pocket and a gremlin in another's?

I believe that one of those qualifiers is total commitment. Total commitment is a protecting tunnel vision. That commitment filters many of the distracting, random, and unforeseen risks that interfere with building equity.

It is an entrepreneur's dedication to a concept beyond any reasonable requirement that results in achievement beyond all expectations. It is this commitment in the extreme that often takes a rather ordinary entrepreneur and allows him to collect a rather inordinate amount of equity.

The repetitive nature of any business will also require from you an ability to endure whatever challenges the marketplace may fling your way. Just like a triathlete, you will need your technical skills and a good dose of stamina to win this contest.

YOU NEED STAMINA

LESSON

STAMINA WILL HELP TO CARRY YOU OVER THE ROUGH SPOTS IN ANY BUSINESS.

Stamina is another quality readily recognizable in successful entrepreneurs. Unsuccessful entrepreneurs are also readily recognized by the absence of stamina in any measurable amount.

All of the risk capital in the world will not give you the stamina you need to build wealth.

Stamina bonds all other entrepreneurial qualities together with epoxy-like certainty. Stamina will keep you building equity long after your competitors have exhausted their own personal reserves. Stamina will allow you to work at your highest level one day after your best investment comes crashing down and you have every right to stick your head in the sand for a month.

It is stamina that guarantees you will recover from financial lightning bolts with your name etched on their fiery tips.

I have seen entrepreneurs who could have succeeded in their business but did not. Their risk analysis was sound, their decisions were good, their expectations were reasonable, and their timing could not have been better. They failed because they lacked stamina. Regardless of their relevant experience, only entrepreneurs with stamina will endure the day-to-day buffeting of their equity for the time it takes to make their business their best investment.

Exactly how long does it take to make your business your best investment? That depends on a number of factors that we will cover in detail later in this book. However, you can move things along in your business a bit more briskly if you have the ability to sell.

YOU NEED TO KNOW HOW TO SELL

LESSON

THE GROWTH RATE OF YOUR BUSINESS DEPENDS ON YOUR ABILITY TO SELL.

You will never bank your first nickel of revenue unless you learn how to sell. Selling is a skill that comes naturally to few entrepreneurs. Most have no formal training in this area and it shows. If you already know how to sell, you have a considerable advantage over many other entrepreneurs.

Melissa sold computers for a restructuring industrial giant. Her boss continually assured her that despite changes in the company's operations, her job was secure. That statement had a hollow ring to it as thousands of employees at all levels were asked to leave:

"It's getting ugly at the office, Mark. I just fired two of my managers this morning. We're now down to eight people in my group and the blood has not stopped flowing."

"Melissa, how do you manage to get any work done there? It seems like a head rolls by your desk every few minutes!"

"That's for sure. Some days I think you could shoot a cannonball through this office and not hit anyone. If our customers really knew what was going on, we'd be in big trouble. I need to get some other business started. I can see the future, and I don't like it."

"So, start your business!"

"Easy for you to say. You already have a business. Where would I start?"

"Well, you must have some idea. Why not look in an area that complements your training or technical skills?"

"That is the problem, Mark. I don't have any technical skills. You'd think that I was a computer whiz, but I'm really only one chapter ahead of our customers."

"Baloney! Do you mean to tell me you manage a group that sells over $60 million per year in electronic boxes to your customers and you don't have a skill?"

"I really don't. All I know how to do is sell. . . ."

And you will need to do that every day to make your business your best investment. The selling never stops. When you are not selling yourself to prospective business partners, you are selling yourself to your banker. When you are not selling yourself to your employees, you are selling yourself to your customers.

In some businesses, you will sell a product. In others, you will sell a service. Which one you sell will depend on the nature of the business opportunities that you identify.

YOU NEED A SELF-EMPLOYMENT OPPORTUNITY

LESSON

YOUR BEST OPPORTUNITY
BEGINS THE DAY YOU INVEST IN YOURSELF.

I have heard many people complain that business opportunities today are just not as plentiful as they were in the past. There is no truth to that remark.

There are more than enough self-employment opportunities for anyone willing to wait in line at the office of their local Business Registration Division.

The line at the Business Registration Division is there because everyone wants a superior return that can result from successfully managing your business.

If you have any doubt, visit your bank to open a savings account. If it is not lunchtime or payday, there are no lines! The absence of any crowd should offer an obvious answer to the demand for riskless, but lower rates of return.

A recent conversation I had went like this:

"Mark, I've got ten more years to retirement. I need to find something to do with my cash that will give me something greater than a 6 percent return. Any ideas?"

"Well, how are you sleeping at night?"

"Great. Why do you ask?"

"It is this 6 percent return that lets you rest peacefully in Never-Neverland. Today, it is a market rate of return, largely without risk, and you never have to worry about it moving against you in a big way. It's also perfectly OK to accept a market rate of return. It lets you sleep like a baby."

"Well, I don't really need that much sleep!"

See what I mean? People have a fundamental anxiety about accepting riskless rates of return. It is not so much that they feel they are cheating themselves, although that is the first point they are quick to acknowledge. Their real objection to a riskless rate of return is that someone with a little more risk is earning a higher return.

Cocktail party conversation for those without business risk can be downright embarrassing:

> "So, Phoebe, what are you doing these days? I never see you at the club any more . . . ."
>
> "You wouldn't believe it if I told you, Willis. Two years ago I welcomed a new family into our neighborhood with a box of homemade candy. My new neighbor insisted I had a product that was beautifully packaged and could compete successfully in a crowded marketplace. When my husband got laid off from work, this part-time hobby became a full-time business for both of us . . . .
>
> "We now have fourteen people working for us in our own 4,000-square-foot factory. The bank has just been falling over itself to lend us money. Our problem, Tibbetts, is that we just don't need the bank's help. Our company now pays us four times the amount my husband ever brought home in wages.
>
> "You know what, Willis? Investing in ourselves was the best decision we ever made. The kids even help out during the summer when they come home from school. Maybe one day they'll take over the business! By the way, what's keeping you busy?"
>
> "Ugh, you know, the same old stuff. I've still got the same job. I've really been thinking about doing something else."
>
> "What do you have in mind?"
>
> "Uh, well, I'm not sure yet, but you've got me thinking . . . ."

Most people dislike their work. It is amazing that they will dedicate a lifetime to a job that brings little personal satisfaction.

Investing in yourself changes that whole attitude. The high points of your career are no longer limited to a salary, fully paid medical benefits, and an annual cost of living adjustment.

Your new entrepreneurial lifestyle will keep you turbo-charged and dancing with risk. You may not be certain when your next paycheck will come. When it does come, however, it will bring with it a special feeling of achievement that a salaried employee cannot buy. The paycheck will also confirm that you were worth the investment.

Wealth that is limited only by the extent of your effort is just one more reason why successful entrepreneurs enjoy running their own business.

SOME BASIC CONCEPTS ABOUT BUILDING WEALTH

2

- ➤ Equity Is Business Wealth.
- ➤ Control Your Investment.
- ➤ Collect Risk Premiums.

It is premature to expect any business to be your best investment without first understanding some simple but basic concepts about building business wealth.

That is one reason why so many businesses fail. The owners of most businesses have started them without any understanding of what it takes to build wealth.

When you understand these concepts and can apply them consistently, you will have in hand some of the primary ingredients for a successful business.

EQUITY IS BUSINESS WEALTH

LESSON

THE REAL EQUITY IN ANY BUSINESS
IS OFTEN AFFECTED BY YOUR ABILITY
TO CONVERT ASSETS TO CASH.

Equity is the business equivalent of wealth. Equity is the value of your business after the assets in it have been converted to cash and everything has been repaid.

If you have not converted your investment to cash, any equity in it is still theoretical. That means you can lose it.

Ellis learned this lesson the hard way.

Ellis owned a business that provided building contractors with thousands of prehung doors each year. Contractors preferred to buy and install ready-made, prehung doors from Ellis than to build, frame, and hang their own.

A recent business appraisal valued his prehung door business at more than $650,000.

"Ellis! How is the prehung door business holding up this year?"

"Not very good, I'm afraid."

"What's the problem? Last time we talked, you were on top of the world. A business valuation fellow gave you a great valuation report, you were running two shifts, and your customers loved you."

"Customers are part of the problem. Now that the construction business has slowed, so has my cash flow. I've laid off the second shift and cut back the hours on the first. That move hasn't endeared me to anyone. To make matters worse, my largest customer just went out of business, still owing me $185,000."

"What a way to ruin your day. . . ."

"What a way to ruin my business . . . ."

Ellis never recovered from that loss and neither did his business. Ellis made only one mistake. He simply failed to collect the money owed to his business by his single largest customer.

The life cycle of any business must ultimately be denominated in cash. That means all business assets have a cash conversion value to which they will move.

When you sell inventory, it becomes a receivable. When you collect that receivable, you have cash.

When a company buys a piece of equipment, that asset becomes part of this conversion cycle. That asset will produce revenue when you use it properly. When you collect that revenue you have cash. When the asset no longer produces revenue, you can either sell the asset for cash or scrap it.

When you cannot convert business assets to cash, any equity those assets represent is fictitious. Equity is fictitious when business equipment that you have acquired does not produce sufficient revenue. Equity is fictitious when customers do not pay the money they owe to your business. Equity is also fictitious when you cannot find any buyer for your business.

Successful entrepreneurs understand the process of converting assets to cash. They also recognize that any event that affects the efficiency of this conversion process also affects their business wealth.

You must learn to convert assets to cash efficiently in order to build equity. Conversion, I must warn you, is an iterative process. That means you will do it thousands of times.

That is also why building equity involves time. Equity is rarely built in one year or on a few well-placed investments. It takes years and it is a lot of hard work.

CONTROL YOUR INVESTMENT

LESSON

IT IS EASIER TO RUN A BUSINESS
WHEN YOU CONTROL THE RISKS IN IT.

Successful entrepreneurs will tell you that the more control they can exercise over the life of an investment, the greater the chance of building equity.

"Wallace, why is it that every time we talk about a new business venture of yours, you always have a majority ownership interest in it?"

"Simple. A majority interest gives me control. That means my vote is the only one that matters. When I control a deal, I have fewer problems sleeping at night."

Control is a feature that is synonymous with owning a majority interest in a business. In fact, that is what it means to be a majority owner.

Controlling your business is particularly crucial whenever your investment is at risk. The element of control is critical when you do not have a high degree of confidence in the abilities of others to convert assets to cash.

When you manage your business properly, you determine the timing and size of the investment. You also determine the nature of some risk elements, their related controls, and the timing and amount of your return.

There are also elements of risk beyond your control: interest rates, trade and budget deficits and surpluses, foreign currency strengths and weaknesses, and recessionary and expansionary economic forecasts.

You can offset these and other risks in your business by receiving risk premiums.

COLLECT RISK PREMIUMS

LESSON

STOP PAYING RISK PREMIUMS.
START COLLECTING THEM.

A risk premium is a fee frequently paid by anyone who wishes to share a risk.

When a vehicle operator wishes to share the risk of driving, he pays a fee to an insurance company for motor vehicle insurance. That fee is a risk premium.

When a homeowner wishes to share the risk of sudden or unexpected damage to his residence, he pays a risk premium for homeowner's insurance.

When a business owner wishes to share the risk of business interruption, he will pay a risk premium for business interruption insurance.

You do not build wealth by paying risk premiums. You build wealth by receiving them!

It is the receipt of these risk premiums from others that can provide you with an overall return superior to those available elsewhere in the marketplace.

Entrepreneurs who are willing to shoulder the risks of business must include a risk premium in the prices they charge their customers. That usually means raising prices.

When Fletcher purchased a stepladder, he discovered that insurance companies were not the only businesses that charged customers risk premiums.

"Thanks for picking up that stepladder for me, Mark. Now, where is my change?"

"Fletcher, there isn't any. You owe me. Here's the bill."

"I don't believe it! Why does it cost so much to buy a stepladder these days?"

"Well, if people would just follow the directions and use them as ladders, maybe they wouldn't cost so much."

"What do you mean?"

"Hardly anybody uses a stepladder like they're supposed to, Fletch. They use stepladders for sawhorses, scaffolding, balance beams, you name it . . . ."

"And those are good reasons why stepladders should be so expensive?"

"Fletch! All you need is one lawsuit for a broken neck and a sympathetic jury to add 30 percent to the price of each ladder! Think of what you pay as a manufacturer's risk premium . . . ."

It is the oversight of many entrepreneurs to insist on receiving these risk premiums that is responsible for the failure of many small businesses.

The risk premiums are always there. This suggests that you cannot eliminate all entrepreneurial risk.

That is fine. You can live with some risk if it is not excessive and if you get paid for it.

The more you understand about these concepts, the easier it is to build equity. But understanding these concepts is not the same as applying them effectively.

Experience will take care of that. There are hundreds of mistakes you will make before you become proficient in applying these basic concepts to your business.

Exactly how these mistakes will affect your business is directly related to your risk assessment capabilities.

PART TWO

Developing Risk Assessment Capabilities

3

HOW TO ASSESS RISK

- ➤ Risk and Yourself.
- ➤ Risk and Your Business.
- ➤ Risk and Your Customers.
- ➤ Risk and the Marketplace.
- ➤ Risk and Dependencies.

Risk is an integral part of building wealth. It is also a significant factor in every business activity.

You can easily convince yourself this is true. Take twenty dollars from your wallet and put it in a jar. Close the jar and put it in the darkest corner of your closet. One day later, the jar will still contain twenty dollars. If you never tamper with the jar, you will always have the twenty dollars. But that is all you will have.

When you take that twenty dollars out of that jar and invest it in your business, you have paired an investment with some element of risk. That element of risk may increase your twenty dollars to a larger amount. The impact risk has on your investment may also make the investment vanish entirely. What risk does to your investment depends on your ability to assess risk.

Risk assessment is a problem for many entrepreneurs. The number of businesses that fail each year should be convincing evidence that the problem has not yet been solved.

You can easily sidestep the question "How do you assess risk?" on your way into business:

> "Tipton! Let's start a business!"
>
> "OK, Woods. What business do you have in mind?"
>
> "Muffins! I've got a great oat bran muffin recipe and I've found a location to sell muffins that's on the way to the shore."
>
> "Aren't there a couple dozen muffin shops on the way to the shore that sell oat bran muffins?"
>
> "Yes, Tipton, but this recipe will be different. . . ."

Some entrepreneurs are unable to identify risk even when surrounded by it. There are several reasons why entrepreneurs have difficulty assessing risk.

Risk assessment skills are not the same skills as those that give you a technical expertise. You may be a professionally licensed businessperson in the eyes of the public, but you may also have a naive view of risk.

Assessing risk requires establishing tolerance levels. Establishing risk tolerance levels can be difficult to do if you have had little previous exposure to risk.

In order to recognize risk, you need to know some facts about it. But facts about risk, like a compulsive liar's alibi, are always changing. The facts about risk may also be of little practical benefit to you after your business has been savaged by it.

It is for all of these reasons that it is difficult to find one formal expression for risk that will satisfy everyone.

Risk is anything that looks as if it has the potential to keep you from making your business your best investment.

Risk is easier to assess when you are certain you know why you are in business.

You are in business to build wealth. You build wealth by taking those risks for which you get paid.

The uncertainty of being paid increases that risk. Determining the likelihood of being paid for each risk you accept is another good step in assessing it.

You do not need a computer and the latest software package to tell you how to assess risk. Assessing risk is a simple matter of knowing something about yourself, about your business, about your customers, about the marketplace, and about your dependencies.

RISK AND YOURSELF

LESSON

THE BIGGEST RISK IN ANY BUSINESS
CAN BE THE WAY YOU
PERSONALLY FEEL ABOUT RISK.

Risk, like fashion, can be a matter of personal preference. That is why it is unreasonable to expect any experienced entrepreneur to be impartial about risk.

Many entrepreneurs new to business are inexperienced in matters of risk. That lack of experience makes it difficult for them to assess risk and its relative levels of severity. Expecting these entrepreneurs to assess risk is like expecting fourth graders to solve differential equations.

Other entrepreneurs are averse to matters of risk. They do not want to assess risk because, like the boogey man, risk frightens them. You can hardly fault these entrepreneurs for their reluctance to greet their nightmares.

There are still others who have been overexposed to matters of risk. Their jobs have been at risk for a long, long time. Overexposure to risk makes these entrepreneurs take risk for granted. As a result, their biggest risks are often viewed as no risk at all.

Assessing risk involves the process of discovery. That means looking behind every assumption to see what risk is hiding there. If you are not certain you have all the assumptions or that you can identify the risks, then you need professional help.

Entrepreneurs, by their nature, are optimistic individuals. That is why it can be difficult for them to ask questions about risk.

Many of these questions have no easy or pleasant answers. What could go wrong? What is the downside? If my assumptions are incorrect, what is the worst that can happen?

Your understanding of risk must be so complete that you are willing to put your best investment on the line for it.

It is unfortunate that many entrepreneurs put their businesses on the line without this understanding, regardless of the level of risk.

RISK AND YOUR BUSINESS

LESSON

ASSESSING BUSINESS RISK INVOLVES FINDING A LEVEL OF RISK FOR WHICH YOU WILL BE PAID AS LONG AS YOU OWN YOUR BUSINESS.

You will certainly find different levels of risk in different businesses. Nevertheless, it is a mistake to believe that risk that is outlandish in one business is acceptable in another. In any business, outlandish risk will produce the same result: the complete loss of your investment.

What makes risk outlandish is inattention to fundamental things that make your business your best investment.

Entrepreneurs frequently focus on that portion of business with which they are familiar. That focus may emphasize one element to the exclusion of all others.

As a result, a business may have a great product to sell, but no general ledger. It may have the industry's finest accounting system, but no working capital. It may have a wonderful cash flow, but dishonest employees. It may have highly efficient employees, but a product that cannot be sold at any price.

You get the picture. The element that you exclude from risk assessment may be the one that will damage you the most. That is the nature of risk.

Large quantities of risk look acceptable for only one reason. Some entrepreneurs are better than other entrepreneurs at insisting they be paid for that risk!

There is just no business in which you can turn your head from risk and still expect to keep your business or your head.

RISK AND YOUR CUSTOMERS

LESSON

EVERY CUSTOMER HAS A SWORD IN ONE HAND
AND A BAG OF GOLD IN THE OTHER.
WHEN YOU HAVE PROPERLY ASSESSED CUSTOMER RISK,
YOU WILL GET THE BAG OF GOLD
WITHOUT FALLING ON THE SWORD.

If you are a cyclist, you have learned not to take vehicle turn signals too seriously.

Entrepreneurs comfortable with assessing customer risk have also learned not to take customer payment promises too seriously.

Customers do not always mean what they say.

Entrepreneurs who have successfully assessed customer risk are not better judges of people. They also do not endorse the usual collection methods: credit manager telephone calls, final-notice letters, lead-weighted gloves, and so on.

Entrepreneurs who have successfully controlled customer risk are those who have simply refused to extend credit.

You will never have more control over your ability to be paid for your risk than the moment before you deliver a product to a customer.

That is why entrepreneurs should follow the example set by real estate escrows. Buyers want their properties without title disputes. Sellers want their proceeds without collection uncertainties. In a customary escrow, both parties simultaneously trade one want for the other.

It is a business deal to which risk has not been invited. Preparing such an invitation list for your own customers is not such a difficult thing to do.

RISK AND THE MARKETPLACE

LESSON

ASSESSING MARKET RISK IS A MATTER OF PAYING ATTENTION TO WHAT IS HAPPENING OUTSIDE OF YOUR BUSINESS.

Market preferences change. When they do, so does market demand. Your ability to anticipate these changes will reduce your exposure to market risk.

Your risk increases when you fail to recognize the beginnings of change in the marketplace. When you fail to make the adjustments these changes suggest, risk flourishes.

When Mother Nature flings a lightning bolt, she may take only the branch at which she was aiming, or she may engulf an entire forest. That is the nature of unadjusted market risk.

There is no business that can achieve its potential without adjusting for market risk. Running a business in a free market will teach you something about that risk.

The moment you start feeling comfortable with one level of risk, the marketplace will no longer pay you for it. The moment you lock in a risk premium, the marketplace will offer greater premiums for less risk.

On rare occasions and for only the briefest moments, the marketplace may relent and offer you returns without commensurate levels of risk. But the marketplace will not tolerate any extended periods of imbalance.

The marketplace just hates to give you something for nothing.

RISK AND DEPENDENCIES

LESSON

YOU CAN REDUCE YOUR EXPOSURE TO DEPENDENCY RISK SIMPLY BY RECOGNIZING IT.

You can also be exposed to a risk you never even considered to be your own. Welcome to dependency risk!

Just like a wild brother-in-law, dependency risk is a relationship that you cannot fully control.

It is the exception where the consequence of any risk that you take is yours alone to bear. Your partners, your customers, your suppliers, your employees, and anyone else whom your business touches all share your risk to some degree.

It is also true that anyone who touches your business has the potential to leave dependency risk along with their fingerprints.

When you order an item for your inventory, you expect a manufacturer to make it using rigid quality control guidelines. That is a dependency. When the failure of that item causes the death of a customer who bought it from you, that dependency becomes a matter of legal record.

The risk in a 50-page legal document also contains dependencies. The quality of the legal talent you have employed to draft the document is a dependency. So is the basic honesty of the other party to the contract.

You share a risk with every dependency. On some occasions, that sharing reduces your exposure to risk. At other times, sharing risk with a dependency increases your own.

If you do not take the time to identify dependencies, you will not know if they are increasing or reducing your risk. Your risk assessment will then be incomplete. What is worse, your assessment of risk will probably be wrong.

After you have learned something about yourself, about your business, about your customers, and about the marketplace, you may have also learned something about risk. When you understand how to recognize dependencies, you will understand much of what you need to know about risk.

Building equity in your business is certainly an easier job once you know how to assess risk. Assessing risk confidently is simply a matter of practice and knowing how you feel about excessive risk.

4

EXCESSIVE RISK

➤ Take the Challenge.
➤ Find Your Tolerance.

Running any business will provide you with ample opportunity to expose yourself to risk. Determining your preference for risk is a logical first step before moving in with it.

If you want your business to be your best investment, you also want to be paid for business risk. **Any risk for which you are not paid is excess risk.**

Excessive risk is not the same as excess risk. Excessive risk is just too darn much risk, whether you are paid for it or not. It is like running cross-country with size eight shoes on size eleven feet. Excessive risk has the potential to cripple your business.

Excessive risk is usually adjusted by bankruptcy court judges. You need not wait that long. When you know in advance your personal risk tendencies, you have a better chance of avoiding excessive business risk.

Some entrepreneurs sleep better with large cash surpluses. Others are comfortable operating within their firm's ability to service debt. A third group prefers sleeping on the edge of maximum leverage where their business assets are pledged to their lending limit.

Clearly, entrepreneurs have a divergence of opinion on the point where business risk becomes excessive risk. That point for you will depend on how you feel about risk today.

How you feel about excessive risk today may not be the same way you feel about it tomorrow.

But how you react to excessive risk today, tomorrow, or next year will have a profound impact on the equity in your business.

TAKE THE CHALLENGE

LESSON

NO TWO INDIVIDUALS FEEL
THE SAME WAY ABOUT BUSINESS RISK.

How do you feel about risk? Read the following questionnaire and score yourself for each question:

4 = Strongly Agree
3 = Inclined to Agree
2 = Inclined to Disagree
1 = Strongly Disagree

1. ______	10. ______	19. ______
2. ______	11. ______	20. ______
3. ______	12. ______	21. ______
4. ______	13. ______	22. ______
5. ______	14. ______	23. ______
6. ______	15. ______	24. ______
7. ______	16. ______	25. ______
8. ______	17. ______	
9. ______	18. ______	Total ______

1. A customer who represents 3 percent of your annual sales tells you that she is now working with one of your competitors. You will carry this disappointment with you for the next few weeks.
2. You have just finished meeting with your banker. The bank will provide you with the credit your business needs if you meet one condition. The bank wants you to pledge your home as security for the loan. Since bank financing is hard to find, you have no choice but to agree to the bank's terms.
3. Being out of work is a fear that keeps you from starting a new business venture. You will probably continue to talk about possible business opportunities, but will not invest much of your money in any prospective business opportunity.
4. You have tried for nearly a week to contact a potential customer who has a problem you believe you can solve. The customer has not returned any of your telephone calls. You are wasting your time to continue to try to contact this customer.
5. A large company has agreed to distribute your product as soon as they take care of a few unspecified matters in their own operations. Although nothing has happened in the last nine months, they keep

telling you they want to work with you. You decide not to press for a definite agreement in order to avoid offending anyone.

6. You cannot make a sensible business decision without all of the relevant facts. If you do not have all of the facts, then you must wait for additional information that will allow you to make an informed decision. A delayed decision with all of the relevant facts is always better than a hurried decision.

7. Cash flow is just a bit tight this month. For no apparent reason, customers appear to have slowed their payments to you. Even though your payroll tax deposits are due tomorrow, there is nothing you can do until your customers send in payments on their account.

8. Events seem to be happening at your business beyond your ability to control them. Many of them are unanticipated and make it difficult for you to schedule your work. You are comfortable planning your work around these events as they develop.

9. You remember the recession that was so hard on your business. Customers were reluctant to part with their money and buy your service. When they did, they always asked for a discount and you gave it to them just to keep their business. You would never dream of raising prices if it meant losing some of these customers.

10. A bank has agreed to provide financing for your business. One of the conditions of that agreement is that you limit the amount of money you personally take from the business. Once you sign the loan agreement, it is OK to ignore this restriction.

11. Your partner has agreed to consult with you before spending any amount over $1,000. When you learn that your partner has recently purchased a $2,500 piece of office equipment without first consulting you, you concede that the business needed the equipment.

12. Your bank approved you for a business line of credit. The rates are competitive with other banks and the terms meet your financing requirements. The bank has asked each of your three partners and their spouses to cosign the borrowing agreement. You see no problem with this request.

13. You finally bought out your partner and now own the entire business. Two years later, your ex-partner sees how well you have done. He also believes he should share your good fortune. You have no agreement

that entitles anyone to share your future profits and you tell him so. Three days later, you get a ten-page certified letter from his attorney threatening legal action. You should consider writing a check to settle this dispute.

14. A new shareholder buys a 30 percent interest in your business. The shareholder wants to receive quarterly financial reports on the business operations. You believe that this shareholder has no right to receive this confidential operating data.

15. You have tried without success to live on the salary you take from your business. Your lifestyle isn't excessive, but you just never seem to have enough money to go around. When you need additional cash, you simply borrow it from your business.

16. Your employees bring you their business problems and their personal ones too. Since you know that the way they personally feel about themselves will influence their work, you lend an empathetic ear whenever they require one.

17. You heard that in any business, you need to spend money to make money. Your business is no different and seems to require a constant infusion of capital. When you have the resources and control the business, investing in yourself is always a good bet.

18. If you only had a little more control over your life, things would be just great. Running your business would give you this control. You could have a four-day work week, take vacations at a moment's notice, and let your employees handle all the details in your business.

19. The revenues of your new business are growing at a blistering annual rate. It has been all you can do to provide customers with the services they require. The last set of financial statements you have is six months old. Since your time is limited and your accountant is overburdened, you are inclined to wait to the end of the year to see how well you have managed your business.

20. Your partner's ex-spouse has a dispute that simply will not go away. When you answer your front door after dinner, a sheriff's deputy serves you with a summons to appear at the federal courthouse with all of your books and records for the last ten years. It is now time to panic.

21. One of your customers has a billing dispute and insists on resolving it with only you. You pass the customer off to a staffperson with

instructions to handle the matter. You really don't have time to personally listen to customer complaints.

22. Your business has developed financial problems beyond your ability to solve them. You are three months behind on your rent, you have not paid your suppliers for over sixty days, your bank refuses to renew your line of credit, and your creditors are threatening to put you out of business. Despite these burdens to your operations, you would not consider filing a bankruptcy petition.

23. Advances in technology have affected the way your customers do business. Computer hardware and software improvements provide you with different ways to manage your operations. Despite the variety of technology available, you are reluctant to invest in an information system for your business that will be obsolete a few years from now.

24. Your friends tell you that you can deduct your business losses on your tax return. You believe that the prospect of having a tax benefit from any business loss is as good a reason as any to start the business.

25. Your folks think you have a great idea for a product and want to lend you the startup capital for your business. You are grateful for their vote of confidence and agree to pay twice the going rate in interest on the loan. All of you believe you have made the best financial arrangement possible.

FIND YOUR TOLERANCE

LESSON

YOU CAN CHANGE YOUR TOLERANCE FOR RISK.

Pain is not necessarily good for you just because you have a high tolerance for it. The same is true with alcohol, noise, and business risk. Knowing your tolerance for risk can alert you to excessive risk long before it rampages through your business.

I will not tell you that the results on this questionnaire are scientific. Nevertheless, the results will tell you how you feel about risk.

What does your total score mean?

- If you scored less than 35, you have a clear vision of how to control the risk in your business. The vision is a result of your previous experience in managing risk.
- If you scored between 36 and 55, you are a little too flexible in your tolerance for risk. You have accepted it as a partner and will never really get rid of it. That is fine, as long as you remember to get paid for the risks you take.
- If you scored between 56 and 75, you lack a good understanding of how to control business risk. This lack of understanding may be the result of your inability to recognize business risk.
- If you scored over 75, risk is running rampant through your business. The high score may suggest you have not yet learned how to manage business risk. It may also suggest that you have given up on running your business.

Whatever your score, you must learn how to identify business risk before you can expect to make your business your best investment. Once you can identify the risks, you have a good chance to make them reasonable.

5

REASONABLE RISK

- Make Risk Reasonable.
- Advance Planning Will Help.
- Change Your Perception Today.

Risk is either reasonable or it is not. Any successful entrepreneur can tell you about reasonable risk. Ivan Boesky can tell you about the other kind of risk.

Ivan Boesky was one of Wall Street's largest risk arbitrageurs with a fatal disease. He was a financially driven entrepreneur, thoroughly enamored with taking questionable risks. The amount of money that he bet was staggering.

His spectacular performance and uncommon avarice were his downfall. Boesky's stock market results were just too good to believe. In fact, they seemed to defy the laws of chance. He seemed to be trading on perfect information. More specifically, Boesky's crime was trading on inside information.

Trading on inside information is an unquestionable risk. Boesky was punished with a fine of $100 million and five years in prison.

You do not need to take these kinds of risks to build your business wealth. All you need to do is be sure that the risks you take are reasonable risks.

MAKE RISK REASONABLE

LESSON

YOU CAN CONTROL BUSINESS RISK.

Risk exists wherever perfect information and the time to analyze it are absent. Risk will always have some unforeseen or unexpected effects on your business. Even with this uncertainty, you can make risk reasonable.

You live with uncertainty every day when you cross the street. You cross at your own risk. As long as you have the benefit of your senses and a little athletic ability to dodge left or right, crossing the street is no big deal.

Accepting business risk is also no big deal, as long as you have reserved your right to adjust this risk.

That is how you make risks reasonable. If you can influence the affairs of your business, you should have some degree of confidence in controlling risk. As long as deflecting unforeseen risks remains an option, you never have a reason to panic.

Successful entrepreneurs have a natural tendency to deflect unnecessary risk. Most would never have a second thought about managing business risk and protecting their wealth.

It is this unsolicited but complete devotion to their business that makes one entrepreneur more successful than another.

ADVANCE PLANNING WILL HELP

LESSON

IT IS EASIER TO CONTROL RISK
IF YOU THINK AHEAD.

It is nice to have the option of adjusting risk in any business. The option is a form of insurance. If your risks are reasonable, then you may never really need the benefit of this insurance policy.

That is OK.

The real risk of any entrepreneurial activity comes from not being in a position to make these risk-reducing adjustments when you need to make them. It is too late to buy any kind of insurance after an airplane's cargo doors have blown out on an overseas flight.

It is that feeling of helplessness that an entrepreneur experiences when he is unable to adjust risk.

That is also why adjusting risk in any effective manner usually requires some planning. In a volatile or an unreliable marketplace, risk adjustments may not work.

Few entrepreneurs like to talk about that risk.

When the marketplace no longer functions reliably, the comforting effect of making any risk adjustment is absent.

A good way to control the risk of drowning is to stay out of the water. When a receding tsunami pulls you into the ocean, your method for controlling the risk of drowning is no longer functioning reliably.

In a terrifying moment, all expectations of controlling risk are dashed. For those entrepreneurs who have experienced this terror, normalcy returns to their business far too late for any comfort.

Planning will help make risk reasonable, but no amount of planning will dispel every uncertainty in your business. Every entrepreneur needs to recognize that there are some unknowns that he cannot evaluate that will affect his business in a manner over which he has no control.

You might have a wonderful convenience store with a great location. Your location could be so great that Wal-Mart noticed it too and bought the forty-acre parcel across the road. That may be the end of your wonderful business.

The use of that farmland covered with corn was an uncertainty about the future. You could not foresee the consequences, let alone evaluate them.

One effective method used to dispel some uncertainty and to make risks reasonable is to spread your investments around. The outright loss of equity in any one investment will surely leave you rankled. It will also leave you in a position to invest again tomorrow.

Smaller diversified investments reduce the overall risk of loss on any investment that fails to build equity. But be practical about diversification. How the theory works and how diversification works for you are probably different.

Your business is probably your single largest investment. Unlike a multibillion-dollar corporation, you may not have the luxury of partitioning it into distinct operating entities that will stand by themselves. That is why you must always look ahead and be serious about controlling risk.

CHANGE YOUR PERCEPTION TODAY

LESSON

DO NOT WAIT FOR A BIG LOSS
BEFORE YOU GET SERIOUS
ABOUT CONTROLLING RISK.

Your preference for risk and your views on making risk adjustments go hand in hand. A willingness to bear greater risk will enlarge the scope of possible qualifying investments. That willingness may require fewer risk-reducing adjustments. It may also require more.

There is a specific time when your attitude toward risk and making risk adjustments changes. That moment first occurs the day an investment moves against you in a big way. Any major loss helps you to redefine risk.

I am not suggesting that a $100 check bounced by one of your customers will change your attitude toward risk. That amount might be enough to buy some politicians a vote or two. It is enough for a short cab ride and theater tickets in New York City. But a $100 loss is hardly enough to precipitate a change in your views toward risk.

It is unfortunate that few of us recognize the value of an inexpensive lesson.

What will grab your attention is the day you discover that $100,000 has slipped through your fingers.

For reasons I cannot explain, some entrepreneurs appear to require a six-digit irregularity to get them to change their views on risk. The change usually insures them against similar future losses of equity, but it does nothing to recover the loss.

Harold, a small food wholesaler, never really understood why he needed monthly financial statements for his business. Each month, Harold sold about $180,000 of inventory and dumped his paperwork on the bookkeeper's desk.

Eldon, the bookkeeper, just loved to keep books. Eldon, in fact, was quite protective about the accounting records. No one, including his boss, ever saw them.

In his customary "I don't mean to bother you" manner, Harold avoided confronting this problem. Harold just asked Eldon when he wanted to know how his business was doing. The conversation went something like this:

> "Hey, Eldon! How are we doing this month?"
> "Fine, Harold, just fine!"
> "That's great, Eldon! Really great!"

The first inkling Harold had of any possible problem occurred three days after he fired Eldon.

Harold asked Eldon to leave for two reasons.

The first reason was that Harold's wife offered to do his bookkeeping without compensation. It is hard for anyone to compete with an offer like that.

The second reason was that Eldon never appeared to be doing any work. Eldon's desk was immaculate! Only the current sports page ever covered the top of it.

Harold's wife discovered that his business was missing nearly $80,000 in deposits. Harold hired a private investigator who confronted the bookkeeper. Eldon explained that he lost the money over a six-month streak of bad sports bets.

Harold could have averted the loss if he had required monthly financial statements and had regularly inspected those statements.

Retaining the right to adjust your risk, thinking ahead, and being serious about risk control are all ways to make risk reasonable.

Despite your understanding about risk, there is no way to guarantee your first business will build any business wealth. You also need the experience of being self-employed and the time to learn from your mistakes.

That is why false starts are inevitable.

PART THREE

Starting Your Business

FALSE STARTS ARE INEVITABLE • LOOKING FOR OPPORTUNITY • DO YOU REALLY NEED A PARTNER? • THE CHALLENGE WITH BANKS • BUYING IN

FALSE STARTS ARE INEVITABLE

6

- ➤ Establish an Independent Business.
- ➤ Refuse That Directorship.
- ➤ Pick Your Customers Carefully.
- ➤ Develop a Technical Expertise.

Building equity in your business is a job for which there are few formal classes. By the time most entrepreneurs decide to work for themselves, the opportunity for formal training has long since passed.

The chance for riskless learning has also passed. The day you start your business is the day that "On the Job Training" takes on an entirely new meaning. Irrespective of the results, you will now bear the consequences of every business decision that you make.

No matter what your experience or where you worked before you started your business, you will make your share of mistakes.

Every entrepreneur's business has been hampered in its infancy by one or more false starts.

ESTABLISH AN INDEPENDENT BUSINESS

LESSON

DO NOT EXPECT TO BE PAID A RISK PREMIUM
WHEN YOU HAVE NO BUSINESS RISK.

A common false start occurs when you fail to start an independent business. Just like your childhood lemonade stand, an independent business is one that stands apart from other operating entities.

Independent businesses are often exposed to risk. When properly managed, these businesses can also receive returns that justify the exposure.

Some entrepreneurs believe it is desirable to reduce risk in a new business by working under the corporate umbrella of an existing enterprise. Sometimes they are right.

There is a consequence to that decision. That reduced risk is likely to reduce any return.

Haley was an energetic, hardworking account executive at a large advertising agency. She enjoyed the status that came with working on major client accounts, but wanted to manage an agency of her own. She believed there was a readily available route that was just waiting for her decision to start a business.

When the timing was right, Haley would walk away from her employer with two or three substantial accounts. If these accounts were willing to share her risk, she just might have an instant business.

Her employers, however, had something to say about that. One morning they discovered a draft of her business plan, which Haley had inadvertently left in the copy machine. They promptly fired her.

Haley was momentarily stunned by the swift change in her employment status, but was not completely unnerved. She still wanted to run her own business. Losing her job was a disappointment, but it just moved her closer to what Haley believed was inevitable.

Haley considered the prospects of soliciting business from several smaller nonagency accounts. That would involve cultivating at least a dozen business relationships for the three or four who might provide her with business. That would also take some time.

Haley did not have the luxury of time. The stack of unpaid bills sitting on her kitchen counter forced her to focus on a single larger account. Haley already had a specific target account in mind.

The target client had a chaotic advertising program. Haley knew how to fix it!

She proposed an agreement to become the client's "in-house" advertising agency and negotiate his media purchases. The client shook hands with Haley and accepted her proposal.

Haley's business grew and so did her client base. Unfortunately, her first client was by far her largest client. The client also occupied the vast majority of her time.

"Mervin! Do you have a minute?"

"Sure Haley. What is on your mind?"

"Mervin, we have to talk about our arrangement."

"So, talk!"

"Fifteen months ago, I agreed to organize your advertising program for about what you would pay an employee."

"You've done a great job, Haley. I'm really proud of you."

"Thanks, Merv. I've figured that by getting the 15 percent agency discount for you even though you are not an agency has saved your business about $150,000 per year."

"That's wonderful!"

"What I want you to know, Mervin, is that I produced this savings for you at no additional net cost to you."

"I know! That's why I agreed to do it!"

"I also want to let you know that I am working nearly forty hours a week on your account to get this savings. That's not giving me a lot of time to develop other business."

"Haley, take a month off and get a few other clients! I won't be able to pay you for that month, of course, but I want to see your business grow."

"I can't afford not to be paid by you for a month, Mervin. You know that! Since I'm saving you such a significant sum, why not just let me increase my billing rate to you? It's only been averaging about $29 per hour."

"I'd have a problem with that Haley. You see, I could hire an employee full time to do for me what you've been doing for me. It just doesn't make good business sense to pay more than the going rate."

"You're not paying the going rate, Mervin! You're paying me $29 per hour! The going rate is closer to $100 per hour!"

"Haley, calm down! Aren't you happy with the office I'm giving you in my store?"

"Yes, but . . . ."

"And the telephone lines you use to make your appointments? I'm also paying for utilities, insurance, parking, and that new copy machine you like so much."

"I know, but . . . ."

"Haley, you just don't have a lot of risk! There's no downside in what you're doing! You don't sweat if my rent goes up. You don't worry if the bank refuses to finance my inventory. All you worry about is typing up your bill so I can pay it at the end of the month . . . ."

"Mervin?!"

"What?"

"Calm down!"

REFUSE THAT DIRECTORSHIP

LESSON

LIMIT YOUR SCOPE OF SERVICE
WITH ANY SINGLE CUSTOMER.

You can make another false start in a matter of courtesy. That occurs when you agree to become an officer of record for a business that you do not control.

"Officer of record" means you are officially on file with one or more regulatory agencies as the officer of a business.

There is a major problem with agreeing to become an officer of record. If it is not your business, you risk suffering through the same kind of attention as the number one duck in a shooting gallery.

If ducks could talk, they would tell you that attention is nothing for your benefit.

Cory started a general business consulting practice with great enthusiasm but no vision beyond his daily list of things to do.

Cory never had a doubt that he would manage a business of his own. He was bright, energetic, and comfortable thinking on his feet. If Cory lacked talent in any single area, it was in clearly defining his role to his clients.

As part of an engagement, a client suggested that Cory serve as the president of the client's restaurant operations. Cory readily agreed with the suggestion.

Several factors influenced Cory's decision to accept the client's offer. Cory had never before been an officer of any corporation. Being president seemed to be a good place to start. The restaurant was also Cory's second client. Cory did not want to risk disappointing this client.

Cory had not yet recognized the risks in failing to set limits on the scope of service to his clients. There are some things you just do not do for any client. Being a corporate officer or director is one of those things.

Most entrepreneurial clients assume you will not object to being an officer of record. That is true even if the position is noncompensatory.

When you agree to their suggestion, you have accepted a Pandora's Box, complete with risk included! There are a number of reasons why this is true.

Few entrepreneurial businesses have the luxury of using their cash to pay for discretionary expenses. A discretionary expense is an expense that is not required for the immediate survival of a business.

Many entrepreneurs consider liability insurance for their officers and directors to be a discretionary expense. That usually means there is no insurance.

The problem goes further.

It is the natural inclination of most entrepreneurs to insist on making their own decisions when it comes to matters that affect their business operations. That is true, even when you are a corporate officer of their business and they are unqualified to make those decisions.

These decisions have a great potential to spill their results all over you.

The restaurant had several serious operating problems. A few months after Cory had examined some of these problems, the state tax authorities sued the restaurant on a payroll-related matter. The disputed payroll tax was over two years old.

Since Cory was now president of record, the state named him in the suit and held him responsible for $18,700 of unpaid payroll taxes.

Cory was dumbfounded! He had not considered the risk that he might be sued for something over which he had no control.

That was a sign of inexperience.

It took Cory several months of corresponding with the state tax officials to convince them they were pursuing the wrong individual. In the act of clearing his name, Cory implicated his client.

That is all the fingerpointing it took for the client to terminate the consulting agreement.

Cory's response was to resign as president. He prepared and filed with the appropriate regulatory agency the documents that formally removed him from that office.

To his credit, Cory recovered from this false start and is looking for new business customers.

You cannot avoid making mistakes in starting your business. However, you can avoid some of the more expensive ones if you take the time to pick your customers carefully.

PICK YOUR CUSTOMERS CAREFULLY

LESSON

DO NOT WORK FULL TIME
FOR CUSTOMERS WHO WILL ONLY PAY YOU
QUARTER-TIME PRICES.

Still another false start can occur when you fail to insist that your limited resources be applied exclusively to the growth of your business. It is an easy mistake to make when you are the victim of inexperience and your assailant, often identified as a customer, recognizes your weakness.

Invariably, some customers will demand your full-time attention. In deference to these customers, you put the welfare of their business ahead of yours and resign yourself to a career of servicing them.

That career usually starts at a modest level of pay. Like a first-floor escalator to the basement, the pay only goes lower.

Ward left his staff position of four years with a regional accounting firm shortly after his annual performance review. It would have been a pleasant surprise if Ward had received a promotion to manager. He did not receive the promotion. Realistically, he had given himself an additional two years to be considered for that position.

What irritated Ward was having his merit increase pegged to the general rate of inflation for a third consecutive year. At this rate, it would take forever for him to build any wealth. Ward just refused to work another year and risk suffering the same disappointment.

It was not difficult for Ward to start an accounting practice. He knew the general differences between debits and credits. Finding clients also came naturally to him. Getting them to pay their bills, however, was entirely another matter.

Ward offset this collection risk and his office overhead by agreeing to work as a part-time controller for one of his clients who owned a waterbed store.

What started as a two-day-a-week job for $1,500 per month rapidly grew to fill the month. His customer thrust the growth upon him. Reluctant to refuse the attention of his largest customer, Ward accepted the additional work for no additional fee.

While he managed the day-to-day furniture operations, Ward found himself doing considerably more work than he had bargained for in his initial agreement. That work included placating irate customers, ordering inventory, and searching for lost headboards and misrouted deliveries.

Ward's efforts were largely responsible for holding together what was otherwise a loosely run operation. That left no time for Ward to service his other clients.

"Ward! Did you order the Thermal Wave heaters for our Winter Wonderland California King models?"

"Not yet, Mr. Riley."

"Have you called that insurance guy about the damage he says was done by one of our delivery vans?"

"I'm waiting to hear back from him, Mr. Riley."

"Well, when he calls, offer him 30 percent of the damage amount he can prove. I also need a printout of our unmatched miscellaneous stock. Do you have it for me yet?"

"No, Mr. Riley. I'll get on it before I go home today."

"When are you leaving?"

"After traffic, about 6:30 P.M."

"I need that report before you go!"

"But it takes three hours to print!"

"Stick around Ward, or I'll see you around! "

It took only one paper jam in the printer for Ward to make the decision he should have made a long time ago. He left the business. Like most boats foundering on a reef, the furniture company fell to pieces.

Ward made a serious mistake in managing a business for a client who demanded full-time attention at quarter-time prices. There were many unfavorable consequences to that single mistake.

The obvious ones were the loss of some professional fees and the loss of his largest client. The damage went considerably further.

Ward's identity as a sole practitioner was thoroughly merged into the failing furniture operations. What few other clients Ward had at that time also left him.

DEVELOP A TECHNICAL EXPERTISE

LESSON

DO NOT EXPECT TO BE PAID PROFESSIONAL RATES FOR AN UNDEVELOPED EXPERTISE.

At some time in their business career, all entrepreneurs share similar disappointments.

Most entrepreneurs will agree that starting a new business is similar to riding in a poorly tuned vehicle that coughs, sputters, and, when it moves, keeps veering to the left. The ride is uncomfortable, and there is simply no power to get the vehicle moving forward with any degree of reliability.

It could be the fault of the vehicle.

In a business, it is usually the fault of the driver, who is inexperienced and probably lacks confidence, an identity, and an expertise. Whatever the fault, you must fix it before you can think about being competitive in wealth-building activities.

Byron could have had a comfortable corporate life anytime he wanted one. His dad owned a business that had gross sales of $30 million a year. Byron declined every invitation his dad extended to walk into a family vice-presidency. Byron wanted to do it his way. Byron's way involved making his business his best investment.

After seven fruitless months of selling insurance products as an independent agent, Byron knew he had a problem.

"Hey Mark! I think I have a problem."
"Only one, Byron?"

"Right now, yes. I need to get some credibility in the next two weeks."

"Why? Are you applying for a home mortgage?"

"No. It's just that every time I try to sell a product I have an identity crisis. Customers ask, 'Why should I buy anything from you? Just who the heck is Byron Lefkowitz?' "

"Byron, you could tell them you're my personal friend. I just couldn't guarantee how much help that would be."

"I'm beginning to think my name is the problem . . . ."

"Byron is a great name! The problem is your expertise. You have none! You need to narrow your focus."

"What do you mean?"

"Tell me what you have been selling to your customers."

"Oh, the typical insurance products: whole life policies, variable annuities, nonqualified employee benefit plans . . . ."

"What have they been buying?"

"Right now, nothing. I've tried selling to individuals, to small business owners, and to major corporations. They all tell me they like the printouts I give them and that they'll get back to me. Unfortunately, they haven't written any checks, yet . . . ."

"Byron, let's assume for a moment that there is no major defect with your product line. The products you sell are standard for your industry. They are also standard for everyone else in your industry who is selling them. You have got to specialize in an area and stop trying to sell every insurance product that was ever developed."

"You may be right. Sometimes I think I'm offering too many things to potential customers. I feel like I'm showing them a restaurant menu and asking what they would like to eat for lunch. If you were me, what would you change?"

"Pick any area that will save your customers money: 401-K retirement plans, employee stock option plans . . . ."

"But I don't have any experience in those areas. Besides, my name isn't exactly synonymous with retirement planning."

"It could be, Byron, but there's a price you would have to pay to get that experience."

"What's the price?"

"All of your short-term wealth."

(Laughs.) "That's not giving up much. I don't have any."

"I'll say." "Besides, you need to have a vision that looks beyond your next paycheck."

"I already do! Otherwise, I'd be working for my dad. One day, I'll be running his business. When that day comes, I want to enter his business from a position of strength, not because I couldn't make it on my own."

"Byron, you can make it on your own. I've never met anyone with your ability to tune out the first twenty 'No, I'm not interested' remarks that you get from a particularly stubborn customer. That ability and an expertise are all you need . . . ."

Byron decided to focus on retirement planning. Two weeks later, a trust company hired him. They gave Byron an office, a desk, a toll-free line, minor secretarial support, and a salary of $3,000 per month. In his three years with the trust company, Byron's base pay never changed, even though he brought in $65 million of new managed pension accounts.

If you had looked at his checking account balance the day he left the trust company to start his business, you would have thought Byron had wasted three years of his time. Byron will tell you differently. He developed an expertise, confidence, credibility, and a reputation as a leader in his field.

Nobody asks anymore, "Just who the heck is Byron Lefkowitz?"

It is disappointing to recognize that you have made a false start. False starts consume your time and other limited resources. That does not mean you have irrevocably damaged your business or your entrepreneurial career.

False starts happen to nearly every successful entrepreneur. Successful entrepreneurs learn from their mistakes. So will you.

Making your business your best investment can be difficult to get right the first few times you try to do it. Building equity in any business is just not a simple task until you have had experience doing it. I might also add that without good results, experience does not count.

You may find that it is easier for you to get the right kind of result by starting with the right kind of opportunity.

7 LOOKING FOR OPPORTUNITY

- ➤ Fight the Risk of Paralysis.
- ➤ You Need More Than an Idea.
- ➤ Walk Away from Interim Work.
- ➤ Start on Familiar Ground.

There are many ways to build your entrepreneurial wealth. Whichever way works for you, one thing is certain: You will begin your business with a combination of ideas.

Ideas are the starting point for all entrepreneurial activity.

The wonderful thing about ideas is that they never have to suffer the constraints of a real world. That means a business in the idea stage does not need to meet any verifiable demand in the marketplace or fret about competition.

There is also no requirement that ideas must pay for themselves. That is why ideas are easy to banter about.

That is also why many entrepreneurs are full of great ideas.

Despite the credit we must give to ideas, there is considerably more to starting a business than having a great idea. Entrepreneurs who agree will freely part with lists of "One Hundred New Business Ideas" in exchange for your certified money order or cashier's check.

Many of the features that make ideas initially attractive usually disappear when you analyze the ideas on paper. There are a number of reasons why this occurs.

An opportunity is what you can do with an idea. That usually means the idea must be within your abilities. It also means the idea must be economically feasible. What you have written on paper may fail to meet these requirements.

Designing a subsonic weapons platform to penetrate hostile radar and remain undetected is an idea. Building a Stealth bomber is an opportunity that is probably within the abilities of a handful of defense contractors. A $550 million price per plane is hardly economically feasible!

The process of converting an idea into an opportunity that is right for you also involves setting a few boundaries. That makes the opportunity manageable.

Simply by providing the first set of boundaries to an idea, the four edges of a single sheet of paper will frequently reduce the potential of most ideas.

The task of quantifying an idea can also be difficult. Some ideas and their related opportunities do not readily lend themselves to numerical analysis. That is why it can be a mind-bending task to translate a visual image of an idea to its business plan equivalent.

Despite the difficulty in converting an idea into an opportunity, the basic requirements for building equity remain unchanged. Building equity in any business involves identifying opportunities with real value and putting capital at risk.

It also involves having the financial muscle to carry those opportunities, periodically adjusting risk, and finally converting any investment in those opportunities to cash.

Your first step in looking for any opportunity is to fight the risk of paralysis.

FIGHT THE RISK OF PARALYSIS

LESSON

PARALYSIS CAN OCCUR WHEN YOU MISTAKENLY BELIEVE YOU ARE THE VICTIM OF OTHER PEOPLE'S CHOICES.

Unfortunately, many bright, aspiring entrepreneurs are paralyzed and unable to start their businesses. They believe they are victims.

They can be victims of the marketplace. How many times have you heard someone say that it is not the right time to start a business? Wait a while. The marketplace will better support your business endeavors when interest rates are lower and the recession is over.

They can be victims of their friends. What friend has not told you that you have a great job? You must be crazy to walk away from a guaranteed paycheck for a bundle of risk!

They can be victims of their families. A new baby, a home mortgage, the responsibility of raising children, and a stack of unpaid bills can temper the dreams of any entrepreneur.

The difference between an entrepreneur and a victim is a simple matter of choice. The entrepreneur chooses to be an entrepreneur. The victim believes there is no choice.

A winter may pass and it may never snow in Raleigh, North Carolina. It is a disappointment to my children when that occurs. During the preceding months, they have dutifully stockpiled a vast inventory of empty containers in the corner of the garage. When it snows, the neighborhood may be paralyzed into believing it is a victim of the weather, but not my children.

"Brittany! What on earth is a five-year-old doing up at 4:30 in the morning?"

"Daddy, it snowed!"

(Turns on outside lights.) "So I see. Who are those vagabonds running around outside?"

"Those are your children! Tiffany, Courtney, and Parker!"

"I might have known . . . ."

"We're picking up snow and saving it."

"Great, Brittany. By the way, I cleaned this counter before I went to bed last night. What is all this frozen food doing on it?"

"We had to make more room in the freezer." (Opens it.) "Tiffany has the top shelf and Courtney has the one below it. This one is mine, and the bottom one is Parker's. Daddy, can we get a new freezer?"

"For all of this food on the counter?"

"No! We need more room for our snow containers! We're filling them up and saving them for summer when it doesn't snow. Then we can make snow cones and sell them . . . ."

(Still trying to wake up.) "Let me talk to Mommy about this one. Hey, Brittany! Where are you going?"

"Back outside. I have another box of containers that I still need to fill . . . ."

A child can teach you many lessons. All you have to do is pay attention. One lesson you will learn is that children are not afraid to take risks. You will also learn there is no such thing as paralysis in the mind of a bright child who has been given an entrepreneurial nudge.

You are not a victim of other people's choices. If you are a victim, it is your personal choice. When you determine you do not like the status of being a victim, you can always change your mind. I encourage you to do so.

The risk of paralysis is a hurdle that you will cross more than a few times as an entrepreneur. All it ever takes to cross the hurdle is a decision from you. Once you have made the decision to be an entrepreneur, you will never again look the same way at a casually spoken business idea.

YOU NEED MORE THAN AN IDEA

LESSON

THERE IS NO OPPORTUNITY TO BUILD WEALTH WITH REASONABLE RISKS BY ACQUIRING NONINCOME-PRODUCING ASSETS AT FAIR MARKET VALUE PRICES.

The plan to acquire an asset is an idea. What you do with that asset could be an opportunity.

The price at which you acquire that asset will affect the overall return from the opportunity. Regardless of the price of the asset, if an asset cannot produce income or be converted to cash, there is no opportunity.

Len failed to recognize this important distinction.

Len looked hard for opportunities that would build his wealth. The lifetime prospect of being a salaried warehouse supervisor was a serious impediment to his personal ambitions.

Len's ambition was to build wealth. His idea was to build it through the leverage that real estate financing can sometimes provide. Real estate seminars that he had attended told him not only how to do it, but where to look for the opportunities.

During their lunch break, a co-worker passed the real estate section of the newspaper to Len. The worker spoke with a combination of despair and hope.

"Len, find us something so we can get out of this job. There has to be an easier way to make money than punching a clock . . . ."

"Maybe there is, Rick, maybe there is. Do you remember that truckload of appliances we delivered to Fairway View condominiums?"

"Sure. That's the project that nobody could afford. Some developer finished building them a year ago and tried to sell them for $255,000 apiece. He sold three or four of them, but I think the highest anyone paid for one of those units was $215,000."

"Right. I heard that the bank recently foreclosed on that project and is now giving the units away to anyone who can qualify for a $135,000 mortgage. All we have to do is help each other qualify for the mortgage, rent the units, hold them until the price goes back to $255,000, and then sell them. Our fortune, Rick, is waiting for us. Let me call my accountant. He may be interested in this deal."

I was not interested. The deal violated a basic wealth-building principle: getting paid for your risk.

It was true that each condominium unit was rentable at the current market rate. That market rental rate, however, was insufficient to produce a positive cash flow. The negative cash flow on each unit at the proposed $135,000 acquisition cost was $1,200 per month.

"That's OK, Mark. We get to deduct the rental loss."

"You're right Len, assuming you meet certain requirements and that Congress doesn't change the tax law again. Assuming they do not, in the worst possible case, are you prepared to carry this negative cash flow indefinitely?"

"But, Mark, you've missed my whole point! We are not going to carry these units indefinitely. We would sell them once they got back to $255,000 and make over $100,000 on each unit!"

"Len, what if they never got back to $255,000?"

"I hear what you're saying, Mark, but what are the chances of that happening?"

I would have told him if I knew the answer for sure. As it happened, I was only 99 percent certain that these assets would essentially be nonincome-producing for the rest of Len's life.

The units were initially offered at $255,000 each. Len assumed that price represented the fair market value of the opportunity. But fair market value is the price at which opportunities freely trade.

These opportunities were freely trading at $135,000. That was the average price of the most recent sales that occurred within the last ninety days. A total of five units during that time period all closed within a few thousand dollars of that average price. On the basis of the size of the negative cash flow, even that price seemed high.

If Len's assumption about initial offering prices and fair market values had been correct, there were far better opportunities available to him. All he had to do was open a *Wall Street Journal*.

Find a stock that was trading at $60 a share a few years ago and is now trading at $10 a share. Buy the stock at the lower price.

When the stock goes back to $60 a share, anyone who bought it at $10 a share would receive a 500 percent return on his initial investment.

Waiting, if you catch my drift, is the key. You may wait five years or you may wait twenty-five years. You may wait until your children have grandchildren and they have great-grandchildren.

After all of that waiting, the stock may still be trading at $10 per share. It might not even be trading.

Len overlooked a simple reason why these condominium units were freely trading at the $135,000 per unit price. Their related negative cash flow had convinced the marketplace that the units were not worth one penny more.

It is true that any investment will involve some kind of risk. One of the risks you do not need is buying a nonincome-producing asset early in your entrepreneurial career.

Until you identify your core business, you will look for interim opportunities where the risks are low and the returns are guaranteed. After all, you have the time and you need the money. An interim investment of your time in an opportunity with a guaranteed return certainly could not hurt your business. The guaranteed return may even lead you to believe you have successfully avoided unnecessary business risks.

Are you ever in for a surprise.

WALK AWAY FROM INTERIM WORK

LESSON

AN OPPORTUNITY WITH A GUARANTEED RETURN IS NOT ALWAYS A LOW-RISK OPPORTUNITY.

You will not be the originator of every opportunity that comes your way. There are other entrepreneurs just like you who are equally bright, comparably ambitious, and competitively aggressive. They will try to convince you that their opportunity can also be yours. It can be hard to refuse them for one simple reason.

Some opportunities are denominated in cash. That means there is no conversion risk. It also suggests that the rates of return are nothing to write home about.

The cash flow requirements of most entrepreneurial businesses usually prompt their owners to accept these interim opportunities.

You accept them because the cash in these opportunities is guaranteed and you have the time to invest.

You do not need to apologize for accepting a low guaranteed rate of return from any opportunity when the attendant risks are small. You may not have a choice. There may be no better investment opportunities with reasonable risks.

A guaranteed return does offer a benefit. That benefit is short-term peace of mind.

You receive this benefit in exchange for another kind of risk. When you accept this return, you may fail to meet your return on equity objectives.

Unfortunately, many entrepreneurs will also accept this guaranteed return without any reduction in risk.

Never let a guaranteed return force you into believing a riskless opportunity exists when it does not!

Garret had an accounting business with twenty-seven customers. Each customer had a different set of service requirements. Some called Garret every week. Others retained him to prepare their monthly financial reports.

There were two customers who came to Garret only when their bank required them to do so. Krupinsky was one of those customers.

Garret was in his office when Krupinsky called about an opportunity with a guaranteed return.

> "Garret, the bank told me that I need a reviewed financial statement again this year. What would it cost me to get it from you this year? I need to decide if I should go to someone else if you're too expensive. The review shouldn't be much of a problem because I hired a temporary employee who put everything on computer this year. All I want you to do is just look at my numbers and bless them for the bank!"

Where Krupinsky came from, blessing was a very big business. Political candidates had their election committees blessed. New businesses were blessed. Building sites were also blessed, sometimes two or three times.

The rate for a standard blessing was $100. If you needed a blessing that provided a greater level of protection against business risk, evil spirits, or just plain bad karma, that was a bit more.

What Krupinsky really wanted Garret to do was to sanctify his financial statements at standard blessing rates.

Garret had not talked with Krupinsky for almost a year. He had a good reason not to. Garret was still fuming over his last job with Krupinsky.

Garret had prepared a set of reviewed financial statements for the first year of Krupinsky's operations. Garret spent $7,300 of professional time, but Krupinsky would only agree to pay for $3,300 of it.

"It wasn't that complicated, Garret. Besides, you'll be doing the review again next year and we're a new company. Give us some consideration on your fees."

Just for the record, the temporary employee doing Krupinsky's data entry work was no accounting scholar. Neither was Krupinsky. Double entry bookkeeping was a concept as foreign to them as clean air is to a resident of Los Angeles.

Their limited accounting skills were a risk that Garret failed to note and for which he paid dearly.

The bank wanted Krupinsky's statements reviewed for two reasons.

The bank has just approved a $1.2 million accounts receivable factoring agreement. As a condition to approving that agreement, they wanted some assurance that the receivables were, well, for real.

They also wanted someone to nail if the blessing did not work.

The bank did not care what Krupinsky paid for the review engagement.

This time, a more cautious Garret started with the Lloyds of London approach in establishing his fee arrangement with Krupinsky.

"Let's see, Krupinsky. What would be the risk premium to insure $1.2 million of assets? One percent of the credit line? That would be $12,000. That's a nice round number. Two percent of the credit line? That would be $24,000. That's even a nicer round number!"

Krupinsky was nonplused. He insisted on standard blessing rates and not one dollar more. He waved the review fee in front of Garret.

"This probably won't cost more than $1,800 this year, right, Garret? After all, you have the benefit of last year's experience and we're now on computer. Besides, I'll even agree to pay in advance!"

"Well, Krupinsky, what's different in your business this year?"

"Not too much, Garret. Our sales volume and inventory have both quadrupled, but otherwise, it's still pretty much the same business."

Garret should have recognized that whatever could go wrong would at least go wrong in size.

Garret determined that the engagement would take about 120 hours of his time. That meant Krupinsky wanted it done for about $15 per hour.

That rate was certainly a good deal for Krupinsky.

Garret pondered the opportunity with some regret. He had just paid a plumber four times that hourly rate for a minor sink repair. Maybe he was in the wrong business. Still, $1,800 was $1,800. Garret had bills to pay and the time to do the work.

Krupinsky paid the $1,800.

Garret took the job and cut some corners. In his haste, Garret never looked at the detail behind a very large account receivable number. The consequence was overstating Krupinsky's accounts receivables by $135,000.

When the bank discovered the error, they terminated Krupinsky's factoring agreement and hit Garret with a thundering lawsuit.

Garrett discovered too late that some opportunities are just not worth the risk.

There are opportunities where you can identify much of the risk in advance. Knowing some of the risks can be useful in controlling them.

Unfortunately, you will never know if these risks are being properly managed when the opportunity is in a business you know nothing about.

START ON FAMILIAR GROUND

LESSON

LOOK FOR YOUR FIRST OPPORTUNITY
IN A BUSINESS YOU KNOW SOMETHING ABOUT.

Building equity can be as exciting and rewarding as it can be frustrating and just plain expensive.

If this is your first serious effort at starting a business, it will no doubt be exciting. Some of the excitement comes from the perceived control of your own destiny.

One of the rewards is the size of your possible return. If the opportunity is in an area in which you know nothing about, just do not expect too much in the way of results.

At age twenty-three, Arlene's worst problem was balancing her checkbook. Arlene had the benefit and the curse of an $800,000 trust fund.

The benefit was the size of the fund. The fund was loaded with blue chip stocks and high-grade bonds. Her father started the fund when a daily market trading volume of 3 million shares was a big deal.

The trust fund's appreciation over the years was also impressive. It was comparable to the appreciation of a collection of pre-Civil War stamps that were initially purchased at their postal values!

The curse was how Arlene came to own the assets. Her parents gifted the assets to her.

The wholesale gifting of large sums of money can be a curse without a cure. It was never intended to be that way.

In its kindest moments, gifting provides children with the financial security that their parents never had. Gifting, unfortunately, also short-circuits about forty years of entrepreneurial lessons and the resulting financial wisdom.

It is still possible for young entrepreneurs to learn these lessons if they have a desire to do so. Despite that desire, parents would roll over in their graves if they knew the prices their children paid for today's lessons.

I have to give Arlene credit. She knew that each month the trust fund increased in value by the stock dividends and bond interest payments that it received. She also knew that she could write checks against that trust fund balance. A lot of checks.

There is a long list of items that are considerably more exciting to a twenty-three-year-old than dividend income and bond interest coupons. One of those items is business risk.

Arlene simply had no business risk in her life.

Arlene looked for an opportunity where she could dance with risk instead of just opening the mail and reading her trust fund statements. She found the opportunity during the family's quarterly retreat at their Incline Village condominium. Eddie, her brother-in-law, talked to her about the opportunity.

Eddie was one of those people who believed he could swing a hammer better than Donald Trump could swing a deal. Never mind that the largest construction project he had ever completed was building a birdhouse to meet his Boy Scout merit badge requirement.

Eddie's opportunity was a historical rehabilitation project. It did not take a great deal of Eddie's convincing for Arlene to believe that it was her opportunity too.

In a remarkable demonstration of her strengths and weaknesses, Arlene handed him a check for $50,000 on a handshake.

With good intentions but disastrous results, Eddie offered to draft the partnership agreement. Arlene accepted the offer.

Eddie took five months just to draft the partnership agreement. During that time, he paid himself a $4,000 monthly management fee.

The partnership agreement allowed Eddie to do to his partner things that a man who believed in justice and fair play would probably consider criminal. The broadest provision of the partnership agreement allowed Eddie to invest in other properties with development potential.

Developing a commercial property has a level of risk considerably greater than buying one that is complete and fully leased. Many events can occur over the development period that might adversely affect the return on investment. You will discover that you cannot control the risks in some of these events.

Town councils can delay or revoke zoning variances. Subcontractors can raise cost disputes, and completion dates can be lost due to inclement weather. Commercial rental markets can soften, and lease commitments can be withdrawn.

In the interim, construction interest on any outstanding loan continues to accrue, further reducing the chances of a possible profitable investment.

Eddie went ahead with plans known only to himself. He bought four properties instead of the single one he had initially proposed. "They were great prices," he explained.

He placed his name on title, and then ran into unexpected difficulty while trying to obtain financing for the rehabilitation construction costs.

The cash flow projections on the projects were simply not good enough for the bank. The fact that there were no prospective tenants for the projects and that Eddie was incredibly inexperienced also hurt the partnership's prospects.

Arlene's trust account saved the partnership. The bank agreed to lend $515,000 to the partnership if it could secure the proposed loan with a lien against the trust fund assets.

Arlene had blind faith in her brother-in-law. "Hey, don't be too hard on him. Eddie's family . . . ."

If Arlene had a little more business experience under her belt, she may have recognized the fatality in that remark.

Arlene had no concept of the effort it took to build the equity in her trust account. Without a second thought, she readily agreed to the bank's collateral requirements.

All of Arlene's trust fund assets were now at risk.

During the next nine months the partnership bounced through a change of architects, construction cost overruns, and loans of partnership capital to Eddie for his personal expenses. There were still no prospective tenants in sight.

Arlene had not yet earned a penny on her investment in the partnership when the bank called the construction loans.

Building equity, just like building a commercial real estate project, is a far more involved matter than finding a prospective opportunity and putting risk capital on the line.

Those entrepreneurs with no knowledge of how to build equity would do just as well to play the slot machines in a Las Vegas casino. The air conditioning is reliable, the excitement is comparable, and the risk of loss is finite. In a casino, you can always walk away when you have spent your last dollar. That luxury is not usually available to most entrepreneurs.

If you look long enough, you will eventually find the right kind of opportunity. When you do, it will be in an area that you understand and where the risks are reasonable.

Before you consider joining forces with another entrepreneur to pursue this opportunity, you need to determine if you really need a partner.

8

DO YOU REALLY NEED A PARTNER?

- ➤ Call Your Own Shots.
- ➤ Grow Beyond Yourself.
- ➤ Make Your Partners Work Effectively.
- ➤ Take Care of Your Money Partners.
- ➤ Balance Your Risk.
- ➤ Retain Your Voting Rights.
- ➤ Talk to Your Partner.
- ➤ Terminate Your Partnership.

There is nothing like the ivory-billed woodpecker. There is also nothing like a partner who works like hell and does not take a salary. One of these has been included on the endangered species list. Both of them should be.

There are two reasons to have partners in your business. Some partners contribute specialized skills you do not have. Other partners contribute risk capital.

There are no other reasons.

In exchange for either of these contributions, you will forego some element of return and its related risk component. That is what it means to have a partner.

The concept of a partnership is nothing more than a risk- and return-sharing agreement.

Loosely speaking, a partner is another owner of your business. That ownership may be in the form of an additional general partner in a partnership. It may also be in the form of an additional shareholder in a corporation. Whatever the form, you may no longer have the right to make independent business decisions.

CALL YOUR OWN SHOTS

LESSON

IF YOU HAVE THE TALENT AND ALL OF THE CAPITAL YOU MAY NOT NEED A PARTNER.

In a business where the magnitude of risk is small, having a partner makes little sense. There is no single rule available to measure this risk other than your personal feeling about your business. When you have all of the talent it takes to manage your business and when you provide all of the capital, what is there for other partners to provide?

Rufus Detweiler could not be convinced to have any partner in his laser printer servicing business.

"How are your customers treating you these days, Rufus?"

"Business is as good as I could ever wish it to be, Mark. I just hired my fourth service technician this morning. If the market demand is any reliable indicator, I may need to hire two more technicians before the end of the year."

"That's great! What about your cash flow?"

"It could always be better, but right now, it's enough to pay the bills and put a little away. I sometimes think about taking on a partner, but I just don't want the complications that come with an additional owner . . . ."

"What are you talking about?"

"My daddy taught me a rule about partners."

"What's the rule?"

"Partners will complicate matters."

"That's all?"

"There's more. There are two corollaries attached to the rule. The first corollary is that a partner will always have an opinion that is different from yours."

"Rufus, a second opinion can be healthy . . . ."

"The second corollary is that a partner will always want to admit more partners . . . ."

"I can't say I entirely agree with those statements. I've seen quite a few operations that work because of the efforts of the partners . . . ."

"Mark, I work nearly eighty hours a week in a business where I call the shots. Any new partner wouldn't agree to work those hours and would want to make his own decisions. How could I allow that to occur after all of the years I've spent growing this business?"

"Rufus, cutting back a few hours a week wouldn't adversely affect your business. Your new partner would pick up the time and, I would add, also bring in additional business . . . ."

"That may be true, but then we'd need some kind of agreement just to make sure we had an understanding of our roles in the business."

"Those agreements are drafted all the time, Rufus. They're called partnership agreements or shareholder agreements. If they're properly drafted, you won't need to pay a referee to settle your business disputes."

"Maybe. But what happens at the end of the month?"

"What do you mean?"

"Let's say I've paid all the bills. What if this other partner wants to be paid?"

"Rufus, he's a partner! You should pay your partner whatever amount he is entitled to be paid. You'll agree on something fair . . . ."

"What if he wants something more?"

"Give me a specific example . . . ."

"What if he wants a loan from the business?"

"Rufus, how you respond to any loan request could be specified in your partnership agreement. Some partnership agreements that I've seen for closely held businesses prohibit a partner from borrowing money from the partnership. That provision is in the agreement because everyone knows that it is easier to feed the residents of a Third World village for a week than it is to feed a cash-starved partner for a single day . . . ."

"What if I wanted a loan from the business?"

"The same provisions would apply to you too. If you don't like the provisions, you and your partner would have to agree on new ones . . . ."

"I think I'm going to continue operating as I have been. I just don't see any benefit to having a partner."

(Sigh) "Suit yourself. It's your business . . . ."

Rufus was steadfast in his refusal to have any partner. He would modify his personal management style and partition his ownership interest for no one.

When the business is larger, so can be the risk in it and the related return. Banking that larger prospective return will almost surely require additional skills and working capital.

In such a business, you may have no choice but to look beyond yourself.

GROW BEYOND YOURSELF

LESSON

SOME LOOK AT THEIR CUSTOMERS AND SAY,
THIS IS MY MARKET.
OTHERS LOOK AT THE MARKET AND SAY,
THOSE ARE MY CUSTOMERS.

You are only one entrepreneur. Irrespective of your enthusiasm, your ability to confront challenges head-on, and your seemingly endless reservoir of energy, there is a limit to what any single entrepreneur can accomplish. You will discover this is true the first time you spend an entire day in your office without crossing out a single item on your list of things to do. You will confirm this a second time the day you get sick. All forward momentum in your business will come to a screeching halt.

You cannot be everywhere and you cannot do everything, even if it is your business. One day, you will need to consider growing beyond yourself.

It can be a frightening proposition to have other individuals in your business. It can be terrifying to have the responsibility for them. Some entrepreneurs never get over these fears.

The support of other capable individuals can help you build wealth in your business. Some of these individuals may be employees. Other individuals may have entrepreneurial talents similar to yours. If you choose your partners carefully, you will eradicate much of your fear in growing beyond yourself.

Select your working partners with a **compatible balance of skills**. Six chemists without an individual who knows how to sell will never bring their product to the marketplace. Six retired colonels and a secretary will never make a decision that forces them into the marketplace. Six salespeople without a business plan will never know if they have reached their sales goals.

You get the idea. A variety of talents with comparable attitudes about building business wealth can be a powerful entrepreneurial elixir. But it is no guarantee.

Dana Greisinger was comfortable with the idea of growing beyond herself:

"Dana, that was a great article I read about your business. Thanks for taking the time to fax it to me."

"Thanks for reading it, Mark. I sometimes wonder where my business would be today if I never took in other working shareholders. I feel silly, now, when I recall how I anguished over admitting other shareholders to my business."

"Not at all! Minority shareholders can make your daytime business a real nightmare. You're fortunate that this has worked for you. What's the secret?"

"Start with good people. Match their skills to specific job requirements and don't compromise on quality."

"That's a nice rule of thumb."

"There's more. Nearly everyone has an entrepreneur on the inside that wants to shout, 'I own a business!' I give everyone who works for me the chance to stand up and say that, but they have to put their capital at risk."

"That means they can lose it . . . ."

"That's absolutely right. It also means they take many of the same business risks to bed with them at night."

"I bet that keeps them working during the day."

(Nods head) "Sure. They work harder during the day because they have their capital at risk. They also avoid making foolish commitments that give the company's products away. It's now their company too . . . ."

"How did you ever learn to let go of your equity?"

"Mark, what's worth more—100 percent of a profitable business that has annual gross sales of $500,000 or 30 percent of a profitable business that has annual gross sales of $10 million?"

"I see your point, Dana. Although your percentage ownership is smaller, the slice of pie is much bigger. What happens if one of your people leaves the business after a year or two? Can they sell their interest to an outside individual?"

"Not at this time. We'll guarantee to buy back their stock according to a formula in our shareholder agreement, but any short-term buyback misses the whole point of the program."

"Which is . . .?"

"Long-term capital appreciation. No one should consider ownership in any business as a quick way to get rich. But over time, if you properly manage your business, your people, and other income-producing assets, the business should increase in value. The formula has worked for my business."

"You've convinced me . . . ."

But you may need to convince your partners more than once. This can be particularly true when you have partners who do not understand the effect of their work on the results of the business.

MAKE YOUR PARTNERS WORK EFFECTIVELY

LESSON

YOUR PARTNERS MUST SHARE SIMILAR WORK ETHICS.

Your business partners do not need to be identical copies of you. Beyond their initial contribution of capital or technical expertise, your partners need only share your burning desire to build wealth in your business.

Your partners must recognize the direct relationship between their work and the results in your business. When they do not recognize that relationship, your business and theirs will suffer.

Your business will benefit from your attention even though your partnership agreement may not require equal contributions in time from your partners. But your business will require similar results from the efforts of your partners. When partners do not share work ethics that produce those results, it is your job to make your partners work.

Beckley, Spofford, and Willis started a telephone message-retrieval service from a proprietary technology that they developed. Their customers were physicians, real estate professionals, and other individuals who required an answering service. Beckley met with me after one particularly frustrating Saturday morning.

"Mark, what are you doing out in your yard this cool spring day?"

"Beckley, if I don't trim the bushes, they don't get trimmed by anyone. Besides, haven't you heard that pruning a bush actually stimulates its growth?"

"My partners could use a bit of stimulation. Can I borrow your pruning shears when you're finished?"

"Sure, but there may be an easier way to jump-start your partners. What's the problem?"

"Remember when I told you that we leased a larger space?"

"Sure. The upstairs loft in your home just didn't have any more telephone line capacity. As I recall, your spouse also wanted to put an end to the company's open-refrigerator lunchtime policy."

"Right. Today, we were scheduled to paint our new office. Spofford and Willis agreed to plan everything."

"So how did it go? If your clothes are any indication, the color looks great! I just hope that some of the paint landed on the walls."

"Mark, it was worse than a donkey rodeo. When I arrived at 9:00 this morning, Spofford, Willis, and three helpers who we hired for the day were sitting around drinking coffee. They were waiting for me to pick up the paint! When I returned at 10:30, Spofford started on the walls without using a dropcloth . . . ."

"I've seen professional painters work that way, Beckley. They have the skill to do it, too. It makes a painting job move along quickly."

"But Spofford was a plumber, not a painter, in his previous life. Now the color of our carpet matches the color of our walls. I was so angry that I had to leave." (Simmers) "And these guys are my partners!"

"Beckley, it sounds like you had a difficult morning, but don't overreact. After all, it was just a botched painting job . . . ."

"If I believed that Mark, I wouldn't be here now asking to borrow your shears. I'm beginning to think my partners have a vastly different concept of work than I do."

"How can you be sure?"

"Willis is in charge of sales. He used most of last week to fill out a home mortgage refinance application. Spofford is our operations manager. He spends the first two hours every morning reading the newspaper. I'm not convinced that either of my partners knows how to work without supervision!"

"So, supervise them!"

"But they're my partners!"

"Beckley, the title 'partner' doesn't exempt anyone from being accountable for a specific task or set of objectives. If your partners do not know how to use their time to produce results, then you must show them how. Make them work effectively!"

"Both partners could use the tips, but Spofford would probably resent the supervision."

"Beckley, it's his business too. When you increase his productivity, you also increase the value of his share of the business. You also share that increase in value. Once Spofford sees the relationship between his work and the value of his partnership interest, he'll begin to develop an entirely new work ethic."

"But what if he doesn't change?"

"Then you know where to borrow a set of pruning shears . . . . ”

Not every partner will need a personal lesson from you in the value of an effective day's work. That reprieve will give you additional time to manage your core business. If you can be successful at that task, your other partners will notice. Your money partners will be the first to recognize that you know what you are doing.

TAKE CARE OF YOUR MONEY PARTNERS

LESSON

KEEP YOUR MONEY PARTNERS INFORMED ABOUT THEIR INVESTMENT RISKS.

Money partners own an interest in your business. It does not matter if their contribution in your business is recorded as equity in a corporation, as capital in a partnership, or as a loan to either entity. It is still the same color irrespective of how you record it. Their money buys you inventory, provides you with credit, and allows your business to grow.

You cannot run your business without their contribution. Let them know you are grateful for their capital.

You can offer many token benefits to your money partners. Some of these benefits may include reimbursements for travel to your business, resort hotel accommodations, private golf outings, and other gestures designed to show your appreciation. Most of these gestures are meaningless. Some of them are offensive. A money partner knows you are using his money to pay for those benefits.

You can return only a single item of any value to your money partners. Their money, of course! Until the day you return their money to them, give them information, lots of it.

Money partners like to be informed. Tell them what you are doing. Tell them why. Make yourself accessible to them at all times. Give them your telephone number and assure them that they can call you whenever they have a question.

Meet with them monthly and talk about the business. Walk them through the business so they see their investment. If there is good news and bad news, get the bad news out first—all of it. If there is more bad news at a later date, put it on the front page of any correspondence to them. Never lie to your partners. Let your money partners have a chance to hear about all of the problems facing their investment in you. You may be surprised at the number of good solutions they offer.

Spivey met with his money partner, Olmstead, about an event that had the potential to affect the future operations of the business.

"Olmstead, am I glad to see you!"

"Spivey, it's always a pleasure. Say, I want to tell you that I really enjoy seeing your monthly pie chart presentation of operating results. It is easy to read and a single picture tells the whole story . . . ."

"It takes me a little more time to summarize the information that way, but I'm glad you find it useful. Of course, you're welcome to wade through our monthly general ledgers, too, if you ever run out of things to do."

(Laughs) "That's OK, Spivey. The day you need my accounting skills will be the day I really start to worry about my investment. What's on the agenda today?"

"The entire business. We may have an uninvited third partner. If we do, it's all my fault . . . ."

"You found another money partner?"

"Not exactly. I received a certified letter from the IRS yesterday. They've issued a Proposed Notice of Intent to Levy for some back taxes."

"How far back?"

"Actually, just a few years. When I left my previous employer, I used all of the pension funds I accumulated at the time to start this business."

"What's the proposed levy amount?"

"Something on the order of $37,500."

(Whistles) "Spivey, I vaguely recall you saying your capital in this business came from a pension fund. I just had no idea that it came with a related unpaid federal tax liability."

"Olmstead, I honestly didn't know I had to pay taxes on that money. I would never do anything to jeopardize this business . . . ."

"I believe that, Spivey. You're the first partner I've ever had who has taken the time to keep me informed about my investment. You always give me the bad news the moment you hear it. I can't tell you how much your honesty has meant to me."

"I just wish I had been smarter, Olmstead. I should have talked to my CPA before I withdrew the money from my pension. It was a $37,500 mistake. I just hope the business can work its way through this levy."

"Spivey, as I read this document, it's strictly a Notice of Intent to Levy. Your problems only start if you don't pay the amount within thirty days . . . ."

"I can't pay the amount in thirty months! I just don't have that kind of savings right now and I can't arrange to borrow that sum in thirty days. A few years from now, it could be a different story . . . ."

"I want this business to have your undivided attention, Spivey. I also want to limit our operations to two business partners, you and me. What would you say if I paid the tax on your behalf just to make the problem go away?"

"Huh?"

"Naturally, it's not a gift to you. It's a secured loan. You'll have to sign over your ownership in the business to me and all the related voting rights until you repay the full amount. You'll also have to pay some predetermined rate of interest for this kind of loan."

"Olmstead, I don't believe what I'm hearing from you. You would agree to bail me out of this problem?"

"Spivey, you're going to bail yourself out. You show up for work every day, you're reliable, and you're honest. It may take a little time for you to repay the loan, but I'm comfortable with the security and convinced that you can do it."

"Thanks for the vote of confidence, Olmstead. I really appreciate it . . . ."
"You earned my confidence a long time ago, Spivey."

It is one matter to convince your current money partner that you are worth the risk. It is an entirely different matter to convince a prospective business partner that you are worth the money. This is particularly true when you are the sole source of business capital and expect to receive a similar division of business profits.

Take the time on your way into business to discuss with your partner the fairness of balancing business risk and business ownership.

BALANCE YOUR RISK

LESSON

INSIST THAT YOUR RETURN IN ANY PARTNERSHIP BE PROPORTIONAL TO YOUR RISK.

So you are going to be a business partner. What an opportunity to make a difference in the growth rate of your wealth! It is also an opportunity to lose your friends, incinerate your savings, forfeit your self-esteem, and forever put to rest your misplaced belief in your good business judgment.

The effect this opportunity has on you will depend on the job you have done in balancing your business risk with your ownership in the business. You can balance this relationship at any time, but it is a task that is best performed by you at the start of any new business.

The act of balancing can be a matter of delicate negotiation.

"Cecile, I hear you're now in the gift basket business . . . ."

"You're absolutely right. One of my tennis partners had the idea. Since there are quite a few businesses relocating to Raleigh, families will follow. They'll need to be welcomed properly to their neighborhoods. A gift basket of local items is the way to do it . . . ."

"You're right about all the new businesses. I think your timing is excellent. How are you proposing to structure this new business?"

"We're going to start off as equal partners . . . ."

"So each of you owns 50 percent of the business?"

"That's right."

"What is the source of your capital for the business?"

"I'm going to provide the initial capital. The exact amount hasn't been finalized, but I think it will be approximately $30,000. We'll use that money to buy inventory, create an advertising brochure, hire a delivery person, etc."

"What is your partner contributing?"

"Oh, well she had the idea! That was her contribution . . . ."

"Cecile, do you have a few minutes?"

"Sure, I don't need to pick up the kids until 3:15 P.M. today."

"What do you know about the concept of proportional interest?"

"Isn't it something about things having a relationship to each other?"

"That's it exactly. In business, many things have predefined relationships. When you don't treat employees fairly, they quit. That's a predefined relationship. When you don't pay your estimated tax payments, you're penalized by the IRS. That's a predefined relationship."

" . . . and when you start a business partnership like ours, you share the profits. I see what you mean about predefined relationships, Mark."

"Cecile, let me modify that last statement of yours. When you start a business, you *may* be entitled to receive some proportional share of the profits."

"I thought everyone shared equally in the profits of the business. My partner, in fact, recommended it. I hear you suggesting that may not be the proper way to do it."

"It is frequently not the proper way, Cecile. Profits are usually shared in some proportion to your risk. The absolute measure of that risk will usually be connected in some way to your capital in the business."

"How do you decide what is fair?"

"There are several things that you should consider before you agree to any division of profits or losses with your partner. Start the process with this question. What happens if in a single moment after you write your check, your business is instantaneously exposed to a massively fatal dose of business risk?"

"Mark, it sounds like you're talking about some kind of radiation poisoning."

"Cecile, that's exactly what business risk is! It is some kind of radiation poisoning. Exposure to business risk in limited amounts has never been known to be fatal. Addictive? Perhaps. Fatal? No."

"When I think of this new business in those terms, I get a little uneasy."

"Can you tell me why?"

"Sure. An instantaneously fatal dose of business risk would make my $30,000 capital contribution go away."

"What effect would the same dose of risk have on your partner?"

"None that I can think of. She'd probably show up at the club and expect to play a few games of tennis the day after . . . ."

"Does that seem fair to you?"

"Not anymore . . . ."

The concept of proportional interest is one of balance. Your business risk should always be proportional to your return. When you discover that it is not proportional, the relationship is out of balance. Take the time and find the balance point with your partner. After all, your capital is at risk!

When you provide 100 percent of the risk capital in a business, you should be entitled to receive 100 percent of the profits in the business, until you have your capital returned to you. If you share in only 50 percent of the profits or losses of a business, your capital contribution should be limited to 50 percent of the total capital exposed to business risk.

Entrepreneurs' investment behavior frequently confirms the fact that many of them know nothing of this concept.

The balance in this risk-return relationship goes beyond capital accounts and the division of possible profits. If your capital contribution is exposed to 50 percent of the risk in the business, you should also retain 50 percent of the voting rights in the business.

RETAIN YOUR VOTING RIGHTS

LESSON

NEVER ACCEPT A MINORITY OWNERSHIP INTEREST WHERE YOU HAVE NO VOTING RIGHTS.

When you are offered a return in profits or losses that is proportional to your capital interest, you still need to look further. It is the first possible sign that you are dealing with an honest partner, but you can never be certain.

Sanford started an automobile dealership. His equal division of equity presumably reflected his sense of fair play. He readily transferred 80 percent interest in the profits, losses, and risk of his business in exchange for 80 percent of the startup capital. He distributed the stock certificates to his business partners in a brief afternoon meeting.

"So, there you have it! Here are your stock certificates. Don't they look nice? Each one of you now owns 2,000 shares of Class A common stock. That's 8,000 shares of Sanford Automotive, Inc., in your portfolios. Here's my certificate for 2,000 shares of common stock. Congratulations on making a fine investment."

"Uh, Sanford? I've got a question."

"Sure, what is it? I hope it's not a legal question. I'm not a lawyer. Every time you have to get a lawyer involved, there's always an invoice that accompanies the advice . . . ."

"How is the company going to pay dividends?"

"Oh, that's one I can answer. We'll take a look at our operating results every quarter. If there are excess funds that we've accumulated beyond the normal and customary needs of the business, we'll pay a dividend just like the larger publicly traded companies do."

"OK. That's all I needed to hear . . . . "

Most customers shopping for a new vehicle understand that the window sticker price is the dealer's initial offer to you. Few dealers expect to sell vehicles at those sticker prices, but then, you just never know who will walk on to your showroom floor.

Sanford loved the business because of the fluid give-and-take of selling a car. Customers offered you their money and you obliged them by taking it.

The real profit to the dealership came from options Sanford offered to each of his customers. Rustproofing a vehicle cost Sanford $70 per car. He offered it to his customers for $290. Sanford paid $45 for acrylic sealing and resold it to his customers for $320.

Sanford offered to extend portions of the original factory warranty on every vehicle he sold to his customers. It was a great deal for Sanford. The original factory warranty covered most of the mechanical risks. As a practical matter, most new vehicles usually worked reliably during the factory warranty period. Consumers, however, freely paid $650 to Sanford for this extended coverage.

A history of increasing sales made the dealership a large one. Sanford never disclosed the real profit of the dealership on financial statements he distributed to the shareholders. He hid most of the dealership's profit from its shareholders in subsidiary companies.

Sanford Automotive, Inc., paid retail prices for the lucrative incidentals ordered by customers. It purchased rustproofing, acrylic sealing, and extended coverage from Sanford's subsidiaries.

After six years of business, Sanford's equity investors had not received a dime in dividend distributions. Sanford balked at paying any dividend distribution.

"Look at the numbers! The dealership is just making ends meet. You tell me where there's any fluff in these operations."

"Sanford, last year, you sold nearly 1,300 vehicles. Why can't we make a profit on that kind of volume?"

"We are making a small profit. Take a look at our income statement!"

"Sanford, I don't know how to read those things. All I know is that I expected to receive periodic quarterly dividends. This arrangement isn't what I had in mind when I agreed to be a shareholder with you."

"I'm doing the best I can. Running a business is tough."

"Why don't you buy me out?"

"If I purchased your stock, then I'd have to offer to do the same for each of the remaining shareholders. I don't have the funds to do that . . . ."

"Sanford, I can't hold these shares indefinitely . . . ."

" . . . and I can't buy you out."

Legal prodding on behalf of the disgruntled shareholders did not initially produce the intended effect. It upset Sanford. It also upset the shareholders. They learned that they could call as many shareholder meetings as they wished. They could also discuss as many issues as they had the energy for. They simply could not vote on any issue. The right to vote was entirely Sanford's.

Sanford had issued two classes of stock when he started the dealership. It was true that Sanford owned only 20 percent of the outstanding shares. Sanford's Class B shares were the only shares with voting rights. The other shareholders simply held attractive certificates with no voting rights in amounts that were proportional to their original investments.

Stock without voting rights is usually worthless.

The shareholders, of course, had the right to sue, and they exercised that option. Two years later, a judge ordered Sanford to sell the dealership and split proportionately the sales proceeds. The nonvoting shareholders received their share of equity and of justice.

Legal battles, however, are expensive. The outcome is never predictable, and these battles are never a completely reliable substitute for good judgment.

That good judgment must show itself before the day your business begins its operations. The judgment is in evidence by the way you select your partners. It is also reflected in the way you resolve conflicts with your partners. Take the time to communicate with your partner. There is no business that can survive an unresolved partnership dispute. Your business cannot survive, either.

When you cannot find the time to talk to your partner, there is no way to resolve amicably any dispute. All you can do then is watch your partner take your business.

TALK TO YOUR PARTNER

LESSON

A 50 PERCENT OWNERSHIP INTEREST
IS NO GUARANTEE THAT YOUR OTHER PARTNER
WILL EVER CONSIDER YOU AN EQUAL.

Minerva and Victoria started an advertising agency as equal 50 percent partners. What followed was a confusing series of events that ended a business with a bright future.

"Minerva, did you get the billing out for last month?"

"I did, Vicky. However, I had to drop all the other projects I'm working on just to do it. It took nearly a week to put the bills together. There has to be a better way to do this . . . ."

"So, what did we make?"

"Enough to pay our rent for another month and take our $1,500 draws from the business . . . ."

"Are you sure you billed everyone?"

"Vicky, of course I did. Unfortunately, there is a limit to what our $30 per hour billing rate planted across fifteen clients will produce."

"Maybe we should raise our rates?"

"That's a possibility. I thought we agreed that we would keep our rates low for the first year until we built up the client base."

"A year is a long time to wait to make some money from this business. How can I ever afford to qualify for a mortgage on our monthly draws?"

"Vicky, we'll do just fine. Give the business a chance to grow."

"Minerva, I'm tired of burning candles at both ends. I've worked fourteen hours a day for the last six months trying to bring in new business. All I ever see you doing is sitting in the office working on one or two projects. I don't understand why it takes you so much time just to prepare the bills."

"Huh?"

"I'm really tired of doing all the work and getting paid for half of it."

"Then let's talk about it, Vicky . . . ."

"Are you kidding? I don't have the time today . . . . "

Minerva never pressed the issue, and Victoria never made the time. The conflict about the value of each partner's contribution to the business simmered. Their blistering-paced schedule never gave them the time to air their grievances properly.

One Monday morning Minerva arrived at her office to find the doors locked and her personal effects neatly arranged in a box sitting in the hallway. Victoria simply refused to open the door.

"But this is our business Victoria!"

"It's mine now, Minerva."

"But I'm a 50 percent partner!"

"So what?"

Victoria wanted to qualify for a mortgage on a condominium more than she wanted Minerva as a partner. In a premeditated manner, Victoria locked Minerva out of the office and filched her interest in the business.

Minerva met with an attorney to discuss the possibility of pursuing her legal rights. The $5,000 retainer for legal fees was unaffordable. An embittered Minerva just walked away from the business.

She did have an earlier choice. Minerva could have talked to her partner long before Vicky changed the lock on the office door.

Not all business ventures end this abruptly. Sometimes, the ventures actually achieve their business goals that build wealth for the partners.

Once this occurs, some partners may feel differently about business risk. Do not be surprised if a current partner is reluctant to participate in a new venture.

Your partner is telling you that there is a time to terminate every partnership.

TERMINATE YOUR PARTNERSHIP

LESSON

WHEN A PARTNERSHIP HAS MET ITS BUSINESS OBJECTIVES, TERMINATE THE PARTNERSHIP.

A partnership is a financial marriage of entrepreneurial objectives. It is this continuity of interest that can make a joint business venture stronger than any single effort.

If I can promise you anything in business, it is that things never stay the same. Interest rates will change. Your feelings about risk will change. Expected business values will change. Why, then, should objectives or goals never change?

The truth is that they do.

Some partners never recognize this. As a result, it comes as a great surprise when one partner proposes to dissolve a business operation that has produced wonderful investment results for all participants. Vigorous objections by dissenting partners usually accompany the proposal to dissolve. Who can blame them? It can be a horrifying prospect to dismember a business that really works. It can also appear to be the irrational act of a partner who, this time, has really lost his marbles.

It is not clear whose fault, if anyone's, it ever is. When the partnership has achieved its objectives and further synergistic results between partners are no longer possible, it is time, then, to reconsider.

Riley and Grigsby were partners in a partnership that owned a small Boston apartment building. Eight years ago, they paid $300,000 for the building. The annual net rental income for the building today was $270,000. Depending on whom you asked, that made the building worth somewhere between $2 million and $3 million.

A month after he bought the building with his partner, Grigsby got on a boat and set sail for unspecified points. Riley agreed to manage the building.

Grigsby was content to let the wind and currents direct his future. At age fifty-six, sailing had given him sea legs second to none and a new view of the world. He was living a year-round adventure with no risk but the open ocean. Additional financial leverage just did not fit in his boat.

At age thirty-seven, Riley had other ideas. Various investment opportunities required the use of his equity capital, which was locked into the partnership. No bank would agree to lend Riley any amount against his partnership equity without Grigsby's consent.

Each partner left his respective world for one week and traveled 5,500 miles in opposite directions to Hawaii. In a three-hour early morning beach walk, they resolved their differences.

Both agreed that the partnership had been a good one. The theoretical equity gains had been enormous and the partnership's equity-building objectives had been met.

Grigsby wanted to reprovision his boat and spend the rest of his life at sea.

Riley wanted to develop commercial property and already had preliminary locations for two small shopping centers.

Neither partner would agree to live in the other's world.

With astute entrepreneurial insight and no regret, the partners agreed to list the building for sale, and bid each other Aloha. When the sale was finalized, each partner received $1.15 million as his proportional distribution.

Not every business venture that you consider will require a partner. But most businesses will benefit directly from the additional technical skills and risk capital that a partner can provide. However, you will not always need a partner to share your business risk. There are other alternatives. Just ask your banker about them.

9

THE CHALLENGE WITH BANKS

- ➤ Welcome to the Risk Transfer Business.
- ➤ You Must Be Trustworthy.
- ➤ It Helps to Be Wealthy.
- ➤ You May Need a Cosigner.
- ➤ Prepare Your Loan Proposal.
- ➤ Quantify the Value You Have Developed.
- ➤ Banks Don't Really Care About Your Business.
- ➤ Find a Banker Who Values Retirement Wealth.
- ➤ Do Not Compete with Your Bank.
- ➤ Beware of Equity Credit Lines.
- ➤ Let Your Fingers Do the Walking.

Working with a partner can have its shortcomings. But those shortcomings will look positively delightful the day you decide to work with a bank.

I do not mean to be critical about most bankers. This is true despite the uncanny, natural ability of a few bankers I have known to make dumb remarks about business with an entirely straight face. It is also true despite the fact that some small business bankers know so little about running a business that it ought to be illegal for them to make any business loan.

There is no better way to ruin your chance of getting your loan approved quickly than by having an assistant bank manager trainee assigned to service your account.

It can be a frustrating exercise to explain to someone who has never seen a balance sheet why the presentation of yours looks different. It can also be a challenge to explain to a new bank employee the business reason for the loan. As an inexperienced intermediary, this individual will almost always omit some critical fact in presenting your request to the loan committee.

Despite my personal feelings about the problem with banks, bankers will nonetheless agree to make business loans to you for two specific reasons. The first reason is to facilitate the transfer of business risk. The second reason is that they get paid for it.

WELCOME TO THE RISK TRANSFER BUSINESS

LESSON

BANKS WILL AGREE TO SHARE YOUR BUSINESS RISK FOR A FEE.

Banks are suppliers of capital. They are also in the risk transfer business. For a fee, they will provide you with debt capital and will agree to accept a portion of your business risk. You can be certain that their business is thriving.

Why is this so?

Entrepreneurs are in the risk-taking business. In exchange for a return, they will accept a certain amount of risk. They will try to balance that risk with any expected return.

When the risk is proportionately greater than the return, there is excess risk. Entrepreneurs will lay off this excess risk on anyone who is willing to accept it.

Aunt Dora, of course, is a good candidate. The two of you have gotten along ever since you could sit in her lap without depositing your breakfast on it. She works downtown, owns her own house, and loves the gallery of pictures by her niece that now cover the door of her refrigerator.

She is also no one's fool. She is a portfolio manager for the state's largest pension fund and knows a thing or two about risk. Getting sixty cents from her for bus money is more difficult than breaking into Fort Knox.

Uncle Fred is another option. Since you were a little child, he has always encouraged you to come to him with your problems. There was nothing you could bring him that an ice-cream cone or a jar of 500 gumballs could not fix.

Fifteen years later, however, Uncle Fred runs a different race. His pacemaker ticks like a clock and he still loves his niece. But his timing and yours are no more closely matched today than the spin rates of the planets Earth and Venus.

That is why banks do a thriving risk transfer business. They are considerably easier to access than Aunt Dora's purse and are generally more reliable than Uncle Fred.

The fee you will pay them will always start from a market-driven level. That is where all similarities end.

Their fees, unlike your expected returns, will have little correlation with the amount of risk you transfer to them. Banks often demand and receive a premium over general market rates for accepting some of your risk.

They do it fully recognizing that your family tree is full of Aunt Doras and Uncle Freds. They do it for another reason, too. Unlike entrepreneurs, they cannot walk away from a really bad bet. It would send a message they do not wish to send to their borrowers.

Banks use this premium as a lightning rod, to deflect an occasional calamitous loan to a cushioned bad-debt reserve.

They also do it in the name of fiduciary responsibility. Do not believe for a minute this is any sense of fiduciary concern on your behalf. After all, you are only a customer.

Their fidelity is first to the preservation of their jobs and then to their shareholders. It is that diverse and largely risk-averse shareholder group that, if the truth be told, has retained loan committee members to build equity on their behalf.

Why, then, should you work with banks at all?

Prudently managed, banks are enduring. They will survive even if your business does not.

Long after Aunt Dora has retired and Uncle Fred has died, these banks will still be accepting deposits and making loans. Their broad equity base and federally guaranteed lending programs have given them an advantage and a longevity that few entrepreneurs will ever enjoy.

Nevertheless, banks are the measure of last resort. You turn to them in despair after all others have turned you away. Get a loan application, fill it out, and walk it over to their office. Someone will listen to your story. That is why they are there.

Before you schedule an appointment, however, you should know a few things about the loan approval process and a bank's own agenda.

YOU MUST BE TRUSTWORTHY

LESSON

DO NOT SIT DOWN WITH A LOAN OFFICER UNTIL YOU HAVE PRACTICED TALKING ABOUT YOURSELF.

A loan officer will never seriously consider your application until she has satisfied herself with your answer to a fundamental question:

"Are you trustworthy?"

Give the matter some thought before you visit a bank office. Presentation is 90 percent of the answer.

When you arrive, it is not a good idea to dress like a crook. It is also not a good idea to act like one. You are there to pass the bank's version of the "smell" test. If you cannot pass this test, you can forget about having to repay the loan. The loan officer will never give you the loan proceeds.

Unfortunately for all of us, crooks today can look and act like anyone, from a bum on the street to a bank president. Few crooks these days ride conspicuously into town wearing black cowboy hats, silver spurs, and a pair of notched six-shooters.

That is another reason why bank loan officers need to know about your past:

"Have you ever been sued for nonrepayment of anything?"

"What does your credit report look like?"

"Tell me a little about yourself."

People who have enjoyed their life cannot stop talking about it. They talk freely and love to tell you what they have done and the successes they have become. It takes little conversational prodding beyond a cup of black coffee and the question, "What did you do before this?" to get them started.

These applicants welcome the chance of addressing a potentially interested and captive audience. They will quit only after they have shown a loan officer all the pictures in their wallet and have long overrun the next appointment.

People who are reluctant to talk freely usually have something to hide.

Once you are judged trustworthy, banks will look at the net worth you have accumulated.

IT HELPS TO BE WEALTHY

LESSON

IT IS EASIER TO BORROW MONEY WHEN YOU CAN DEMONSTRATE YOU DO NOT NEED IT.

What is the primary source of repayment for the loan and how do you propose to repay what you will borrow? If you are borrowing $300,000 for working capital in a new business startup, the bank likes to see that you are independently wealthy:

"How may I help you?"

"My name is Dr. Pettigrew. I'm a neurologist at Weston Medical Center. I'd like to apply for a $300,000 business loan."

"Is the loan for your medical practice?"

"No. It's for a new business. I'm going to start a poultry farm that specializes in raising ostriches as an alternative food source . . . ."

(Pause) "May I ask what your wife does, Dr. Pettigrew?"

"She's a radiologist."

"Why don't you make yourself comfortable in our executive dining room while I have the loan documents prepared. Will a twelve-ounce cut of prime rib and a bottle of 1985 Australian Merlot be adequate?"

That wealth gives loan officers some assurance that you can service the full amount of the debt from your stock dividends and bond interest coupons. When they see that wealth, they also worry less about the ultimate success of your proposed operations.

Most entrepreneurs, of course, would like to win the state lottery. The chances of that occurring are not what you should consider to be a high probability event.

If your net worth looks too modest, then finding someone to cosign the loan with you may improve your chances of receiving it.

YOU MAY NEED A COSIGNER

LESSON

THE EASE OF BORROWING MONEY INCREASES IN DIRECT PROPORTION TO THE NUMBER OF QUALIFIED LOAN GUARANTORS.

"What is the secondary source of repayment?"

It is always a better deal for the bank if you are married and your spouse works as a salaried heart surgeon or chief executive officer and is willing to cosign the loan. Parents and relatives who cosign loan documents are also nice secondary repayment sources.

A word of caution may be useful. Cosigning a loan is a great way to break up a family.

That single act has created an oversupply of prodigal sons and daughters. The actions of too-kind parents or in-laws have also resulted in the forfeiture of many homes, bonds, and businesses.

If you can provide satisfactory answers to a loan officer's questions, then the bank will probably take a serious look at your loan application. Be sure your loan proposal is complete.

PREPARE YOUR LOAN PROPOSAL

LESSON

YOUR LOAN PROPOSAL MUST LOOK SERIOUS
IF YOU WANT TO BORROW SERIOUS MONEY.

The standard two-page bank loan application is no longer adequate for anything more than a standard auto loan. If you want to borrow serious money, you must have a comprehensive loan proposal that shows you know what you are doing.

This loan proposal will be a direct reflection of your management style. It will also be a subtle indicator of the way you view your banking relationship. Take the time to do it right and include the following items in a bound and indexed report:

- Loan request
- History of your business
- Current personal financial statements
- Individual tax returns for the last two years
- Business financial statements for the last two years
- Business tax returns for the last two years
- Current business plan and a twenty-four-month operating budget

You cannot prepare the contents needed in this proposal over a long weekend "The Bank Needs This Report by Our Tuesday Meeting" session. If you have not previously taken the time to prepare business financial statements, business tax returns, and a sensible operating budget, you have a job ahead of you.

There are no shortcuts. If you have a finance and accounting background, it may take you a few weeks to put the information together. If your strengths are in different areas, you will need to find someone to help you. Entrepreneurs who are successful in obtaining bank financing almost always have a certified public accountant coaching them through this process. It is worth the expense and the effort. You will not receive the financing if you cannot demonstrate that you know your numbers.

Your numbers may not tell the entire story. If they need some window dressing, attach an analysis that quantifies other hidden values in your business.

QUANTIFY THE VALUE YOU HAVE DEVELOPED

LESSON

DRAW A PICTURE OF THE ASSETS THAT ARE NOT ON YOUR BALANCE SHEET.

Service businesses are some of the most difficult operations for banks to analyze. There are several reasons why this is true.

A service business usually does not have a guaranteed market for its service. The absence of that guarantee means that customers are not always repetitive.

The day you apply for a loan, a banker will tell you something that you already know. Today's customers cannot be relied upon with certainty to provide your business with tomorrow's revenue.

Time is the primary asset of any service business. A successful service business is usually one where its owner has been efficient in converting that primary asset to cash.

That efficiency usually means there are few remaining assets parked on a balance sheet that a banker can use to secure any business loan.

The bank's problem and your dilemma are further compounded when one of those remaining assets is goodwill.

Entrepreneurs will usually agree that there can be a considerable amount of goodwill in any successful service business. Bankers will unanimously agree that goodwill can be elusive and hard to value.

Goodwill in any business can be a sizable asset.

When you buy it, it is an easy asset for a banker to see on your balance sheet. The dollar value they see under the caption "goodwill" represents the amount you have paid for a bundle of income-producing assets.

When you develop the income-producing capabilities in your business, you have produced goodwill. Unfortunately, this type of goodwill cannot be readily seen as an asset on a traditional balance sheet. No matter how effective you have been building business wealth, bankers will usually not agree to secure any loan with assets that they cannot see.

It is your job to make sure your banker can see the goodwill you have developed. It is a simple three-step task:

1. **Quantify the value you have developed using units.**

   Units are easy to count even for those individuals who have difficulty with math.

2. **Convert those units to dollars with a multiplier.**

   Bankers like to determine if your current operations are growing. The multiplier allows them to measure the possible size of your future revenues.

3. **Draw a picture. You may need more than one.**

   A set of convincing graphs will validate your numbers.

Griggs and Loftin built a law practice specializing in plaintiff personal injury litigation. In their typical case, there was usually no question if damaged occurred. It was merely a matter of quantifying the amount of damage.

Their Los Angeles law firm started from a desk in the second bedroom of their co-op. In six months, it took over their living room and kitchen. When the neighbors complained about unauthorized vehicles in their parking stalls at all hours of the day, Griggs and Loftin knew they had to move to a larger office.

The growth rate in this new office was phenomenal. The rate of growth was influenced in part by the quantity of referrals from satisfied clients. Griggs and Loftin received nearly ten new cases a week.

It was also influenced by their willingness to file complaints on behalf of their clients. Insurance companies will settle a case promptly only if it looks serious. A case usually looks serious if there is personal injury and the plaintiff has hired an attorney who, in turn, has filed a lawsuit.

Griggs and Loftin worked entirely on a contingent-fee basis. They were paid only on the results of their good efforts. These efforts resulted in approximately $3,300 per settled complaint. Despite their success, Griggs and Loftin found themselves short of working capital and wanted to ask their bank for a $50,000 loan.

"Mark, I know firms ten times our size that can't get bank financing. What do you think our chances are of getting the loan?"

"That depends on a number of items, Griggs. How do you intend to use the loan proceeds?"

"Mostly to pay for complaint filing fees, certified court reporter fees, expert witness fees, investigation expenses, and other expenses on behalf of firm clients."

"What is the fee for filing a complaint?"

"It is $135 and it's worth every penny of the expense. We make a statement to the insurance carrier each time we file a complaint. They know the plaintiff is serious. Rather than go to court, the insurance company will try to settle our typical case within sixty days."

"Is there a difference in the timing of the settlement if you don't file the complaint?"

"Oh gosh, yes! If we just write letters on behalf of a plaintiff, it could take a year to settle a case. Some cases take two years or longer to settle. That is a long time to compensate a plaintiff for his injuries. When we file a complaint, our clients always receive a larger and more prompt settlement."

"So how many cases do you have in inventory for which you would like to file complaints?"

"Currently 386 . . . ."

(Pause. Then slow whistle.) "That's quite a number. Filing fees alone would amount to $52,110."

"True, but the contingent fees to this firm would also amount to $1,273,000 . . . ."

"Griggs, any bank would love to make this loan. Let's figure out how to show them the way you intend to convert these contingent fees to assets."

A few hours and graphs later, we had the principal contents of a convincing loan request. The first graph showed three years of increasing revenues. The second graph showed three years of increasing partner net income. The third graph showed the potential contingent-fee value of case filed in each of the three previous years. The third graph also showed the contingent-fee value of the 386-case inventory. The firm expected to file these cases within a month after receiving the loan.

They delivered their proposal to the bank on a Monday. When the banker called that afternoon and expressed an interest in visiting their new office, Griggs and Loftin knew they had won another case.

Unfortunately, there are two sides to any loan proposal.

Even if you know your business, there is simply no assurance that your loan officer will share your understanding. The loan officer may lack your good business sense. If this is true, it is now your responsibility to educate a bank employee about your business. If you want the loan, consider your time at this task as a nonreimbursable cost of doing business.

There are some loan officers who cannot be educated about any business. There are other loan officers who do not want to be educated about your business. If either of these individuals sounds like your loan officer, you should listen to what the bank may be telling you about its commercial lending policies.

BANKS DON'T REALLY CARE ABOUT YOUR BUSINESS

LESSON

BANKS WILL TRY TO SECURE THEIR LOANS SO THEY DO NOT NEED TO WORRY ABOUT THE RISKS IN YOUR BUSINESS.

Some banks know a great deal about managing risk. That is why, despite advertising to the contrary, a bank really has no interest in your business per se. Business loans can be risky. Some banks are risk control fanatics.

There are banks that will agree to make entrepreneurial loans once they have attached the appropriate risk premiums to them. These premiums are usually described as loan origination fees, standby commitment fees, and, of course, high interest rates.

When banks can diversify the lending risk by securing independent sources of repayment, they have usually made a great investment for their shareholders.

In an elegant manner, they have positioned themselves away from discussions about the relative merits of your business and your estimate of its expected success.

They have also softened the impact of their massive collateral requirements by raising that issue at the latest possible moment.

> "Oh, I should probably tell you that our five-year certificates of deposit are now paying 4.35 percent annual interest. Although $100,000 of the loan proceeds will be restricted, they'll still be earning competitive interest that will be credited to your account."

Banks, you see, do not really want noncash collateral. They need to get court approvals to sell this collateral at market-driven prices that may only return to them ten cents on the dollar.

It is mechanically easier for a bank just to make a bookkeeping entry that zips $100,000 out of your account and applies it to any unpaid loan balance. It is then your burden to initiate any legal action that may be necessary to reclaim what may have been wrongfully but readily taken.

Smart bankers, on behalf of their shareholders, will also squeeze you harder the more apparent it becomes to them that you need their money. Many will require this certificate of deposit or a similar compensating balance arrangement throughout the amortization period of the business loan.

There is an injustice that leaps from this requirement, although I am not sure that any judge would ever rule that an agreement between a bank and a consenting customer ever created an injustice. While the loan principal is reduced through amortization of the monthly payments, the certificate of deposit requirement is not.

When this occurs, the value of the bank's security increases out of all proportion to the outstanding loan balance. The divergence on some loans can be so wide that it starts to look similar to a point spread offered in a Nebraska-Northwestern football game.

There are other alternatives to working with a banker who will not take the time to learn about your business. One of those alternatives is to find a loan officer who understands the effort it takes to build retirement wealth.

FIND A BANKER WHO VALUES RETIREMENT WEALTH

LESSON

A LARGE RETIREMENT ACCOUNT BALANCE REVEALS THAT YOU HAVE BEEN SERIOUS. ABOUT BUILDING WEALTH.

A properly managed service business usually has a retirement plan that the owner has funded for his personal benefit. Where this owner has managed his business for several years, the funds accumulated in the retirement plan can be considerable.

Unfortunately, most bankers do not acknowledge the wealth in these plans when they are evaluating your business credit. There are several reasons why this is true.

Retirement plan wealth does not appear on any business balance sheet. What is not on your business balance sheet is also excluded from the net worth of your business. That is the only reason that any banker needs to disqualify it as an asset.

At the time you make them, retirement plan contributions are a deductible business expense. That expense reduces your business net income. To those loan officers who do not understand how you build entrepreneurial wealth, that makes your business appear less profitable. Never mind that you are reducing your business income taxes by paying this retirement plan contribution to yourself.

Most bankers have a difficult time recognizing wealth that you have removed from your business. To many of them, the assets in your retirement plan are no more real than a phantom on Halloween night. The typical phantom asset discussion with a banker goes something like this:

"Alan, this is Throckmorton at Federal Savings Bank. I just finished looking at the application for your line of credit renewal."

"Great, Throck. I bet you're calling to tell me it's been approved. When can I sign the papers?"

"That's what I wanted to talk to you about, Alan. I think we have a problem . . . ."

"Oh? What's the matter?"

"Well, the kind of credit line you have is secured in part by your business net worth."

"And?"

"Well, you're only showing a $67,000 net worth and your business had only a $17,150 net profit this last year. Your credit line renewal request is for $130,000. The last time we had lunch, you led me to believe things were going OK . . . ."

"Things are more than OK, Throck. They're great! This is the best year I've ever had."

"Not according to these financial statements, Alan. Where is the profit? Where is the net worth? I can't renew this line of credit when the numbers look as poorly as these do . . . ."

"Hold on a minute, Throck. The profit is there. I just reduced it by putting the maximum amount possible into my defined-benefit pension plan. Last year, that amount was $42,000. The year before, it was $47,000. I don't remember what the contributions were before that, but they've averaged somewhere around that figure for the last seven years."

"Oh, then where is the money?"

"It's in my retirement trust. The last time I looked, I had $530,000 accumulated in it, and I'm the only beneficiary."

"But where is it on your business financial statements?"

"It's not on those financial statements. I've got a separate account over at my brokerage firm where I keep the funds invested in stocks, bonds, money funds, you name it."

"This may come as a surprise Alan, but that doesn't help your credit renewal request."

"Why not?"

"Federal Savings Bank doesn't officially recognize those retirement plan assets."

"You're kidding!"

"Not at all. Even though they may be your golden year funds, we don't consider them to be part of your net worth for credit purposes."

"Unbelievable . . . ."

Sad to say, most banks penalize you for building your wealth by saving for retirement. It is noteworthy and to their credit that some banks do not.

Even when you find a bank that recognizes retirement wealth, you still cannot be certain you have found someone to share your business risk. This is particularly true if your proposed business will compete directly with the bank.

DO NOT COMPETE WITH YOUR BANK

LESSON

BANKS ARE RELUCTANT TO FINANCE THEIR COMPETITORS.

Banks want you to believe that they are equal opportunity lenders. That is to say, each loan applicant has an equal probability of transferring business risk to the bank. In theory, no applicant would receive preferential or detrimental treatment.

That is not the case if your dad is president of the United States, Treasury secretary, or a congressman.

The theory also ceases to apply when you propose to enter the bank's own marketplace. It does not matter that they have been inefficient or unsuccessful in meeting market demand. Banks are scared to death of entrepreneurial-driven competition.

First Mortgage Corporation (FMC) was a proposed mortgage banking business that Benning funded with $300,000 of equity capital. The company proposed to solicit first mortgage applications, make the loans to qualified borrowers, and then sell the loans to the secondary market.

One of the state's largest banks provided Benning with a verbal commitment for a $2 million warehousing line for his business. The company's equity would secure the warehouse line. So would any first mortgage production.

When Benning started to get the necessary federal and state business approvals, someone at the bank asked another loan committee member if it was prudent to encourage competitive mortgage lending.

After all, the bank was already in the mortgage business. The bank determined the loan commitment to FMC was not in the best interests of the bank. They decided to withdraw the verbal commitment.

The bank faced an unpleasant task. They had to tell Benning, "We didn't really mean to say 'Yes' to you." They also had to do it in a manner that avoided a lawsuit from Benning and the related public embarrassment.

The solution was made for a financial soap opera.

Soon after they hired Harvey, the bank assigned him to review Benning's loan request. Harvey was one month out of graduate business school. He had just finished learning which elevator bank to take to his office. One day later, he met with Benning about his loan commitment.

"Mr. Benning, what kind of experience have you had in the mortgage banking business?"

"It's in your loan application file, Harvey. Did you have a chance to read it? I was a bank loan officer for ten years. Then I accepted a position as a loan originator at a mortgage banking company, where I worked the last six years. It is amazing what you can learn watching how inefficient the marketplace is in processing home mortgage applications. That's why I want to start this business."

"What do you mean?"

"Harvey, have you ever owned a principal residence?"

"No, but I plan to just as soon as I can save enough from my bank job for the downpayment."

"Let me tell you from personal experience. If you work for a bank, that may take you a while . . . ."

"Huh?"

"Let me also tell you something about getting a mortgage. Filling out a mortgage application is an incredibly difficult task for most borrowers. Evaluating it is a remarkably lengthy process for most lenders. I've bought the finest mortgage banking software package in the industry to help prospective borrowers fill out the applications and to evaluate their financial data. It should take weeks of time and a bundle of subjectivity out of the process."

"Benning, at our bank, mortgage lending is an art, not a science. You just can't use mortgage banking software to determine if a prospective loan applicant meets or fails to meet various qualification requirements."

"Harvey, you are talking to someone who has worked in banking since the day you entered third grade. The statement you just made couldn't be further from the truth . . . ."

"Uh . . . well . . . thanks Mr. Benning. I guess that will be all for today. I have another appointment down the hall. Let me get back to you later this week after the committee meets . . . ."

Benning was not misled nor intimidated by Harvey. Benning found secondary mortgage packagers who agreed to piggyback FMC's mortgages on their first mortgage inventory. This arrangement readily provided a source of liquidity for any first mortgage inventory that FMC might accumulate. It reduced risk considerably.

Other secondary buyers agreed to buy FMC's first mortgage production directly as soon as the mortgages were funded and a complete set of documents delivered to them by a bonded and insured courier.

Under the bank's instructions, Harvey stonewalled. He focused his objection on the narrow possibility of an inventory of nonconforming, unsalable loans that failed to meet minimum mortgage banking standards.

Benning would fail to meet those standards only if he ignored his common sense, sixteen years of lending experience, and the results of millions of dollars of development that went into the mortgage banking software that he had purchased.

Benning's persistence and preparation finally forced the bank to grant a commitment with terms that could never be met.

"Harvey, you're a difficult man to reach by phone. Those loan committee meetings must be keeping you busy."

"They sure are. Sorry I'm a few weeks late in getting back to you."

"That's OK. Tell me, what good news do you have for me?"

"The bank has agreed to give you the commitment . . ."

"That's wonderful!"

". . . subject to a few conditions."

"Naturally. So what are the conditions?"

"We'll give you the $2 million warehouse line at the prime rate of interest plus two points."

"That's a bit pricey . . . ."

"That's what it took to get it through the committee."

"I suppose I should be grateful for your efforts. Is there anything else?"

"Yes, one other condition. You need to maintain a similar amount of compensating deposits or marketable securities to secure the line. Do you have the assets to do that?"

(Gets ready to explode.) "Harvey, that's $2 million! If I had that amount of assets, I wouldn't be here talking with you. There has to be a mistake. The commitment would be fully secured by the underlying conforming first mortgage inventory and the equity in my business!"

"I know, but that's what it took to get this through the loan committee. They agreed to take a second look at the compensating balance requirements in another two or three years."

"What a thoughtful group of people . . . ."

"Huh?"

In the act of protecting their own interests, the bank flushed from the marketplace one more entrepreneurial competitor.

There may be an easier way for you to obtain a business loan than by prostrating yourself before a loan committee. If you own a home, you may wish to consider an equity credit line. Unfortunately, it also has its own set of risks.

BEWARE OF EQUITY CREDIT LINES

LESSON

DO NOT BE CASUAL ABOUT ACCEPTING THE TERMS OFFERED IN AN EQUITY CREDIT LINE.

Equity credit lines are a wonderful way to increase your financial risk. With little more than a nod of your head and a personal signature, you can put at risk all of the equity in your principal residence.

Have you ever wondered why banks go out of their way to make it easy for you to do this? There are no points, no closing costs, and no appraisal fees. They will even validate your parking.

Banks like to issue equity credit lines for several reasons.

A principal residence usually secures the credit line. It is an asset that even the most nearsighted banker can see.

It is an arm-breaking task to persuade most entrepreneurs to deliver meaningful business financial statements supporting the use of loan proceeds. A home equity credit line solves that problem. A casual drive by an oceanfront property is convincing evidence that at least the loan security is above water.

It takes some effort to approve a $10,000 auto loan. It takes little additional effort to approve a $100,000 home equity credit line.

Unlike the cars that they drive, most entrepreneurs are reluctant about turning the keys to their home over to the bank. Banks recognize this reluctance. They find a comforting measure of risk control in knowing that a borrower will usually dispose of all other assets before he will voluntarily agree to leave his home.

Some equity credit lines really are not credit lines at all. Rita discovered this after she signed the documents for a $65,000 home equity credit line.

"If you'll just give me your checking account number, Rita, I'll have the funds transferred tomorrow morning."

"Oh, that's OK. I don't really need the money yet. I simply wanted to take care of the paperwork this month, while I had the time. I really appreciate your quick response to my application, but I probably won't start drawing against those funds for another few months."

"Unfortunately, we do have to transfer the funds tomorrow. That's our standard policy."

"I don't understand. This isn't a second mortgage, it's a line of credit! If your bank issued me a credit card, I could draw the funds as I needed them. I wouldn't have to draw them all at once . . . ."

"Rita, let me explain. This **is** our equity credit line. You can make monthly payments in any amount at any time. The only requirement is that we must issue the entire $65,000 amount tomorrow. Naturally, it will accrue interest on the entire balance once we transfer the funds."

"I think we need to talk this one over. What you refer to as a line of credit is not what I had in mind . . . . "

There is no need to despair if a bank will not accept your business risk or will agree to do so only after you have pledged the future income stream of your first-born child. Your bank is one of thousands in the marketplace. There is a good chance that you can find at least a dozen different lenders who are interested in working with you. All you have to do is let your fingers do the walking.

LET YOUR FINGERS DO THE WALKING

LESSON

A FINANCIAL DATA BASE
WILL LEVEL THE PLAYING FIELD.

The access to capital markets is largely a relational matter. Larger companies have a chief financial officer, whose job is to schedule golf outings with any number of prospective lenders. The game of golf gives them the opportunity to negotiate multimillion-dollar credit lines while strolling smartly down the fairway.

If you do not play golf and cannot afford the luxury of a chief financial officer, you cannot begin to imagine the amount of time that you will spend looking for capital for your business. The pursuit of capital is a frustrating puzzle for even the brightest entrepreneur.

When you follow the recipe to bake a loaf of bread, the results are predictable: a warm loaf of goodness that will melt the toughest slice of butter. But there are no proven recipes for loan proposals. Even after you mix the ingredients, you can never be certain that you have anything on which a lender would like to nibble.

Any entrepreneur who has managed a business for more than a few years will tell you the task of finding capital is not a simple one. The task can also be an unpleasant one. Despite a string of successes in your business, a single loan request may force you to suffer through the indignity of more than a few rejections. Where do you look when your bank turns you away?

You look at a financial data base of lenders. With this data base, you can level much of the playing field and soften some of the indignity you are forced to suffer.

"Whatever happened to you Warshawski can't be bad enough to explain the way you look. Did you have a death in the family?"

"I feel like that's what happened. I got turned down on a loan request by my own bank! Do you believe it? I've been a loyal depositor with them for the last six years . . . ."

" . . .and they didn't trust you enough to lend you some of the cash you have on deposit with them."

"I can't tell you how helpless that makes me feel, Mark. I used to believe I knew what it took to get a loan approved. I don't believe that any more."

"Warshawski, most banks don't go out of their way to tell their depositors the criteria for approving business loans. If they did, they would risk losing their depositors."

"That's a fact."

"What type of loan request did you submit?"

"I'm not sure the proposal ever made it to the loan committee. If the speed they pitched my loan request back to me is any indication, you'd think I wanted them to fund the riskiest deal on the street. All I needed was $450,000 to buy out a shareholder."

"Don't despair, Warshawski. A single rejection doesn't mean you've been turned down by the entire lending community . . . ."

"But I don't have the time to hand carry this request to the entire lending community! I also have a business to run and a shareholder who wants out . . . ."

"Chill out, Warshawski. If you've got thirty minutes, I can give you the names of a few lenders who would consider looking at your request."

"How do you propose to do that?"

"With some nifty computer software that lists over 6,000 different lenders and the deals they're interested in. The lenders run the entire financial spectrum: venture capital firms, banks, financing and factoring companies, private lenders, etc. If they lend money on a regular basis, they're in this data base."

"Let's do it. Where do we begin?"

"All we have to do is enter our financing requirements and answer a few questions . . . ."

"Can you turn the screen so I can see it too?"

"Sure. Here we go. Let's search all lenders. (Click.) Let's look for debt capital in the amount of $500,000 with a maturity of less than five years. (Click, click, click.) "What do we want to call this type of financing? Hmmm . . . it's not startup financing, first-stage financing, second-stage financing, mezzanine financing, private placement, syndication, debt offerings, equity offerings . . . here it is! Buy-out acquisition financing. (Click.)"

"That's it?"

"Not yet." (Click, click.) "We have to wait a minute or so while the computer screens the lender profiles based on our financing requirements . . . ."

"Amazing!"

"Right. Now you know how a Third World country that has just acquired favored nation trade status feels. Hey, will you look at this? The computer found thirty-two matches for our search criteria."

"How do we contact them?"

"Let's print a summary list." (Click, click.) "That will give us the names of the lenders, the individuals to contact, and their phone numbers. We can also print the details on each one of these lenders. That information will tell us what specific information they want to see included in a proposal, what specific rates of return they're looking for, and how long they'll take to get back to us . . . ."

"I don't feel so helpless anymore, Mark. You just leveled the playing field. Thanks!"

"My pleasure."

But getting a lender to make a loan is still a relational matter. You do not necessarily need to push divots down the fairway with your lender, but you do need to be convincing. Honesty and full disclosure will take care of most of that.

The marketplace is filled with other readily available financing sources. Someday every business that prospers will be sold. The sellers of those businesses will usually agree to finance a portion of the sale. That is why buying a preexisting business can be a great way for you to begin your entrepreneurial career.

10

BUYING IN

- ➤ Find an Owner with a Reason to Sell.
- ➤ Learn to Be Patient.
- ➤ The Future Is Yours.
- ➤ A Premium May Be Warranted.
- ➤ Climb Within Your Limits.
- ➤ You're No Henry Kravis.
- ➤ You Need an Edge.

Not long ago, there was an affluent Japanese family visiting the United States. The father, mother, and their three children did their share of sightseeing, including a trip to Disneyland.

A few days before their scheduled departure, the father asked his three children what each would like to have as a souvenir of their trip. He addressed his first son:

> "Kenji-san. What gift would you like to receive?"
> "An airplane!"

The father called Boeing and placed an order for one of their new 767s. He then turned to his second son:

> "Kitaro-san. What gift would you like?"
> "A racing car!"

The father located a Lamborghini Countach, bought it, and had it crated to ship home for his son. He then turned to his little daughter:

> "Moriko-san. You have been a very patient girl on this trip. What gift may I give to you to show my appreciation?"
> "A Mickey Mouse outfit."

So the father telephoned his investment banker and authorized an all-cash tender offer for the controlling interest of a mismanaged publicly traded corporation.

A business need not be mismanaged in order for it to be a possible acquisition candidate for you. However, it is no small coincidence that many entrepreneurial operations that are mismanaged are also for sale. It is a fact that in each of those operations, some owner has taken a business to a point beyond which he is no longer capable. That is an adequate reason for an owner to want to sell any business.

That single reason should not necessarily disqualify any business from your possible interest in buying it. After all, even a mismanaged business may have hidden value. Many of them do. Equally important, if you are buying a business, you have to start somewhere.

FIND AN OWNER WITH A REASON TO SELL

LESSON

EVERY BUSINESS OWNER WILL ONE DAY HAVE A REASON TO SELL THE BUSINESS.

You are at the start of the process once you find an owner who is willing to part with his business. Now all you need to do is to convince the owner that today is his lucky day.

That can be a difficult task if you are new to business. Your lack of previous relevant experience suggests you may be missing some of the qualities that are crucial to entrepreneurial success. Even if you believe you have all of the qualities, you are in for a bruising game if you have never purchased a business. You can overcome that deficiency by asking a certified public accountant (CPA) to block and tackle on your behalf.

There are tens of thousands of businesses that are for sale on any given day. Your professional advisor will do far more than help you to identify a possible business that is right for you. A professional will give you the credibility you need to receive confidential seller information. An experienced professional will also analyze your proposed acquisition for you in ways you have never dreamed.

Can you trust the sellers? Are you capable of analyzing them? Do their numbers suggest manipulation? What kind of negotiators are they? Can we confine price negotiation to the real world? Can you out-wait them? What are they really thinking? Why are they willing to consider selling?

Do they understand that losses, despite their deductibility, are never preferential? Do they understand that income, regardless of taxes, is better than no income? Should you get involved in their tax problems?

What are their personal motives and how are they hidden? Should you get involved in their personal problems? What private requirements for funds do they have? Are they looking for an "out"? How are they going to react to changing their business name?

How far will they go? Can you get them to do the dirty work of firing unproductive employees? Will they train their successors? How important is their reliance on a few customers and vendors? What information do they seem to suppress? Can you tie them up so they will be around if you later discover unrecorded liabilities? How risky is this deal?

And those are just a few of the questions your CPA will ponder on your behalf. It is worth the professional time to be certain you are taking a solid entrepreneurial step. After all, you are in business to build equity. You build equity by making good investments. After you have successfully converted the equity in these investments to cash, you look for other good investments. Everything else that you do in your company is merely a means to that end.

Your advisor will also help you price your proposed acquisition within acceptable limits of risk and your savings account balance. How you price an opportunity is far more than a matter of style.

The day that the price of oil inched past $24 a barrel, a Dallas oilman called in his company treasurer:

> "Horton! My oldest boy is big enough to play with blocks. I want you to go out and buy him some, say, about half a dozen, between Main Street and Akard . . . ."

Most entrepreneurs, however, lack the style and do not have the resources of that Dallas oilman. Their approach to buying a business must be different. That approach is usually slower and more measured.

LEARN TO BE PATIENT

LESSON

DO NOT RUSH TO CLOSE THE DEAL
WHEN YOU BUY A MISMANAGED BUSINESS.

There is a better way to buy a mismanaged business than rushing to meet a closing date with little regard for the price you will pay. When you buy a mismanaged business, do it patiently, and for as little as possible.

Kelsie's parents wanted her to own a business. Owning a business, they believed, was a good way for Kelsie to pay off her student loans and build for her future. That is why they agreed to help her buy a veterinary practice. They provided Kelsie with the equity capital and the assurance she desperately needed. Both items reaffirmed that someone believed in her.

Kelsie found a small animal practice with annual revenues of $75,000 listed for sale in a trade journal. In response to her brief letter of inquiry, she received an invitation to inspect the practice. Over a long weekend visitation, she met with the current owner and a few customers. All of them confirmed her newfound belief that people who liked pets were nice people. Emboldened by her good judgment, she also met with the seller's lawyer to look at the historical operating data.

When Kelsie finished examining numbers that she did not understand, she discussed the offering price in fifteen seconds.

> "Now what amount did he want for his business?"
>
> "He would agree to sell his practice to you for $110,000. If you wanted the equipment that went with it, that would be another $25,000."
>
> "Do you think that is a fair price?"
>
> (How naive is this lady?) "Seems reasonable to me!"
>
> "OK. Where do I sign?"

Kelsie paid for her inexperience and lack of patience for the next five years.

The net earnings of the practice were negligible at the time Kelsie acquired the business. That suggested there was little value in the business operations. When Kelsie found it difficult to make the monthly payments on her business acquisition debt, she knew she had paid too high a price.

Through five years of diligent efforts, Kelsie doubled the gross revenues of the practice. She also paid off the business acquisition debt. These were accomplishments.

Those achievements came at a cost. The continual strain of managing day-to-day operations was just too much. Kelsie had burned herself out. Kelsie explored the possibility of selling the practice to other interested buyers. None would agree to pay what Kelsie paid five years ago for a business that was profitable and now twice the size!

When you acquire a company, you are buying some tangible and intangible assets for a price. If you are in a hurry to make a deal, you will pay a far greater price for these items than the price they may be worth.

Letting time pass will never hurt you when you are buying someone else's mismanaged business.

You do not change operational behavioral patterns in a mismanaged outfit in a day. If the business is losing money today, it will probably continue losing money tomorrow. If the business is wasting assets today, it will waste them tomorrow. If there is no sensible risk control program in place today, it will not magically appear the following morning.

These and other behavioral patterns will continue to exhaust the seller's resources. When the air is finally out the balloon, a seller will be relieved that you made any offer.

THE FUTURE IS YOURS

LESSON

WHEN YOU BUY A BUSINESS,
PAY ONLY FOR WHAT IS THERE TODAY.
THE FUTURE OF THAT BUSINESS
AND WHATEVER VALUE IS HIDDEN THERE
ALREADY BELONG TO YOU.

When I look at a possible business acquisition for a client, one of the first conversations I have with the client goes something like this:

> "What price are you willing to pay for tomorrow's value?"
> "What are you talking about, Mark?"

A seller will always try to receive some premium over what his business is worth today. That may be a forward motion premium, a future potential premium, or a combination of both.

A forward motion premium is an incremental value that a buyer may decide to pay for a forward-moving operation.

A forward-moving operation, bluntly, knows where it is going. There is not a lot of indecision in the way the business is run. It is run to build equity for its owner. There is no other reason that the business exists.

A future potential premium is an incremental value that a buyer may agree to pay for the future.

A seller who knows where his business should be will often request a future potential premium.

Wherever the business should be, it is not there today.

Most sellers try to receive a forward motion premium. Only a few sellers are entitled to receive that premium. Many sellers also try to receive a future potential premium. No seller is entitled to receive that premium!

Paying for future potential is just as ridiculous as paying $300,000 for a house that, in today's market, is only worth $200,000. The possibility that it might be worth $400,000 in ten or twenty years does not warrant an additional $100,000 premium to the seller.

The future always belongs to the buyer! That is why it is difficult for me to agree with any seller who argues he should receive an additional premium for the time he is not at risk.

There is another good reason to pay only for the value that is in a business today. Most buyers will overlook this reason and most sellers will not discuss it. Nevertheless, it is possible that the future value of a business can be far lower than its value today.

A PREMIUM MAY BE WARRANTED

LESSON

A SELLER MAY BE ENTITLED TO RECEIVE A PREMIUM WHEN HE HAS SOLD THE BUSINESS BUT HAS KEPT THE RISK.

There is a readily identifiable point where the buyer is entitled to receive all of the returns from a newly acquired business. That point occurs at the moment the seller transfers the business and all related risks to him.

Where the buyer can keep the seller at risk, the seller may also be entitled to receive some of the future returns of the business. One way to keep the seller at risk is to insist on the orderly transfer of the seller's risk to the buyer over time.

You can achieve that orderly transfer of risk by an installment sale.

A properly drafted installment sale does considerably more than defer cash payments to which the seller of a business may be entitled. In exchange for these cash payments, an installment sale can also defer the transfer of the seller's risk to you.

There is a benefit in declining to accept all of the seller's risk the day the deal closes. If you are buying a seller's business today, what value does it have tomorrow when the customers leave for a competitor?

An installment payout to the seller that is proportional to the number of customers retained in the business will keep the seller at risk. Your risk is that the customers will leave. The seller's risk is that if the customers leave, he may not be entitled to receive his full installment payment. Such an arrangement effectively holds the seller personally responsible for the transfer of customers in his business. You can be reasonably certain that where their wallets are concerned, most sellers will give you their personal attention.

When you expect sellers to act as a bank by agreeing to finance some or all of your acquisition cost, it should not surprise you if the sellers start behaving like one. They may agree to retain some business risk in exchange for a risk premium. The premium may be reflected in a higher acquisition price, in the interest rate, or in a consulting fee that you will pay.

The premium, of course, is without cost to you unless there is an enforceable agreement for you to pay it. Unless you have personally guaranteed the acquisition price, the enforcement of any possible claim stops at your corporate doorstep.

Banks know this. That is why a bank will want security and a personal guarantee beyond the value of the equity in the business when a bank agrees to finance your acquisition.

Most sellers also know this. Yet, in their rush to take leave of their business, some sellers also take leave of their senses. These sellers will accept any signed contract regardless of the value behind the guarantee!

A knowledgeable buyer may offer a pledge of the assets and the stock in the business he is proposing to acquire. It is the exceptional case when that offer includes a personal guarantee.

When a buyer can persuade a seller to restrict the seller's security requirement to stock in the transferred business, the buyer has effectively acquired something for nothing.

As a practical matter, a buyer will always expect to pay some amount for a business. That involves some financial risk. The absence of a personal guarantee leaves that risk at the office.

CLIMB WITHIN YOUR LIMITS

LESSON

IT IS EASIER TO TEACH THE
CONSEQUENCE OF POOR RISK CONTROL
200 FEET ABOVE THE GROUND.

There is a fundamental danger in buying any business instead of starting one from infancy. The difference, of course, is the amount of equity immediately at risk.

It costs money to buy a business. You usually need a down payment.

That means cash. You may also have a requirement for additional working capital. That also means cash.

What you do not pay in cash, you borrow from the seller, an investor, also requires cash.

Large enterprises meet some of these cash requirements by selling off pieces of the business they acquire. You can, too, but you may have considerably less to sell.

Indeed, it may be impossible for you to sell a portion of the business without increasing the chances that the core business that you retain will fail.

That is one more reason why there is risk in buying a business.

Buying a business may place at risk a considerable portion of your financial resources. If you have made a poor investment decision, you stand to suffer a large financial loss. That is not necessarily true if you start a business from its corporate infancy.

Rock climbers recognize the distinction. When you are one foot off the ground, you are hardly at the point of no return. You can reduce your level of risk by taking one step down and planting both feet firmly on the ground. It is entirely another matter when you suddenly discover you have a fear of heights nine pitches into a fourteen-pitch climb.

The risk of a poor decision on a 5.12 rated climb has life-threatening implications. That is, of course, unless your name happens to be Henry Kravis.

YOU'RE NO HENRY KRAVIS

LESSON

FAIR MARKET VALUE IS THE MOST
YOU SHOULD PAY FOR ANY BUSINESS.

Never pay more than fair market value for a business. After all, you are no Henry Kravis.

Who is Henry Kravis? With little more than an eye for undervalued companies and $25 billion, Henry Kravis engineered the largest takeover in the history of Wall Street.

What did Henry Kravis see? Theoretical equity that was out of this world!

A price tag that large is nothing that Wall Street had ever seen before. It is larger than the gross national product of New Zealand. It is also larger than the combined gross national products of the Sultanate of Oman, the Dominican Republic, the Republic of Panama, and the Kingdom of Jordan.

If you laid each dollar end to end, it would extend 2,367,424 miles. Driving that distance in a car at 55 miles an hour would take you 43,044 hours. That is 1,793 days of continuous driving without rest stops, fill-ups, or vehicle maintenance checks.

If you invested it in long-term 9 percent Treasury bonds, the interest alone would be worth $2.16 billion per year. That amounts to $5,917,808 per day!

Unlike Henry, you live in a microeconomic world.

You are reasonably pleased when you can go six months without a major car repair. You are ecstatic when you can meet payroll for a year and still have cash in the bank. You are complete when you have made the maximum contribution to your pension plan even after all of this.

I am too. That is why we can let Henry do the big deals without wondering what is left for us. It takes 24,000 $1 million deals to do an RJR Nabisco. At some price, each one of those 24,000 deals will warrant our interest.

What is that price? That price is not fair market value. Never, never pay fair market value for any business!

Paying fair market value is like buying a house for $200,000 that you can sell for $200,000. There is no equity for you in that transaction.

The results are entirely different when you can buy a home for $120,000, repaint it, replace the mail box post, and then sell it for $200,000 a few months later. If there were enough homes to buy at the lower price, even Henry Kravis may be interested.

YOU NEED AN EDGE

Lesson

IF YOU CANNOT NEGOTIATE AN ADVANTAGE IN A PROPOSED BUSINESS ACQUISITION, YOU SHOULD EITHER HIRE THE SELLER OR WALK AWAY FROM THE ACQUISITION.

The great Japanese swordsman, Musashi Miyamoto, told his soldiers to fight with the sun at their backs.

It is no more than a matter of positioning that will give you an edge. When the stakes are high, you need every advantage that you can get.

Acquiring a company is no different. When you buy a business, you need an edge.

One reason for this requirement is to compensate you for the risk of illiquidity. Most businesses are not known for the speed at which an investment in them can be converted to cash.

A second reason is to pay for transaction costs. Those costs include audit fees, legal fees, transfer taxes, and income taxes.

A third reason is to compensate you for a possible error in judgment. The day you sign the document closing the deal, you would like to think you have made the correct decision in buying this business. Regardless of your previous experience, you will not always make the right decision!

A fourth reason is to cushion the inherent unpredictable nature of business risk. There are some risks that you will never see. You will discover these risks the day they come crashing through your office window.

You can look for your edge in the company's market penetration or in a unique product mix. You can search for your edge in the specialized skills of employees or the general chemistry of the operations.

Wherever you find some established base of competence, you will find value. Quantifying that value is difficult. You are never really certain of the potential in the value you find.

That is why I never look beyond the acquisition cost for my edge. It is one number that I understand. The lower that number, the better my edge.

The bigger the edge is, the better it is, too. You will certainly have to negotiate for it. That will involve pounding a table in ways you have never done before.

You must also prepare yourself to walk away if you cannot find an edge. Without an edge, you are simply accepting the transfer of self-employment risk. That transfer is occurring at fair market value from a seller to you. There is no equity for you in that exercise.

However you decide to start your business, once you begin, customers will play a decisive role in it. They will actually pay your way! The first step in getting them to do this is understanding how to create value for your customers.

Part Four

Working with People

11 CREATING VALUE FOR YOUR CUSTOMERS

- Show Them the Value.
- Measure Their Relief.
- Increase Your Return.
- The Time Has Come for Value Billing.
- Price the Value Fairly.
- Where's the Value?
- Price, Quality, Speed (Pick Two).

Most tourists have a good feeling for value. That feeling of theirs is the result of making a few dozen judgments about value during the course of any given vacation day.

A tourist can tell you about the best hotel packages, the best car rental deals, the best shops to visit, and the best brunches in town. A tourist can tell you where to go to spend your time enjoyably, and how to avoid those tourist "traps" that are sure to waste your time.

A tourist can tell you if last evening's $60 dinner is worth the same price tonight. Ask a tourist and she will tell you what she would change to make the dinner worth $60 every night.

A tourist can also tell you if she has found so much value that she is planning to return on her next vacation!

Value is the reason that a tourist will part with her money. The absence of value is also the reason a tourist will save her money and spend it another day.

Customers are like tourists. They have money to spend, and they are not foolish. That is why customers will flock to businesses where they see value. Value can be judged only through the eyes of your customers.

When you have something of value to offer to customers who will pay you for that value, you have discovered a simple way to increase the wealth in your business. Unfortunately, the fact that every business does not have a waiting room full of new customers should tell you something about the difficulty of creating value.

The difficulty is there because customers have their opinions about value. Those opinions usually will not be the same as yours. Irrespective of any differences, if you can show them the value, you may have the chance to change their minds.

SHOW THEM THE VALUE

LESSON

CUSTOMERS WILL PAY FOR VALUE
ONLY WHEN THEY SEE IT.

Milligan knew how to put a house together. He learned the construction trade from his father who, in turn, learned it from his grandfather.

Of course, a lot had changed over the years. Air compressors now powered equipment that drove nails faster and farther than a 28-ounce framing hammer and in a fraction of the time. Materials had changed too. They were lighter, more durable, and, in many instances, preassembled. Milligan's dad built the windows for his homes on the job site. Milligan simply telephoned a window supplier and ordered elaborate window configurations that slid into the fitted locations previously framed for them.

It would be unfair to say that Milligan was a perfectionist. However, he knew the technical side of his work and tried to build each house better than his last one. Milligan looked at each house he built as a bundle of value. He looked at himself as the delivery boy. Milligan's job was to deliver a bundle of value to his customers and get the customers to pay for the delivery.

Getting customers to pay for the delivery had never been a problem until now. Milligan explained why.

"What do you think of the house, Mark?"

"There's nothing like walking through a newly constructed home, Milligan. I don't know what I like best, the smell of sawdust, the look of new paint, or the fact that no one has lived here before."

"Maybe what you like is the fact that you don't have to make the monthly mortgage payments on this home . . . ."

"Good point, Milligan! What are you doing in this room? The floor looks wet . . . ."

"Watch where you step, Mark! We just finished applying the first of three coats of acrylic sealer on the floor. My flooring subcontractor wouldn't like to see a size ten footprint in this room tomorrow morning . . . ."

"Oh, right. Sorry. What's downstairs?"

"A walk-out basement, a home office, and the utility room. We put in two hot water tanks. Each tank has a 120-gallon capacity. The owner of this house will never have an argument with any family member about using all of the hot water."

(Pause.) "This is a beautiful house, Milligan. Have you sold it?"

"Not yet. We've had quite a few individuals express an interest in it. They like the large rooms, the bright kitchen, the landscaping, and the way the house sits back on the hill . . . ."

"Are there any parts of the house they don't like?"

"Only one part: the price! They tell me the house is priced approximately $25,000 to $35,000 above the market."

"How can that be, Milligan? It's a beautiful home in a picture-book setting."

"Everyone who has walked through this house readily acknowledges the obvious values. The difficulty I am having is convincing them about the values that are not so obvious."

"I don't know what you mean. Can you give me an example?"

"How many examples do you want? Before I put on the exterior siding, I wrapped the entire house with an industrial-strength polyvinyl barrier. You will never feel a draft in this house. Unfortunately, customers can't see the wrap because it's covered by the siding. That is a $2,800 improvement they can't see."

"Anything else?"

"Sure. Before I closed up the walls on the inside, I had two individuals apply caulk to every exterior joint. The only way heat will escape from this house in the winter is if the owners open a window. That improvement cost approximately $850."

"These all sound like quality improvements to me. What about your heating and cooling?"

"We have three heat pumps at the side of the house. We also installed a radiant barrier on the underside of the roof rafters. That barrier reflects 97 percent of all radiant heat back into the home in the winter and out of the home in the summer. It also cost a cool $1,750 to install . . . ."

"Can I see what it looks like?"

"I'd have to tear out the ceiling to show you."

"I'm beginning to see your dilemma. By the way, where did you get your windows?"

"That's another improvement customers don't appreciate. These are triple-pane windows. The insulating value of these windows is far superior to your standard double-pane windows. But when customers stand where we are and look through the windows out to the yard, all they see is a clear pane of glass. So much for the additional $3,900 that I paid for these windows. Do you need additional examples?"

"No! Milligan, what's wrong with people shopping for houses these days? Every improvement you have described has a definitive value. The improvements will also reduce the monthly utility bills for the next sixty years . . . ."

"Mark, customers want value that they can see. When they can see the value, they know their neighbors can see it too."

"Oh! I think I understand now. It's like paying $30,000 for a new car, and then burying it in a hole in your backyard. It's nearly impossible to convince anyone you have $30,000 of value in the middle of your backyard. However, if you park the vehicle in the circular driveway in front of your house, the value is easier to see."

"That's the problem I'm having with selling this house . . . ."

"And if the new owner walked through this house with his neighbors pointing out invisible joints that were caulked and then covered by the interior walls, his neighbors would think he was daft . . . ."

"Exactly!"

You cannot charge for value when you are the only one who sees it. You also cannot be paid for value even if everyone except the customer sees the value. The customer must see the value because the customer writes the check.

Even when your customer sees the value, your customer may not agree with the way you have priced that value. It can be easier for you to price your product or services if you can first measure the relief that your customer receives.

MEASURE THEIR RELIEF

LESSON

THE VALUE OF A SERVICE IS DIRECTLY RELATED TO THE LEVEL OF RELIEF THE CUSTOMER RECEIVES.

When your business is service-related, establishing a market value for your services can be a frustrating job. Markets drive prices. It does not matter if your business is selling cars or selling cookies, or giving legal advice or giving advice on how to pitch manure. The marketplace will tell you the value of your service.

If you price your service too high, the marketplace will ignore your business and will seek out lower prices. If you price your service too low, the marketplace will embrace your business and strangle your operations with its affection.

A few consultants suggest that you should price your services somewhere in between. That would be at a point where you can sell your services to customers without giving away equity. These consultants base their advice on the premises that a market rate of return is your target rate of return.

If a market rate of return does not make you do back flips, the balance point for you is not where these consultants think it should be.

The difficulty in establishing value effectively in a service business is that individual customers and clients pay your bills, not the marketplace.

Each customer will evaluate you, rightly or not, on his perception of the tangible value of a largely intangible service. That perception can be measured by the level your customer's relief.

Some entrepreneurs rightfully argue that it is easier to measure this relief if your customer comes to you in two pieces. When you can sew a severed hand back to a wrist, your patient will recognize the value he has received and will not usually quibble about your professional fees:

"Dr. Beegle, I want to thank you for reattaching my hand after the accident."

"I'm glad we had the technology and the skill to do it. Aren't you relieved that the operation is over?"

"Oh, yes!"

"OK, that will be $83,592."

In nonlife-threatening situations, measuring that relief can be far more difficult to do:

"Davenport! Are you relieved now that you've eaten an entire bag of potato chips?"

"What are you talking about? It was just a bag of potato chips."

"OK, that will be $1.98."

Despite this difficulty in measuring a customer's relief, it is still your job to convince your customers that they receive value from your business.

You can lie to your customers about that value and be convincing. That approach will work only once. When customers discover you have lied to them, you will lose them as customers.

You can also tell the truth to your customers about that value and be convincing. Customers who recognize value will also recognize the truth. Those customers will be your lifetime customers as long as you own any business.

Whatever you sell to a customer must include value if you want the customer to return to you instead of returning to the marketplace.

There is an obvious advantage to having a value-based business. The day your customers recognize the value is also the day you are ready to increase your rate of return in a very big way.

INCREASE YOUR RETURN

LESSON

WHEN YOU INCREASE YOUR RATE OF RETURN,
YOU ALSO INCREASE YOUR BUSINESS WEALTH.

How fast you may build your business wealth can depend on your timing, your luck, and your rate of return.

It is difficult to control your timing. You are either present and available when an opportunity arises or you are not. Having a good sense of timing means you have not overextended yourself, you are flexible in your scheduling, and you have the resources necessary to support a new investment.

It is nearly impossible to control your luck. Blowing on a set of financial statements or carrying around the first dollar that you earned will not make you lucky.

Successful entrepreneurs agree that you can find luck in those uncommon situations where preparation meets opportunity. Preparation is a lot of hard work. You already know how difficult opportunities can be to develop.

Despite these difficulties, some entrepreneurs have no problem in building their wealth. They are successful because they have increased their rate of return, and they have done it without swallowing a mouthful of risk.

There are many good reasons why you too may wish to increase your rate of return.

There is a big difference in the rate that your wealth grows at a risk-free 6 percent rate and risk-adjusted 20 percent rate. The lower the rate of return that you accept from your investments, the longer it will take for you to build business wealth.

All entrepreneurial activities carry risks and related risk premiums. If you bear the risk, you are entitled to receive the risk premium. These risk premiums will build your wealth.

That is why most entrepreneurs would prefer to receive the higher rate of return even with the higher risk that accompanies it.

At an 8 percent annual growth rate, a modest initial investment of $10,000 will be worth $46,610 in twenty years. That is the value of a rate of return on an investment that is largely without risk.

At a 20 percent annual growth rate, that $10,000 initial investment will be worth $383,376 in twenty years.

If you like large numbers to describe your business success, that is one more reason why you need to increase your rate of return beyond market levels.

Value billing allows you to do just that.

THE TIME HAS COME FOR VALUE BILLING

LESSON

VALUE BILLING IS A GREAT WAY
TO INCREASE YOUR RATE OF RETURN.

There is nothing difficult about applying the concept of value billing.

Value billing permits you to receive a rate of return for your work that is commensurate with its value to a customer. You cannot find that turbocharged return on any hourly rate schedule.

Value billing is more of a stumbling block for entrepreneurial professionals than it is for their clients. A significant majority of clients have already been trained from adolescence to look for value.

A hungry teenager knows there is value when he can buy two hamburgers and two servings of French fries, all for two dollars. His growling stomach tells him there is value in the lunch he just purchased. You can almost hear his relief after he has consumed the entire meal. Value can be total satisfaction.

Safety-conscious drivers know there is value in a car that can support six other cars on its roof. That convincing demonstration of strength tells these drivers there is value in this vehicle. The driver knows she will feel great relief in walking away from a collision. The collision need not occur. If the anticipation of relief is powerful enough, the driver will gladly pay for the value. Value can be emotional safety.

A defendant who has received a sentence of one year's probation and a $500 fine instead of ten years in prison will gratefully acknowledge the value of his attorney's efforts. Value can be a second chance at life.

A taxpayer whose CPA has settled a $92,000 tax assessment for $4,000 will also recognize the value he has received. Value can be money saved.

Where, then, is the difficulty with value billing? To those customers of entrepreneurial businesses who do not recognize value, it is a tough concept to explain.

Parents usually complete a child's toilet training, with minor lapses, by the age of five. You cannot reach this milestone without the commitment of patient parents, willing children, all kinds of accidents, and several hundred loads of laundry.

It is no less difficult to teach some customers how to recognize value. It is a burden to teach the concept of value to customers who know nothing of it. Your instruction time alone will diminish the return that you receive under a value billing arrangement. That may put you right back at an average rate of return.

Where services or goods are generically available, it is also difficult to sustain any hope of value billing. That is why you rarely see anyone willingly pay $18 for an extra tasty hamburger. The generic equivalent is available for considerably less.

Where the billing is excessive, value billing is also difficult to sustain. An extreme example of excessive value billing occurred recently in the $25 billion takeover of RJR Nabisco.

The investment banking firms involved were livid when someone suggested that their $300 million fee might be subject to negotiation.

I will be the first to admit that only the participants really knew the time it took to put the RJR Nabisco deal together. Perhaps it required one hundred professionals to work ten hours a day for five months.

In a brief moment of madness, you might have agreed to pay those professionals at the hourly rate of $500. That hourly rate is more than most people earn in a week.

If the firms involved chose not to reduce their fee out of courtesy to a very good customer, your bill for those hours would have amounted to $75 million.

The firms involved thought they were worth four times that amount!

Other items may have been factored into this proposed $300 million fee arrangement. I am certain it included a risk premium for possible damages in the event of trailing legal actions. Whatever else it included, it was not enough to prevent someone from asking, "Are these guys really worth it?"

It should go without saying that value billing must be for a product or level of service that is superior. The amount of the bill must also be reasonable. If you leave reason behind on a value billing arrangement, people will also wonder if you are really worth it.

Value billing clearly allows you to increase the speed at which you can make any business your best investment. However, you must price value fairly for your customers if you wish to receive the full benefit of value billing.

PRICE THE VALUE FAIRLY

LESSON

VALUE CAN BE JUDGED THROUGH
THE EYES OF THE CUSTOMER.

The value in any value billing arrangement is not always denominated on a single invoice. The full benefit of any value billing comes from retaining the eternal loyalty of your customer.

You can price your services in a manner that makes this possible:

"Hello! This is Hollyfield Water Pumps."

"This is Mark Peterson. I know it's one o'clock in the afternoon. I'm on a well system and I have a water pressure problem. None of my faucets work.

There's also no water pressure to flush a toilet. At 7:00 tonight, I'm having an Indian Princess tribe party here to celebrate the end of the season. Can you help?"

"Water pumps are my business. Do you know what kind of water pump you have?"

(Pause.) "No. If you tell me where to look, I'll find the name of it for you."

"It's at the bottom of your well. Do you know how deep your well is?"

(Shakes head. Thinks of canceling the party.) "No. I'd guess somewhere between 100 and 300 feet. Does that sound right?"

"I don't think your estimate is off by more than 50 percent. I can still work with the situation . . . ."

"Good! Can you come out today?"

"I have another job that I should finish by three o'clock. Would that time be OK?"

"Are you kidding? Sure!"

Hollyfield fixed the well. A lightning bolt had fried the pump. It took a superbly muscled Hollyfield and a crew of two to pull the pump from the bottom of my 210-foot well. They replaced the pump, 210-feet of PVC, all of the wiring, and even the house water filter. Nearly three hours later, after adding a spigot at the wellhead, they finished.

"Here's your bill. The total is $629. I'll warranty all of my work for two years."

"Is there anything I need to do?"

"No. I'll be back in a few days to change your house water filter again. I'm sure I stirred up the sediment in your well. It will be a while before it settles . . . ."

"What will I owe you for that?"

"Not a cent. It's part of the job."

The party went off as planned. Hollyfield returned to change the filter, and I haven't had a problem with the water pressure.

My relief was measurable. Hollyfield could have charged a few hundred dollars more and I would have gladly paid it. With his kind of value billing, Hollyfield has me as a lifetime customer.

If you like the idea of lifetime customers, consider a change in the way you bill your customers. Show them the value, measure their relief, and price the value fairly. When you apply this concept to new customers, focus on those customers who understand something about value.

WHERE'S THE VALUE?

LESSON

YOU CANNOT RECOGNIZE VALUE
WHEN YOU KNOW NOTHING ABOUT IT.

You cannot apply the concept of value billing to a customer who cannot recognize value. Send this customer to a competitor. This customer will not tolerate even your standard billing arrangement.

Clayton called to tell me he was starting a wholesale meat business.

"Who's your partner, Clayton?"

"You'd never believe it if I told you."

"Try me . . . ."

"I met Garland Ratcliff III a couple of weeks ago. We had a few drinks in the lounge next to the office where I work and we talked about business. He had this great idea for opening a cold storage walk-in shop that sells beef in bulk, precut, prepackaged quantities."

"Any idea what it will cost to start one of these shops?"

"He seemed to think about $80,000. I'd put up $40,000 and Garland would put up the other half."

"Where are you going to get $40,000, Clayton? You don't earn that much in a year!"

"My partner suggested taking out a second mortgage on my house."

"Interesting. Have you found a location for the shop?"

"Well, it wouldn't be here. My partner says he has the perfect spot already picked out in Canada."

"Canada? What's your partner's background, Clayton?"

"You know what? I don't really know. He said he owns Ratcliff Packaging, Inc., a company based in Seattle. His company also has an office in Houston. I could tell by the way he talked that he knew a lot about business . . . ."

"Clayton, hold on to your money. You and I have a little talking to do."

Clayton had never owned a business. That kept him from building any wealth. It also insulated him from business risk. That insulation clearly affected his judgment about risk.

I could see the dollar signs dancing inside his head. That is why I spent an hour telling Clayton how his partner, Garland Ratcliff III, would probably steal his capital. That was not what Clayton wanted to hear from me.

After Clayton left my office, I started my work. I called information in half a dozen states looking for a telephone number listed under Ratcliff, Garland. There were no published or unpublished listings. I ran a data base search through 81 million residential telephone numbers with the same result. I called the Business Registration Division in Washington state and Texas. There were no official records of any filings for Ratcliff Packaging, Inc.

My worst fears were confirmed. The man and the business did not exist. I called Clayton and left a message on his voice mail.

I must have been convincing because Clayton never parted with his $40,000.

Two months later, Clayton had still not paid my bill for $125. The note I received from him explained why.

> "Please write this one off your books. I strongly feel this bill went out mistakenly. To help you recall the situation, I asked you a question regarding a business venture in Canada. You then got into talking about some other deals that didn't work. Nothing really came out of our conversation."

Clayton failed to recognize there was about $40,000 of value in our conversation. Like some entrepreneurs, Clayton needs to make expensive mistakes just to appreciate the skill it takes to avoid them.

Clayton, I am sure, will have the opportunity to make those mistakes.

My mistake was providing Clayton with information that I thought should have been valuable to him. You can solve this problem by letting your customer make the choice of what is valuable before you begin any work.

PRICE, QUALITY, SPEED (PICK TWO)

LESSON

LET YOUR CUSTOMERS PICK
TWO OF THE THREE SERVICE COMPONENTS
THAT ARE VALUABLE TO THEM.

Contrary to what others may have you believe, you do not build equity by giving your products or services away.

Building equity in a business is never an easy job. However, it is easier to build equity in your business when you know how to stop giving it away to your customers.

Most entrepreneurs do not realize they have been giving their wealth away.

If you must convince yourself this is true, pull out a current telephone directory. Call a few quickprint shops. Tell them you have a printing job for which you are getting a few bids.

Like most entrepreneurial businesses, the first shop you reach will probably want the work. They will also tell you why they are the best deal in town. If they do your job, they will give you the best price, the best quality, and the best speed.

"Beta Graphics! How may we solve your printing problem?"

"I'd like to receive a bid on printing 200 sets of a 60-page presentation."

"Is that one-sided or two-sided?"

"If the printing won't bleed onto the reverse side of the page, two-sided copying is fine. That would make the final product 30 pages in length."

"May I recommend our classic linen, 25 percent cotton fiber, 24-pound, brilliant white paper?"

"That would be nice, yes!"

"May we bind it for you along the edge?"

"I don't think so. However, I would like the sets stapled once in the upper left-hand corner."

"You'll be happy you chose Beta Graphics. When would you like the work done?"

"As soon as I've had a chance to get two other bids. If you would fax me your bid, I could get back to you by next week . . . ."

"Let me suggest something. We have the best price in town. If, by chance, you find a better price, just tell us. We'll match it!"

"Well, I want these sets to look great . . . ."

"We don't skimp on quality, either. We want you to look great. The printing we do for you will reflect that commitment . . . ."

"Would it be possible to have these sets tomorrow?"

"Just name the time. Two hundred sets will be ready."

"OK. Fax me your price quotation and I'll call you in an hour . . . ."

"Thank you for choosing Beta Graphics!"

Now call one of their competitors. The competitor will tell you to bring the job over that morning. She wants the work, too.

She will also promise to deliver the best price, the best quality, and the best speed.

Now call a few other telephone numbers in the telephone directory just to be sure there really is no better deal. You may discover that many of those numbers are no longer in service.

Many of these shops are out of business for one simple reason. These shops gave away their equity! They gave to their customers price, quality, and speed.

It is possible to provide customers with value and still build business wealth. Building wealth in any customer-related business is a simple matter of keeping either price, quality, or speed.

This is how you do it.

Tell your customers when you meet them that there are three components to your service. Those components are price, quality, and speed. Customers can pick any two of these components for themselves.

They will pick whatever is valuable to them.

Keeping any one of the three components is valuable to you. That will allow you to stay in business. It will also allow you to provide customers with the other two components as long as they wish to remain your customers.

That means if a customer wants a top-notch printing job done by tomorrow, he is telling you that quality and speed are the components of his choice. If you can deliver those two components to the customer, the customer will receive value.

Pricing then, is not really open to discussion.

If a customer wants a $300 dollar printing job for tomorrow and only wishes to pay $150 for it, then he is telling you that speed and price are his two preferences. Those two preferences will give the customer value.

You must tell your customer that when your ten-year-old daughter's school day ends, you will get her started on his job. The job's quality is your decision.

If a customer wants this $300 job for $150 and wants it to look first-class, he has just told you what is important to him. The combination of price and quality will give him value.

You must tell your customer that once every couple of years your business association has a winter conference in Hawaii. There is a pretty good chance that you can find an association member who might like to earn a few extra dollars while on his vacation. Speed, then, is your decision.

Value-conscious customers are understanding when you offer them choices like these. The choices are fair to your customers and are fair to you.

Customers will choose what is valuable to them and they will have no problem paying for that value.

Building wealth involves delivering value to your customers. But not every customer will recognize that value. You will have a better chance of building business wealth when you can successfully identify those customers who are right for you. Customers who are right for you are opportunities for your business.

12

THE OPPORTUNITIES WITH CUSTOMERS

- ➤ Analyze Your Customers.
- ➤ Upgrade Your Customers.
- ➤ Cross-Sell Your Customers.
- ➤ Ask for Permission.
- ➤ Identify Their Pain.
- ➤ Propose an Extraordinary Solution.
- ➤ Balance Your Customer Portfolio.
- ➤ Prospect for New Customers.

What is left for you to do besides running your business? There is plenty for you to do. You can start by analyzing your current customers. Customers will provide you with more opportunities to build business wealth than you could ever imagine.

ANALYZE YOUR CUSTOMERS

LESSON

NOT EVERY INDIVIDUAL WHO REQUIRES YOUR SERVICES DESERVES TO BE YOUR CUSTOMER.

You must determine what each of your customers means to your business. There are many ways to do this.

Some of the normal and customary methods of analyzing customers can be useful. You can categorize your customers by annual gross billings, type of work, total annual person-hours required to service them, and the level of technical skill required. You may also wish to classify them by the frequency of your work for them. Are their requirements for your service recurring or nonrecurring? Can their work be scheduled throughout the year or is it seasonal?

All of these methods can be useful, but all have the same shortcoming: Once you have the facts, what do you do with the information?

Tamra didn't know what to do with this information, either.

"This has been some exercise in forensic accounting, Mark."

(Laughs.) "Tamra, is this the first time you've had to exhume a set of accounting records?"

"I've had to reconstruct fact patterns that were never recorded just to get the information I needed to analyze my customers. I even went back to each bank deposit slip to summarize the amounts individual customers paid me last year."

"That's one way to start, Tamra . . . ."

"It was an impossible task for me to determine the number of hours I worked for each customer. I simply didn't have the information. So I estimated the hours in most instances. I don't have a lot of confidence in these estimates."

"Tamra, do you recall that last year I recommended you install a reliable billing system? That system only cost a few hundred dollars and should have captured all of this data. Instead, you've spent the better part of three days compiling this information, which may not be accurate! Where is the system now?"

"Here it is. It's still in the box. I've spent so much time servicing my customers that I never had the time to install the system."

"How do you know they deserve to be your customers?"

"You've got to be kidding! They pay me. Isn't that enough?"

"Tamra, there's more to having a customer than depositing their check. Even if your customers pay you, that may not be enough."

"What am I missing?"

"You're missing the effect that each customer has on your business. You're also missing the opportunity to develop better customers. Do you have the time for a brief action-sensitive analysis?"

"OK, show me where to start . . . ."

"Divide your customers into three distinct levels. Begin with your Level I customers."

"And Level I customers are . . ."

". . . your most profitable customers. They are compatible with the service capabilities of your firm and your business development plan. They are fully sold on you. There are no other service providers retained by them. They are fully penetrated with your services. They are also grateful for the service that you provide. Their businesses would have to fail before they ever hired someone to replace you . . . ."

"That's my kind of customer! I have one or two of those . . . ."

"What would you say if I told you that all of your customers should be Level I customers?"

"I'd say, 'You must be dreaming!' "

"Make it your goal, Tamra, to develop all of your customers into Level I customers. If you can achieve that single goal, your business will prosper beyond belief."

"What about my other customers?"

"Start with your Level II customers. Level II customers are those with the potential to be converted to Level I customers."

"I thought every customer had that potential . . . ."

"Not really. Level II customers are still profitable customers. They are also compatible with your firm capabilities and your current business development plan. However, you have not fully sold these customers on your service. In fact, they are probably using other service providers, too. Although they are not looking for a service provider to replace you at this time, if they had a relative in your business, they would consider making a change."

"That's not very reassuring . . . ."

"That's OK. You can still keep them as customers, but there's a lot more you can do for them. They haven't had the chance to receive the benefit of your work. They simply can't be moved to Level I without the opportunity to watch you do your stuff."

"How can I get these customers to become Level I customers?"

"Service the bejeepers out of them, Tamra. You've got to spend time with these customers. Earn their trust. Get to know their families. Ask them about their goals, their problems, and their requirements. Show them they are your most important customer . . . ."

"Does that mean I have to give my services away to them?"

"Absolutely not! But make it easy for them to do business with you and do a great job for them. One day, they will recognize that even considering a change of service providers is a task with so much complexity that they will be better served by remaining your lifetime customer."

"I'm embarrassed to say that I have some other customers too . . . ."

"Those are your Level III customers. Unfortunately we all have them at some time. It doesn't matter what you do for them. Level III customers will one day leave you."

"That's for sure. There's just no stopping a Level III customer who is ready to leave . . . ."

"Level III customers, Tamra, are not particularly reliable customers. They may call for an appointment and arrive forty minutes late. They will tell you that they have the capability to do what you are doing for them. Any compatibility they may have had with your firm capabilities and business development plans occurred years ago. You have grown beyond them. Level III customers usually make partial payments on your invoices and always pay late. They will never agree to pay interest or any late payment charge."

"Should I let them go?"

"Tamra, they will leave soon enough. Don't worry yourself with their departure. But don't compromise your fees, your time, or your current business development plans to make these customers happy. You cannot satisfy them and they cannot be converted to Level II customers."

"Mark, what I like about this analysis is that once I associate a customer with a particular level, it makes my decisions for me. I'm not guessing what I should do with any customer."

"That's the benefit of performing an action-sensitive analysis, Tamra. The analysis forces you to move customers to a higher level."

"My new philosophy about customers will be to move them up or move them out . . . ."

"Right! ”

When you discover your time is in short supply, it is probably time again for you to analyze your customers. It is an exciting process each time you do it. Your business will always grow from the result. When you upgrade your customers, invariably, you will say good-bye to a few.

UPGRADE YOUR CUSTOMERS

LESSON

SAY GOOD-BYE TO YOUR LEVEL III CUSTOMERS.

There are some customers you must not keep. You already know just how much work is involved in servicing your Level III customers. You have nearly made a career from accommodating their unique circumstances and special requests. You have also suffered through their invoice disputes and late payments. But your business has grown beyond them and so have you. You can no longer afford to invest time in customers who will never be more than Level III customers.

It is always a difficult task to ask customers to leave your business or to recommend them to a different service provider. Turning customers away from your business seems to be almost the irrational act of a misguided entrepreneur. After all, how can you make your business into your best investment without customers?

The truth is that making your business your best investment is a task that is far easier done without the additional burden of Level III customers. Unfortunately, every entrepreneur recalls the disproportionate amount of effort spent in getting that first customer. That first customer may have even been a Level III customer. It is your recollection of this effort that you makes you reluctant to return a Level III customer to the marketplace.

Many Level III customers know they have used you at an early stage in your business. Some make a practice of seeking out inexperienced service providers and punishing those providers with their service requests. They know that one day, you will grow more experienced and they will have to move on. You must move on, too. When you identify your Level III customers, take a deep breath, then let them go.

Sidley owned a landscaping service. He started his business by cutting the lawns in his neighborhood. When a few residents asked him to manage the lawn service at their Beltline offices, Sidley was on his way to building a larger business. In little over a year, he had added nine office complexes and five homeowners associations. It was time for Sidley to say good-bye to his Level III customers:

"Sidley, I saw your new pickup truck last week. 'Sidley Greene Landscaping Services' has a nice ring to it . . . ."

"What do you think of the color, Mark?"

"I've never seen any business with more color uniformity than yours. Between your uniforms, your tools, your trucks, and your stationery, you've covered just about every shade of green in a box of sixty-four crayons. Now that you're color coordinated, what challenges are left for your business?"

"I can think of a few, Mark. Scheduling is one challenge that stands in front of all the others. I'm having a terrible time with it . . . ."

"Sidley, what is so complex about scheduling your commercial jobs? I thought you had them signed up for a twelve month service contract. Unless rain made your work impossible, I thought you just showed up once a week and started your engines . . . ."

"The commercial jobs are not the problem. My smaller residential jobs are the ones that must cause 80 percent of my scheduling problems. I'm beginning to think I should get out of the residential business."

"If scheduling is the problem, Sidley, I'm sure we can solve it."

"I think most of my residential customers also happen to be Level III customers . . . ."

"That statement makes a difference, Sidley. What makes you think these customers are Level III customers?"

"It takes five or six calls to schedule and confirm an appointment with most residential customers. Invariably, there's a communication problem . . . ."

" . . . between you and the customer?"

"No! Between the customers! We'll do the job that one homeowner asks us to do. The next day, I'll get paged at another job by the other spouse who also thought we were going to weed by the side of their garage. Both of them will expect us to return and do the weeding without charging them for the work simply because they couldn't find the time to talk to each other."

"So your residential customers are essentially making their marital problems your business problems?"

"That's about right. A few years ago, I had the time to deal with these people. My commercial jobs have changed my perspective. These days, I don't have the time to do a job twice and get paid for it only once."

"How many of these Level III customers do you have?"

"We service 12 to 15 of them on an as-needed basis. None of them are under contract . . . ."

"That's good. The absence of any contract may also be your solution to the problem. How much revenue do they represent?"

"They're somewhere between 8 and 10 percent of my annual gross sales."

"How much profit do they represent?"

"I'm not sure there is any profit in servicing these customers. In fact, they require so much attention that I believe I'm losing profit on the new customers I can't service because I don't have the time. I could handle four or five additional Level II commercial customers if I didn't have these residential parasites."

"That's a fact, Sidley. If they haven't referred you any commercial business, cut them loose . . . ."

Level III customers are dead weight for your business. You will not need their checks for your revenue to grow. When you have the entrepreneurial talent that it takes to make your business your best investment, all you may need to do is cross-sell to your current customers.

CROSS-SELL YOUR CUSTOMERS

LESSON

A QUALITY PRODUCT OFFERED AT A FAIR PRICE MAKES IT EASY TO CROSS-SELL ANY CUSTOMER.

Guy built the best picnic tables you could ever hope to buy. His *Signature Series* model was 10 feet long, nearly 4 feet wide, and every bit as solid as a rock. If you measured the quality of his tables by weight, they were impressive. More than 40 pounds of carriage bolts and lag screws fastened almost enough lumber to build the frame of a carport. The tables were fairly priced: at $395 apiece, they would last for 40 years.

Guy also knew how to cross-sell his customers.

"Mark, I've sealed your table with two coats of a satin acrylic sealer and leveled it. How does it look to you?"

"Guy, I think this is the first time I've seen a picnic table that can accommodate sixteen people. That's about the right size for a Brownie troop . . . ."

"In case you haven't noticed, there's extra room in the center of the table. You can easily put half a dozen serving dishes and all the condiments down the middle of the table and still have room to set your plate squarely on it."

"Guy, you've done a great job for me, but why do you overbuild these tables? If I took this one apart, I could reassemble three smaller tables from the lumber you've used . . . ."

"I don't think of it as overbuilding, Mark. I think of it as having the room to accommodate extended family, guests, friends, and neighbors without ever having to look for that elusive card table and folding chairs."

"I see what you mean. We're going to have an absolute ball this summer eating our meals out here. You've put it in a shaded area that's far enough away from the house. The kids will have to finish their meals before they leave the table . . . ."

"Now that you mention it, Mark, where do they go after supper?"

"They play in the yard for a while and then go inside . . . ."

"Do you want to keep them in the yard until you're ready to call them inside for bedtime?"

"Hey, if you have the secret to doing that, let me in on it. I could use the extra quiet time."

"Well, you may want to consider a swing set . . . ."

"That's a good idea. I'll look for one this weekend."

"How long do you want the swing set to last?"

"The swing sets I've seen rust over in a few years and the children outgrow them. If I can get two or three years use from it, that would be fine."

"How would you like a swing set that will keep their interest while they grow and will last until your grandchildren go to college?"

"Can you show me a picture?"

"Sure. Look at these 8 x 10 color photographs."

(Gasp.) "That's some swing set!"

"It's part of my *Backyard Signature Series*. The four swings situated across a 16-foot crossbeam will put an end to all bickering about whose turn it is. The vertical posts are anchored 4 feet into the ground with 1,800 pounds of concrete at each anchor point. Each piece of lumber in the *Signature Series* is a pressure-treated piece of 6 x 6-inch stock. These swings will never lean or sag. The chains for the swings are 10 feet long and are made from quarter-inch stainless steel links."

"I can see my grandchildren using this swing set thirty years from now. Would you have the time to build it later this week?"

"Oh, sure. It will take a few days, but your kids will confirm that it was worth the wait."

"What's the cost, Guy?"

"With installation, $895."

"That's a bit more than I had in mind for a swing set . . ."

". . . but since they last forty years, that's still less than $2 per month. Can I start on Saturday?"

"What do you need from me?"

"Just show me where you want the holes . . . .""

When a customer is fully sold on your services, cross-selling is almost just a matter of asking for the work. Many of your current customers may be logical candidates for this service. However, before you cross-sell any customer, be absolutely sure you have that customer's permission. All you need to do is ask for it.

ASK FOR PERMISSION

LESSON

OBTAIN THE CUSTOMER'S PERMISSION
BEFORE YOU SOLVE HIS PROBLEM.

It is no wonder that customers do not always think highly of recommendations by service providers. That circumspect conditioning is the result of having received self-serving recommendations from dishonest service providers.

It can also be the result of receiving recommendations that the customer is forced to accept without having first granted permission to the service provider to make those recommendations.

"Mr. Geisler, we've completed our 14-point inspection of your vehicle."

"I didn't ask for a 14-point inspection. All I wanted was the oil changed. I've got to get to a meeting in fifteen minutes!"

"At Enviro-Lube, it is the job of all lubricating technicians to make sure our customers are safe and their vehicles are protected from unnecessary wear and tear. There's no charge for the 14-point inspection, but we did notice a few items that you may want to consider replacing . . . ."

"Such as?"

"Look at these wiper blades. I've removed them so you could see how worn they are. In another hundred miles, they won't wipe the rain from your windshield. I want you to see where you are driving even if it rains. That's what safety is all about."

"How much is a new set of wiper blades?"

"$12.95."

"Fine, add it to the bill and get me out of here. I have that meeting."

"Oh, there are two additional inspection points that your vehicle failed. Here's your air filter. Do you see all the dirt on it? Your engine can't run efficiently unless this is clean. You really should think about replacing it."

"Can't you just clean it with compressed air and put it back in?"

"It's really better if you replace it, Mr. Geisler. It's only $8.95 and it will last you another 20,000 miles."

"OK, put in a new air filter and then button up the vehicle. I've got to get going. I'm already late for my meeting. My checkbook is in the car. Let me get it."

"Oh, Mr. Geisler . . . ."

"HEY! Where are my tires?"

"That's our other inspection point that your vehicle failed. I thought you'd want to know that your brake pads are worn on all four brake shoes. You risk suffering an accident while trying to make an emergency stop with these old pads. There's practically nothing left on them. See?"

"What will a new set of brake pads cost?"

"$345 . . . ."

"Get me out of here!"

It is a rude business practice to offer a solution when you have not first received permission. It is also a risky practice. The customer may rightly decide not to pay you.

Ask for permission before you solve a customer's problem. It is a necessary step in building customer trust. It is also a critical step. Without permission, the customer may not accept your solution.

Once you receive that permission, take the time to ask the customer where it hurts.

IDENTIFY THEIR PAIN

LESSON

ANY PROPOSAL BY A SERVICE PROVIDER MUST START BY CORRECTLY IDENTIFYING THE CUSTOMER'S PAIN.

Watney complained about the pain in his lower back. The medical specialists he consulted tested him as if he was their only patient, without success. Prescription drugs did not work. Back braces did not work. Special exercises did not work. Relaxation therapy did not work. Infrared heat therapy did not work. Ice packs did not work.

Three years and $4,225 later, Watney had exhausted all conventional diagnoses and the wisdom of a few medical professionals.

"Watney, how's the back feeling today?"

"I feel like an old man, Mark. I know that running a business can take a physical toll, but I'm beginning to wonder if it is worth the price."

"It's not worth the price, Watney. There is no business that justifies becoming a physical wreck. Actually, you look normal when you're on your feet . . . ."

"I feel normal when I'm on my feet, Mark. It's just that after I sit for long periods of time, my back starts to go out."

"You're welcome to stand during our meeting. I'll stand with you if it would make you feel more comfortable . . . ."

"That's OK. I don't mind sitting for a while."

"Watney. Why are you sitting like the leaning Tower of Pisa? You're tilted to the left . . . ."

"I don't have so much pressure on my lower back if I sit that way."

"Well, if that makes you more comfortable, fine. Say, did you bring a picture of your new baby?"

(Takes out wallet.) "Sure. Here she is, all eight pounds seven ounces of her."

"Wow. She's a big girl. Looks smart too, just like her daddy. What's her name?"

"Witney."

"What a beautiful name! Practical name, too. You won't have to buy her new luggage when she goes away to college. Hey, you've straightened up. What happened?"

"What do you mean?"

"You're sitting like me. How does it feel?"

"Fine, for the moment. The pain always comes back though. There's no treatment I've had that works."

"Watney, I'm an accountant, not a physician. I don't want you think of this as medical advice, but we may have found the source of your problem. Take a look at your wallet . . ."

"It's on your desk. My wife gave it to me as a Father's Day present three years ago. (Sigh.) I felt so much younger then . . . ."

"When did this back pain start?"

"Actually, a little after that Father's Day. Nice wallet, isn't it?"

"It's also two inches thick. What do you keep in there?"

"The usual stuff. Business cards, credit cards, pictures of my children, spare change."

"I think your back has been protesting your act of sitting on a wallet that can barely fit into your pocket."

"Do you really think so?"

"Let's find out. Keep your wallet on my desk until our meeting is over. I promise I'll keep my fingers out of it."

Watney's physical problem came from three years of sitting on a wallet that was as thick as a brick. Anyone who had taken the time to identify the source of the pain should have seen the cause of his problem.

When you ask a customer where it hurts, be sure you treat the cause and not the symptom. You should also be certain that your solution makes their pain go away. You need not go to extraordinary measures to provide an extraordinary solution.

PROPOSE AN EXTRAORDINARY SOLUTION

LESSON

CUSTOMERS WILL GLADLY AGREE TO YOUR SOLUTION IF IT MAKES THEIR PAIN GO AWAY.

When you service a customer, you have an opportunity to meet a unique set of requirements. Entrepreneurs frequently will meet those requirements by providing their customers with goods or services in an amount sufficient to meet specific customer demands.

But you can be much more than just another service provider to your customer. You also have the opportunity to be an extraordinary service provider. As an extraordinary provider, you will reaffirm the customer's trust in you. When you provide extraordinary service, you have the chance to upgrade a Level II customer to a Level I customer in a single meeting. That single event can also provide you a lifetime of customer loyalty.

Any service provider can be extraordinary, but few actually achieve that distinctive status. The key to receiving an extraordinary service grade from your customer is in recognizing which problem the customer wants solved. Many entrepreneurs inadvertently propose solutions that solve problems but don't make any pain really go away.

All you have to do to be extraordinary in the eyes of your customer is make their pain go away. As simple as it sounds, it takes an ability to reassemble existing pieces of a business into a remarkable result. When you can propose a solution that stops the customer's suffering, you have convincingly demonstrated why you stand apart and above all other service providers.

The solution, of course, must be nonlethal. A customer will view with disbelief any recommendation that proposes to end suffering by permanently disposing of the patient.

Hoover and Mizelle sold antique furnishings. The antiques were priced at the high end of the market and provided Hoover and Mizelle a business that grossed nearly $500,000 per year. The partners located a large century-old house on the corner of a busy street for their new showroom. That location assured them of high visibility to all who passed by. The renovations were extensive and exceeded their initial renovation estimate in a very big way.

"Hoover, how's the antique market today?"

"That all depends if you're buying or selling."

"Neither. Right now, I'm just looking and trying to visualize what a customer would see in that hand-carved sofa. By the way, your renovations look fabulous. Somehow, you and Mizelle have managed to take a residence built in 1890, update it a hundred years, and keep all of the charm . . . ."

"The renovations should look fabulous. At $210,000, the renovations cost $20,000 more than the initial price we paid for the house."

"Hoover, I know that's a large number, but you'll be paying it off over the length of the mortgage."

"I wish that were true, Mark. The bank wouldn't agree to give us a mortgage."

"Then how did you manage to pay for your renovation? It's nearly impossible to receive approval for a construction loan if a bank can't first be assured that a long-term lender will take out their position . . . ."

"Mizelle and I paid for all the improvements by taking cash advances on our credit cards . . . ."

(Pause.) "That's quite a few credit cards . . . ."

"Thirty-seven to be exact."

"How are you going to pay those credit card balances?"

"We thought you would have an idea. Right now, I just make the minimum monthly payment on each credit card statement . . . ."

"Do you mean to say that you write 37 checks a month just to pay for the interest on your improvements?"

"Mark, believe me, I know it sounds far-fetched, but we just didn't anticipate the renovations costing so much . . . ."

"What are your minimum monthly payments on the credit cards?"

"They total about $7,200 per month. The underlying first mortgage is an additional $2,150 per month."

"Hoover! Run to your bank today and get an application to refinance this property. Use the additional proceeds from the refinancing to pay off all of the credit cards. It would also lower your cost of borrowing from an average interest rate of 18 percent to somewhere south of 9 percent."

"We tried to refinance. The bank said we didn't have enough equity in the project."

"You must be joking. Do you mean to tell me that after you paid $190,000 for the property and added $210,000 in improvements there isn't sufficient equity for you to refinance this property?"

"Their appraiser said our improved property is worth $200,000."

"That's a nice round number. What did the appraiser do? Add together your initial cost with your improvements and then divide by two?"

"The appraisal said most of the houses in the neighborhood are priced between $175,000 and $200,000. The appraiser said he valued our improved residential property at the high end of values for our neighborhood."

"Hoover, I don't mean to suggest that you should be ungrateful. But this is a mixed-use neighborhood. There's a law office across the street and a medical practice next door to you. You're using this property as commercial space. The appraisal has understated the value of this property by at least 100 percent."

"What can I do?"

"Tell me what you intend to do with this property."

"It's our showroom for the business. Mizelle and I own the property. We'll continue to use it as a showroom for as long as we're in business."

"How long will that be?"

"At least another twenty years. It's as good a commercial location as we will ever find. Our customers walk in our store, see an end table, and write a $1,200 check for it. I can't anticipate changing locations."

"Do you have a lease agreement?"

"Not at this time. Do you think we should?"

"Hoover, a noncancelable long-term lease would make a big difference. You're using this property entirely for business. The appraiser should have valued this as a commercial property. What are comparable commercial rates for this kind of space?"

"We looked into lease rents. We could have leased a space just half a block down the street, similar in size to the 4,500 square feet we now have, for $2.10 per square foot per month."

"Your monthly lease payment would be $9,450 . . . ."

"Right."

"The solution is obvious to me. Draft a noncancelable lease with four equal five-year terms. The lease rent for your initial five-year term will be $9,450 per month."

"Do you mean we have to write a check for that amount?"

"That's exactly what I mean. You're also going to pay a late charge if your monthly payment is more than five days past due. The advantage with this lease is that you're writing the check to you and Mizelle, not the credit card companies. It's also a single check instead of 37 different ones."

"But how do we get the mortgage?"

"Give a copy of your lease to a commercial appraiser approved by the bank. Your appraiser will have the simple task of valuing a twenty-year stream of cash flows . . . ."

(Thirty days later.)

"Mark, it worked!"

"You mean you finally sold that sofa?"

"No. Our refinancing came through. A different bank made us a commercial loan for $410,000 using an appraised value of $550,000. The credit cards are paid off and our monthly payment is only $5,210 . . . ."

"What do you and Mizelle do with the $4,240 of additional rental income you receive from the business?"

"We get to keep it!"

"Extraordinary."

Each one of your customers will appreciate your extraordinary service. The experienced customers will recognize your exceptional work. They know quality of that magnitude is not readily available elsewhere.

Unfortunately, it is not enough to have just a few great customers. If a few are sufficiently large, you must balance their size with smaller customers.

BALANCE YOUR CUSTOMER PORTFOLIO

LESSON

A BROAD MIX OF CUSTOMERS REDUCES YOUR EXPOSURE TO BUSINESS RISK.

It is a luxury to choose your customers. When that opportunity is yours, make the most of it.

A broad mix of great customers will make your business interesting. Customers that represent a variety of industries will help you grow professionally. They will also expose you to challenges unique to those industries.

You will also win the battle with boredom when you service a variety of customers. There is nothing more numbing than business as usual. A broad mix of customers will both test and stimulate the farthest corners of your entrepreneurial mind.

There are other equally important reasons to have a broad mix of customers. The principal reason stands above all others. A broad mix of customers will reduce your exposure to business risk.

When you are a handyman who provides fix-it services to a single estate, where is your business when you lose that single customer? When you are a personnel agency that supplies temporary labor to a single industry, what occurs when federal regulation stagnates the growth of that industry? When you manufacture electrical components and the U. S. Department of Defense is your largest customer, what happens when

Congress reduces its defense budget? If all of your patients and your spouse's family are named Smith, how will a divorce affect your business? When all of your customers reside in your community, what occurs when there is a strike at the largest employer in town? If all of your customers require only tax return preparation service, what occurs if Congress ever passes a real tax simplification act?

An imbalanced portfolio of customers kept Lutkus awake at night.

"Come on Mark, pick up the phone. I know you're there. This is Lutkus."

"Hello? Lutkus?"

"You're not asleep yet, are you?"

"Not anymore, Lucky. What time is it?"

"It's nighttime and I can't sleep. I keep dreaming about my business."

"Welcome to the entrepreneur's nightmare . . . ."

"Does it ever end?"

"You never stop dreaming about your business. The nightmares, however, don't have to be part of the dream. What part of the dream do you remember?"

"It's the day before I have to make a transfer from my operating account to my payroll account. I stop by to visit with my largest customer and they're not there anymore . . . ."

"Where are they?"

"I don't know. Their business no longer exists. I keep driving along the road where their offices should have been and their address is missing. It's almost like they have been swallowed up by their competitors."

"I think you're having an anxiety attack about your customers."

"I don't know how that could be. My customers are all Level I and Level II customers. How can anyone lose sleep over that?"

"Lutkus, you're not losing sleep over the levels. You're losing sleep over the size of your customers. How big is your largest customer?"

"Forty percent of my annual gross revenues."

(Pause.) "I can see why you're having difficulty sleeping. The thought of losing that customer would be a daytime nightmare for anyone."

"What can I do about it?"

"Tonight? Not a whole lot. Tomorrow, start prospecting for new Level II customers . . . ."

"There just aren't that many large customers in the marketplace."

"Then prospect smaller customers . . ."

"Wouldn't that be a waste of time?"

"Not at all. You cannot exclude little customers from Level II status by distinction of their size. Lutkus, each Level II customer has the potential to be converted to Level I. Six new Level II customers will take the fright out of your dream. An even dozen new Level II customers will make the nightmare vanish."

"Do you really think so?"

"Sure! You haven't compromised your business development plans by balancing your customer base with additional customers. The balancing has actually reduced a few elements of risk in your business."

"That makes a lot of sense. I feel much better. But now I've got another problem."

"What's that?"

"You've got me so excited about prospecting that I don't think I can get back to sleep."

You lose nothing by trying to balance your customers. You also have everything to gain. You've stretched your thinking as an entrepreneur. Now stretch your customer base. Look for Level II customers in other industries and in other geographical regions who require other levels of service.

Your customer base is not properly balanced if:

- A single customer provides more than 15 percent of your revenue.
- Five or fewer customers provide more than 50 percent of your revenue.

Balancing your customers will involve prospecting for new ones. You can use the shotgun approach to find those customers, but you will waste a prodigious amount of powder. Consider, instead, a few well-placed shots.

PROSPECT FOR NEW CUSTOMERS

LESSON

PLACE YOUR SHOTS AT NEW LEVEL II CUSTOMERS.

Everyone cannot be your customer. Nor do you want everyone as a customer. That is why it is futile to prospect for new customers using mass mailings. Most mailings promise the recipient you will be everything to them, if only they will be your customer. The wrong kind of customer always responds to these mailings.

Level III customers just love coupons and free initial consultations. You already know that Level III customers will consume your resources beyond your capability to service them. Level III customers are not your target customers.

The shotgun approach to prospecting is popular among those entrepreneurs with a few cases of cartridges and no better alternative. There is a better alternative. My mom impressed that lesson upon me at twelve years old.

My mom taught me about gun safety. She also taught me how to place my shots. She could have used the type of modern rifle that you load once in the morning and fire all day. Instead of the customary BB gun or .22 caliber rifle, she chose a .69 caliber muzzleloader. It was made in 1832, kicked like a mule, and could drop a buffalo at 500 yards. Of course, if you couldn't hit the broad side of a barn, those statistics didn't mean a great deal.

"Mark, you're going to learn about placing your shots today. Here's a single bullet I want you to load. Put your powder in first, then the bullet, then your ramrod. Seat your bullet on the powder with nice steady pressure."

"OK, Mom, I'm ready."

"Mark, remember to remove your ramrod from the barrel or you'll set a world record in the javelin throw for twelve-year-old children."

"Oh, right. I'm all set now."

"Where do you want your bullet to go?"

"Into the tree where we nailed the target."

"Fine. All clear on the firing range? Commence firing . . . ."

(Aim, flinch, Ka-Boom!) "Wow, Mom! What a kick! Where did it go?"

"You tell me. Here's the spotting scope."

"I don't see a mark on the target. Maybe it shoots a little high . . . ."

"Let me see the spotting scope. Your shot hit the tree about three feet above your target. Let's try again. Clean your rifle and reload."

(Five minutes later. This time, I remember to take out the ramrod without parental reminder.)

"OK, I'm ready . . . ."

"Where is this shot going to go?"

"In the target."

"Just somewhere in the target?"

"In the black circle?"

"Just somewhere in the black circle?"

"Sure! It'd be in the black!"

"Mark, that black circle is still nine inches wide. If you had to feed a family of seven on that single shot, you had better put your bullet in the middle of that circle."

"Mom, I can barely see the black circle. How am I going to put a bullet in the middle?"

"Here, let me show you." (Ka-Boom!) "Take a look through the spotting scope. What do you see?"

"Nothing . . . wait a minute. There's a hole right in the middle of the target. How'd you do that?"

With a bit of practice to be sure. After all, when you are on the firing line, it doesn't hurt to be a national rifle champion. It also doesn't hurt to have the motivation of feeding a family of seven.

You have your family to feed, too. That is why when you prospect for a new customer, look for a Level II customer. That means the customer has the potential to be a Level I customer. Then place your shot so it hits the bulls-eye.

If you do it properly, finding a new Level II customer can be as easy as falling out of a tree. All you need is a good word from a Level I customer. Ask for it!

You cannot imagine the impact of a good word to a prospective customer from a current Level I customer. Level I customers already know your abilities. They know you will respect their confidence and will treat their referral with all of the reverence accorded a potential Level I customer. They will endorse your service and you will spend little time in explaining to a referral the services you provide.

The referral knows you have the capability to provide service at the highest level. They also respect the good judgment of the Level I customer and will waste none of their time reviewing that customer's decision to retain you as a service provider. When you can personally meet with the referral at their place of business, the referral will recognize the effort you have made. They will also be reassured that you will continue to service them even after they agree to be a Level II customer.

Make your initial contact productive. Ask for permission to talk with them. Identify their pain. Propose an extraordinary solution that makes the pain go away. It is that simple. These kinds of customers will help you build your business wealth.

There is more to working with customers than recognizing the opportunities they offer and taking advantage of those opportunities. Some customers will not offer you any opportunity. Level III customers will bring you problems and lots of them. Some of the problems can be lethal. In order to make your business your best investment, you must develop the ability to recognize and avoid the potential problems some customers will try to bring to your business.

THE CHALLENGES WITH CUSTOMERS 13

- Large Customers Can Be Your Worst Customers.
- Small Customers Can Be Your Worst Customers.
- Bill Them Promptly.
- Teach Them to Pay on Time.
- Protect Yourself from Customer Theft.
- Rocco Will Sue You!
- Beware of Professional Customers.

A business without customers is like a cruise ship without passengers. There is no hope of a profitable cruise and, therefore, no reason to put to sea.

A business with too many customers is like a swimming pool full of barracuda. It is nice to have the pool, but only a suicide would swim in it.

Therein lies the dilemma with customers. The cure can be life-threatening!

You can avoid much of the confusion about customers. Customers are not yours. They never have been. They may buy your product or engage your services. That does not give you any exclusive rights of ownership to them. Customers belong to the marketplace. In fact, customers are the marketplace.

That is a blessing. What the marketplace brings to your business, your business can return to the marketplace.

If you take care of customers, they will take care of you. All that customers require from you is comfort. They need to know that you care. You reflect that care in the attention that you provide them. You also reflect it in the quality of your products or professional services.

You do not need to give away the equity in your business to show customers how much you care.

There are some customers you cannot satisfy irrespective of what comfort you provide them. These customers are unhappy because you have given them your professional best and have asked them to pay for it.

Customers like these make it difficult for you to make your business your best investment. You need them like the city of Buffalo, New York, needs snow.

There is no shortage of good customers in the marketplace. There is no shortage of bad customers. There is also no shortage of firms in the marketplace that cannot tell the difference between the two.

These firms will sell inventory to customers when the chance is remote that customers will pay for it. These firms will also service customers after the customers have declined to pay for the service.

If you let them, some customers will be a curse on your business too. When a customer is a curse on your business, waste none of your time with apologies or regrets. Send them back to the marketplace.

That is true, even if they are your largest customer.

LARGE CUSTOMERS CAN BE YOUR WORST CUSTOMERS

LESSON

LARGE CUSTOMERS LOSE MUCH OF THEIR LEVERAGE WHEN YOU DIVERSIFY YOUR CUSTOMER BASE.

Wilcox was in the import-export business. He bought toys from Hong Kong manufacturers for the Christmas holidays and sold them to his customers in the United States at wholesale prices.

The success of his business depended in part on the mad dash for holiday cheer that traditionally begins the day after Thanksgiving. Parents dash to the store and select toys for their children. Store clerks box them and gift-wrap them. Parents pay for the items and then stack them under the Christmas tree.

On Christmas morning, children open these presents. In their enthusiasm to discover every engineering defect, they unintentionally break these toys. Once the damaged toys are discarded, parents have reacquired the closet space to plan for the next holiday season.

Each year, Wilcox traveled to the Far East and ordered new toys for his customers. The toys had a wholesale value of about $2 million.

These toys also had a shelf life of less than one season. If retailers did not sell them in the course of the holiday season, they returned the toys to Wilcox for full credit to their accounts. What merchandise Wilcox did not return to his suppliers usually fell apart in his warehouse.

Wilcox had a talent for buying. This was no small accomplishment considering the planning involved. He obtained customer purchase orders in June. He placed his orders with the overseas suppliers in July. He received the merchandise in September and delivered it to his retailers in October.

His customers usually paid him in December and January, after they sold his merchandise.

The Far East suppliers knew how to make their business their best investment. They did not extend any unsecured credit to Wilcox. They required a letter of credit from his bank before they would ship the merchandise. A letter of credit (also known as an LC) is essentially a bank's commitment to pay a supplier for merchandise that it delivers.

Wilcox agreed to provide the bank with his personal guarantee. That was worth something. After all, his grandfather founded the bank and Wilcox still had the benefit of some name recognition. Wilcox also agreed to provide the bank a fully secured interest in the inventory, accounts receivables, and other assets of his business.

But Wilcox was not entirely certain how to make his business his best investment. When the bank agreed to provide Wilcox with all the LCs he needed at the prime rate of interest plus seven points, he gratefully accepted.

You have to be something of an idiot to agree to borrow at seven points over any base rate. But the relationship is also symbiotic. You also need a bank with the loyalty of a financial mercenary who is willing to bear your business risk at soldier of fortune rates.

Banks are frequently willing to accept this role as long as their financing agreement is not contingent upon the sale of this merchandise as the only source of repayment.

Wilcox delivered this merchandise to his customers under extremely generous credit terms. Wilcox also accepted just about any story that explained why his customers could not pay him promptly.

> "Wilcox, I like the products you've delivered, but our rent has just increased. Since your items are receiving prime display space in our stores, I would like you to give our customers a chance to buy your merchandise so we can pay you for it."

Or:

> "You are a new vendor to us. We have established relationships with other vendors who are also waiting to be paid. You need to wait at the end of the line until we pay our other vendors."

Wilcox's risk in extending this wholesale credit increased the day his largest customer pointed out to him:

> "Gee, I think we're you're largest customer! In order for you to be competitive with our other suppliers on a long-term basis, you are going to have to consider reducing your profit margin on our account. Say, from 25 percent to 10 percent . . . ."

In order to keep this large customer, Wilcox lowered his margins. In order to increase his profit, Wilcox sold this customer more merchandise on credit. After one particularly poor Christmas season, his largest customer filed for bankruptcy, still owing Wilcox about $330,000.

Wilcox learned a few good lessons.

If you agree to lower your margins, payment terms need to be specific, guaranteed, and enforceable. Otherwise, a customer who represents a disproportionate amount of your revenues and profit can force you to jump through hoops faster than three dogs in a carnival show.

At some point, it is no longer financially prudent to continue building revenues at the expense of declining operating margins. There are certain levels of business that are just not worth developing. The reduced operating returns from customers at these levels never adequately offset the incremental risks.

This is particularly true if you work with small customers.

SMALL CUSTOMERS CAN BE YOUR WORST CUSTOMERS

LESSON

REQUIRE ALL SMALL CUSTOMERS TO BE CASH-PAYING CUSTOMERS.

Julie owned a copy shop with a prominent downtown location. It was located within walking distance of several major law firms, the federal and state courthouses, and six major banks. Its first-floor location made it readily accessible to pedestrian traffic.

That was a mixed blessing.

"Hi Julie! How are you doing today?"

"This spring weather is really something, isn't it? Some light showers, warmer weather . . . just what my flowerbeds need. So what can I do for you today?"

"I need some copies of this canceled check. The phone company misposted my last payment. Naturally, they don't believe they made a mistake. Until I can prove that I paid their bill, I'm going to remain on their list of irresponsible customers. Here's the check. I guess I need two copies of its front and back."

(Makes copies.) "So here you are. That will be 40 cents . . . ."

(Examines copies.) "Julie, don't these look a little light to you? You probably need to darken the print density on your machine. I can barely identify the check amount. Maybe I should also use a black pen the next time I write these checks. Would you mind making the copies so the phone company can read them?"

(Simmer.) "You're right about the pen. How do these copies look?"

"Those are much better. That's still only 40 cents, right? By the way, where do you buy your flower bulbs? I'm thinking of planting a few this year."

"It's a bit late for spring planting, but Homestyle Nursery has everything you need at great prices. If you do enough business with them, they will even set up an account and bill you. Say, how do you want to pay for your copies?"

"Why don't you just bill me, Julie. Since I come in at least once a week, I may as well set up an account here. Just send me a bill. Hey, if you're not doing anything this weekend, can you come by my home and show me where you think I should plant some flowers?"

There was more to the cost of this job than the first-class postage Julie paid to mail out an invoice for 40 cents of photocopying work. Julie entered the customer's billing data into a computer file and followed a series of procedures to ensure the collection of that 40-cent account. Julie recognized the extent of her mistake with her credit procedures after she spent an entire Saturday afternoon calling 40-cent customers for their payments.

If you have enough of these small customers, they will hammer the nails in your corporate coffin.

Julie corrected her mistake by providing a self-service machine that any customer making fewer than 30 copies could use. She reduced her conversion risk by requiring cash payments for all orders under $50.

She also billed the remaining customers promptly.

BILL THEM PROMPTLY

LESSON

DO NOT EXTEND CREDIT
UNLESS YOU ARE PREPARED
TO BILL ALL CUSTOMERS PROMPTLY.

Pauline left her hospital job as a salaried physical therapist to start a physical therapy practice of her own. After a year of success with a single facility, Pauline opened a second office.

The gross revenues of Pauline's business increased after she hired two additional physical therapists to staff the new office. Despite the addition of these therapists and the large number of customers whom others referred to her business, cash flow from the business operations suffered.

The additional salaries nor the additional lease rent of the second office did not cause the cash flow problems. The cash flow difficulties were a direct result of Pauline's failure to install a reliable and timely patient billing system before she expanded her business.

Billing promptly for your services is a key step in the process of converting business assets to cash. Jumping over that step just increases your business risk.

It also increases the likelihood that you will join the sizable group of entrepreneurs who are now the reluctant owners of marginally performing businesses.

Most of Pauline's business activity depended on receiving reimbursements from third-party insurance carriers for treating workmen's compensation claimants. The treatments Pauline provided to these claimants usually involved several forty-minute sessions with each patient over a two- or three-week period.

When Pauline finished treating a patient, she usually looked to the insurance carrier for the payment of her fees.

Like most entrepreneurial businesses, Pauline's operations were out of balance. Treating her patients was a high priority and billing them was a low priority.

At six-month intervals, Pauline billed the insurance carriers. She sat at her desk and prepared the required insurance reports from her patient records. She mailed these reports to the insurance carriers for their approval and payment.

Anyone who has ever filed an insurance claim will readily agree that third-party reimbursers live in a different time zone. You can more effectively clock the speed at which most insurers issue reimbursement checks by using a calendar instead of a stopwatch.

Pauline's dependency on the timetables of various insurance carriers delayed for an additional three months the conversion of $85,000 of third-party receivables to cash. Pauline could have avoided this nine-month delay. All she had to do was prepare and batch her patient reports every week, then mail them to the insurance carriers.

There is no entrepreneur who can afford to increase business risk by slowing the process that converts business assets to cash. Indeed, there is a good reason why successful entrepreneurs will promptly clear any conversion blockage once they recognize that blockage.

Getting paid is a major reason why these entrepreneurs are in business.

TEACH THEM TO PAY ON TIME

LESSON

BE FIRM ABOUT GETTING PAID.
YOU CAN GO TO THE BEACH FOR FREE.
WHY SHOULD YOU WORK FOR FREE?

Lester was incredibly casual about the way he managed his business. He never hurried to meet a customer deadline or to complete a business project.

Despite his outward appearance of being a methodical and thorough individual, Lester had difficulty remembering things. Those individuals who knew Lester also knew that his memory difficulty was not contrived for convenience.

I am sure you have met one or two customers with convenient memories. Normal-appearing in all other aspects, these customers will remember to ask you for business credit and will then conveniently forget to pay you for your work.

In Lester's case, his memory disability existed for a much more critical reason. Lester's difficulty in remembering was an emotional fail-safe that protected him from his own incompetence.

How does someone who is entrepreneurially illiterate manage to end up owning a business?

He inherits one!

Lester's memory disability and my tolerance of it continued for the four years that I prepared monthly financial statements for his business. His disability almost made my work for him a full-time career. Lester insisted that I depend upon him for complete and accurate accounting data, and he was not capable of delivering it!

One month Lester forgot to summarize cash disbursements. The next month he failed to reconcile his bank accounts. The following month, he forgot to include all in-transit raw materials in inventory. One month later, Lester excluded his revenue and accounts payable figures from the information that he agreed to provide me.

It was impossible for me to work with Lester on a fixed-fee basis. There was just no reliable information from one month to the next that I could use to compute a fixed monthly fee with any degree of confidence.

As a result of receiving incomplete information every month, I billed my time to Lester by the hour. The bills were substantial.

Lester treated my bills to him with the same recklessness he used in running his business. If I made no effort to collect the unpaid amounts, Lester forgot them too. Icebergs would find their way to the shore of Texas before Lester volunteered to pay my bills.

When I finally asked to be paid, the accumulation of several months of fees worked against me. Lester always found it harder to pay for work that he could not remember being done.

In an effort to "jog" Lester's memory and to collect the total amount due, I invariably offered to make a downward billing adjustment. That adjustment lowered my effective billing rates. It also established the precedent that all of my bills were negotiable.

I got smarter as I got more experienced. I insisted that Lester pay each bill when he received a finished product. The theory sounded great. At the worst, it forced me to address the issue of getting paid by Lester every month.

My secretary called Lester to tell him his work was ready. She also told Lester to bring to the meeting a check for his unpaid professional fees.

This arrangement worked with some success until I changed it. I inadvertently allowed Lester to receive some work without first paying for it. That mistake only encouraged Lester's regressive behavior.

Lester's excuses the next four months included a misplaced check, a sick bookkeeper, an unexpected vacation, and temporary cash flow problems. In no time at all, Lester had succeeded in pushing me back to ninety days past due on $3,800.

Tootsie-Pop, move over. I was now the world's greatest sucker!

Collecting my fees became such a large part of the engagement that I felt compelled to bill Lester for my collection time. He objected and invariably raised the issue of my fees in every meeting. The fee issue was always accompanied by the subtle threat of changing accountants.

At a meeting that shortly followed, Lester proposed a new payment schedule to clear the large unpaid balance. He offered to pay me half of the outstanding balance at the conclusion of the meeting and the other half thirty days later.

The applicable condition was that I release his company's current financial statements that I had just completed. His bank required these financial statements to process Lester's business loan request.

Four years of billing adjustments, collection problems, and the frustration of being manipulated by an individual who was otherwise incompetent, flashed through me in an instant.

With a sense of fairness and the wisdom of Solomon, I placed a ruler down the middle of the financial statements and tore them in half!

I gave the half with the account descriptions to Lester and thanked him for his 50 percent down payment. I also told him I would deliver to him the side with the numbers when he paid the other 50 percent.

Lester was stunned but got my drift. I was disengaging!

Three days later I received the other 50 percent and had his bank guarantee the check. I carried the check to my bank, deposited it, and then mailed out the other half of Lester's financial statements.

I learned some valuable lessons about getting paid.

Fixed-fee billing agreements are fine for customers without memory disabilities. Under a fixed-fee filling agreement, additional bills always accompany additional work requests.

Never adjust your bills after presenting them to a customer unless you intend to establish the precedent that all future bills are negotiable. A customer will surely negotiate if he believes you will permit him to do so.

Collect your fees in full when you deliver a product. Otherwise, you are competing with a bank by extending credit.

A bank will always beat you in a credit war. Their asset base is far larger than yours, and they can afford to offer special deals to selected customers. Despite what some customers would have you believe, you cannot afford to offer similar deals.

If a customer insists on receiving credit from your business, do yourself a favor. Tell the customer you have signed a noncompete agreement with his bank and let the bank have his credit business.

PROTECT YOURSELF FROM CUSTOMER THEFT

LESSON

EXAMINE A CUSTOMER'S CREDIT REPORT
BEFORE YOU EXTEND SERIOUS BUSINESS CREDIT.

Some customers will expect you to finance their business growth and share their business risk.

Welcome to the undercapitalized customer.

An undercapitalized customer is an entrepreneurial business owner who does not have sufficient cash to pay his bills. You do not need another more chilling reason to stay current on collecting your accounts receivable.

The most common maneuver will appear to look like a standard business transaction. This customer will request an increase in the amount of credit that you have already extended to his business. You will grant this credit request, believing you have found a good customer.

A handful of other businesses will also agree to provide additional credit to this customer. With no more than $1,000 of equity capital at risk, an undercapitalized customer can pillage seven or eight businesses for goods and services worth many times that amount.

A customer who has financed his business operations through his creditors has committed no punishable crime. That is true even when his business fails.

All this customer has done was convince you and a few other unwary entrepreneurs to finance a bundle of risk that no bank would agree to touch!

Insufficient working capital is usually symptomatic of a poorly managed, marginal business operation.

The operation that must rely on receiving creditor-supplied working capital usually has an adverse reaction to any cash flow reduction. When that reaction is severe, it usually results in the failure of that customer's business.

When that loss occurs, the customer will lose his initial capitalization. That amount can be as little as $1,000.

Your loss will be significantly higher and could be the full amount of credit that you have extended.

A customer will compromise whatever amount he owes you when he settles his business affairs under one of the federal bankruptcy provisions.

Creditors will file their legal claims. A bankruptcy trustee will total those claims. When the court rules on those claims, you may receive in settlement only a fractional amount of every dollar of credit that you extended. The bankrupt estate may pay that fractional amount to you in penny increments over several years.

Yet there is no point in being overly optimistic about the court's decision. In most bankruptcy cases where you are an unsecured creditor, you should expect to receive nothing.

Avoiding customer theft of your equity requires anticipatory behavior. That is why banks insist on receiving credit reports and audited or reviewed financial statements from their business customers.

If you must extend credit to customers, your requirements should be nothing less.

ROCCO WILL SUE YOU!

LESSON

STAY AWAY FROM CUSTOMERS
WITH LITIGIOUS HISTORIES.

Rocco made his living by stealing equity. Anyone who was hapless enough to do business with Rocco supported his habit. The extent of Rocco's activities were staggering.

"Mr. Peterson. Techtel Leasing has retained our firm, Shenstone, Coulson, and Hammerbeck, to represent their interests."

"Fine. What side are you guys on?"

"We represent the plaintiff."

"Who is the defendant?"

"Rocco Johnstone."

"No kidding!"

"You're smiling, Mr. Peterson. Why are you shaking your head?"

Rocco Johnstone, also known as Rocco Johnson, Roscoe Johnsten, Roland Johnnson, Ricardo Johnstone, and Richard Johnston.

"Is Rocco still in town?"

"Yes, Mr. Peterson. As a matter of fact, he's been very active the past six years."

"What is Rocco doing now? The last time I heard from Rocco, he was trying to sell me a $4,000 shake roof renewal job with a fifteen-year guarantee."

"Oh, that's one we don't know about!"

"What has he been doing?"

"Practicing law, mostly."

"Rocco's not an attorney."

"We know that. Rocco's expertise seems to be in the area of settling lawsuits filed on his behalf. Do you know he's filed over seventy lawsuits in the last six years?"

"That's one a month!"

"That's right. To say he is a litigious individual would be an understatement. My firm believes Rocco is running out of friends. His last five attorneys have not yet been paid. We also discovered Rocco is in this country illegally and has never filed a U.S. income tax return."

It is easy to recognize individuals like Rocco before the sheriff's office delivers a subpoena to you on his behalf. These individuals never pass the smell test. Something you can never put your finger on is not quite right.

Maybe it is the way they interrupt their conversation to check the number on their digital pager. It could be the way they cancel their appointments with you at the last minute and never seem to reschedule. Their wallets are thick and are always filled with dog-eared business cards that say they manage a variety of thinly capitalized businesses. Their confidence and their speech will surely fool you into believing you have found a new customer.

Whatever it is, you ignore your better judgment and strike a deal. At Rocco's pace, you should be hearing from his attorney in the next thirty days.

If you know what you are doing, you can avoid customers like Rocco. Unfortunately, it can be difficult for you to avoid professional customers. Just like you, they also know what they are doing.

BEWARE OF PROFESSIONAL CUSTOMERS

LESSON

PROFESSIONAL CUSTOMERS WILL PICK YOUR POCKETS.

A professional customer thoroughly enjoys the role of being your customer but for all the wrong reasons.

He knows you are new to managing your business. He knows you need him as a customer. He also knows his rights as a customer and is not reluctant about abusing them. A professional customer will use your inexperience to build wealth in his core business. It is always at your expense and it is always an expensive lesson.

Karen started an architectural consulting practice with low professional rates and long days as her only guarantees. Her first client, Thatcher, was a commercial building contractor.

Thatcher was also an experienced architect, a professional customer, and Karen's worst nightmare. Thatcher taught Karen a great lesson about running her business: *Never trade horses with a professional customer!*

Thatcher asked Karen to prepare the initial set of plans for a series of extensive commercial renovations. He also dangled a lucrative carrot in front of her nose. He told Karen she could prepare the numerous layout and design changes that each customer would inevitably request.

Karen's good fortune at finding such a large job quickly faded when she presented her bill. As her professional customer, Thatcher insisted on trading horses with Karen before he paid the bill.

The first trade cut Karen's fee in half. If Karen worked in Thatcher's office, she could bill for her work. Karen's travel time and her out-of-office work failed to pass this test. Thatcher scrawled this first downward adjustment on her bill.

When Thatcher walked around his desk, Karen knew the rest of her bill was also in trouble. Thatcher was the kind of contractor who looked as if he wrestled horses instead of just traded them. He used his overbearing size in the second trade to squeeze an additional 20 percent fee reduction.

For eight months Karen let Thatcher corral her into trading horses. Karen stopped trading with Thatcher the day she recognized the extent of her gambling losses. *The New York Times* had just advertised a round-trip first-class airfare from New York City to Honolulu for $985. Karen's losses had a market value approximately equal to thirty round-trip first-class airfares!

Karen would have thoroughly enjoyed Thatcher's gregarious behavior if he had not been her customer. As a customer, however, Thatcher knew exactly what he was doing. He effectively disarmed Karen with his "Howdy, Partner!" greeting one moment before he picked her pocket.

Actually, Thatcher never really picked anyone's pocket. Just like a schoolyard bully and an experienced professional customer, he made you put your hand in your pocket, pull out your equity, and hand it to him.

Karen could have avoided this difficulty altogether if she had provided Thatcher with a written fee-arrangement letter. The fact that she did not prepare such a letter was a sign of Karen's inexperience.

No entrepreneur can afford a professional customer. Professional customers are expensive beyond what they pay you, and their control over your business can sometimes be downright scary.

When you discover you are being bludgeoned by a professional customer, get rid of the customer.

Customers will always challenge your ability to deal with them. You will not always win these challenges, but you need not hide from them either. Your employees can also help you with your customers. The right kind of employees will not only help you retain your existing customers, but also build your business by finding new ones. That is why there are opportunities with your employees.

14

THE OPPORTUNITIES WITH EMPLOYEES

- ➤ Pay, and You Shall Receive.
- ➤ Find Their Strengths and Use Them.
- ➤ Keep Your Worker Bees.
- ➤ Let Your Road Warriors Sell.
- ➤ Offer Them Golden Handcuffs.
- ➤ Make Them Your Partner.

With the right combination of tools, materials, labor, and supervision, you can build practically anything. You can also build one heck of a business with the right combination of employees. Good employees can provide you with a unique opportunity to multiply the results of your entrepreneurial efforts many times over.

What does it take to hire good employees? Luck and the law of averages will always be involved. You may be fortunate and find a great employee in the first job applicant you interview. You may also need to interview forty job applicants before you identify a single employee who is right for your business.

Prospective employees will also try to determine if your business is right for them. Most will consider the nature of your business, their job responsibilities, the opportunity for advancement, the commute, and the working environment. But those considerations are usually secondary. All employees will rightfully want to be paid for their contribution to your business. When the cordial probing of a job interview is nearly finished, most prospective employees will want to know how the bundle of intangibles that you offer them can be denominated in dollars.

PAY, AND YOU SHALL RECEIVE

LESSON

GOOD EMPLOYEES DRIVE THEIR POSITIONS.

It is a time-tested rule that where employees are concerned, you get what you pay for. Really good employees cost more. They are usually worth the premium.

Experienced entrepreneurs will tell you there is always a demand for qualified employees. They will readily confirm that there is a shortage of employees with specialized technical skills and a positive attitude about work. They will also confirm that there is a shortage of employees who are capable of driving their own positions.

Employees with the ability to drive their positions free you from the burden of doing their job.

Top-flight administrative assistants can be as reliable as a German-engineered vehicle and nearly as expensive. However, in addition to doing their job, they will probably do much of yours, too.

Great receptionists are an open door to your business. They will convince your customers that your company is ten times its size and are smart enough to recognize that satisfied customers are the most valuable part of any business.

Intrepid salespeople will push your products into new marketplaces and lead your competitors into believing you have more offices than all of theirs combined.

Any of these results can only have a positive effect on your business.

You will not need to chauffeur good employees through their work day. Good employees drive themselves. When you find those employees, take time to explain their jobs to them, answer their questions, and then hand them the keys.

> "Merkle! How is your new administrative assistant working out?"
>
> "I can't believe I waited so long to hire one, Mark. Having an assistant like this one has saved me hundreds of hours in just the last few months."
>
> "What were your initial reservations?"
>
> "My objections seem silly now. I thought that at $2,300 per month, she was a bit overpriced. I also thought I would have to plan my day and every moment of my assistant's day. That burden kept me from hiring anyone."
>
> "It also kept you from developing your business . . . ."
>
> "That's for sure. I don't know where I found the time to do my job and run the office, too. I know my work suffered because I lacked the administrative support. I'm just glad my customers stayed with me."
>
> "How much time do you spend supervising your assistant and scheduling her work?"
>
> "Very little. My assistant does a great job at driving herself."

You do not have to have an experienced employee to have one with the ability to drive her position, but it helps. That ability usually comes with some experience. It can also come from a desire to do an exceptional job.

You should expect to pay more for that ability. Employees who can drive their positions offer you capabilities and strengths that you can immediately use in your business. In the long run, hiring those employees is usually a better deal for your business.

It is always a better deal for you when you can hire employees with the ability to think. Employees with that ability will usually identify the most efficient way to convert a set of instructions into productive results. Employees will also complete the entire conversion process. All it takes is using the head that accompanies them to work every morning.

FIND THEIR STRENGTHS AND USE THEM

LESSON

THE HEAD IS THE MOST IMPORTANT PART OF ANY EMPLOYEE.

You receive a bonus every time you hire an employee. In addition to two arms, a strong back, and a reliable set of feet, you also get a head. That head is the most important part of any employee.

You will find the strengths of every good employee inside that head. You do not need a degree in human relations or a fourteen-pound personnel manual to unlock those strengths for your business. In most cases, all you need to do is ask your employee to use them.

"Shalinski! We need to drum up some additional translation business before the end of the quarter. Why don't you put together a letter and mail it to some prospective customers?"

"Thy will be done, oh hallowed one. Are there any specific points you'd like to see included in the mailing?"

"Tell them about the capabilities of Wyker Translation and Printing Services, Inc., in a single page. Let them know that we translate anything into Japanese. Whatever we translate, we can also print: business cards, letterhead, announcements, wedding invitations, menus, instruction manuals, parade banners, etc."

"I get the idea. I'll be sure to tell them about our two-day guaranteed turnaround or their next order is free. Is it OK if I also include a coupon in the mailing that offers a 10 percent discount for orders placed before October 1?"

"Good idea. Print one side of the coupon in English and the other side in Japanese. Can you get 50 of these letters in the mail by tomorrow?"

"Why only 50?"

"Shalinski, it's going to take you a few hours to draft the letter and print the coupons. It will probably take the rest of the day to pull addresses of prospective customers from the telephone directory."

"Uh, that may be true if I have to do the job your way . . . ."

"What other way do you have in mind?"

"I have a computer at home with one of those CD-ROM telephone directories with over 90 million business and individual listings. I use it to update my high school alumni telephone directory."

"That's one heck of a data base. How would that help us?"

"It would certainly help us identify prospective customers. We offer Japanese language translation and printing capabilities. I'll just use the words 'Japan' and 'Japanese' as the search criteria. We'll see how many matches I receive on the data base."

"How long would it take to do this search?"

"I'll need about an hour for travel time and an additional hour or two for computer time. Why don't I leave for home now? I'll meet you back here with your favorite lunch by 1:00 P.M. and let you know what I find . . . ."

"See you later, Shalinski."

(Two hours later.) "I'm back! Here's that cheesesteak sandwich . . . ."

"Hey, thanks. What do I owe you?"

"That depends if you're paying me for the cheesesteak or this wonderful customer list (waves it in the air). I discovered that in the northeastern United States, there are 832 businesses that begin with the word 'Japanese.' There are an additional 102 that have the word 'Japan' in their name. Each one of those businesses could be our customer. Here is a listing of their names and telephone numbers."

"Great work, Shalinski! I'll find someone to type up the mailing labels. That task may take a week to complete, but with the market that you identified, I'm sure it is well worth the effort."

"May I make a suggestion?"

"Sure. What is it?"

"My software has the capability to print mailing labels. Here they are, all 934 of them. Why don't you consider using them?"

(Pause.) "Shalinski, your next cheesesteak is on me. Why doesn't everyone learn to use their head the way you do?"

They will learn. You must take every opportunity to remind them. Tell them it is their job. Let your employees know that you expect them to exercise their initiative and unique talents on a regular basis. The more frequently they exercise those abilities, the stronger employees they become.

You may even be fortunate. Some employees will finally tire of your continual reminders and will eventually remember to bring their thinking caps to work with them.

When you take the time to continually encourage a single employee to arrive mentally prepared to give you his best, you will receive great results. When all of your employees follow that example, the results and the productivity increases are nothing short of remarkable.

You don't need a six-digit salaried employee to have a strong employee. Someone has to open the mail, answer the telephone, and straighten out the office at the end of the day. Just as they are invaluable to the environment, worker bees are also important to your business.

KEEP YOUR WORKER BEES

LESSON

EVERY HIVE MUST HAVE ITS SHARE OF WORKER BEES.

There is no rule that you must promote your employees beyond their capabilities to perform effectively. An individual with the skills to restore fine antique furniture may have a great eye for detail and a priceless knowledge of finishing technique. That vision and knowledge, however, does not necessarily qualify him to be the general contractor for a $500,000 principal residence. An accounting clerk may be a possible candidate for a full-charge bookkeeper. That candidacy does not make the clerk the logical choice to be your next chief financial officer.

Every company must have its share of employees who are good at their level of work and satisfied with that responsibility. It is a key role and one that must be filled with qualified and reliable individuals. You cannot run a business without your share of Worker Bees. Identifying them is not difficult. When you offer them opportunity, many will take the time to tell you they want to remain Worker Bees.

"Lee, you've been a great corporate order specialist for us. How would you like a promotion to office manager?"

(Pause.) "If you're suggesting that I have a choice, I'd prefer my current position."

"You must be kidding! Why? You'll earn more as an office manager and have broader responsibility. You won't have to travel and your schedule will be more predictable. Besides, if the letters of commendation about you that we've received from our customers are any indication, the company is not making the highest and best use of your skills."

"I really appreciate your recognizing my contribution. I'm also glad that some customers have taken the time to write, but I like my job just the way it is. I enjoy meeting new customers and working with our current ones. I also like the local travel and the customer contact . . . ."

"But Lee, what about the growth of your career? The office manager position would be an important step up the ladder."

"I don't mean to appear ungrateful, but my family needs me home at 5:00 every day. I'm also satisfied with my work. You've provided me the opportunity to earn some performance-based pay in my current position. That recognition and the flexibility to be home in time to sit with my family around our dinner table is fine for now. In fact, I'm sure I could do even a better job as a corporate order specialist if you would agree to give me a little more support."

"Sure. What do you have in mind?"

"My job is to prepare proposals for your sales staff and answer specific customer questions. If you could reassign the morning telephone responsibilities, I would have more time to work with the sales department and handle customer inquiries. I'm sure I could prepare six to eight additional customer proposals a week if you would agree to this change."

"Let's try your recommendation for the next thirty days, Lee. I appreciate the suggestion."

"Thanks for understanding."

Worker Bees who drive their positions are also good employees. They may be assigned clerical functions, marketing support, production jobs, and even sales support. But Worker Bees do not generally make good salespersons. For that job, you really need a Road Warrior.

Selling is a part of every business. This is particularly true if you want your business to grow. When you require the skills of an employee who must sell, your only alternative is to find a Road Warrior.

A Road Warrior is an awesome spectacle. He lives for the thrill of a sales order. The next sales commission is the only motivation he requires. When dressed for combat in the marketplace, a Road Warrior with a cool head, a thick skin, a cellular phone, and other tactical capabilities will help you defend market share and increase your sales.

All you need to remember is to keep your Road Warrior on the road.

LET YOUR ROAD WARRIORS SELL

LESSON

EVERY DOLLAR HAS AN EMOTIONAL VALUE.

Hunger is a great motivator. A hungry individual will stand with sign in hand by a freeway exit ramp in severe weather just to serve notice that he is looking for work. But a hungry individual will always think of his appetite before he thinks of your business. Even a full stomach will not change the natural order of his thinking.

Fear is also a great motivator. An employee fearful of the next round of company layoffs will work a Herculean schedule just to demonstrate her dedication to your firm. But a fearful employee has one eye on you and the other on her work. Is it any wonder that during massive corporate restructurings, current period earnings are always first to be damaged?

There are better tools than hunger and fear to motivate your employees. Money is the best motivator for employees who sell your services. Every dollar has an emotional value. As owner, it is your job to make the most of each dollar.

"Barney! Your financial statements for the last three months look positively malnourished. In this robust economy, they should have a healthy color to them. What's going on?"

"Sales are a little slow, Mark, and I don't really know the reason why, either. You would think that with the addition of a Road Warrior six months ago, our orders would be taking off. We've had a modest increase in sales, but it still hasn't been adequate to pay for the salesperson's guarantee. I'm beginning to think I made a mistake in hiring one."

"Don't be so tough on yourself, Barney. Everyone makes mistakes. Your mistake was listening to the voice of inexperience and believing that Road Warriors run on guarantees. Road Warriors run on emotion. They love the thrill of combat and they love their independence. Speaking of guarantees, how much are you paying your Road Warrior?"

"I'm paying him $2,500 per month plus mileage reimbursement at 28 cents per mile. He needed that guarantee so he could make his house payments . . . ."

"That's some payment! Where does this guy live?"

"In Killworth Hills. It's a gated community of single-family residences. He's unmarried, but basically needs the funds to make his mortgage and car payments."

"Barney, it doesn't take a psychiatrist to recognize that you have a case of an employee who has essentially made his problems your problems. That high guarantee has also diminished most of his incentive to call on your customers. He's shamelessly comfortable sitting at his desk answering the telephone for you. You can hardly blame him . . . ."

"Now that you mention it, he's usually in his office at least half the day."

". . . and isn't that an odd place to be for a Road Warrior? I think you need to make a few minor adjustments."

"What do you recommend, Mark?"

"First, get him out on the road. Tell him his office is in the field, starting tomorrow. He'll schedule his appointments, write his sales orders, and complete his mileage logs all from the climate-controlled comfort of his red BMW. Take his desk away and return it to the office supply store that delivered it to you."

"What if he quits?"

"That's a possible risk, Barney, but at this time, it wouldn't be a great loss for you. Besides, his mortgage and car payments probably won't permit him to leave tomorrow, even if he believed that quitting was the proper thing to do. By the way, you also need to adjust his mileage allowance."

"But isn't he entitled to some mileage reimbursement?"

"Sure, Barney, but not for driving to the office. The first commute and the last commute of the day are on him. Give him a mileage reimbursement for the distance he drives in excess of fifty miles per day. That arrangement should keep him from thinking of this reimbursement as another form of compensation . . ."

". . . or as another way to finance his BMW. I'm now paying him nearly $720 per month just in mileage reimbursements. I like your idea."

"We're not finished, Barney. He also needs to know that at the end of thirty days, his monthly guarantee goes away."

"Do you mean to say he'll be paid by straight commission?"

"Absolutely, Barney! He's a Road Warrior! Give him a sliding commission scale that increases with the amount of monthly sales so his paycheck will have some potential for earnings acceleration. He should be making at least $60,000 per year instead of $30,000. You've inadvertently punished him and your business by taking away all of his incentives."

"All of this sounds good to me, Mark, but I don't think he's going to agree with most of the changes."

"Then hire a new Road Warrior, Barney. And this time, let him sell . . . ."

The combination of a high monthly guarantee and high monthly personal living expenses is an infallible way to derail the effectiveness of any Road Warrior. A Road Warrior with the burden of high personal living expenses cannot focus on sales. He will spend more time comparing his slim checking account balance with the thick payment booklets piled next to it than he will making sales calls. The specter of having large personal financial obligations will also insert its uninvited tension into any sales presentation. Customers usually recognize when a Road Warrior "needs" the sale and will seldom respond favorably to the presentation.

As a practical matter, most Road Warriors will require an initial guarantee for a brief period of time. There is no absolute measure of the correct guarantee amount, but it should always be less than the amount that the prospective sales candidate requests. It should also comfortably fit within the parameters of your operating budget.

Never lead a Road Warrior into believing that you will extend a guarantee beyond the initial ninety-day period. If he believes you will extend it, he will build a convincing pattern of hardship that will support his request for the continued security of a financial safety net.

The history of failed commission agreements can be a reliable indicator of what will happen to you. When you extend a Road Warrior's guarantee beyond the first ninety days of employment, you will not usually recover the extended advance through additional sales. If your Road Warrior is not making his guarantee within that time, you may not have properly motivated him. You also may have hired the wrong person for the job. Either way, the fault is yours. Let him go and enlist the services of a new Road Warrior.

Employees who know how to sell are an elite group of individuals. They are competitive and they know how to drive their positions. These individuals are confident in their skills, their products, and their ability to ask for the sale. They are comfortable working without any guarantee. They will trade the promise of a fixed salary for a higher commission rate. You should usually agree and make the trade. Qualified Road Warriors will proudly wear their commission agreement with you as a badge of courage that lets others know their ability to sell is the only safety net they will ever need.

You will recognize one day, in an interesting turn of events, that you are the one who needs a safety net with a specific employee. A fifty-dollar spiff, the shirt off your back, or a weekend trip to your summer house at the shore may simply not be adequate adhesive to bind this individual to your business. The moment you recognize you have such an employee, handcuff that person to your business.

OFFER THEM GOLDEN HANDCUFFS

LESSON

HANDCUFFS MADE FROM GOLD
DO NOT REQUIRE ANY KEY.

The job of building business wealth is a task made easier when you have key employees who can do the job for you. When you recognize that you have such a key employee, offer that person golden handcuffs on the spot:

"Susan, drop what you're doing! I need to talk with you for a few minutes!"

"Uh, sure. Is everything OK?"

"We just had our ninth consecutive month of record sales and you ask me if everything is OK? It's GRRRREAT!"

"Whew! For a moment, I thought I was in trouble."

"Susan, if I had a red carpet in my office, I would roll it out just for you. Last year you brought in 38 percent of our new business. This year you brought in 42 percent of our entire business and kept the integrity of our gross profit intact. You deserve to be treated like no other employee."

"That's nice to hear. How about giving me a day off tomorrow? It's my birthday and the kids have the day off from school. I thought I would take them to the art museum . . . ."

"Done! But I have something better in mind. Do you like jewelry?"

"Of course!"

"How about a nice set of golden handcuffs for you?"

"Huh?"

"Look. I know your family comes first. I can live with that as your first priority. But I couldn't live with myself if you ever left my company to work for a competitor. These golden handcuffs are a preemptive strike against that possibility."

"How do they work?"

"Your earned commissions for this year look like they're going to come in near $60,000. I'm going to give you a bonus of 50 percent of that amount . . . ."

(Whistle.) "That's $30,000!"

"That's right. I've decided that under this program, I'll pay you that bonus in equal installments over the next five years. All you have to do is continue your fine performance and stay with the company."

"You've got my attention. What's the catch?"

"Beyond what I've already described, there is none. If you meet your sales budget next year, naturally you'll receive your standard sales commissions. You'll also be entitled to receive an additional bonus of 50 percent of those commissions under this program."

"Let's go through an example. If my commissions are $80,000 next year, a 50 percent bonus is $40,000, right?"

"Right! And at the end of the year, you'll receive a bonus check of $14,000: $6,000 as your second installment of the previous year's bonus and $8,000 from your first installment on this year's bonus."

"I'm speechless. You're doing this for me?"

" . . . and no other employee. The program is intentionally discriminatory in favor of continued superior performance. I want to remind you that your continued employment at this company is a key ingredient of this program. If you ever leave the company for another job, you'll lose everything that has not yet been paid to you."

"I'd have to be crazy to ever consider leaving the company."

"That's the idea. The bonus program is a set of handcuffs that are intended to keep you from having any reason to read the "Employment Opportunities" section of the newspaper. The handcuffs are also intended to keep you permanently linked to this company. However, since they're made from gold, I sincerely hope you'll consider wearing them."

"Wait until my husband hears about this piece of jewelry . . . ."

The golden handcuffs program is a discriminatory program. You will decide who participates in it. You will also reserve the right to terminate even a participating employee for negligence, bad faith, dishonesty, or other violation of company policy.

The program is fair. Your employee must earn the bonus. The bonus is directly related to performance and annual earnings. It is paid over time and it is subject to continued employment. It will cost you a far greater sum if you lose such an employee to a competitor.

The program is also easier to administer when you can compute the operating profit on the employee's contribution. If you inadvertently use gross revenues as the measure of performance, there may be no profit. There will almost certainly be no cash available to pay any bonus.

Even this bonus program may not be adequate for the exceptional employee. When a key employee starts thinking like an owner, the employee may be partner material. If you have such an employee, consider making him/her an offer.

MAKE THEM YOUR PARTNER

LESSON

EMPLOYEES ARE PARTNER MATERIAL
WHEN THEY CONSISTENTLY OVERPERFORM
AND BEGIN THINKING LIKE AN OWNER.

The transition from employee to partner can be a difficult one. Employees, as a general rule, do not have unlimited amounts of investment capital. That lack of capital prevents them from investing in your business or starting one of their own. Despite having a proficiency in technical matters that may far exceed your own, as another general rule, employees do not think like owners. That deficiency may keep them classified as employees indefinitely.

Considering the inclination of most employees simply to pick up their check, it is noteworthy that some are actually partner material. When employees think like future owners in your business, you will note a new change in the way they value themselves.

An employee who is paid a salary of $100,000 may think of herself as being worth $100,000. That way of thinking is what keeps this individual an employee. When an employee who is paid the same salary of $100,000 recognizes that she is really worth $300,000 or more in gross revenues to you, then you have a possible partner. When this employee consistently produces those gross revenues and starts using phrases like "risk control," "adding value," and "gross profit integrity," she is putting you on notice that if you want to reduce your risk, continue to add value to your business, and keep some of the profit, you will do it with her as a partner.

Tread lightly. The decision to add a shareholder or a partner can be a sensitive decision for everyone involved. It takes a delicate hand to deal with a kaleidoscope of egos, finances, emotions, and valuations. It can be a complex task to change the capitalization of your business. It can also be an eye-opening task to work with shareholders new to co-ownership. If you are new to this process, consult with a professional to coach you through it.

There are other ways for you to identify employees with partner potential. They have a strong sense of fair play and a limited tolerance for mistakes. They are results-oriented and bottom-line conscious. They have a creative way of thinking that you cannot find in any professional advisor. They have an excitement about work that an annual performance review simply cannot buy.

They also have the fearlessness to catch any bullet fired at you and spit it back at the assailant.

In many ways, your employees will be your extended family. They will bring you great joy and more than a bit of sorrow. The parental responsibilities that you must assume are not casual ones. Even good employees will continually test the boundaries you have given them and the limits of your patience.

Knowing how to be a good parent helps. You must always be firm with them. You must also be fair. That way, you will also avoid many of the challenges with employees.

15 THE CHALLENGES WITH EMPLOYEES

- ➤ Do You Want to Be Coach?
- ➤ Hire Qualified Employees.
- ➤ Stop the Feeding Frenzy.
- ➤ Let's Talk About That Raise.
- ➤ Fire That Employee.
- ➤ Take the Last Walk Together.
- ➤ Pay Me Now or Pay Me Later.

The employees of your business can be a bus-riding crowd or a winning team. Both groups are competitive. One group holds umbrellas when it looks as if it is going to rain. The other group holds state championship titles. The difference is in the coaching.

DO YOU WANT TO BE COACH?

LESSON

BE SURE THAT YOU ARE QUALIFIED TO COACH BEFORE YOU HIRE ANY EMPLOYEES.

When you start your business, it is not enough to decide that you are ready to take some risks. You must also decide if you want to have employees. If you have employees, that means becoming a coach.

Coaching is not for everyone. Some entrepreneurs readily admit they do not have the skills to coach and to run a business successfully. The skills are not the same.

If you decide to coach, you have made the decision to work with a team. The team will build your equity. That job is no longer yours. Your job is to coach the team.

Coaching is the fine art of motivating skilled team members so they achieve a common goal. A good coach knows how to push the performance specs of each team member. A great coach will do this year after year.

The winning record that a great coach has is no surprise.

No matter how great the coach, a team with limited skills will not always achieve. That is what makes individual skills important.

That is also what makes transforming a bus-riding crowd into a member of the *Inc. 500* difficult. Many employees do not have the relevant skills for such a transformation.

Not all employees recognize they will benefit if the team reaches its goal. Therefore, it is a coach's job to see that each employee knows there is a personal benefit.

When the coach has done this effectively, employees will have at least one reason to contribute to the team at their highest possible level. Whether an employee makes this contribution is entirely another matter. Coaching in an entrepreneurial business also involves time. The days when you could show up at game time, toss out a ball, and point to the opponent's net ended when pee-wee soccer leagues began. Coaching now involves tactical and strategic planning. Transmitting those game plans effectively to a diverse group of employees with differing levels of enthusiasm is a full-time job.

Peter's greatest problem as a coach was keeping his win/loss record intact during the time that it took to build his team.

"Peter, why do you look like you've just returned from the front lines in Sarajevo?"

"I look that bad, huh?"

"You know me, Peter. You want the truth, you've got me. You want a yesman, go buy a rubber stamp."

"I feel like I've been under constant bombardment for the last month . . . ."

"Hey, take a break! It's not like you're the only guy in your business. You've got fifteen other employees."

"Yes, I know. I meet with them first thing in the morning. I then call my customers and handle their requests. In the afternoon, I check back with my employees and put out their fires. I have performance reviews, salary reviews, and motivation sessions. It just doesn't end. By the time I finish my work for the day, it's already tomorrow."

"Same old grind, different day. You need to rethink a few items."

"What do you mean?"

"Why are you in business?"

"To sell my products and pay my rent?"

(Pause.) "Not exactly, Peter. You're in business to build equity. That's possible if your employees do their jobs. Are they doing their jobs?"

"If the way I feel is any indication, they must not be doing their jobs very well . . . ."

"Are you building any equity?"

"That's a good question. I don't know the answer. My bookkeeper hasn't had time to prepare a financial statement for the last four months."

Coaching is sometimes so consuming that you spend more time on coaching mechanics and the personal problems of the players than you do looking at your win/loss record. It is easy to understand how this occurs.

Entrepreneurs who accept a coaching role are far more than just a coach. They are likely the business manager and the owner. They hold at least three jobs, although they are paid for only one of them. Professional sports teams have these roles clearly defined and usually separated. This luxury is not available to smaller, privately held businesses.

If you decide to coach, having some coaching talent does not hurt. Whether it is a natural talent or one that is learned, some coaches are better than others. As a result, it is not particularly remarkable that some entrepreneurial businesses are also more profitable than others.

Starting an employee-intensive business without coaching talent is similar to synthetic yachting. Instead of standing in a cold shower and tearing up $100 bills, you will tear them up sitting behind your desk.

HIRE QUALIFIED EMPLOYEES

LESSON

LIST ONLY RELEVANT JOB REQUIREMENTS WHEN YOU ADVERTISE FOR EMPLOYEES.

Employees with the appropriate level of relevant skills will make your coaching job far easier. All you will need to do is coach these employees. They will do the work. If both of you do your jobs, you will build equity.

When you are unclear about your requirements, it is difficult to find talented employees.

Austin started a telephone gift service by installing a toll-free 800 number. Local vendors supplied Austin with a good selection of merchandise and reasonable credit terms. Austin's six employees not only answered the phone but also pulled stock from the warehouse. He still needed more employees.

"Austin! Have you hired your additional telephone and warehouse people?"

"Not yet, Mark. I'm working on the advertising copy. I want to make sure I spark interest in just the right people!"

"What requirements are you posting?"

"You know, my usual high standards: enthusiastic, pleasing personality, likes to work with people, nonsmoking, vegetarian . . . ."

"Vegetarian?!"

"Vegetarian."

"How will being a vegetarian help your employees answer the phone or pull stock from your warehouse?"

"For starters, I'm a vegetarian."

"That's funny, you look normal to me. Go on . . . ."

(Scowl.) "I think that individuals who are serious about the food they put in their bodies reflect that seriousness in their job performance."

"That's an interesting theory, Austin. How do you test that theory in a job interview? Offer them a hamburger for lunch and see if they eat it?"

"That's one way. I'm sure I'll think of others . . . ."

"Wow. I just didn't realize that eating smoked salami made an applicant unqualified for a job."

(Ignores remark.) "Besides, I already have two other vegetarians working for me. One of them is so strict that he refuses to put his lunch food in the same refrigerator holding any meat products. It would be easier for all of us if the other people we hired were vegetarians."

"No kidding?"

"No kidding!"

Two vegetarians replied to the ad after it ran in the paper. Both applicants did a better job of discussing their diets than discussing the job requirements. Both were equally unqualified for either position. That was a result of the focus of the ad and the small number of applicants who replied to it. It was not a result of their diet.

When Austin dropped the vegetarian requirement and ran the ad a second time, he filled both positions.

STOP THE FEEDING FRENZY

LESSON

NO ONE HAS THE RIGHT TO EAT YOUR PROFITS.

There was a time not too long ago when employees were grateful just to have a job. Somewhere along the line, they started receiving benefits. An expense account, a company car, medical insurance, sick days, mental health days, and an assortment of other items all confused matters. The once distinctive line between normal and customary wages and incentives for superior performance simply disappeared.

When employees think of the incentives you offer as entitlements, you need to promptly set the record straight.

"Brenda, we need to talk about your food costs."

"What's the problem? Our restaurant just finished having a record month for gross revenues. I thought that with the inventory system we set up, we would finally get our food costs under control."

"Oh, I think you have them under control. Unfortunately, they have been consistently five percentage points over budget."

"That can't be! That's almost $6,000 per month! How do you figure?"

"Well, I know the additional costs aren't the result of theft. Your locks on the walk-in refrigerator and freezers see to that."

"It couldn't be in the size of our servings either. The chef weighs everything before it's prepared. I'm confident the right amount of food gets served to our customers."

"So how do you feed your employees?"

"Most of them just grab something to eat during a break in the day. Usually they'll just grab a plate and fill it with whatever is ready to eat. We give them their lunch as a benefit and don't charge them anything for it."

"I think you've just found your problem."

"What do you mean?"

"Brenda, the food you serve isn't pasta salad and lettuce wedges. It's chicken skewers, shortribs, pastrami sandwiches, etc. Those are all high-cost items. Your employees are eating your profits by the plateful!"

"Hmmm. Now that you mention it, I see what you mean. There's probably $4 or $5 of food cost on a luncheon plate. Most of the time, the employees will have seconds. They may even eat more than one meal here. Whatever food they don't finish eating here, they usually wrap and take home."

"So how many employee meals do you serve?"

"About 40 meals a day; say, 1,200 a month . . . ."

"There's your answer! Why not charge them $2 a lunch and limit the food service to a single plate of more reasonable cost items?"

"But what if they don't want to pay for the meals?"

"Brenda, what you are asking them to pay amounts to less than $45 for a month of hot lunches. If they complain, then let them pay the same prices you charge your customers!"

Whenever you eliminate an entitlement, a vocal minority will always object. Brenda's decision was unpopular for a few days, but not even the vocal elements quit their jobs. They were too busy thinking how to ask for their next raise.

LET'S TALK ABOUT THAT RAISE

LESSON

WHEN YOU HIRE EMPLOYEES, TELL THEM HOW AND WHEN THEY WILL BE EVALUATED FOR MERIT INCREASES.

Employees will acknowledge having a job makes them feel secure. From the comfort of their employer's office, they can apply for home mortgages, plan vacations, or pay for the education of their children. That is why many employees want to keep their jobs.

Working effectively at that job may or may not be a condition of keeping it. That is why job security is a hotly contested point in many union negotiations.

All employees have paid some price for this security. In protecting themselves against self-employment risk, they have also barred themselves from receiving any related entrepreneurial returns. When they feel the price they have paid has been too high, they ask for a raise.

"Margaret, you said you wanted to see me today, before you went home. Here I am! What's on your mind?"

"Uh, can we close the door?"

"Sure, if it makes you feel more comfortable."

(Big breath.) "I've been meaning to talk to you about a raise."

"Don't let me stop you, Margaret. Get it out of your system! Do all the talking you need to."

"I've been working for the company for the last four months. I've never been late for work and I've never called in sick when I wasn't."

"And?"

"And, I think that based on what I've been doing for you, I need a raise!"

"Just for discussion purposes, Margaret, what amount did you have in mind?"

"Say, an additional $10,000 per year."

"Refresh my memory Margaret. What have you been doing for me?"

"Well, I have here an extra copy of my job description. As you can see, I've done everything I've been hired to do . . . ."

"I would have expected you to! If I had any doubt about your ability in this area, I would have hired another candidate!"

"Yes, but I've done them very well."

"That's great, Margaret! Why do you believe you are entitled to a raise?"

"I'm very good at what I do . . . ."

"I knew you would be, Margaret. That is another reason why I hired you. You have confirmed my hiring decision by meeting the minimum standards of your job. I'm paying you for meeting these minimum standards."

"But how about some kind of raise?"

"Margaret, when you were hired, you agreed that your starting salary would be effective for the next twelve months. You still have eight months to go."

"Well, would you consider some form of company stock ownership instead? Say, 20 percent?"

"MARGARET!"

A salary discussion, even when held behind closed doors, is more public than a posted "No Trespassing" notice. If your employee is happy with the discussion and better paid because of it, everyone will know. Other employees will want raises too. If your employee is not happy with the discussion and no better off because of it, everyone will also know.

You must be clear about the conditions affecting subsequent raises. It is easier to do this at the time you hire an employee.

You must also be fair. When an employee has earned a raise, pay it. When he has not, you must decide if he should still be your employee.

FIRE THAT EMPLOYEE

LESSON

FIRING AN EMPLOYEE IS USUALLY THE END RESULT OF A POOR HIRING DECISION.

By whatever name you call it, firing an employee can be difficult for many entrepreneurs.

You do not need to be friends with your employees. You just need the chemistry to work together. Firing them is certainly easier if you are not friends.

That, unfortunately, is where you may have made a mistake. You may have hired a friend where some chemistry was already in evidence. It is not usually the right kind of chemistry for your business.

That is why you are now pulling the trigger.

Dewey is your controller. You went to the same college, drank the same beer, and settled in the same town. Dewey, however, has smelled like gin for the last six months, the petty cash box is missing, and so are the deposits for the last three days.

Firing Dewey might be the best thing you can do for your friend. It may also be one of the most difficult things for you to do.

There may be other employees you have hired without carefully matching their skills to the related job requirements. Like most entrepreneurs, you hired them before you formalized any job requirements. When their skills are no longer adequate and their motivation to develop new skills is not there, a change is in order.

Firing an employee, however, can be a thankless job. That is clear by the way you avoid it at any cost:

"I want you to fire Daisy this week."

"Why me?"

"You're the general manager, that's why!"

"But we need Daisy!"

"What specifically does she do?"

"She doesn't do just one thing. She does many things! I don't know the specifics of her job, but I know she does some things for me. She's always busy . . . ."

"That's the problem. No one has ever been able to figure out just what Daisy does!"

"Have you asked her to put together a job description?"

"I did two years ago. I just checked back with her last week. She's still working on it."

"We can't fire Daisy! She's been with the company ever since it started . . . ."

"She also gets paid $26,000 a year and gets four weeks of vacation for doing something that even you can't figure out."

"Yes, but that's only about $2,200 a month . . . ."

"What about benefits?"

"All right! Say $2,800 a month. That's still less than a lot of people who are only half as busy . . . ."

Whether you have a Dewey or a Daisy, there is only one way to ask someone to leave. That is with finality. Incredible as it may seem, when some people pull the trigger, they never hit the target at which they are aiming.

TAKE THE LAST WALK TOGETHER

LESSON

WHEN YOU FIRE AN EMPLOYEE, GIVE HIM YOUR COMPLETE ATTENTION UNTIL HE IS OUT THE DOOR.

Some entrepreneurs believe firing an employee is a messy job. That is why they let other people do it.

Other entrepreneurs do not like the sound of screaming employees in their office. That is why they shoot them over the telephone.

There are still others who anguish at the pain that firing an employee can cause. That is why they shoot rubberbands instead of bullets.

When I hear that an employee of a business has shown up for work after three consecutive Friday afternoon terminations, I know the message is not getting across. Both parties may be at fault.

You can be compassionate about firing an employee. It does not have to be a job for an executioner. However you choose to fire an employee, it is a task made easier when you remember why you are doing it.

You invest capital in every employee through the salary, benefits, and training that each receives from you. You are entitled to receive a return on that investment that is sufficient for you to build business wealth. When employees are no longer providing you with an acceptable return on your investment in them, either retrain them or fire them.

When firing an employees, you must get your message across clearly.

Tell them they are being terminated. Tell them why. Make it effective immediately. Thank them for their contributions and give them their final paycheck. If courtesy or law requires it, make arrangements for extended medical coverage. Require they pay for this in advance. Have them sign a terminating agreement. Ask for their keys and walk them to their desks. Watch them clean out their personal effects in ten minutes or less, and escort them to the door.

If employees will sign a terminating agreement, that may be of some value. It certainly establishes closure. It also lets them know they are no longer employed by you. If your reasons are insufficient or contrived, they may contest your action and may argue that you forced a signed confession in exchange for a final paycheck. They may be right.

If you are firing someone for negligence, irresponsibility, or dishonesty, be certain you have sufficient, competent evidential matter.

Stealing a carton of milk is a dishonest act. It may or may not warrant firing. Before you make that decision, you should understand that firing as the result of petty theft can be the substance that makes headlines.

Never lose control of an employee you are terminating. That is why you should escort the employee at the end of your meeting to the front door.

While on his way out of the office, one recently fired employee stopped at the color copy machine and photocopied his last paycheck fifteen times. The company's auditors discovered the ruse when they examined a bank statement one month later. They noticed that the same check number and amount cleared the bank sixteen times.

It can sure be a challenge to fire employees, even if they deserve nothing better. When they leave, some will try to take their office with them. You can understand removing family pictures that once stood in a row on the credenza. But how can you identify who owns those crystal ashtrays, vest-pocket telephones, and desk clocks? Sometimes, you just cannot.

You must realize that the loss of a few disputed items may actually be a small price to pay. After all, an unproductive employee in your business is certainly no bargain.

Yet even when they leave your office with their arms full of belongings, you may not be finished paying them. They may believe they are entitled to receive unemployment benefits.

PAY ME NOW OR PAY ME LATER

LESSON

AN EMPLOYEE WHO YOU DISCHARGE FOR MISCONDUCT IS NOT ENTITLED TO RECEIVE UNEMPLOYMENT BENEFITS.

If you have done a poor job of terminating your employee, you will continue to pay him in absentia. Where you permit him to do so, a terminated employee may file for unemployment benefits. Where you do not contest the filing, he will receive those benefits.

The unemployment office will note the precise language you used when they determine if an ex-employee is entitled to receive unemployment insurance benefits. If your employee quit without good cause, he cannot receive any benefits. If you fire him for misconduct connected with work, he cannot receive any benefits. If he fails to accept other suitable work that you may have offered him, he cannot receive any benefits.

Firing, then, is a matter of style.

"Look. I'm not at all happy about being told I'm out of a job."

"I didn't say you were out of a job. I said you were fired for misconduct."

"Yes, but everyone makes a few personal long distance telephone calls from the office!"

"Not $850 worth a month."

"Well, you knew I was in the middle of planning a vacation to Acapulco next week. You could have waited until I returned."

"Why would that have been the more responsible thing for me to do?"

"I don't know if I can afford to take the vacation now. I'm certainly going to need one before I start looking for another job!"

"Sorry. You're just going to have to make other arrangements."

"Tell me about it. Say, couldn't you just say that my job was eliminated? That way, I could file for unemployment, which would pay for part of my vacation. Once I got back and found a job, I'd go off unemployment."

There is a problem if you agree. Unemployment insurance has a real cost to your company. You pay it in the form of insurance premiums to a state insurance agency. That agency credits the premiums to an insurance reserve for your business.

Like term life insurance, the premiums you pay have no cash surrender value. Like auto insurance rates, if you are a good driver, your premiums may go down. Like homeowner's insurance, if there is a break-in every three months, you will pay a higher premium.

That is the problem with permitting someone to file for unemployment who really should not receive it. Any unemployment claim disbursement will result in an immediate charge against your reserve. It may also result in a higher current premium that you will be required to pay.

As a business owner, there is no reason to feel bad about contesting an unemployment insurance claim. You did pay your employee while he worked for you. When he stopped working, you fired him. There is no need to pay him further. After all, there is no point in giving away equity when you are trying to build it.

Building wealth successfully is also a matter of avoiding the traps that can keep you from building it.

Unfortunately, it is not possible to identify all of these traps in advance. No matter how diligent your risk-control efforts, there is always one new trap that remains undiscovered until the day you put your foot in it.

Knowing in advance about some of the more avoidable traps, however, may be just what you need to know to keep from shooting yourself in the foot.

PART FIVE

Running Your Business

HOW TO AVOID SHOOTING YOURSELF IN THE FOOT • YOUR TIME IS MONEY • TIME DECAY • CAPITAL INVESTMENTS • COMPUTERIZING YOUR BUSINESS • SOME FINER POINTS OF RUNNING YOUR BUSINESS •

16

HOW TO AVOID SHOOTING YOURSELF IN THE FOOT

- ➤ Draw the Line.
- ➤ Stop Entertaining Customers.
- ➤ Do Not Let Customers Entertain You.
- ➤ Discontinue Employee Advances.
- ➤ Avoid Cosigning Loans.
- ➤ Beware of Contingent Liabilities.
- ➤ Correct Your Unfavorable Variances.

One way that entrepreneurs build their wealth is by taking reasonable risks.

As simple a task as recognizing risk might appear, it takes the discipline of a saint and the luck of a lottery winner for anyone to do this consistently.

What no entrepreneur needs to do is to injure his wealth discreetly by shooting himself in the foot. Shooting yourself in the foot is embarrassing, it hurts, and you will not receive any medals for self-inflicted wounds.

You take aim at your foot whenever you fail to let a business relationship control your business matters.

DRAW THE LINE

LESSON

KEEP YOUR BUSINESS RELATIONSHIP SEPARATE FROM ALL OTHER RELATIONSHIPS.

Maintaining business relationships is a delicate balancing act. When business relationships are between friends, the balancing can be difficult.

I do not mean to discourage you from starting a business with a friend, or from accepting a product order from your neighbor. The difficulty in having more than one relationship is that few entrepreneurs have the ability to draw the line that separates a business relationship from all other relationships.

There is considerable nuisance potential that results from failing to separate your business relationship from all other relationships. That potential for confusion and operational damage can be far greater than any expected return that you may receive on your investment.

Many entrepreneurs do not take the time to establish distinct relational boundaries. You complicate the task of making your business your best investment when it is no longer clear which relationship is the controlling one.

Sometimes a friend with whom you do business will ask you to leave your good business sense at the door. If you agree to do this, you have punished your business. If you do not agree to do this, you have punished a friend.

Who needs a choice like this?

Fenton was a general partner in a cable TV venture. He and fifteen other partners were bound by a general partnership agreement. In thirty-seven pages, the partnership agreement set forth the responsibility of each one to the partnership.

Percy was one of those partners. He was also a vendor to the partnership. That meant he had two readily identifiable relationships with the partnership. He was a general partner who shared an unlimited amount of business risk. He was also a supplier who sold $200,000 of TV programming each year to the partnership.

The partners met monthly at a private downtown dining room to review the business operations. There they discussed partnership matters in a two- or three-hour meeting before their evening meal. When it was time to eat, the partners unwrapped their utensils and shelved unfinished business.

It was at one of these meetings that Percy asked the partnership to pay his programming bills faster. Percy thought that as a partner in the venture, he was entitled to receive preferential vendor treatment. That treatment would neither be considered nor extended to other vendors.

"What a wonderful meal. It's hard for me to imagine a more fitting end to our monthly meeting. Anyone for dessert? Maybe a little green tea ice-cream?"

"Sounds good to me, Fenton. I've always liked the color green. It goes great with my wallet. Say, there is one more item of business I'd like to get resolved . . . ."

(Gets out pipe.) "Sure, Percy. What is it?"

"Can I stop by the station tomorrow and pick up a check for $28,300? The partnership is behind in its payments to me."

"Oh? How so?"

"I have two outstanding invoices. The invoice for $9,600 is almost forty days past due. The other invoice for $18,700 will be thirty days past due in another week. I thought I'd save your accounting department the trouble of writing checks at two separate times and just pick up one for the full $28,300 amount."

(Fills pipe.) "Oh, no trouble at all, Percy. I'm sure they don't mind writing out two separate checks, but that was a very kind gesture on your part. When the accounting department personnel process your invoices in the normal course of business, I'm certain they will mail the checks to you."

"But Fenton, they're past due!"

(Lights pipe.) "Percy, I'm not so sure you're correct. You know it's the station's policy to pay all programming vendors on a net sixty-day basis. That means we pay your invoices sixty days after we receive them. We would be violating that policy if we issued checks to you before that time."

"I know that, Fenton, but these invoices are different. I'm a partner and my invoices deserve preferential treatment."

(Points pipe.) "Let me stop you right there, Percy. I think you'll agree we have several relationships. One of our relationships is as partners bound by a partnership agreement. That agreement tells us in very clear language what our responsibilities are to each partner and to the partnership."

"I know that, Fenton, but come on! We own the business! We deserve to be treated differently . . . ."

"Like our elected congressional representatives? Not in this partnership, Percy. That is because we have a second relationship: that of a vendor and a customer. You supply us with merchandise which, I might add, we buy at expensive prices. We pay for this merchandise in the normal course of business. The normal course in this business is sixty days."

"But Fenton, why does it have to be that way? Can't we bend the rules just a little bit? Isn't there a small privilege I'm entitled to receive as a co-owner?"

(Lights pipe again.) "If it was my decision alone, Percy, I would do it for you. However, I have a responsibility to my other partners. I simply can't permit you to be paid outside the normal course of business."

"What about our friendship? What better reason do you need to have the accounting department cut me a check a few weeks early?"

"I'm glad you think of me as your personal friend Percy. I truly am. That friendship is our third relationship. We sit in the same pew at Sunday services. Our families socialize with each other. We dine together. We are both interested in the welfare of each other's children and grandchildren."

"Great, so can I pick up the check at the. . ."

(Points pipe again.) " . . . but don't call upon the strength of one relationship to offset a weakness in another relationship. None of the relationships we have will then be strong enough to stand on their own. I would rather have one strong relationship, a business one, than three weak relationships."

The matter may have been open to further discussion between Percy and the other partners, but Fenton left no doubt in anyone's mind that he had already made his decision.

Fenton always knew that the business relationship was the controlling one for all partnership activities. The partnership prospered under Fenton's distinctive leadership and his narrow focus on the business relationship with his partners.

All it took was some confidence and a commitment beyond all

objection to the right way of managing a business. That commitment is all you need to moderate your entertainment expenses.

STOP ENTERTAINING CUSTOMERS

LESSON

ELIMINATE ENTERTAINMENT AS A NORMAL AND CUSTOMARY BUSINESS EXPENSE.

The next time you inspect your monthly credit card statements, you may discover that you have been infected with an entertainment bug. This infection can have a tragic impact on building business wealth.

When you begin to think of yourself as an entertainer instead of as an entrepreneur, you no longer understand why you are in business.

Valerie had heard someone comment that making money involved spending money, even if there were no immediate measurable returns.

That is a dangerous attitude for a general manager to have.

Nevertheless, the enjoyment Valerie received from entertaining customers made it difficult for her to resist spending an average of $2,000 per month on business entertainment.

Valerie believed that if you bought a set of tires for a prospective customer, that customer would owe you. If you provided sporting event tickets to another prospective customer, that customer would owe you. If you took other prospective customers to lunch, they would also owe you.

As the theory went, customers would repay your kindness by giving you their business. A few times it worked that way. Most of the time, customers simply repaid in kind. That meant the customers gave you a set of tires, sporting event tickets, or ordered you lunch.

Valerie's employees were quick to adopt her behavior. They promptly expanded the scope of their personal entertainment activities. Entertainment was no longer an activity reserved solely for the benefit of customers.

Salespersons started entertaining each other. Cross-entertaining, they agreed over lunch, was beneficial for employee morale. The practice of cross-entertaining reached idiocy levels when the accounting department started entertaining other members of the accounting department.

The owner of the business finally curtailed the obsession with entertainment by a memorandum. The memorandum required the business manager to approve all customer entertainment one week in advance.

From the reaction of Valerie and the offending employees, you would have thought that an insensitive employer was violating basic human rights.

Before the memorandum was issued, basic wealth-building principles were certainly being violated.

It is true that making money will occasionally involve spending money. When you spend that money on income-producing assets, a business will usually build wealth for its owner. When you spend that money on entertaining, it generally will not.

Entertaining for the sake of entertaining is an incredibly poor use of working capital.

Customers who insist on being entertained are not your kind of customers. The equity they burn on your behalf is often more than enough on which to retire. What you save when you stop entertaining these customers will certainly buy you a new car every few years.

Do not believe that you can control your business entertainment expenses any better by transferring those costs to your customers. When you permit a customer to buy you lunch, you risk damaging your return on that customer for years to come.

DO NOT LET CUSTOMERS ENTERTAIN YOU

LESSON

A CUSTOMER WHO BUYS YOU LUNCH
HAS JUST ESTABLISHED THE VALUE OF YOUR TIME.

You cannot solve the entertainment dilemma by letting customers take you to lunch. If you value your time, you lose at least twice when you accept that invitation.

You lose the first time when you are unable to bill for your time at the table. Business issues may be the only matters that you discuss at lunch. Irrespective, you will not always be successful in passing to a customer the cost of your time at the table.

Customers with whom you are dining believe they are entertaining you. You reduce their lunchtime enjoyment when they must pay for the lunch and for your time. Can you blame them?

You lose the second time when those customers make the connection that it is less expensive to buy you lunch than to buy your professional time.

When a customer pays for a $60 lunch that lasts two hours, he has effectively established a $30 per hour billing rate for your time. That sets a precedent that will be difficult for you to overturn. As a result, it will be hard for you to bill that customer at a rate that is higher than your recently established lunchtime professional rate.

"Let's do lunch" has always produced an immediate reduction in my equity. It is a game that if I choose to play, I know I cannot win. A full stomach and dining in company five days a week are just not adequate substitutes for building my business wealth.

Business lunches are also a far more effective sedative than swallowing a few sleeping pills or counting sheep. After a long lunch, I would prefer heading back to bed for a nap instead of returning to the office.

For all of those reasons, I canceled my business membership at a private dining club and have stopped taking business lunches altogether. I now have the freedom to reschedule my late afternoon appointments and, if I choose, to end my day a few hours earlier. It is a flexibility that I have earned and a benefit my children enjoy.

If you have children, your commitment to them will not be lost on your employees. In many entrepreneurial businesses, employees feel like part of the family. In some businesses, employees are each other's family. You will know for certain they have adopted you as a parent the day they ask you for an advance.

DISCONTINUE EMPLOYEE ADVANCES

LESSON

DECLINE ALL EMPLOYEE ADVANCE REQUESTS.

Professional athletes usually receive a signing bonus at the time their future employers draft them from their collegiate training camps.

Gordon was not a professional athlete. I am not even sure if he graduated from college. Those points did not stop him from insisting that he deserved a signing bonus of $15,000 the day that Kevin hired him.

Kevin declined to pay this signing bonus for several specific reasons.

Gordon had not earned the bonus. That is a great reason not to pay one. When you pay a bonus that an employee does not earn the recipient will always consider that payment part of his nonnegotiable, non-reducible base compensation.

Paying Gordon a bonus would have distorted the monthly financial statements if Kevin treated the bonus as an expense. Only a weakly contrived argument and a generally accepted accounting gimmick would allow Kevin to treat that bonus as an asset.

Paying a bonus would certainly deplete the company's working capital. Replacing that working capital would involve increasing Kevin's business risk.

However you considered Gordon's request, there were just no compelling reasons to justify any bonus payment.

Kevin thought the matter was closed. Three months later, Gordon presented Kevin with a new employee advance request.

"Kevin, since the company is doing so well, I think you need to reconsider our agreement."

"What are you proposing, Gordon?"

"Well, I just had my 1995 tax returns prepared by my CPA. I thought I would be getting a refund, but instead, I owe about $10,000 in federal and state taxes."

"How does that affect our agreement, Gordon?"

"My agreement with you provides for the payment of an incentive amount at the end of the year based on meeting specific profit objectives. It looks to me that we've exceeded those objectives. It would be a great personal favor to me if you would pay me a bonus today sufficient in amount to pay for these taxes. I've earned it, and I think the company has the money to pay for it. A check for enough to net me $10,000 after withholding would be fine."

"Gordie, your recollection of our agreement is fine. The point you consistently overlook is the following one. Your bonus is based on your cumulative performance through the end of the year. If, for whatever reason, the profit goes away, so does your bonus."

"Kevin, I know that. But we are $200,000 ahead of where we're supposed to be. What are the chances of that going away?"

"Gordie, old buddy, I have no idea. That's why our agreement is based on a calendar year!"

Kevin knew he had been fair to Gordon in the initial employment agreement. Kevin, in fact, had been unnecessarily generous. That generosity may have been one reason why Gordon tried to obtain further personal financial benefits.

Successful entrepreneurs know what it takes to build equity. Personal favors in the form of five-digit employee advances just do not figure into any equation that works.

Two months later, Gordon was at it again. He asked for a loan to pay for the second installment of his 1996 estimated taxes.

"Kevin, I need $8,500 net by tomorrow or I will be late on my estimated tax payment this year!"

"Gordie, don't get excited. The IRS will still accept your late payment whenever you have the money to pay it. In the meantime, they'll simply charge you interest as if you borrowed the money from them."

"Well, won't they charge me penalties too?"

"Yes, there will be some penalties. Haven't you saved anything that you earned?"

"Some, but I've had a lot of bills to pay. The company has the money, Kevin! Why don't you just lend it to me, and I'll repay it from my end-of-year bonus?"

"Gordie, we're no longer $200,000 ahead of budget. The way you're going, there may not be an end-of-year bonus . . . ."

"Well, I could sign a note for it and pledge the pension plan benefits from my old job as collateral."

"I have two comments on that offer, Gordie.

"In this state, creditors have no rights to any vested pension plan amounts. The law, which was written for your protection, does not allow you to pledge these assets. If you did pledge them, the law would also not allow me to enforce my claim against them.

"Further, you are asking me to take a risk that requires the use of my firm's equity capital in an area that is entirely inconsistent with my business. Banks are prepared to accept this risk, Gordie. Why don't you go to a bank?"

Untested and less experienced entrepreneurs would have caved in to Gordon long before his second or third employee advance requests.

In the face of a persistent adversary, it is easy to lose sight of the reason to bear risk. That reason is to receive a commensurate rate of return.

It is also easy to lose sight of the reason to be in business. That reason is to build business wealth.

Those are also two good reasons why alarm bells should ring whenever someone asks you to cosign a loan.

AVOID COSIGNING LOANS

LESSON

NEVER COSIGN A LOAN UNLESS YOU PUT THE ENTIRE LOAN AMOUNT INTO YOUR BUSINESS AND YOU CONTROL THE BUSINESS.

Crocker entered the marketplace like every other entrepreneur who is eager to develop a niche in the professional service field. Crocker tried to stay busy, waited for the telephone to ring, and wondered where he would find his first customer.

Then he found Gene.

Gene was a professional at using other people's money. He was also something of a professional in real estate development.

Gene's real estate activities always operated around the fringes of risk. Although he never developed a real estate project of his own, Gene would agree to consult with several other developers in return for a relatively riskless monthly consulting fee.

That consulting usually involved providing recommendations to developers on how to use other people's money.

Gene believed he had something to say to the investing public about using other people's money. That is why he asked Crocker to assist him in preparing material for the seminar that Gene entitled, "The Money in Them!"

Crocker agreed and went to work. His previous job as a copywriter had already conditioned him to long hours. He expected to work a similar schedule with Gene during the next few months, and he did.

When the materials were nearly complete, Gene put the project on hold for a number of vague reasons.

Crocker could not wait any longer to be paid. He timidly approached Gene about paying his fees that were now three months past due.

Gene assured Crocker that writing a check was only a temporary problem. Gene left it unsaid that he would solve the problem once he decided how to apply a few principles from "The Money in Them!"

If you had listened to their conversation, you would have thought that Crocker was a well-heeled trustee for a charitable foundation.

> "Crocker, I'd like to get you paid, but I'm a little short of cash right now."
>
> "That's OK, Gene. Is there anything I can do to help?"
>
> (Looks at ground.) "No, not unless . . . ."
>
> "Gene! Why don't I help you get a loan?"
>
> (Looks at Crocker.) "That's a great idea, Crocker! Are you sure you wouldn't mind?"
>
> "It's no big deal, Gene. I'll just cosign a second mortgage note on your house and you can make the payments . . . ."
>
> "That's a swell idea, Crocker! You'll get paid and I'll have some additional cash to develop my seminar. When you think about it, we're just using someone else's money."

Two weeks later, Crocker cosigned a $20,000 second mortgage note with Gene and received a $2,800 check for his past-due fees. Crocker was overjoyed at how easy it had been to collect finally this large unpaid balance.

Crocker certainly had no premonition of what would follow.

Although the custom varies from thrift to thrift and from state to state, when you borrow someone's money, it usually goes without saying that you have also to repay it. That is what it means to borrow.

When you cosign a loan for another individual, you usually have agreed to repay whatever that individual does not.

Almost four months from the date Crocker deposited the $2,800 into his business account, he received his first call regarding Gene's second mortgage.

"Crocker, this is Myles Costanzo from Nick's Thrift and Loan. Your second mortgage payment is twenty-seven days past due. May I pick up a check today?"

"I don't know what you're talking about, Myles. I don't have a second mortgage and I've never missed paying any bill in my life! Are you sure you've got the right person?"

"The document I am looking at, Crocker, says you cosigned a second mortgage at our office about four months ago."

"Oh, that! Yes, of course! I did it for a client of mine."

"Well, you are now twenty-seven days past due."

"I don't understand!"

"We have a record of receiving only two payments. The first was sixteen days late. The second was twenty-two days late. I am calling you because we have not yet received the third payment."

"Myles, you need to call Gene. He was really the borrower. He makes the payments. I just cosigned for him."

"That makes you responsible for his debts, Crocker."

"Haven't you tried to reach Gene?"

"He refuses to take my phone calls or to return them, Crocker."

"Can I get back to you tomorrow, Myles? I have a phone call I want to make."

"You'll then be twenty-eight days late."

"Right, Myles. I'll get back to you at nine o'clock tomorrow morning."

Crocker picked up the phone and dialed Gene's office telephone number.

Gene's apology was smooth. Crocker accepted it with the further assurance that Gene would try to make his monthly payments on time.

The difference between trying and actually doing can be considerable.

Gene's erratic payment behavior continued for the next five months until Nick's Thrift and Loan called the loan. The thrift issued to Crocker a demand letter for payment.

Just as when you discover that a horrible dream is no dream at all but a real-life nightmare, Crocker could not believe what was happening to him.

Inexperience and the cash flow requirements in Crocker's new business momentarily blinded him to the consequences of unnecessary business risk. Now Crocker was living those consequences.

Crocker had some difficulty accepting the fact that Gene was not overly concerned with the credit implications of late mortgage payments. Gene's credit history would soon become Crocker's unless Crocker did something to prevent that from occurring.

What amazed Crocker further was that Nick's Thrift and Loan looked pretty serious about collecting their money.

Crocker ran his billfold of credit cards to the limit to get the cash he needed. He bought the second mortgage loan from Nick's Thrift and Loan for the sum of $20,300. That amount included the unpaid principal loan balance plus the thrift's legal and collection fees.

With justice in mind, Crocker hired an attorney who promptly exercised what were now Crocker's legal rights and foreclosed on Gene's second mortgage. Crocker was at the courthouse steps to bid for Gene's house.

Crocker never intended to buy Gene's residence at the foreclosure auction. If the crowd's behavior warranted, he might have moved the bidding along, but just enough to cover his second mortgage position.

His worries were unfounded. The bidding was competitive and when the auctioneer's hammer fell, Crocker was relieved to recover his $20,300.

Crocker's experience left him with a lifetime lesson about cosigning loans. Unfortunately, that lesson can be shouted down when a group of entrepreneurs, chasing a deal, combine their borrowing power.

BEWARE OF CONTINGENT LIABILITIES

LESSON

NEVER GUARANTEE A LOAN FOR AN INCOME-PRODUCING ASSET BEYOND YOUR PROPORTIONAL INTEREST IN THE ASSET.

Perry was an orthodontist. Four other dentists who practiced independently from the same office asked him to share the cost of a $72,000 package of specialized equipment.

Sharing the cost of the equipment between group practitioners initially seemed like a good idea. Sharing the equipment would allow them to participate in the additional revenue this equipment could provide at only 20 percent of the cost.

The supplier required the full advance payment before he would ship the equipment.

A bank agreed to provide the five dentists with 100 percent financing. Each dentist provided the bank with a set of personal financial statements. Each dentist also signed the bank's $72,000 equipment loan agreement.

The bank's work at risk reduction was both excellent and elegant. The bank requested and received the personal guarantee of five professionals, each of whom guaranteed the full amount of the $72,000 note.

Perry had made an enormous mistake. His financial statements, more specifically, his investment portfolio, made him the strongest guarantor of the group. If the other four dentists failed to make their prescribed portions of the monthly payments, the bank would look to Perry for performance on the note.

I encouraged Perry to have each member obtain his own $14,400 unsecured but personally guaranteed loan. Each professional would then have limited his financial risk to 20 percent of the loan amount. That made sense because no one would receive more than 20 percent of the revenue from the equipment.

The other group members, all of whom were unable to obtain a $14,400 signature loan overruled me. People without credit will be the first to tell you that your risk control efforts are complicating matters.

The immediate effect of this joint guarantor arrangement was the dilution of the borrowing power of everyone involved. Each borrower was contingently liable for $72,000—100 percent of the acquisition debt.

The final effect of the arrangement has yet to be played. The first few payments were made according to schedule. I already know and Perry will discover what is likely to occur when business is just a bit worse and cash flow a bit tighter.

There is simply no compelling reason for you to increase your business risk when you do not have the opportunity to also increase your related return. Common sense, in fact, requires you to continuously examine your risk and return relationships.

Where those relationships are not proportional, you must take the time to readjust them so they are correct. That rebalancing takes time, but it is always a less expensive alternative than continuing to pay for any unfavorable variances.

CORRECT YOUR UNFAVORABLE VARIANCES

LESSON

YOU CANNOT SOLVE A PROBLEM
BY THROWING MONEY AT IT.

Beaver-Duckworth Partners had a business plan that included an annual operating budget. Unfortunately, those employees with profit and loss responsibility considered the budgeting exercise little more than a time-consuming accounting drill.

The Beaver-Duckworth accounting department prepared monthly comparative financial statements. They took the time to isolate and analyze favorable and unfavorable budget variances by individual expense categories.

Despite all of the good intentions, the variance analysis might well have been put into a capsule and launched into outer space. No one did anything with the results of the variance analysis.

In a business that is losing money, it is not smart to ignore unfavorable budget variances. Ignoring those variances is like taking a shower in 40° water, confirming the temperature with digital precision, and then waiting for the water to run out or for hypothermia to do you in.

As a result, what little working capital momentarily found its way to Beaver-Duckworth was promptly gobbled up. That left the business manager holding $80,000 of computer-prepared checks with no cash to cover them.

The business manager's suggestion to resolve the problem was easier than printing your own money but no less criminal: Issue a cash call to each Beaver-Duckworth partner.

The Beaver-Duckworth partners who paid the monthly cash calls did not think highly of this solution.

Each partner received a one-page worksheet showing the monthly cash deficit and his pro-rata share of the cash shortage. There were no payment options or terms. A 30 percent partner had to deliver a check for $24,000 payable to the partnership within ten days from the receipt of an $80,000 cash call. A 3 percent partner had to deliver $2,400.

These monthly cash calls continued with more persistence than an after-supper telephone solicitor. The Beaver-Duckworth partners paid nearly $8 million in cash calls over a six-year period!

In an effort to avoid violating the provisions of the partnership agreement and to keep Beaver-Duckworth solvent, some partners ran their six-digit credit lines to the limit.

In a desperate attempt to redirect the monthly cash calls away from them, other partners considered selling their partnership interests. These partners were sellers at almost any price.

If the partnership ever agreed to enforce its operating budget, each partner could have slept easier and left his credit line untouched.

There is no point in having a budget unless you hold someone accountable for every material budget variance. That person will worry about keeping his job. He will also worry about controlling unfavorable variances.

As a practical matter, in many small entrepreneurial businesses, the owner is the only one who can comply with this requirement. As an owner, controlling unfavorable variances becomes a simple matter when you recognize that you pay for every unfavorable variance from your pocket.

The daily operating expenses of your business are not the only items that can produce unfavorable variances. The single largest recurring investment you will make in any business is in your people. The way your employees use their time will determine how productive they are for your business. Like children in any family, they will look to you, their corporate parent, for an example of the way they should value their time. How you value your time will affect not only your employees, but also the rest of your business.

17

YOUR TIME IS MONEY

- ➤ Value Your Time.
- ➤ Get Out of Your Million-Dollar Chair.
- ➤ Delegating May Not Be the Answer.
- ➤ Stay on Your Feet.
- ➤ Avoid Drifting Salespeople.
- ➤ Manage Your Time Selectively.
- ➤ Cancel This Meeting.

Many entrepreneurs fail in business because they do not understand the value of time. Your time is worth money. All you have to do is believe it.

VALUE YOUR TIME

LESSON

CUSTOMERS WILL LEARN TO VALUE YOUR TIME ONLY WHEN YOU DO TOO.

"Rod! How is your consulting business coming along?"

"Well, you know I've been working on three projects. The most promising one involves putting together a U.S. marketing plan for an East European company. When the Cold War ended a few years ago, the requirement for producing tens of thousands of artillery pieces simply disappeared."

"And so did the demand for the only product that hundreds of companies knew how to produce. I suppose there just isn't a big demand for gun tubes any more."

"That is absolutely right. My job is to determine what products may be compatible with their existing production facilities and training. Once I identify those products, I'm going to prepare a marketing plan to sell the production in the United States."

"What a job! What is your time frame on this?"

"It's fairly flexible. I've put in the better part of six months getting started on this project. I leave later this month for my second trip to Kiev."

"Too bad you couldn't wait until warmer weather. By the way, how the heck do you get paid for something like this? Do you bill them in dollars or rubles?"

"I haven't billed them anything yet. I'm really not sure how I'm going to handle that. The currency situation over there is so uncertain . . . ."

"Rod! You're not a college graduate student doing research for a dissertation! You're self-employed! How can you put in six months of professional time on an engagement in a country that has defaulted on billions of dollars of U.S. loans and not know at what rate or how you're going to get paid? "

There is one explanation. You have to be either independently wealthy or value your time at zero.

There are occasions, however brief, when it is permissible to value your time at zero. When you run a business, however, you cannot permit any customer to attach such a trivial value to your time for any extended period.

Your time can be worth something every minute of the day. The amount of money that your time could be worth is staggering.

GET OUT OF YOUR MILLION-DOLLAR CHAIR

LESSON

YOU CAN EASILY CREATE WEALTH WHEN YOU TURN OFF YOUR TV SET.

If you have any doubts about the value of your time, relax in your TV chair. Settle yourself, get a good grip on your remote control, and fast-forward thirty years into the future.

Welcome to the Twenty-First Century.

You are still sitting in the same chair, but a bit closer to the floor. Your proximity to the ground has no more to do with gravity than it has to do with the additional weight around your middle from thirty years of eating chip dips and microwave popcorn.

You are sitting lower in your TV chair simply because you have given the springs in its seat cushion more of your personal attention than you have given your business.

TV programming is still the same. Sprinkled throughout all those reruns are forty-year-old classics: The Star Wars Trilogy, Ghostbusters I–IV, and Rambo I–IX.

You have sat in your TV chair for four hours a day, every day, for thirty years. That amounted to 1,460 hours a year, or 43,800 hours for thirty years.

You do not need a premium billing rate to convert your TV chair into money. Let's face it. You may not have the skills of an electrician, but even your TV chair time is worth something.

At $10 per hour, your TV chair time is worth $14,600 per year. That sum, invested annually by you for thirty years at a tax-free rate of 9 percent is worth $1,990,082.

At $20 per hour, your TV chair time is worth $29,200 per year. That sum, invested annually by you for thirty years at a tax-free rate of 9 percent is worth $3,980,164.

If you are willing to accept a little more risk, your TV chair could be worth considerably more. Add a third digit to those two-digit hourly rates and you now have the undivided attention of even the most skeptical couch potato. Is it any wonder that you can lose a tremendous amount of equity when you fail to properly manage your time?

Their reluctance to kiss these potential earnings good-bye is a major reason why successful entrepreneurs scrutinize their use of time.

There is also another reason. Unlike capital assets, time is one of the few inventoried items you have as an entrepreneur for which there may be no carrying cost. Selling no-cost inventory at retail prices will build your equity faster than selling inventoried items to which significant cost elements have been attached.

Therein lies the potential for real wealth.

Entrepreneurs are the first to observe that having a few good employees can effectively multiply these earnings. In theory, this is true. Delegating work to employees will almost certainly free some of your time. Your customers, however, will always have something to say about how much you can delegate.

DELEGATING MAY NOT BE THE ANSWER

LESSON

CUSTOMERS WILL PAY YOU MORE
FOR COMFORT THAN ANY OTHER TECHNICAL SKILL.

When you can manage your time effectively, wealth is not far behind. Delegation, however, is not always the ideal solution to every entrepreneur's time management problem.

The limitations of delegating are readily apparent to any entrepreneur in a service business.

A patient rarely feels comfortable when an intern and not a surgical specialist performs an operation. That is true for even an operation as standardized as removing a gall bladder.

A defendant's stomach falls to new lows when an associate attorney, not the partner who held the fee discussions, shows up unannounced in the courtroom.

Most customers cannot explain why receiving your attention is important to them. They do know that they feel a certain kind of comfort when talking to you. They also know that the quality and level of the comfort they receive by talking to a hired employee are just not the same as the comfort they receive from you.

Customers will always be willing to pay you for comfort.

That is why you must manage your time effectively if you wish to maximize the contribution that time can make to building your wealth.

Banking that wealth is certainly no more difficult than working hard, long hours. You expect to do that in a business of your own.

Those long hours are one of the reasons why entrepreneurs who run their own businesses successfully find any restriction of time both limiting and frustrating.

STAY ON YOUR FEET

LESSON

YOUR APPOINTMENT WILL SEE YOU SOONER IF YOU STAY ON YOUR FEET.

When you control the office turf, you have a reasonable chance of managing your time efficiently. The chances of managing your time efficiently can diminish sharply when you visit another office.

How do you tell your appointment that, rather than sitting on a sofa in the reception area, you would prefer to begin your meeting? How can you let someone know that you just do not have the time or inclination to page through magazines that are nine months old?

Getting out of the reception area and into your next appointment can be a difficult thing to do. That is particularly true after you have accepted your second cup of coffee and used the lobby phone to reschedule your next meeting. After receiving treatment fit for a visiting head of state, any display of impatience would appear to be ungrateful.

Staying on your feet is one way to see your appointment sooner. When you courteously decline the offer to "Have a seat," you send a clear message that you have a different destination than the reception area.

Sheldon started each day with a customer call list of different destinations. The fact that those destinations were often miles apart left little time for him to reread the morning paper in the office of his next appointment. Sheldon was sure to arrive at his appointments promptly and insisted that his customers do the same.

"Good morning. I have a 9:00 appointment with Mr. Rankl. It's now 9:00. May I ask you to show me to his office?"

"You are . . .?"

"Sheldon! Mr. Rankl knows who I am. We talked earlier this week about some business matters. He agreed to see me at 9:00 this morning."

"Oh, Mr. Rankl is busy right now. If you'll just have a seat, I'm sure he'll get to you."

Any receptionist who has met Sheldon before knows that for the next five minutes, he will stand in the most conspicuous spot, fiddle with his necktie, and then reintroduce himself.

"Excuse me, but Mr. Rankl and I had a 9:00 appointment this morning and it is now 9:05. Would you please buzz his office and let him know that I am waiting?"

"I'm sorry, Sheldon, but Mr. Rankl just picked up another line. I think it's a long distance call. I'll let him know that you're still waiting when he gets off the phone."

With a little red at the tips of his ears beginning to match the color of his necktie, Sheldon will methodically inspect the reception area. Five minutes later he is back at the desk for his last time:

"Yes, I know. You are Sheldon and you are here to see Mr. Rankl."

"Yes. It is now 9:10, and Mr. Rankl and I had a 9:00 appointment for which he is now ten minutes late. I have something of great value to discuss with him. I am absolutely certain he would want to know about it before I leave. Would you please point me to his office? This way? Five doors down the hall, take a right turn, and his is the first office on the left? No, don't bother to get up. Thanks!"

Scheduling your time will help you be more productive. Arriving on time practically guarantees it. There is no point, however, in pushing matters to extremes by arriving an hour ahead of schedule. Your arrival is sure to conflict with the normal and customary work day of your appointment.

Some dare call that drifting.

AVOID DRIFTING SALESPEOPLE

LESSON

DO NOT AGREE TO ANY SALES DEMONSTRATION THAT YOU HAVE NOT PERSONALLY REQUESTED.

Salespeople, particularly those on guaranteed salaries, can be a thoughtless group of individuals. Time is all they have, and they are usually eager to share it with you.

They are hardly reliable. They request a 10:00 appointment to give you a free demonstration of their product and show up at 9:35.

"Good morning, Mr. Widney. I'm here for our 10:00 appointment!"

"It's only 9:35."

"Yes, I know, but I just thought I would come a little earlier just in case you were free."

"I am free at 10:00. That is why I agreed to schedule an appointment with you at that time."

"Oh, well, I'll just wait then."

"Not at my desk you won't!"

Salespeople will talk to your staff and use your telephone, but they will never offer to pay you for the time they have filched.

They will also take whatever time you give them. A request for thirty minutes of your time rapidly spills past an hour:

"You know, I appreciate your visiting my office. It is now 11:05. You have been talking to me for over an hour and I still don't know the price of what you are asking me to buy."

"I'll get to that, Mr. Widney. That is in the later part of the presentation."

"But you said it would only take thirty minutes!"

"I meant thirty minutes for me to find out about your requirements before I told you how I could meet them."

"How much longer do you need?"

"Do you have another thirty minutes of time?"

"Sure I do. Do you have a check to pay for it?"

"Huh?"

Yes, your time is worth money. It is more than a principal asset. It is also a limited resource. You have every right to earn a return on anyone's use of it. It is a simple matter of asking to be paid for it.

You can also manage that principal asset by selectively screening requests for large pieces of it.

LESSON

MANAGE YOUR TIME WITH THE WORD "NO" AND YOUR "TO DO" LIST.

The notion that every entrepreneur's time is valuable is a bit presumptuous, if not a little incorrect.

Time, just like any other business asset, must enter and exit the conversion process before it has any value. You now know that process is converting business assets to cash.

What you do with your time may give it value. When you convert that value to cash, you build business wealth.

Despite what numerous time management speakers will tell you, it is not true that entrepreneurs are short of time.

Entrepreneurs have plenty of time.

The frustration that entrepreneurs have with time is that most of them never put enough of their time into the conversion cycle. That means much of their time never gets converted to cash.

The result is that many entrepreneurs are paid for only fractional amounts of their time.

The magnitude of the time management problem is made obvious by the way some entrepreneurs will try anything to organize their time.

"Carol, what are all those notebooks on your desk?"

"Oh, hi Mark. Those are my new time management portfolios . . . ."

"Wow! I thought they were some new unabridged version of the *World Book Encyclopedia*. How do you use them to manage your time?"

"Well, every day I prioritize my activities into five different categories. I have a black notebook for each category. The categories essentially range from the things I must do, to the things I'd like to do if I had the time, to the things that don't really matter even if I do them."

"What's the red notebook for?"

"The red notebook is full of things that other people have asked me to do. Those things may or may not be important, but they're going to require my time. Once a week, I go through the red book, sort the activities into my other time management categories, and then transfer the activity sheets to the appropriate binder."

"Sounds like a full-time job, Carol. How long does something like this take to keep up?"

"Oh, it's really not that involved. An hour a day is the most that it ever takes."

"Carol, what ever happened to an appointment book and a To Do list?"

"I have an appointment book. That's the green notebook. What's a To Do list?"

"A To Do list just lists the things you have to do! There is only one priority. Everything on that list gets done before you finish your day."

"Doesn't that make for a long day?"

"No way! Only the items that build your business wealth ever find their way onto that list. When you know you're building wealth, there's no such thing as a long day."

"What about all the other items?"

"Carol, as far as the rest of the items go, it doesn't matter if they are ever put on anyone's list . . . ."

"Is it a difficult system to use?"

"Carol, it's not a system. It's a single sheet of paper! Using it is no more difficult than brushing your teeth in the morning. You should try it . . . ."

"Sounds like it might work, but I just paid $395 for my time management portfolios! What will I do with all those notebooks?"

"You want my advice? Dump them at your next garage sale. Since they're in pretty good condition, you might get $2 apiece . . . ."

Putting your time into the conversion cycle can be difficult enough without using an encyclopedic diary or a piece of computer software that requires a few megabytes of memory just to document your daily schedule.

Most entrepreneurs take a misguided step when they try to make a career out of managing a system for managing their time. All you really need is a simple system to schedule your activities.

You cannot get much simpler than a single sheet of paper.

Businesses, unfortunately, can be notoriously uncooperative with your good intentions of scheduling your time productively. You do not help that matter by being unfocused or easily distracted.

You also further complicate that matter by being a de facto member of the human race. Let's face it. To some degree, all entrepreneurs like to socialize. Social activity is not noted for the income it produces in any business.

If you have any doubt about the expense of socializing at the office, just remember that a whole watercooler industry was built from business customers like you.

How you spend your time at work is always a matter of choice.

You do not need to agree with anyone's argument that interruptions of time are just a part of business. Inefficiently used time may be a part of a marginal or an unprofitable business, but it does not need to be a part of yours.

You can pass along that message to anyone who requires your time by being selective about the way you use your time.

Being selective, bluntly, means saying "No" to most requests for your time.

Most entrepreneurs do a poor job of filtering the activities that require their time. You probably do too. Out of kindness, ignorance, or fear, you are simply afraid to say "No" to an activity that does nothing to build your business wealth.

For each activity that will build wealth, there are many activities that will not. That means you will say "No" far more often than you will say "Yes" to any requests for your time.

Learning how to say "No" is a basic requirement for entrepreneurial survival. How else do you think Center City residents can walk a few blocks in Philadelphia and still keep the change in their pockets?

Just like the Center City residents who learned quickly how to deal with panhandlers and their never-ending litany of requests, all you need is a little practice. Look in the mirror and get started. It is as simple as that.

Where should you spend your time?

In your business, building wealth.

Spend your time in those activities that either reduce business risk, accelerate the conversion of business assets to cash, or, in general, build your business wealth.

Otherwise, you are making poor use of your time and the opportunities in your business.

Your friends and your employees may not always agree with your intensity and the way you focus on managing your time. That is one reason why many of your friends do not own businesses that build wealth for them. That is also a reason why some employees will never be anything more than employees.

You can be selective about the use of your time without being remote or inaccessible. Just let everyone know that all of your time at work goes into the conversion cycle. If they can pay for your time, they can have it.

CANCEL THIS MEETING

LESSON

YOUR EMPLOYEES WILL HAVE TIME TO DO THEIR JOBS WHEN THEY STOP ATTENDING MEETINGS.

Meetings, I believe, were invented by an eighteenth-century politician who was looking for a new way to spend his time until the overseas mail arrived.

It is a tribute to this politician that people who attend meetings today still jockey for position around the conference table.

Meetings can be an expensive way to manage your business assets.

Employees are your most expensive business assets. Few entrepreneurs will argue otherwise. With the prices they demand these days, employees must be income-producing just to pay for themselves. Arranging your employees around a conference table several times a week will not always help you to achieve that goal.

Meetings can be a time-consuming event.

It takes several hours of time to prepare properly for a meeting. Even with a well-planned agenda, a typical meeting can easily last the morning.

Meetings can also be a social event.

There are always new introductions and there are also occasional farewells. Unless you limit the seating, any meeting that you schedule will also occupy the time of employees who have no business attending the meeting.

Many entrepreneurs do not recognize the true cost of unproductive meetings they schedule with their employees. When you think of your employees as income-producing assets, computing the price of an unproductive meeting is a straightforward exercise. Simply compute the revenues you have lost and the expense you paid to lose that revenue.

The Real Cost of Unproductive Meetings
(in thousands of dollars)

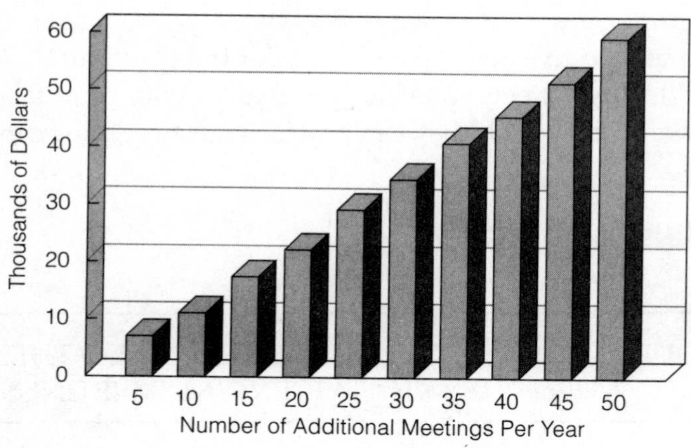

Suppose you own an electrical contracting firm. Five electricians attend a three-hour meeting. Normally, you bill their time to customers at $60 per hour. That meeting has $900 in lost revenues attributed to it.

If you pay each one of those employees an annual salary of $30,000, their $15 per hour cost to attend that meeting amounts to $225.

Like most other federal and state compliant entrepreneurs, you will also be required to pay the benefits for those employees in attendance. Those benefits amount to another $45.

Your grand total for a three-hour meeting is $1,170.

How do you ever pay such a bill? The wealth that you fail to put in your pocket will pay for this meeting and for every other unnecessary meeting that you wish to schedule.

At these rates, having one more meeting than you need every week for a year will cost your business $60,840.

Thirty years of those meetings, and, well, you get the picture.

For all of those reasons, I hate meetings that last longer than ten minutes! So do other entrepreneurs who already know what to do with their time.

Nothing of substance is accomplished in most meetings that could not be accomplished quicker by the same people knowing their jobs and just doing them.

I have discovered that not much ever changes in any business even after several hours of meeting around a table. That should not be a surprise. After all, the marginal utility of any meeting falls sharply after all of the jelly doughnuts have been eaten.

I also hate meetings for another reason. The people I need to reach are always in them.

It does not take a statistical genius to recognize that there is a high correlation between meetings and job status in most mature businesses. You can easily see that correlation at the trust company where Hargrave works.

As a trust company officer, Hargrave was paid $46,000 per year to attend meetings. She may have had other responsibilities, but you would never know it. As a customer of hers, all I knew was that she was in a meeting whenever I called.

I suspect that Hargrave worked her way onto a few different lists of key people who should attend meetings. Her attending these meetings no doubt visibly increased her job status. Attending these meetings also allowed Hargrave to find new tennis partners and to recommend times for future meetings.

I could be excessively critical about meetings and I could be just plain wrong about Hargrave. Maybe the meetings also helped Hargrave to do her job. If the meetings did help her, the customer in me sure failed to receive any of the benefit.

Hargrave's obsession with attending meetings was a continuous source of frustration to me. Some days, I was fortunate to reach her at the end of one of her meetings. Most of the time, all I could do was leave a message and hope for a return call. Hargrave was on her way again to another meeting.

I took my business away from Hargrave and the trust company. Many other customers did too. When I stopped playing telephone tag with Hargrave, I also preserved a limited business asset: my time.

When you can limit the frequency of meetings and the time that you agree to spend in them, you have made a good start in managing your time. You may even make your customers happier by being more available to them.

You will certainly have an appreciation for the value of time and the contributions that efficiently managed time can make to your business.

Do not mourn the fact that you did not learn how to effectively manage your time sooner. At least you have taken your first step in understanding how time decay affects your business.

18

TIME DECAY

- Avoid Bad Time Decay.
- Make Time Work for You.
- Learn How to Wait.
- Complacency Can Be Dangerous.
- Do Not Scorch Your Balance Sheet.

Once you appreciate the value of your time, it is easier to understand the impact of time on building business wealth. The expiration of time and its effect on the equity of your business is a concept more readily recognized as time decay.

The term "decay" is not a nice-sounding word. The harsh connotations bring to mind neighborhoods littered with last year's garbage, broken glass, and boarded-up storefronts.

That comparison is not lost on entrepreneurs who have failed in business because they did not manage their time.

Time decay is a simple concept for retirees to grasp. Time is a resource that appeared in great abundance earlier in their lives. Now it does not. The size of their retirement portfolios and the extent of their postretirement activities are largely a reflection of how successful these retirees used time to build their wealth.

"Harley! What are all those brochures?"

"Oh! Hi Fred! The Mrs. and I are planning a six-week trip around the southwestern United States. We're going to rent one of those motor homes. This time, we are traveling in style. The trip is something we've always wanted to do. We'd love to have you guys join us . . . ."

"Thanks Harley, but I just don't see how we can afford it. We can barely scrape by on our retirement income now. I'd have to leave my part-time job, and I'm not sure the job would be there when I returned."

"Oh, come on Fred! You had your own business for twenty years before you retired. That should have made you a wealthy man."

"Harley, if I only knew then what I know now . . . ."

AVOID BAD TIME DECAY

LESSON

BAD TIME DECAY IS THE CONSEQUENCE OF MANY MINOR MISTAKES.

The abundance of time makes time decay a difficult concept for younger, inexperienced entrepreneurs to take seriously. There always appears to be enough time to fix whatever needs fixing in a new business, and there is usually enough money to pay for those adjustments.

If an employee you hired with great expectations has failed miserably to meet them, you fire that employee and hire another.

If the computer software you bought does not meet the standards of the job, you simply buy another software package.

If someone knocks on your door with a new business deal, you agree to meet with him, putting your business aside to discuss your possible interest in something you know nothing about.

Events like these will occur in most business operations.

The cost of these events also appears to be minor. Besides a little inconvenience, all you have really done is issue a few more checks, right?

Most entrepreneurs believe these costs are a necessary part of running their business. That attitude is just one more reason why most new entrepreneurial businesses fail.

A $500 mistake today that could have earned interest at a 9 percent rate will have reduced your wealth by $6,634 in thirty years. Ten of those mistakes in one year will have reduced your wealth thirty years later by $66,338. Make a similar amount of mistakes every year for thirty years and you have reduced your wealth by $681,538.

Welcome to bad time decay.

You can readily identify bad time decay by the accompanying cash flow deficits, net operating losses, and, in general, a business that consumes investment capital at a rate that would make a congressman proud. Bad time decay is simply the result of many poor business decisions.

Entrepreneurial losses to bad time decay have a tendency to be far greater than modest $500 errors in judgment. Many entrepreneurs will privately concede they have lost more wealth than they have kept simply by ignoring the compounding effects of time on their mistakes.

There is respite for those entrepreneurs who cannot bear to see their equity savaged by time. The kind of time decay that will occur in your business is largely a matter of choice.

MAKE TIME WORK FOR YOU

LESSON

TIME WORKS FOR YOU WHEN YOU KNOW
YOUR COSTS AND UNDERSTAND YOUR RISKS.

Good time decay is no accident. It is the result of paying attention to your business. That means managing your operations.

Good time decay can occur in your business if you have a comprehensive business plan, a market for your product, readily accessible distribution channels, a budget, adequate equity capital, income-producing assets, a pension plan, and a burning desire to run your business effectively.

It takes work to put these pieces in place. It also takes time. In their first year of business, few entrepreneurial businesses will have the managerial talent or the available hours necessary to develop the operational chemistry for good time decay.

That is why it is a rare event for any new business to build a large amount of equity in its first year.

The payoff will certainly take longer than a year. It usually takes several years. If you do not know your costs or understand your risks, you may never be paid off.

In the meantime, you need the savvy of a riverboat gambler and the patience of a vacationing fisherman to make time work for you.

Unlike the casual fisherman, however, you do not have the luxury of sitting on a riverbank and dangling your hook and line in your favorite fishing hole. You work dozens of lines in different rivers at the same time. First you bait and then you wait.

When the fish bite, you have a chance to build wealth. When they do not bite, you keep your lines in the water, clear any snags, and keep looking for other good spots.

Mostly, however, you wait. That takes a patience that many entrepreneurs do not have. However you learn to do it, waiting always pays off.

LEARN HOW TO WAIT

LESSON

WAITING FOR YOUR BUSINESS TO
BUILD WEALTH CAN SOMETIMES BE
THE MOST DIFFICULT THING TO DO.

Successful entrepreneurs know how to wait. On the floor of any options exchange you can find a unique breed of entrepreneurs who understand the value of waiting. Officially, they are called market makers.

A market maker has only two goals. The exchange that approved the market maker's membership will tell you that one of those goals must be to help keep the marketplace liquid. All market makers will publicly concede that this is a goal.

Market makers will privately tell you that their other goal is to build equity. If they cannot build equity, they will not need to worry about any other goals.

When trading is active, market makers may or may not be active, but they will always make markets. They make markets for public customers by quoting prices at which they will buy and sell option contracts.

Some public customers may not wish to buy or sell option contracts at prices that allow market makers to build their wealth. When that situation occurs, a patient market maker does nothing. He waits and adjusts his markets based on his preference for risk.

Then he waits some more.

Just like a successful market maker, wealth can be the result of being patient with your business.

Just like unsuccessful market makers, impatient entrepreneurs can be a burden to their businesses.

Many entrepreneurs expect instant results. That is precisely the kind of behavior you want to avoid in your business.

Your impatience is unfair. Good time decay just does not work that fast.

If you plan on making your business your best investment, you must learn to wait for results. It's not like putting a quarter in a slot machine, pulling the lever, and knowing your payoff in six seconds or less.

Any entrepreneur who cannot wait for results can damage his business by forcing on it the wrong kind of attention at the wrong time.

There are, of course, easier ways for time decay to damage a business. Ignoring your business is just one more way for bad time decay to flourish.

COMPLACENCY CAN BE DANGEROUS

LESSON

PAY ATTENTION TO YOUR BUSINESS.

It is true that equity capital, risk, and time are basic ingredients in any business.

It is also true that quality ingredients have the potential to support a quality business. Starting with the right ingredients of sufficient quality, however, is no guarantee of a successful business.

Making any business your best investment also requires your undivided attention. If you cannot provide that attention, when time decays, so will your business.

Kent owned a temporary personnel agency.

During the slow part of a business cycle, his agency had a large pool of temporary employees to offer to his customers. The size of the pool increased when other businesses laid off or terminated their employees. Many of these employees were the qualified but unfortunate victims of operating expense reductions.

During the fast part of the cycle, the size of the employment pool decreased. Companies hired Kent's temporaries to build business wealth. They also paid Kent a placement fee for the temporary employees that they removed from the employment pool.

There was not a great deal of complexity to Kent's temporary employment agency. The risk was largely self-adjusting and the return was predictable.

Variable expenses are one component from which entrepreneurial fortunes are made. Kent's expenses were largely variable. That meant if Kent did not have the revenue, he did not have the related expense.

To build the wealth in his business, Kent paid temporary employee expenses only while they worked for his customers.

All Kent had to do was let these temporary employees work for his customers or be hired by them for full-time positions. Either event produced wealth for Kent.

The danger in predictability is the boredom that sometimes hides there. Kent soon tired of making these low-risk, equity-building investments and decided instead to play a riskier game. Kent spent his working capital on cocaine.

Three years later, Kent owed the IRS nearly $400,000 on past-due payroll taxes for his business. Kent's cavalier management style, his drug addiction, and his lack of interest in his business accelerated the day of reckoning.

When that day came, Kent lost his business. He also lost his credibility and his sense of self-worth. Today, a more docile Kent has nothing but time on his hands and now is content to let others take the risks.

Kent had nearly every component for a successful business. Time decay could have increased his wealth. Instead, each day that passed took some of his wealth with it until there was nothing left.

Kent could have avoided the total failure of his business if he had simply paid attention to it.

But there are some situations where even a generous amount of attention is not enough to make time work for you. This is especially true in a business you know nothing about.

DO NOT SCORCH YOUR BALANCE SHEET

LESSON

TIME USUALLY WORKS AGAINST YOU
IN AN UNFAMILIAR BUSINESS.

In any business, a scorched balance sheet is the consequence of bad time decay. A balance sheet looks scorched when much of the equity on it has gone up in smoke. A business you know nothing about has the potential to do just that.

Stan started a gift shop that sold greeting cards and novelties. He leased a ground-level, downtown location, with plenty of off-street pedestrian traffic.

Stan figured he had learned just about everything the day he received his Ph.D. degree in economics. That set of credentials made it easier for the landlord to accept Stan's personal guarantee on a fifteen-year lease.

Anyone whose business brains are not in working order can personally guarantee a lease for fifteen years. Just because a landlord accepts your guarantee does not mean you know what you are doing.

Just like the performance limitations of our own congressional representatives, not every economist is qualified to balance revenues and expenses. Stan understood the theory about balancing, but knew very little about the practical aspects of running a business.

As an entrepreneur, you either find the balance point that leaves you with a profit in line with your risks or you are out of business.

The two largest revenue weeks for any greeting card shop are Christmas and Valentine's Day. The numbers will tell you why. Nearly 2.2 billion Christmas cards are sold every year. Almost 900 million greeting cards are delivered each Valentine's Day.

During those two holidays, Stan filled his store with customers. He also sold most of his greeting card inventory. Those holiday sales represented 80 percent of Stan's annual gross revenues. That revenue had to pay most of his business bills for the rest of the year.

Stan understood many of the pro-deficit spending arguments offered by federal budget deficit supporters. The prospect of deficit spending in his business was horrifying to Stan after only one year of operations and a five-digit operating loss.

Stan closed his doors for good later that summer. He also hired an attorney to settle the long-term lease commitment with his landlord.

Stan is still paying that settlement and his legal fees. Every Christmas and Valentine's week, you can see Stan on downtown street corners, hawking $2 helium balloons just as fast as he can inflate them.

If you ask him, Stan will be the first to tell you to stay away from a business you know nothing about.

Stan will also agree that sensible entrepreneurs can learn from their mistakes. You can too.

In a competitive marketplace, however, you may not have the luxury of learning as you go. The learning curve not only takes time, but it is also expensive.

Time decay will affect every business. If you are uncomfortable with the way that time may affect your business wealth, you are probably uncomfortable with your risks and with the way you have managed your business.

There are other changes you can make that will affect the way you manage business risk. Learning how to make an informed capital investment decision will help you do just that.

19

CAPITAL INVESTMENTS

- ➤ Make Your First Capital Investment.
- ➤ Control Your Capital Spending.
- ➤ Recover Your Costs.
- ➤ Examine the Numbers First.
- ➤ Equipment Leasing Can Destroy Your Budget.
- ➤ Residual Values Are Always a Burden.
- ➤ Do Not Buy Your Office.
- ➤ You Can Be a Blue-Collar Entrepreneur.

Capital investment decisions play a major part in positioning your business for future growth. Unlike many other decisions that you will make, the consequences of most capital investment decisions will stay with you as long as you own your business.

MAKE YOUR FIRST CAPITAL INVESTMENT

LESSON

EVERY BUSINESS REQUIRES AN EQUITY INVESTMENT.

The first capital investment decision that any entrepreneur will make is the amount of equity capital to put at risk in a business. No entrepreneur has an unlimited amount of equity capital.

It does not matter if you were previously an officer of a major corporation or are the new entrepreneur on the block. When you start a business, you will put at risk much of what you have saved.

You may, of course, need to risk far more than your savings to start a business. You will need to buy assets and you will need to meet minimum working capital requirements. A family loan or a premature retirement account distribution may give you the additional capital that you require.

The additional capital comes at a cost. You must repay the family loan. The withdrawal of retirement funds may be penalized and will definitely be taxed. It is a wonder that any business can succeed when you start it under these conditions!

That is another reason why considerable thought must accompany your first capital investment decision.

The initial equity capital for most entrepreneurial businesses is usually insufficient. That is hardly a surprise. The only equity capital guidelines available to most entrepreneurs are their preincorporation checking account balances.

Lending money to your business does not increase your equity capital. When you lend money to your business, you become a creditor. That means you expect your business to repay what it has borrowed from you. If the amount that you lend is significant, you must charge your company interest. That interest expense will further reduce the equity in your business.

You look more serious about your business when you start it with a substantial amount of equity capital. That commitment is also not lost on your creditors. Any firm that extends credit to your business will look at the size of your investment in it. The bigger your investment, the more credit they will extend.

Some entrepreneurs limit the equity they contribute to their business, believing they have reduced their exposure to business risk. Without much additional thought, they later agree to guarantee personally any credit extended to their business. That just increases their risk.

Do not be so eager to put all of your wealth at risk by personally guaranteeing your business credit. It is a far better alternative to contribute additional equity capital. If you were to lose all of the equity capital in your business, at least you have set a ceiling on the maximum financial loss that you may suffer.

There is a further benefit. When creditors see a large investment in your business, many will forego their personal guarantee requirements.

You will also find it difficult to earn a greater return on this capital than what you can earn when your business is your best investment. Each additional dollar of equity capital that you contribute to your business will earn this return.

Those are all good reasons why the equity capital in your business should be no less than one year of your expected salary.

Your initial equity capital contribution may need to be a far greater amount. That may involve having other partners or investors to share your risk. They will also share your return.

If sharing the return achieved in your business through your personal efforts does not excite you, consider a more modest approach. Simply limit the scope of your business plans to those that you can fund with a smaller initial capital investment.

One year's salary is usually a number that is large enough to get you up for work in the morning, to warrant your attention, and to comfort your creditors.

CONTROL YOUR CAPITAL SPENDING

LESSON

THE ONLY REASON TO BUY AN ASSET IS FOR THE INCOME IT PRODUCES.

Most aspiring entrepreneurs have no opinion about lawyers. That will change the day you incorporate your business. For $500 and one hour of professional time, an attorney will make your new business a matter of legal record.

If you were previously incapable of recognizing a debit from a credit, that will not change the day you incorporate your business. For $500 a quarter, someone who may know very little about your business will agree to compile your financial statements.

When you finish meeting with your lawyer and your accountant, you then go about your business, believing that you have forever put to rest your capital investment decisions. This belief, for many entrepreneurs, is the beginning of the end.

Not one tenth of the amount of thought that went into a decision to start a business ever goes into a decision to buy other business assets! Owners usually acquire these assets on the basis of want. Few owners take the time to consider the long-term cost of these assets or how they will be utilized.

In any failed business, it is sad to see the vast array of hardware on the auctioneer's block. You can see cars, desks, file cabinets, computers, copy machines, telephones, and other paraphernalia. All of these items represent capital investments that are now worth little more than a fraction of their initial acquisition cost.

What happened?

There are many ways to dilute the return of any business. Buying assets that cannot pay for themselves will do just that!

When assets cannot pay for themselves by producing enough income, positive cash flow will decrease. That smaller cash flow increases business risk.

Left unchecked, that increased risk can be enough to put any business out of business.

LESSON

INSIST ON FAST PAYBACKS
FOR ALL ASSET ACQUISITIONS.

Weldon had a lifetime ambition of being a surgeon with hundreds of grateful patients. His college education and postgraduate studies qualified him to perform that surgery on four-legged patients.

Weldon's patients were horses!

Weldon wanted to buy a specialized $12,000 surgery table for his veterinary practice. The proposed cost of this surgery table represented nearly 40 percent of the assets on Weldon's balance sheet. That meant this surgery table was a big investment decision for Weldon's little business.

Weldon did not perform the volume of specialized surgery that warranted such an investment. In fact, the revenue that Weldon earned from specialized surgery the last five years was less than 1 percent of his total revenues! That low percentage suggested that it might take a few years before the surgery table started paying for itself.

It did not require much analysis to see that this surgery table was not going to be one of Weldon's best investments. Weldon could have reached the same conclusion if he answered a few simple questions:

- Do I really need the asset?
- How will I pay for it?
- How long will it take for this asset to pay for itself?
- Will this asset provide a return that meets my business requirements?

Weldon had the answers to the first two questions:

"Yes, Mark. I need a surgery table. Besides, my bank has even agreed to finance it for me."

"Those aren't great answers, Weldon. What are the chances that this surgery table will pay for itself in the next four years?"

"But isn't a four-year payback about a 25 percent annual return?"

"That's close enough . . . ."

"I think that return is extreme and unrealistic."

"Why do you say that, Weldon?"

"Nobody gets that kind of payback on this equipment."

"That certainly explains why every equine veterinary practice doesn't own a surgery table. Maybe that's also telling you something about the equipment . . . ."

"But at least I would have it when I needed it. Besides, you always tell me that taking risks is a part of running any business . . . ."

"Weldon, I agree that you're going to take some risks when you run any business. You should also be paid for those risks. Your modest salary does not pay you for most of those risks . . . ."

"Yes, but I think I can increase the profit in my business and my salary. Wouldn't that make a difference?"

"It sure would, Weldon, but those two new competitors who just opened an equine clinic two miles away at Countryside Stables will probably have something to say about that."

"Hmmm . . . ."

"All I'm suggesting is that you are entitled to returns that are in line with this bundle of risk. That is why even as a one-person business, you need to look at a capital budget before you just go out and buy any asset that you'd like to have or you think you need."

EXAMINE THE NUMBERS FIRST

LESSON

ANALYZE THE PROFIT CONTRIBUTION OF EACH ASSET BEFORE YOU BUY IT.

An integral part of building business wealth is a capital asset budget. Capital budgeting is a systematic and rational method of planning for fixed asset purchases and retirements. It is a practical, analytical exercise, separate and distinct from an operating budget.

There are several acceptable methods of capital budgeting that have been fully tested. That means they work. Whether you choose to use the payback method, net present value method, or internal rate of return method is largely a matter of preference.

The payback method computes the number of years it takes for an asset acquisition to pay for itself. Do not buy an asset if it takes too long to pay for itself.

If you cannot recover the cost of an asset in less than five years, the asset has taken too long to pay for itself.

I prefer to recover the cost of most assets in one year or less. That one-year period can be a difficult target to meet for any business. Nevertheless, it keeps me from buying assets that are marginal from an income-producing point of view.

The net present value method computes today's value of all future net income that an asset will produce. That net present value tells you if an asset will recover its cost. Do not buy an asset that will not recover its cost.

The interest rate you use in your net present value computation will have a considerable impact on the computation's result. Your choice of interest rates should reflect the higher of your borrowing costs or the return that you would earn on other available investments with comparable risk.

The internal rate of return method computes a rate of return as if the asset were an investment and the future net cash flows produced by that asset were annual dividends. The internal rate of return tells you the rate of return on your investment as if it were a stand-alone business. Do not buy an asset that has a low internal rate of return.

A low rate of return for a self-employed individual is any rate that is less than 25 percent. I consider that rate of return the minimal acceptable rate for any entrepreneur with moderate business risk.

Common to all of these methods are an initial cash outflow and subsequent cash inflows. The cash outflow occurs at the time you acquire the asset. The cash inflows occur over the income-producing life of the asset. There are, of course, other characteristics applicable to each method. Any good finance textbook will outline these for you.

The concept of responsible capital budgeting rests on no more than a single point: Any asset you acquire must be income-producing.

If you buy an asset that never produces income, you can never recover its cost. If the income it produces is inadequate, you can be certain that you have failed to build wealth with that asset.

Good intentions are just no substitute for good results. That single statement dispels any argument you may offer that you intended to produce a specific level of revenue with these assets. For whatever reason, you did not.

Economists know that you can create a statistic to support any conclusion. Failed entrepreneurs also know that you can create on paper a series of cash inflows to support any proposed capital asset acquisition.

That is why you must be realistic about the net cash inflows from any proposed capital asset acquisition. At their best, future net cash flows are uncertain. At their worst, they are totally unreliable.

Still, some analysis is better than none at all.

Kritzer's board of directors approved his proposed $147,000 capital budget. Halfway into the year, Kritzer purchased an additional $180,000 of assets without board approval.

For that indulgence, the board should have promptly fired Kritzer.

Kritzer negotiated the financing for these unapproved assets. The supplier agreed to accept a 10 percent down payment and the remaining balance in equal monthly installments, without interest, for the next three years.

Suppliers of business equipment are not generally recognized for their fairness to their customers. A supplier who agrees to receive his payments in installments without interest has already increased the asset price to reflect the foregone interest!

Ten days after he signed the purchase commitment, Kritzer received a bill for $6,300 of additional shipping charges. The supplier would not agree to prepay the shipping charges or combine them with the unpaid principal balance.

Kritzer also failed to identify other equipment-related costs. The company did not have sufficient space for these assets until it paid $26,000 for a last-minute room addition. The company also hired a new $42,000 employee without whose attention the asset would never produce income.

Kritzer's mistakes were not unique, but they were unnecessary. The company could have avoided the mistakes by analyzing costs and profit contributions before they purchased the assets.

When you skip the analysis, you run the risk of paying two or three times more than what a supplier tells you an asset will cost.

EQUIPMENT LEASING CAN DESTROY YOUR BUDGET

LESSON

EQUIPMENT LEASING OFFERS A VARIETY OF WAYS TO MAKE POOR CAPITAL INVESTMENTS.

Some entrepreneurs believe equipment leasing is a successful substitute for their capital budgeting program. It is easy to understand why they are so excited about leasing. Equipment leasing is a great way to circumvent any capital budgeting program.

You are one possible source of risk capital when you buy an asset. You do not need a better incentive to negotiate vigorously the price of an asset with a vendor. After all, you will keep what you do not pay to the vendor.

A bank is another logical source of risk capital to finance an asset purchase. If you have never prepared financial statements for your business, the bank will expect to receive them from you when you ask them to finance an asset purchase.

With that single request, the bank has successfully diverted your attention from the price of the asset and the loan interest rate to the loan approval process. That process is something else. As most entrepreneurs will confirm, it is a great relief just to know that you can complete the bank's standard business loan application.

Leasing is the worst of all worlds. Glossy promotional literature will usually offer to finance your equipment acquisition at attractive rates. Sincere leasing agents will also tell you that leasing permits you to conserve capital and preserve lines of credit for other operating and investment purposes. That can be true, but leasing is frequently more costly than owning equipment.

Leasing is far too easy. The offer of leasing something for nothing down is attractive bait that few entrepreneurs will ignore. That is true, even when these entrepreneurs know there is a hook hidden in the bait.

As long as you do not plan to use the proposed equipment in a restaurant or a fitness center, there is a good chance the bank will approve your lease application.

Leasing is the silent killer of capital budgeting. With little more than your personal signature, you can bind your business to a sobering contingent obligation. That obligation is the residual value that someone must pay at the end of the lease.

You probably think that a 30 percent residual value means you have agreed to lease an asset for 70 percent of its useful economic life. That is not true.

What you have likely done is agreed to pay, in monthly installments, 70 percent of the acquisition cost of an asset. The day you make your last payment, the asset may have no more useful economic life. That makes the asset worthless.

At the end of the lease, you must return the equipment to the lessor, who may sell it at used equipment prices. If the price they receive is less than the residual value, you will pay the difference to the lessor as an additional expense.

That additional amount is an expense for which you may have received no revenue. No leasing company will clearly explain this risk to you until they bill you for it at the end of your lease. By that time, it is usually too late for you to object.

RESIDUAL VALUES ARE ALWAYS A BURDEN

LESSON

YOU ALWAYS PAY FOR THE FLEXIBILITY IN A LEASE.

Residual value is a creative, flexible, and dangerous concept.

Lessors use residual values to make assets under lease agreements look affordable. A leased asset with low monthly payments looks affordable.

Lessees use residual value as a veil to hide long-term debt obligations. Few entrepreneurs will voluntarily disclose to their creditors any of their lease obligations or the potential liabilities for any unpaid residual values.

Whatever the residual value, both the lessor and the lessee must agree on the same amount.

You could agree on a residual value of 10 percent. That would make your monthly payments large for the reason that you will pay 90 percent of the equipment's cost before the last day of the lease.

That may be prudent because the equipment may have no useful economic life at the end of the lease period. If you cannot sell the equipment for its residual value, there is only a small additional amount to pay.

That may also be foolish because you may have other opportunities to earn a greater return on your equity capital during the lease period.

If a leasing company were willing, you could agree on a residual value of 90 percent. That would make your monthly payments small for the reason that you will pay only 10 percent of the equipment's cost before the last day of the lease.

That may be smart because you have the use of an income-producing asset without an equivalent cash outflow.

That may be unwise because there are few assets that you can use in a business and then sell at 90 percent of their acquisition cost several years later.

One way or another, you will always pay.

In the manner that Secret Service agents will protect a visiting head of state, a leasing company will guard disclosure of its interest rate. That way, you can never really compare the true cost of leasing to other alternatives.

"Hello! Beckworth Leasing!"

"Yes, good morning. My name is Norton Filmeister. I want to lease two delivery vans for my company, Filmeister Electronics."

"That's why we're here, Norton."

"What is the cost of these two vans?"

"Say, $40,000 for the two of them."

"Have you ever leased anything before, Norton?"

"No, I haven't."

(Grin!) "Well, let me figure this out. I think that with a five-year lease term and a 30 percent residual, we can get your monthly payments down to $853 per month. How does that sound?"

"Gosh, those are low payments. What interest rate are you using?"

"Interest rates, Norton? I think you may be confused. We're a leasing company, not a bank."

"But how did you figure out my monthly payment?"

"Oh, now I understand your question. Your lease has a cost per thousand of $21.32. Does that explain everything?"

"Well, no. Isn't there some interest rate all these numbers were figured on? How can I compare this to bank financing if I don't know the interest rate I am paying?"

"Norton, I'm not sure you'd want to compare this to bank financing even if you could. It's like comparing yellow fire trucks with red fire trucks. They're two entirely different colors!"

"Yes, I know that. Look, I know you're trying to be helpful, but I'm getting a little frustrated. I know there has to be an interest rate here somewhere. I've got to talk to someone else. Can you transfer me to Mr. Beckworth?"

"You're talking to him, Norton."

See what I mean? Leasing companies are in business for the same reason that you are. That reason is to build equity. If they disclosed to you the interest rates on their leases, you might decide to get out of your business and get into theirs.

If you do not have the cash for an outright asset purchase or a down payment on your purchase, your business is telling you something worth listening to: Leasing can be hazardous to your wealth.

DO NOT BUY YOUR OFFICE

LESSON

UNLIKE WELL-MANAGED BUSINESSES, THERE IS AN OVERABUNDANCE OF OFFICE SPACE.

Frantic Realtors are the first to encourage entrepreneurs to buy a business office. Buying an office condominium, these realtors explain, allows you a guaranteed location from which to run your business. You never have to worry about renegotiating a lease or increasing office rents.

That is where most advantages to owning your office end. Buying an office for your new business can be a mistake for several reasons.

You probably do not realize that you are starting a second business when you buy an office condominium and rent it to your business. Office condominium ownership is a business that has its own unique risks.

You do not need additional risks unless they are reasonable and unless you are paid for them. The only way you can realistically expect to receive any payment for these risks is to charge your business a higher rent. That higher rent decreases risk in your rental business. It also increases the risk in what you are trying to make your best investment.

Realtors will tell you that depreciation from a personally owned office will shelter your business operating income from taxes.

These realtors do not understand that when there is profit in a business, there are far better ways to shelter it. Since many entrepreneurial businesses today are only marginally profitable, these businesses do not have any requirement for sheltering operating income.

An office condominium purchase frequently involves an immediate capital investment. Realtors call that investment a down payment. When you make that down payment, you divert working capital from your basic business.

The result of making that down payment is that you have accomplished little more than pay a realtor a commission for selling you a bundle of risk that you do not need.

I know very few entrepreneurs who will claim to have adequate business working capital or sufficient personal borrowing power. When you buy an office, you reduce your personal borrowing power by the amount of the office mortgage.

What is worse, the burden of servicing that long-term debt is also yours. You and your new business do not need that burden.

It is a mistake to rely on the possible future appreciation of your office condominium to build your wealth. It is the exception where the appreciation of an office condominium will exceed the rate of return from a properly managed business.

The space requirements for your business may also change. A two-room office condominium may no longer provide sufficient space for your business operations. When you move to a larger facility, you must also find a new tenant for your old office. If there is a large inventory of unleased commercial property, finding that tenant will be difficult.

Every business has a life cycle. That means it will not be your best investment forever. There is a point where other opportunities will offer greater returns. Unfortunately, there is no assurance that those opportunities will be in the same marketplace as your office condominium.

Office condominiums are also not known for their liquidity. That means they can be difficult to resell. An unsold, nonincome-producing office condominium can be more effective than a deep recession in preventing you from seizing a new business opportunity.

That is also why renting your office usually makes good business sense. You can pick the office size and lease term to suit your requirements. You can also pick your location. Generally, there is no dilution of future personal borrowing power. While it is true that you may have committed yourself to a long-term lease obligation, lenders do not look at that commitment the same way as they would a first mortgage obligation guaranteed by you.

When your business is finished, if you were fortunate to sign the lease as a corporate officer, there is also no personal obligation to settle any remaining unpaid lease obligation.

That is risk control at its finest.

There is another way to lease the office space your business requires at an affordable price. If you are willing to modify your business hours, you may be surprised at how efficiently you can run your operations.

YOU CAN BE A BLUE-COLLAR ENTREPRENEUR

LESSON

YOU DO NOT NEED A DAYTIME OFFICE
TO HAVE A FULL-TIME BUSINESS.

Inefficient use of capital assets is a crime against building equity. That crime occurs as frequently as the 5:00 P.M. mass exodus to the company parking lot.

Visit any office complex at 2:00 A.M. to observe what is happening. The maintenance crew has long departed. Apart from the occasional snoring of the night watchman, only the hum of the power plant offers any indication of activity.

Every floor is deserted. Millions of square feet of office space are quiet. The criminals, just like you, are probably at home, asleep.

Those who have worked with such diligence at their business think nothing of letting one of their largest expense items produce revenue only 40 percent of the time!

Why are entrepreneurs not making more productive use of their facilities?

I believe one of their reasons is their disdain for blue-collar entrepreneurship.

Blue-collar entrepreneurs are rather ordinary. They are not given to displays of wealth. They drive to work in a car that more closely resembles a rustbucket than a badge of their success. They do not have cellular phones because there is no telephone call that cannot wait until they reach the office.

They are generally less gregarious and more independent than their white-collar counterparts. They do not require the reinforcement of being recognized and greeted by an associate as they walk down the street.

These blue-collar entrepreneurs are not socially inept individuals with personality defects. They are innovators who have discovered a simple way to increase the rate of return in their business operations.

Like many other entrepreneurs, their business is service-related. They own a computer, a fax machine, and have one or two telephone lines. That is all. A large portion of their work requires their personal attention and no one else's.

These entrepreneurs increase the return on their equity capital by sharing a facility during nonpeak hours.

There are several reasons why you may wish to do the same. The rental rates can be considerably less. Lease terms are flexible and without long-term liability. Distractions and interruptions are minimal.

Blue-collar entrepreneurs have little more to worry about than making their business their best investment.

There are other points that make sharing a facility as a blue-collar entrepreneur more attractive than a home office command center. Space is one of those points.

Many homes do not offer the dedicated space required for a functional home office. You cannot focus your attention on your business if you do not dedicate the space to that single use. That will affect your profitability. If you do not want to be profitable, you should not be in business!

Your customers will take you far more seriously if they know that you have a real office. You can still empty your own wastebasket at the end of the day and have a real office. A real office needs only a location similar to your competitors.

For many businesses, that rules out a home office.

Your family will take you far more seriously when you have a real office. There is something of a part-time, "You are not very serious about work" stigma when you have the freedom to gaze out the window without getting rapped on your head.

That is unfair, but it is also the truth.

Children also have a hard time understanding that the big flat board in Mommy's room is a drafting table and not a Play-Dough workshop.

You will also take your business far more seriously away from the home. However nominal, you will have a monthly overhead. When the location of your office is separate from the location of your home, it will also be easier for you to distinguish between work and the other activities in your life.

There is also a psychological benefit. When the sun rises and you leave the office for the day, you carry with you that great feeling that you have been the first that morning to build wealth.

You have every right, in fact, to feel downright ebullient about it. Toss a wave to your traffic-locked competitors, get on the freeway, and head on home. You have earned it!

The act of making informed capital investment decisions will control some of the risk in your business. But getting serious about knowing the numbers in your business is an act that is crucial to effectively controlling the risks in it. Computerizing your accounting system will help you accomplish that.

COMPUTERIZING YOUR BUSINESS 20

- ➤ Automate Your Accounting System.
- ➤ Identify Technical Support Risks.
- ➤ Sounds Like a Hardware Problem.
- ➤ Update Your Procedures.
- ➤ An RFP Will Reduce Your Risk.

It happens to every entrepreneur and it will happen to you. You will discover that your accounting and information system is restraining the growth of your business. The multiple-column ledger books that were state of the art forty years ago are just not doing the job very well anymore.

Oh sure, a few office supply places still sell oversized ledger paper from their vast stockpiles. You can even find some bookkeepers who are entirely at ease with a four-foot-long accounting binder opened across their desks. Those individuals, however, are getting older and are harder to find these days.

The alternative to hand-posting your accounting transactions is to automate your accounting system. In its simplest, least expensive form, automating a small business would require you to spend a few thousand dollars on hardware and a few hundred dollars on accounting software. It is not such a bad alternative. It can also be a great improvement over a hand-posted set of books for one convincing reason.

Obtaining a meaningful set of financial statements from a hand-posted set of books is a mind-bending task. This is true even for those individuals who have not yet retired and still remember how to do it. Those who remember how to do it also know that time cannot be a factor in any request for financial statements.

"Madeline! How are the June financials coming along?"

"I'm working on them, Steve. We've had a bit of a problem closing December's, but I hope to have that done by next week. Why do you ask?"

"Well, this is July. I just thought it would be nice to know how the company did last month. I might add that it is also six months since December. What is taking so long?"

"I'm only one person, you know, and we're short-handed. Has the bank asked for any financial statements?"

"As a matter of fact, yes. I've told them that our temporary bookkeeper has taken a leave of absence and that the replacement just wasn't up to snuff. I don't know how much longer they are willing to wait before they cancel our line of credit. Do you have an estimate of what it would take to close December and then bring us up to date through the end of June?"

"I've thought about it for a while. I think we need to buy a computer system . . . ."

Hold on to your checkbook until you think about it for a while. Buying a computer may be just the thing you need to help you manage your business. It certainly is an easy step to take. After all, how much effort does it take to visualize a computer processing your recurring business transactions?

Unfortunately, buying a computer is only one step of many that you will take when you decide to automate your accounting system.

AUTOMATE YOUR ACCOUNTING SYSTEM

LESSON

THERE IS MORE TO AUTOMATING YOUR ACCOUNTING SYSTEM THAN BUYING A COMPUTER.

The computer system that you buy is no more than a box that performs repetitive mathematical computations and other accounting functions at speeds that were unheard of only a few years ago.

The box has a wonderful memory. A floppy diskette that can fit in your shirt pocket can store tens of thousands of transactions. An internal storage device that is about the size of your hand can store millions of transactions.

As long as a continuous, uninterruptable supply of electrical current is available, the box will show up for work every day. It will never call you to tell you it is sick, that it missed the bus, or that it needs a vacation. It will always do what you tell it to do, in the exact way, every day.

If boxes are so wonderful, then why doesn't every entrepreneur have an unimpeachable computerized accounting system? The answer to this question rests with the fact that people who know about boxes must tell the boxes what to do. In nearly every small business accounting system, your employees must still tell the boxes about the accounting transactions in your business. They do that by touching the box's keyboard. That is one point where the computer system has its first opportunity to fail.

"So, Madeline, what do our June financials look like?"

"I'm not there yet. You know, this computer system is a great deal more work than I thought it would be."

"What's the problem?"

"Well, for starters, I don't have a good place to put it. It takes up too much room on my desk. Now I don't have anywhere to put my office supply catalogs. When I move the keyboard around, it's always knocking something over. I'm no klutz, but this keyboard has knocked over two of my chocolate shakes."

"No problem, Madeline. We'll reimburse you for the chocolate shakes. We'll even get you an extra work table for your office. By the way, do you have any idea how much of your time this system is going to free up?"

"This system doesn't really save any time. Someone still has to reconcile the bank statements, prepare journal entries, and then enter the information into the computer. None of that can be done until we set up certain reporting options in the system. The manuals that we received with the software don't really tell us how to do that, and I'm not a computer expert."

"Did you try calling the software company's technical support number?"

"You bet! I haven't been able to get through for the last four days. Let me show you . . . ."

(Dials technical support number.)

Welcome to Ridgeway Technical Support Service. If this is your first time using Ridgeway Technical Support Service, please listen to the entire message before pressing any of the buttons on your telephone.

Enter your seven-digit technical service contract number followed by the pound sign. (Madeline enters contract number.)

If you are calling from a touch-tone phone, press 1.

If you wish to receive information about our software support contracts, press 2.

If you wish to order disk or documentation replacements, press 3.

If you have a hardware interface problem, press 4.

If you know the name of the party you wish to speak with, press 5.

If you are calling from a rotary phone, please stay on the line and an operator will be with you shortly.

If you would like to hear this message again, press 9."

The profit in technical support services is one reason why vendors price accounting software packages so inexpensively. It is also a major reason for the ongoing proliferation of poor software documentation.

IDENTIFY TECHNICAL SUPPORT RISKS

LESSON

TECHNICAL SUPPORT CONTRACTS
WILL INCREASE THE COST OF YOUR SYSTEM.

Competition by vendors in the software industry has squeezed nearly every last bit of profit from the business of selling a product. Survival-minded vendors have been forced to search for new ways to boost their sagging revenues. They have found one additional source of revenue in technical support service for their products. All it takes to create a technical support department is a few new lines on an employee's job description and a toll-free telephone number.

If you are in the software business, there is a very good reason to offer technical support to your customers. The revenue from technical support will not cannibalize the revenue from software sales. Technical support revenue is an entirely separate stream of revenue.

Besides, there is now considerably more profit in supporting many technical products than there is in selling the products. It should be no surprise to you that many software vendors know this and will practically give you twenty pounds of manuals and computer diskettes in exchange for their right to bill you for technical support.

The first thirty days of technical support are usually free. That is only fair because if the truth be known, sometimes it takes that long to get past the person initially screening your call.

"This is Pinetree Technical Support. May I have your customer number please?"

"Where do I find that?"

"Take a look on your invoice. It's in the upper right-hand corner. It's also on the original copy of the diskettes that were purchased with the Pinetree Complete IV accounting package."

"Oh, I see it now. It's 106170."

"Hmmm. We're not showing a 106170 on our system. Are you the original purchaser of the diskettes?"

"Sure. I'm Laura Keckley. I placed my order with a salesperson named Beth about three weeks ago."

"Are you sure your salesperson's name was Beth? We have several Beths here, but none work in the sales department. Do remember her last name?"

"No, I don't, but I know it was Beth who took my order over the telephone. Look, all I really want to do is talk to someone in technical support. I'm having some difficulty setting up the system and wanted to talk to someone in that department."

"Laura, we still don't have anyone named 'Keckley' listed as a licensed user of our Pinetree Complete IV accounting package."

"Then there has to be a mistake on your end. Somebody obviously didn't enter my customer number or my name in the file. How else could I have your manuals, diskettes, and thirty-day guarantee right in front of me?"

"I wish you wouldn't place any blame on us. If you were a licensed user, Ms. Keckley, we would have you listed on our system."

"I don't believe it! This conversation is going nowhere. Let's start over and let me ask the question another way. What do I need to do to receive technical support for your product?"

"Oh, well, there are several alternatives available to you. You can call one of our licensed support centers and for $270, they will provide you with unlimited technical support for up to three hours. We can also provide you with a support contract. Our annual support contract, for $670, will entitle you to receive up to ten hours of technical support over the next twelve months . . . ."

"But your software only cost $235! Aren't your support fees more than a little out of line?"

"We're competitive with the industry, Ms. Keckley. You just need to decide how valuable your time is and if you want your software to work . . . ."

If you have no previous experience setting up an accounting system, you may need more than just technical support from the vendor who sold you the software. You may actually need someone to do the on-site installation and the conversion work.

SOUNDS LIKE A HARDWARE PROBLEM

LESSON

"SOUNDS LIKE A HARDWARE PROBLEM" IS REALLY TECHNICAL SUPPORT'S WAY OF LETTING YOU KNOW THEY ARE IN OVER THEIR HEADS.

No matter whom you have helping you with the installation of your computerized accounting system, there are sure to be a few setbacks and other glitches. The computer industry just has not yet reached the point where you can buy a box loaded with the software you need, plug it in, and have it work exactly the way you heard it would.

Unless accounting software and computer consulting are your core businesses, you are going to need some technical support. The individual who provides that support can physically show up at your office doorstep each morning until the conversion to a fully computerized and operational accounting system is complete. That individual can also coach you through the installation process by instructions provided over the telephone.

Most technical support people sound smart, particularly to someone who knows very little about computers or the software they just purchased. In a business where $90 per hour is the minimum technical support fee and the sky is the limit, you need to have some way of determining the relative skill level of your technical support representative.

How do you know if your technical support representative is qualified? Often, they will tell you themselves.

"Kimberlee, thanks for returning my call. Do I ever feel like I could use some technical support!"

"I don't know how much help I will be because I just started in tech support last week and everyone else has left for the day. What seems to be the problem?"

"Well, we've finally set up the accounts payable system. I've entered in the computer over 900 invoices this past week, and I'm trying to print checks for the ones we're going to pay. Each time I go to the print menu, however, I get a message on the screen that reads: 'Access Denied. Call Your Tech Support Representative.' So here I am!"

"Oh, that's something I know how to fix. Once a month we have to dial in your machine by modem and unlock the check print feature. If your modem line is clear and there's no one on the machine, I'll do it now. Do you have any other questions while I'm dialing in and clearing the lock?"

"As a matter of fact, yes. Why is the lock there in the first place? There's nothing written about that in the manual for your accounts payable module . . . ."

"The manuals you probably have are for our old software version 2.1 We're now on version 5.3 and haven't had the time to update the manuals for nearly two years."

"Is there any way I can get the check print lock feature removed?"

"Unfortunately, no. The programmers put that in just to make sure the monthly software maintenance fees were paid. If you're more than thirty days past due, the lock stays on until your account with us is current. It's really just a formality because your account is current. There! The lock is now off and you should be able to print your checks."

(Repeatedly tries to print checks, no success.)

"Kimberlee, the accounts payable check-printing feature doesn't seem to be working. What's wrong?"

"Hmmm. When the lock is off, the checks should print. Is your printer plugged in?"

"Yes, it's plugged in! We've used it all day today printing other reports from your software. I don't understand why the software is not working now."

"Did you purchase the hardware from us?"

"No, just a $50,000 accounting information system software package that, like your tech support department, doesn't appear to work after 5:00 P.M. . . . ."

"Well, if you were printing with it all day, the software works. Sounds like a hardware problem to me . . . ."

Did you really hear those last few words? Your technical support representative just disclaimed all responsibility for the performance of their product on your office computer. The "sounds like a hardware problem to me" dilemma is the start of a rapidly deteriorating technical support relationship.

You have a few choices. You can sue them. That will take time and you may never get this system up and running. You can toss the manuals and the diskettes in your office recycling bins and chalk up the software investment as an expensive lesson. You can also get your hardware checked for any possible defects, get on your knees, and try to get your vendor's technical support people to like you.

Whatever you decide, if you want to take full advantage of any accounting and information package that you buy, you are going to have to make some changes in the way you do business.

UPDATE YOUR PROCEDURES

LESSON

YOU CANNOT AUTOMATE AN ACCOUNTING SYSTEM THAT HAS NO INTERNAL CONTROLS.

Computer hardware and application software have become incredibly fast and efficient in recent years. Today, more likely than not, your employees and your company's current procedures are the weak elements in your accounting system.

This is true for a number of reasons.

The children of your current employees probably know more about computers than their parents. Education today has mandated computer training at an early age. Most parents will learn how to use computers only if it is a requirement in order to retain their jobs. That requirement has not yet been mandated by all entrepreneurial businesses.

Most small businesses have no formal accounting position. Those businesses that do may be fortunate to have a full-charge bookkeeper. Larger entrepreneurial operations may have a controller and a set of accounting procedures that are no more than a loose conglomeration of the controller's ten most-recent memos.

Sometimes these procedures are well designed and have the required internal controls to safeguard the company's assets. You must record a sales order before any credit memo can be issued. You must use a purchase order to buy all inventoried items. You must receive inventory, tag it, and enter it into stock before you can sell it. You must record a vendor liability before you can issue a check to pay that liability.

Most accounting software packages are designed around the highest level of these control features. Many existing accounting systems in entrepreneurial operations are notable principally for the absence of **any** of these control features. That means you will probably have a software compatibility problem unless you modify or redesign your existing procedures. It is premature to automate your accounting system until some form of internal controls are in place in the existing system. If you don't agree, just ask the Venuto brothers!

Bobby and Rich Venuto inherited an import/export business from their dad. Late last year, the Venuto brothers attended a trade show for their industry. After a single day of being schmoozed by a software vendor, Bobby and Rich purchased an integrated accounting package for Venuto Imports for the tidy sum of $55,000.

In addition to his responsibilities as vice president of operations, Bobby Venuto agreed to oversee the installation of the accounting package and the complete conversion of their existing manual accounting system. He knew he had a problem the first day he opened the software manuals.

"Rich, come here and take a look at this."

"Hey, nice-looking manuals! Dad would be proud of us . . . ."

"Not the manuals you idiot! Look at this list!"

"So?"

"I was just reading the inventory manual to get an idea of how long it would take to get this system up and running. I prepared a list of some things we have to change before we can start printing the purchase orders off this system. The manual says we have to have a stock number for every single inventory item."

"But that's over 700 items from 120 different vendors!"

"No kidding. It's going to take some time to set up those stock numbers. I don't have the time for all of this."

"Well, can you ask Norma to work on it? She knows about computers."

"Hey, Norma! Can you come in here a minute?"

"Sure, Bobby. What do you need?"

"Norma, do you know anything about setting up inventory?"

"Well, I know that you have to be able to identify specific individual inventory items that we sell. You also have to know what is selling and how much stock is left so you know what to order."

"How do we do this now?"

"Every morning, the warehouse guys give me a stroke count of everything that's on the floor. Delivery gives me a stroke count of everything that's scheduled to go out the door. The difference is basically what I have to reorder."

"That's what I thought. Do you have the time to set up the inventory package?"

"Time? Who has time for anything around here? Just kidding. Sure, I'll set it up. It may take a while though because on Mondays I have to do the purchase orders, Tuesdays I record receivings, . . ."

"Norma, we know your schedule. Just do your best and tell us when inventory will be up and running."

(Two weeks later.)

"Bobby, I'm still finding dozens of new inventory items. We have 1,135 items listed so far, and I still haven't entered all the items from this stack of sales orders."

"Do you have any idea when this is going to be finished?"

"Hopefully this week . . . ."

"Norma, the software vendor said we didn't have to spend time identifying every item. We could set these items up as we found them and enter them 'on the fly'. Let's try that! That way we can get started entering our sales orders. The sooner we get our sales entered, the sooner I'll get the marketing information that I need. Have a couple of people in the office help you with the sales order data entry."

(Later that week.)

"How is the new system working, Norma? Do you have any marketing reports for me yet?"

"Not yet, Bobby. We're having trouble with the printer. We also found out that the system won't allow us to enter a sale for inventory items that we have not yet recorded as being received."

"Well, set those sales orders on the side and be sure that we're entering the inventory receivings first thing every day. I'll just remember that the merchandise reports don't include some of the sales orders."

"I don't know, Bobby. There's at least 200 sales orders that we can't enter in this stack alone. We haven't even started on the transfers, the special orders, the back orders, and the returns and exchanges . . . ."

"Norma, don't get so animated! How did we handle those items before the computer?"

"Well, you know those piles of sales orders on my credenza? Each pile is a separate type of nonstandard transaction. When I had the time, I'd go through some of the information in those piles and try to handle them. At most, we were probably a few weeks behind in our work, but I've got to tell you, with this computer conversion going on, I think I'm going to need some additional help."

"Can you hire a temporary person until we get caught up?"

"I'm getting the feeling, Bobby, that being behind is not going to be a temporary thing."

Venuto Imports hired four different temporary employees, each with different data entry abilities. Although the employment agency "certified" the data entry skills of all the temporary employees sent to Venuto Imports, the agency must have used a very loose certification procedure. Only one of the temporaries was comfortable using more than two fingers at a time on the keyboard.

"Bobby, we've got to have a meeting about the computer system."

"Sure, Rich. Hey Norma! Can you come in here for a minute? We're going to have a meeting about the computer."

"Bobby, when you and I bought this system for the business, the vendor told us we should have all of the different modules up and running within ninety days. It's now seven months after we sent them our first installment for the system and we're still no closer to getting your merchandising reports or my financial information off the system. What's the problem?"

"Well, the people who sold us this system are a bunch of jerks. They keep telling us we have to change the way we do things to accommodate the software. I keep telling them we've never had a problem with our current procedures in the ten years we've had the business. I think we should stop paying these guys and ask for our money back . . . ."

"OK! Let's call them. Here's your phone."

Venuto Imports did ask for its money back. The software vendor had already spent the money and thought the refund request was unreasonable. A panel of arbitrators will hopefully hear the facts of this case in the next few months.

Before you part with your money for a computer system, it is always a good idea to match the requirements of your accounting and information system with the capabilities of the software vendors. A request for proposal will allow you to do just that.

AN RFP WILL REDUCE YOUR RISK

LESSON

A REQUEST FOR PROPOSAL OFFERS SOME ASSURANCE THAT THE SYSTEM YOU BUY WILL ACTUALLY MEET YOUR SPECIFICATIONS.

The affordability of computerized accounting systems today is the principal reason for their popularity. Dollar for dollar, it is hard to find a better payback for any investment in your business.

It is also hard to argue about the performance capabilities of a properly installed computerized accounting and information system. It is quite possible to run the accounting system of a $10 million business on a $5,000 investment in hardware and software.

However, even a *PC Computing Best Buy* system has its limitations. You will discover this as the volume of your accounting transactions increases. Running a general ledger with twenty-three departmentalized profit-and-loss statements on a $235 accounting package is theoretically possible. To be sure, it is a lesson in the skill of your CPA.

It is also a lesson in pushing the performance specs of a software package. The people who wrote the software may have designed it to do far less than you have a right to ask of it or to expect of it. It is no different from using the engine from a Volkswagen Beetle to power a bus carrying the high school football team. It should be no surprise to you if the system stops working altogether.

You should expect to pay considerably more for automating your accounting information system if you are essentially asking it to carry the high school football team. If the anticipated cost of your system is over $50,000, there is only one way to be certain you have properly controlled the risks in purchasing your computer system. Call John Frazzini of British American Consulting Group in Lisle, Illinois, at 708-505-5775 and have him prepare a request for proposal (RFP).

John will tell you that a comprehensive RFP is the only way to be certain that the computer system you ultimately purchase will meet your specifications. I am inclined to agree with him.

If you want your computer system to have a perpetual inventory system, put it in the RFP. If you later determine that the system sold to you does not have such a capability, the vendor has an obligation to fix the software and put in that capability or to give you your money back. An RFP provides you with clauses that will protect you on warranties, copyrights, and other matters that are crucial to maintaining your investment in the system.

An RFP's role in the purchase and delivery of a computer system is the same as a blueprint's role in the acquisition and ownership of a custom-built house. If a vendor has met the terms of the RFP, there are no surprises. It is the only way you can really be sure that the vendor has delivered a product that precisely meets your specifications.

When you ask a group of vendors to respond to an RFP, you are telling them that you know your business and your information requirements. In a professional manner, it also lets the vendor know what you need most from him: the vendor's best price on your specifications.

You may wonder what challenges remain once you have successfully computerized your business. Perhaps no single remaining challenge is as massive or as frustrating. None may be as complex or as time-consuming. Nevertheless, there are some finer points you still need to know about running your business.

21

SOME FINER POINTS OF RUNNING YOUR BUSINESS

- ➤ Lead with Integrity.
- ➤ Take Some Credit.
- ➤ Soften Your Rough Edges.
- ➤ Write Your Annual Plan.

There are some finer points about running a business that focus on you more than they focus on your business.

Hard-charging entrepreneurs may be inclined to skip these points as elective, personal matters. After their fortunes are made, they believe they will have plenty of time left for personal development courses.

Do not be misled.

The way you feel about yourself and your personal goals and objectives will affect the way you feel about your business. Anything that affects your business will also affect the way you build equity in it.

These finer points are subtle points. They are also the kinds of points that you can appreciate without first being an entrepreneur for twenty years. For many, these points are connecting links between their personal and entrepreneurial lives.

LEAD WITH INTEGRITY

LESSON

YOUR INTEGRITY WILL MAKE YOU A LEADER.

There are entrepreneurs who have the glittering talent to attract money partners. These entrepreneurs are at ease whether speaking to one partner or 400 shareholders. They are also convincing. They present investment opportunities with color slides and laser-powered pointers. They even talk about risk with respect and reverence. Every gesture of theirs confidently displays the potential of a successful business.

But most partners want to see more of you than your newly pressed suit and freshly polished teeth. Wherever they look, they want to see that your entrepreneurial style is grounded in integrity. That bedrock is more convincing than any chart that you can produce.

There are other entrepreneurs who can create a product that almost any customer will buy. These individuals are peerless in their ability to anticipate the needs of the marketplace. They will match customer requirements with new product development in a way that gives them an insurmountable lead on their competitors.

But customers want more than just generic computing technology that sits in a desktop box. If integrity is not part of the packaging, customers will remember your omission and will not buy any more of your products.

There are even a few entrepreneurs who have the accounting skills to compile a set of financial statements that will get them a business loan at nearly any bank. They can integrate last year's operating results and a five-year forecast with three-dimensional color graphs that will remove much of the doubt from any lender's mind.

Regrettably, forecasts occasionally need to be met not only for the good of the business, but also for the satisfaction of the lender. If there is no integrity in those forecasts, no bank will ever renew your business loan.

A few entrepreneurs even have the skills to recruit employees who will dedicate their evenings and weekends to your business matters. These employees will routinely contribute sixty-hour work weeks in exchange for little more than an encouraging word from you.

However, once they discover that you really do not mean what you say, they will stop sacrificing their lives for the sake of your business.

You can be an entrepreneur without integrity, but I do not recommend it. Your business already offers enough challenge without the burden of an owner with a rudderless sense of fairness and responsibility.

Besides, every business needs a leader. It is a fact that you cannot lead without integrity. The concept of integrity is more than a word. For those entrepreneurs with integrity, it is a way of life.

"Kimball, I sure hate to lose you as a shareholder in my business. You've been a wonderful co-owner who has always believed in me and the long-term development of our business. That belief made it easier for me to focus on developing the business instead of developing relationships with new shareholders."

"I hate to sell my stock, Mark. Unfortunately, my dad is aging and needs my help. I just couldn't foresee the additional medical costs that I would need to pay to take care of him."

"I'm surprised that he's still ambulatory at eighty-nine years old. I wish companies today would build that kind of reliability into their products . . . ."

"And I'm amazed that most parts of him still work. The only operation he ever had was for a new hip joint a few years ago. He just requires the full-time attention of a health care worker so he doesn't wander off on his own. Even with the benefit of some health care reform, that degree of attention is going to cost me approximately $4,200 per month."

(Whistles.) "Kimball, that's nearly $50,000 per year! We started this business ten years ago on less capital than that."

"Believe me, I know. With annual recurring health care charges like that, I may just consider starting a home health care service business."

"See me first, if you're serious, Kimball. I'd like another shot at being your business partner."

"Thanks, Mark. By the way, are there any details we need to finalize regarding this buyout?"

"A few. I received my copy of the business valuation we requested and have a few comments on that report. I know you wanted to settle everything within the next thirty days. That's fine with me. Where do you want the funds from the sale of your 25 percent interest in the company's stock to be sent?"

"If it's OK with you, just have your bank wire them to my bank. That's probably the most expedient way to move $467,500 of funds."

"Fine. Now tell me something, Kimball. What do you really think about that business valuation?"

"The appraisal firm obviously knew what they were doing. They're the recognized experts in valuing firms in our industry. They valued the total equity in the company at $2.2 million. That made my 25 percent interest in the stock worth $550,000. After subtracting a minority ownership discount of 15 percent, they computed the adjusted value of my shares to be $467,500."

"That's what the report says, Kimball. Unfortunately, I have a problem with paying you the $467,500 as the value for your stock."

"Oh?"

"The whole concept of a minority discount is really an estate tax planning tool. It's the argument that tax attorneys offer to Internal Revenue Service agents in order to reduce the value of closely held stock in any estate. When you can reduce the value of an estate, you also reduce the estate tax liability."

"Although I hate to argue against myself, Mark, there is some truth to the argument that produces the lower valuation. Most shareholders with a minority ownership interest have little to say about the operations of any business. That would be obvious if you put any business matter to a shareholder vote. I suppose that's the reason why business valuation experts have a tendency to discount minority ownership interests."

"Kimball, I can't argue with the theory. As a practical matter, that's not how you and I ran the business. We were co-owners, alike in every aspect except our ownership percentages. I owned 75 percent of the company and you owned 25 percent. Does that lower percentage ownership of yours justify penalizing you $82,500 for not having a controlling interest?"

(Sigh.) "Who knows? But we agreed to have an appraisal determine the value in the event of any buyout."

"We sure did, Kimball. But we didn't agree to accept the concept of a minority discount in that valuation. In our company, each dollar of your equity was exposed to the same risk elements as each dollar of my equity."

"That's true . . . ."

"We both took the same elements of risk to bed with us for the last ten years. I don't care how the appraisal report of our company justifies penalizing you $82,500. That's stealing in my books and I won't permit that to occur. I'll wire the full $550,000 for your 25 percent interest on Monday."

(Pause.) "You're certainly not required by our shareholder agreement to do that, Mark. I don't know what to say . . . ."

"You can say that my parents gave me some fundamental lessons about business that were grounded in fairness and integrity. In those lessons, all shareholders are created equal. It's been great having you as a shareholder, Kimball. I know we'll do it again. By the way, I hope everything works out for your dad."

When you have integrity, everything else will also work out for you. Your employees, customers, bankers, and any other individuals who touch your business will all recognize your integrity and the high standards of fairness that you use as the platform on which all relationships must stand.

They will also recognize that you have been worth the risk.

TAKE SOME CREDIT

LESSON

TAKE THE CREDIT
WHEN YOU HAVE BEEN WORTH THE RISK.

There is far more to credit than the nod of approval that any bank will give you when it wants your business. Credit is what you deserve when you know you have been worth the risk.

At the end of a long day or after the results of a particularly difficult month, you deserve some credit. Take the credit you have earned. After all, you have survived.

Taking credit often means congratulating yourself. Self-congratulatory accolades are frequently the only comfort or recognition beyond the accumulation of wealth that you will ever receive.

You do not need a special occasion to tell yourself you have been worth the risk. You just need to believe it.

TV personalities send gifts to themselves all of the time. They do it as a reward when the ratings for their shows are high. They also do it for medicinal purposes when the ratings for their shows are low.

In the first case, they earned the flowers. In the second case, they need the flowers. Whatever the ratings, they recognize they have been worth the risk.

Every candidate for an elected political office will tell you that you cannot get enough of the right kind of recognition. Some businesses that rely heavily on entrepreneurial talent recognize this need for recognition and go out of their way to meet it.

Margaret owns and operates a highly profitable employee placement franchise. The last time I visited with Margaret, I counted forty-seven achievement awards hanging behind her desk.

The physical limits of Margaret's office walls prevented her from displaying other awards that I am sure were already framed and available. I do not doubt that Margaret's personal need for recognition has ever been better met or better deserved.

Louis is another entrepreneur who will stop just this side of breaking his arm while reaching to pat himself on the back.

As a starving architect only a few years earlier, Louis lived in abject poverty until a general building contractor noticed his work.

Today, Louis has his own share of professional awards and a list of devoted admirers. I have always kidded Louis that the top ten names on that list are his own.

But there is a sobering second reason for all of this recognition. That reason goes beyond the element of personal need.

When a business investment sours, no one will come forth to share the failure with you. They will, in fact, do everything they can to preserve their equity at the expense of yours.

Being unemotional about your business failures will help to cushion some of them.

SOFTEN YOUR ROUGH EDGES

LESSON

DO NOT OVERREACT TO CHANGES
IN THE PERFORMANCE OF YOUR BUSINESS.

The movement of equity values in your business is no more predictable than the behavior of an adolescent teen.

You will have a definite reaction to good and bad business decisions. When your equity soars, so will your hopes. When your equity crashes, the effect will also not be lost on you.

It is one thing to ride the volatile behavior of the marketplace. It is entirely another to let it consume you. If you are an emotional entrepreneur, you should consider a personality change. There are a number of reasons why.

An employee will never bear the same risk as the entrepreneur who hired him.

That is not to say that an employee's job is secure. An employee may still have some exposure to the effect of market conditions on his employer, but that is a broader market risk. The employee has the option of leaving this risk at the office at the end of every day.

Upon arriving home, an employee greets the spouse, plays with the children, mixes a drink, and watches the news. To any observer, that behavior would appear, well, normal!

That behavior usually changes when you own a business. When you leave your office and walk through the parking lot, risk is sitting on your shoulders. When you put your car in gear to drive away, risk takes the empty seat next to you.

Your spouse will recognize the appearance of risk by the sound of your grunt as you walk through the door. Your pet will keep its distance and so will your children.

As you stare at the ceiling from your bed, you will wonder,

"Do I really need this?"

No, you do not. It is stressful, it is nerve-racking, and medical specialists will tell you it is unhealthy. They are right. You can avoid all of these conditions by being an unemotional entrepreneur.

There is a definite balance point between risk and return in every business. You may have discovered the absence of that balance point for the first time when a business in which you ignored risk collapsed on top of you.

There is also an emotional balance point that will leave you largely unaffected by the whipsaw changes in the levels of your business risk and wealth.

That is not to say you will not care anymore. The favorable and unfavorable results of your informed business decisions will always affect you. You can still grin when your equity grows and grimace when it does not.

When you are unemotional about your business, you have simply purged yourself from the extremes. The euphoria and the rage are no longer there.

Developing that unemotional style is not a difficult task. All you need is confidence in running your business.

Leave operational changes alone if they do nothing to increase your rate of return. When risk is out of proportion to your expected return, get rid of the excess risk. When asset values have been maximized, convert these assets to cash.

Being unemotional is not the same as being indifferent. You certainly have an interest in the directional movement of your equity. If you were indifferent, you simply would not care.

As an unemotional entrepreneur, it is easier for you to accept the results of your decisions without an accompanying case of the heebie-jeebies. Leave those frantic reactions to your competitors.

WRITE YOUR ANNUAL PLAN

LESSON

THERE IS MORE TO BUILDING YOUR EQUITY
THAN THE ELEMENT OF FINANCE.
BALANCE THE OTHER ELEMENTS
OF EQUITY GROWTH WITH AN ANNUAL PLAN.

There is far more to your equity than the numbers a banker sees on your financial statements. That single number is one measure of financial equity. There is also social equity, spiritual equity, personal equity, and physical equity. You build them the same way as financial equity, by making good investments and adjusting risk over time.

No entrepreneur can be complete without a balance among all of these equities. An annual plan will direct the growth of these five equities.

I can offer perfectly valid reasons why there is time to build financial equity, but there is no time to build the other equities. The reasons, of course, will be convincing until the divergence between these equities is so great that all growth comes to an end.

If you need to convince yourself that this is true, try building your social equity to the exclusion of the other equities. Party every night. Drink whatever is in your glass, meet as many people as you can, and dance until the sun rises. Take the risks that are fun for you and walk away the next morning from the ones that are not.

After a year of celebrating, you will feel like a rental car that has been driven without maintenance checks. You may have covered a lot of ground and be vaguely familiar with the scenery. The truth is that you have been parking in a different stall every night and at best you have aged no better than the car.

Then try building your spiritual equity to the exclusion of the other equities. Join an ashram. Practice yoga and chant from four in the morning to late at night. Sleep on a tatami and forsake all material things.

Your spiritual soul may belong to Buddha, but where is the balance? You are as thin as a pencil, poor as a monk, and cannot carry on a normal conversation without inviting someone to meditation.

Now try building your personal equity. Read every book you can find about improving your life and attend every workshop you hear about on becoming a better you. Practice what you learn, but do not try thinking for yourself. Leave that to your group discussion leaders.

In no time, you will have accumulated a vast array of personal reference material. You will also be at the top of the "Seminars for Suckers" mailing list.

Now develop your physical equity to every other equity's exclusion. Buy an eighteen-speed carbon-frame bike and a pair of running shoes. Ride 100 kilometers a day and then run twenty after that. Alternate your speedwork days with interval training. Perfect your swimstroke and hypoxic breathing in open ocean water. Enter every fun run for practice every weekend and a mini-triathlon every month.

Your body fat will measure 6 percent or less and your VO_2 max will be pushing seventy milliliters per kilogram. You will not have time for a full-time job and your family will get tired of traveling like gypsies. The day you do not finish a race, you will wonder if there is any life left for you after competition. The way you have ignored everyone else, there may not be.

Financial equity extremists have the same incongruities. They have superb credit references and can cherry pick signature loans. They can eat on the run, sleep at the office under their balance sheets, and win any race for owning the most toys.

Their spouses, however, are sleeping under different sheets and their children will never know how it felt to play with two parents. Their clients will own whatever the banks do not and when these financial extremists die, only the tax collector will care.

Building equity also means striving for balance, for being whole, for being complete, and for achieving the most that you can accomplish. It means being the best that you can be, given the risks you are willing to take with whatever you are willing to invest. There is no measure for success other than your own, and even that is never absolute or final.

I write an annual plan every year in order to be sure that I balance my equities. The process is several notches above a typical list of New Year's resolutions. It is also a few notches below the specifications list for building a Trident nuclear submarine. After all, there is no point in having a plan which far exceeds the resources you can afford to allocate to it.

Take five sheets of paper, one for each equity. List on each sheet the investments you will make for that equity. Be specific with people, topics, events, dates, and amounts.

You will discover that when you take the time to ponder your mission for the future, your annual plan will give you the direction and the momentum you need to step smartly from one year to the next.

But I cannot see the future. I have always added additional investments along the way that have increased some form of equity. I have also failed to make all of the investments that I hoped I might. I have averaged about an 85 percent success rate in crossing items off the list.

The 1994 Olympic figure skating gold medal winner, Oksana Baiul of Ukraine, surely would have scored better than that, but she was blessed with a technical expertise I never had.

A few years ago, a younger Lee Iacocca may have reached the investments faster, but he would have the essentially unlimited resources offered by Chrysler Corporation.

Donald Trump surely would have made larger ones, but he sleeps better at night with risk than I do with my pillow.

I start my annual plan early in December and revise it as many times as it takes to get it right. I set the plan in mortar before the start of the new year.

My annual plan is as important to me as the bagman with the nuclear missile launch codes is to the president. The plan is never more than ten feet away, and if it is not on my desk, it is in my pocket. Having instant access to it at all times provides compelling direction and keeps me away from bets I have no business making.

By the end of the year, the plan has been notated, folded, dog-eared, and coffee-stained, but there are lines through most of the items. When the year has turned, I have a subtle reassurance that for all of the risks I have taken, I have built and balanced equity.

The task of successfully running your business will require you to make decisions about partners, capital, customers, and employees. The decisions you make in these areas are all part of an ongoing process in managing business risk. There is no such thing as a normal and customary decision when it comes to controlling business risk. That alone can make running any business a challenge. But decide you must, if you are serious about controlling business risk.

PART SIX

Managing Business Risk

22

RISK ADJUSTMENTS

- ➤ Here's When to Adjust Risk.
- ➤ Doing Nothing Can Be Expensive.
- ➤ Make the Adjustment Promptly.
- ➤ Some Adjustments Are Too Little, Too Late.
- ➤ You Cannot Micromanage Risk.

You have a problem when you have difficulty sleeping at night. It could be the spicy food you ate for supper, the pesky mosquito flying about your room, the energy-efficient thermostat you set at seventy-eight degrees on the hottest night of the summer, or the sagging mattress on your bed.

If you are an entrepreneur, it is likely more than that. When you are an entrepreneur and you cannot sleep at night, you probably have too much risk.

HERE'S WHEN TO ADJUST RISK

LESSON

MAKE THE ADJUSTMENT IF IT HELPS YOU SLEEP BETTER AT NIGHT AND IS LESS EXPENSIVE THAN YOUR FUTURE LOSSES.

When you have too much business risk, sleep is out of the question. Find a large memo pad and a pen that works. List your business risks and place an asterisk next to those risks that are not reasonable. Write down the reasons why.

Make your risk adjustments within the next three days.

Some people will tell you that you cannot adjust risk that fast. Others will say you are premature and are overreacting. A third group will insist that nothing is wrong with the level of risk in your business.

Most of these contra-consciences have never known the meaning of risk. They certainly do not know what risk means to you. Your sleep-deprived body is telling you differently. That is to whom you must listen.

The use of risk control is an excellent substitute for throwing money at problems. It is a fact that risk-reducing adjustments are a significant and an integral part of building equity. They are also easy to do unless you have let the risk in your business increase out of all proportion to the wealth your business produces.

Where you once could have initiated a six-month hiring freeze, you must now fire five people.

Where you could have installed a simple system of inventory controls, now you have $35,000 of excess or obsolete stock that you must sell for scrap.

Where you had the opportunity to collect your receivables when you delivered your product, you must now pay an attorney to collect an amount that is one year past due.

Adjusting your risk in the normal course of business is a simple matter of preserving a reasonable risk-return relationship.

Variables affecting your business change over time. So does your business risk.

Waiting until the last possible moment to reduce risk can be completely ineffective. It is like going away on vacation for two weeks and leaving your hot iron on the ironing board. You could be lucky and find your house is still standing, or you could find no more than a foundation covered with ashes.

Last-minute risk adjustments have the potential to be either.

Some entrepreneurs offer a reason to wait before reducing risk: Given time, anything can happen. That is true. A horde of IRS agents could overrun your strongest competitor. An electrical fire could wipe out your largest creditor and his records from the marketplace. Even the venerable Ross Perot may die and, as a surprise to everyone, name you as the beneficiary of his estate.

Those individuals who have made their business their best investment have a difficult time stepping out of the real world to rely on acts of God or other divine intervention to adjust business risk. They know that God, like any banker, has far more important things to worry about than a single business customer.

DOING NOTHING CAN BE EXPENSIVE

LESSON

IT MAY BE LESS EXPENSIVE TO PAY FOR THE ADJUSTMENT THAN TO PAY FOR THE CONTINUAL EXPOSURE TO RISK.

Grady took large sums of money from his business to pay for a variety of real property investments. The investments could not support themselves. Those cash withdrawals of Grady's hurt his business and did not help his real property investments.

The cash flow from the properties was not sufficient to pay their underlying mortgages.

A quick look at the cash flow from any investment will tell you who is paying the premium for risk. In a positive cash flow environment, an investment pays you a premium for the risk of ownership. In a negative cash flow environment, you pay the bank a premium for the privilege of ownership.

Grady paid $18,250 a year of negative cash flow for the privilege of owning his properties.

"One day, Grady, you are going to be rich."

"What do you mean by 'one day'? I've got a good business and a great portfolio of real estate investments. I figure that if the properties only increase in value by 9 percent a year for the next twenty years, I'll have one heck of a retirement portfolio."

"Grady, have you read a paper lately?"

"Sure. What's the big deal?"

"Real estate values have been flushed down the toilet. Exactly how far down depends on where you live. Where are these properties?"

"One of them is on Emerald Isle. Two are condominiums in Waikiki, Hawaii. The last one is a cabin we purchased outside of Murphy, North Carolina."

"Grady, the way I see it, your tax returns are telling me that you have some serious negative cash flow."

"What are you talking about?"

"It looks to me like you've been handing out $50 a day for the last four years. Is that true?"

"No! Where did you hear that?"

"I just looked at your tax returns for the last four years. The numbers you reported on those returns include some hefty rental losses. The way I figure, the negative cash flow alone on those properties has cost you about $50 a day. That's an expensive way to fund your retirement portfolio . . . ."

"Are you kidding me? I thought my old accountant was doing a pretty good job. I mean I never really looked at the returns before I signed them, but my accountant looked like he knew what he was doing. In fact, he recommended some of the real estate investments . . . ."

(Shakes head.) "I don't know what to say about that, Grady. All I'm telling you is that you should have about $73,000 more in your pocket with none of the risk. . . ."

"What? Is there any way we can amend the returns? Maybe I should sue the guy! What kind of idiot would make a $73,000 mistake?"

"Grady, here's a mirror. Say 'Hi' to yourself!"

Grady wanted to own these properties when he retired. Unfortunately, Grady had ten more years to retirement. That was $182,500 of additional negative cash flow. No amount of prayer or meditation would change that fact.

Grady was reluctant to list the properties for sale because of the soft real estate market.

Deferring a risk adjustment until the market strengthens is like continuing to sleep on a bed of nails because you are still tired. The sleep you receive will be restless. The damage that may occur also has the potential to be far greater.

Those are all good reasons to make your risk adjustments promptly.

MAKE THE ADJUSTMENT PROMPTLY

LESSON

THE MARKETPLACE WILL TELL YOU AT WHAT PRICE TO MAKE YOUR RISK ADJUSTMENT.

Once you determine that a risk adjustment is in order, do it now.

Do not quibble about the price. The marketplace will decide at which price to make the adjustment.

That price will usually be fair market value. You do not build wealth by buying or selling assets at fair market value. But fair market value is a great price at which to reduce business risk.

If you discover that your business owns too many nonincome-producing assets, either make them produce income or sell them. When you sell them, take what the market will give you. Do not insist on getting the price that you paid for those assets.

There is no surer way to prolong unnecessary risk than to make a risk adjustment contingent on an arbitrary price. When you insist on pegging a risk adjustment to an arbitrary price, you are depending on hope to bail you out.

There is one minor problem with depending on hope to adjust your level of risk. You cannot build equity on hope. You build equity by adjusting risk at market-driven prices.

Nothing short of adjustments today at market-driven prices will make you competitive, improve your record, keep your job, and position you for great future opportunities. Entrepreneurs with poor win-loss records need to adopt "the future is now" attitude with respect to making risk adjustments.

When you decline to make a prompt risk adjustment, you also agree to accept risk for which you may never be paid. When you agree to work without compensation, you are forgetting why you are in business. If you postpone making risk adjustments long enough, you may not be in business.

SOME ADJUSTMENTS ARE TOO LITTLE, TOO LATE

LESSON

ALL RISK ADJUSTMENTS REQUIRE TIME TO WORK.

The day he moved his corporate headquarters into an 8,500-square-foot office penthouse, Garrett thought he had it made. He had a sweeping ocean vista, a personal secretary, his own controller, and a $3 million gross revenue business.

Selling commercial and residential solar installations came easier to Garrett than molecular physics did to Enrico Fermi. There was a year-round demand in the marketplace, and the consumer utility savings were distinctive.

Garrett took a solar system for which he paid $900 and sold it to a consumer for $5,000. The consumer had $2,500 returned to him through federal and state tax credits. The net consumer cost was, therefore, $2,500. That net cost would have been the fair market value of Garrett's standard solar installation.

The solar tax credits were nothing more than legislatively mandated manna for Garrett's business. If Garrett sold and installed forty solar systems a month, he received the tidy sum of $100,000 in federal- and state-subsidized tax credits beyond the fair market value of his product! Drinking nectar with the gods is a heady experience.

I met with Garrett to discuss the result of his financial statements that I had reviewed.

"Hi, Dorothy. I'm here to see Garrett."

"Oh, he's been waiting for you. He wants to walk these financial statements in to the bank this morning. Here he is."

"Garrett, good morning. I've got your reviewed financial statements for you."

"Great! How did we do?"

I winced at Garrett's choice of words. The business was his, the tax windfalls were his, and so were the results of operations.

"Mark, it says we lost $250,000 this year! How can that be?"

"Where do you want me to start?"

"With the good news!"

"Garrett, there is no good news. Your controller kept your books on a cash basis. I simply accrued the revenue you didn't collect by December 31 and the expenses you didn't pay. The net effect of those accruals is a $250,000 operating loss."

"What is this prior period adjustment of $95,000?"

"Oh, that amount reflects some payroll taxes and related penalties that are over one year past due."

"You mean we haven't paid our payroll taxes for over a year?"

"Two years is more like it, Garrett."

"Why wasn't that picked up last year?"

"I'm not entirely sure, but I have an idea why. Your controller, like your salespeople, works under an incentive program. She earns a bonus of 20 percent of the pretax net income. Deleting $95,000 of expenses the last two years was an easy $19,000 bonus-motivated decision for her to make."

"That's not possible! Our financial statements were reviewed last year! What could have happened?"

"Garrett, the fees you paid to the guy who reviewed your financial statements last year amounted to $750. For that amount, I could take you to a leisurely $250 dinner and bill you at my professional rates for the time it took us to eat it. I can't imagine how anyone could review a set of financial statements for a company with annual gross sales of $3 million in only four hours . . . ."

"But we can't show these statements to the bank! They'll call their loan!"

"You're right, Garrett. We can't. They're downstairs, waiting for you . . . ."

Garrett, unfortunately, stopped thinking about his business the moment he moved into that office penthouse. His employees followed his example.

Garrett rode the elevator to his office at 10:00 each morning. His office staff invariably arrived a few minutes earlier.

Garrett's residential sales manager was an avid water sports enthusiast. When the surf was up, sales were down.

The company's traffic department employees scheduled their weekend social activities far better than they did residential solar installations.

A competent installation crew of three could handle one job a day. That, of course, assumed that their installation packages were complete.

Garrett's crews never operated close to any theoretical efficiency. One member from each crew was always in transit to the warehouse for additional parts.

It was a wonder that consumers accepted at face value Garrett's fourteen-year installation guarantees. The warranty work alone, for which nothing had been reserved, was potentially frightening.

Garrett's concerns, however, were far more immediate.

"What can we tell the bank, Mark?"

"I think you can tell them you are terminating your office lease and moving back to your warehouse where you belong."

"You mean I have to move these offices?"

"Not if you want to go out of business!"

"What?"

Garrett, like many entrepreneurs, never wanted to face the consequences of his own bad decisions. Locking his administrative overhead inside an office penthouse was a bad decision.

Three months after his controller left, Garrett moved his business back to the warehouse. Two months later the allowable solar federal tax credits expired, and by the next month Garrett's business failed.

For some businesses, it is just too late to do anything.

YOU CANNOT MICROMANAGE RISK

LESSON

DO NOT SPEND YOUR TIME AND EFFORT ADJUSTING FOR EVERY MINOR RISK.

Every entrepreneur will look at risk differently. What is a minor risk to one entrepreneur can be a major risk to another. How entrepreneurs see risk will certainly affect what they do to adjust it.

If fixed overhead is too high, some entrepreneurs will reduce it by reducing the size of their operations. If the level of manufacturing payroll is too great for a product demand that never materialized, others will reduce risk by firing people.

There is another group of entrepreneurs who will adjust for any risk, no matter how minor it is. Just like vacationing in a large city, every risk adjustment has its cost. Even if you make these adjustments efficiently, the equity of the original investment will change.

Moving from one facility to another half the size is a major risk adjustment. There are expenses directly related to that move. There is considerable downtime involved and there are start-up expenses at the new location.

You will definitely lose the theoretical benefit that could have been yours with the larger facility. The assumption, of course, is that the larger facility at some future time would have operated profitably and at the larger capacity.

There is also an expense associated with the reduction of your work force. Those individuals now unemployed will require their accrued sick and vacation pay, and other possible termination incentives. They will probably file for unemployment compensation, which may increase your state unemployment insurance premiums.

Those employees who survived the cut may not be the same gregarious group that brought doughnuts every morning to the office. Some will be furious that you terminated their friends. Others will worry about the security of their jobs. The quality of work may suffer, and your equity may further decrease.

These are some of the possible adverse consequences of any major risk adjustment.

But there are also major benefits that you receive when you make major risk adjustments. Your fixed costs will be lower; so will your payroll. When you make risk reasonable today, your business has a better chance of building wealth tomorrow!

Risk adjustments are necessary in any business. Too many risk adjustments, no matter how you make them, can be thoroughly confusing. Adjusting for every minor risk is exhausting work and it does not make you money.

Micromanaging risk is the real-time continuous adjustment of minor business risk. Its focus is on risk alone, not the impact or the cost of the risk adjustment on your wealth.

Want some examples?

A $342 receivable falls into the sixty-day past due column. You schedule a two-hour meeting with your management group to discuss the creditworthiness of the account.

The bank raises its base interest rate by .5 percent on a $17,000 five-year equipment loan. You call the bank and spend the next three days putting documents together for them to convert this variable-rate loan to a fixed interest rate.

Revenue fails to meet budget for the first time in eight months. You propose temporary staff reductions and subleasing 30 percent of your office space.

A newspaper columnist writes that stocks may be a bad investment. You hurry to your discount broker's office and sell the company's entire investment portfolio the following morning.

Micromanaging risk is a contest you can never win. Every risk demands some adjustment. For all of the attention they require, microfine adjustments never really reduce risk because they never pay for themselves.

Sometimes it costs more to analyze the impact of a proposed risk adjustment than the savings it will produce. When that occurs, it is probably a good idea to forget the analysis and the risk adjustment.

If you do not, before the year is over, you will have microtuned your way through your business, overadjusting for every minor risk. What was once a reasonable equity building business may no longer be recognizable.

When your business is no longer recognizable, neither are your risk and return relationships. It is your responsibility to set things straight.

Sometimes, you can reestablish these relationships without unduly upsetting your operations or employees. Other times, only a corporate execution will get this point across.

23

NOW HANG HIM!

- ➤ Bring Back Yardarm Justice.
- ➤ Make It Your Job.
- ➤ Hold Them Responsible.

Some business owners will act responsibly and try to control the risk in their businesses. They will make this effort despite knowing very little about risk and even less about controlling it.

These limitations certainly do not help risk control efforts.

When employees are responsible for risk control, controlling business risk can be considerably more difficult.

Few employees really understand critical risk control issues in their employer's business. That is true, even when you pay the employees to understand these issues.

Many employees also do not understand how important it is to be consistent in controlling risk. That is also true, even if you take the time to tell them.

Most employees operate under the assumption that there is always a second or third chance to control any business risk.

Those chances will always cost you money. They may also cost you your business.

It is your fault when the message about risk control just is not getting across to your employees. You need to do a better job of showing them the consequences of their behavior.

When those consequences affect them personally, employees usually take notice.

Yardarm justice will show the guilty just how wrong their assumptions about having extra chances can be.

BRING BACK YARDARM JUSTICE

LESSON

THE CONSEQUENCE OF IGNORING BUSINESS RISK SHOULD BE A HANGING OFFENSE.

Many years ago, a frigate encountered a terrible storm. Heavy seas tossed the ship. One of its guns below deck careened around the inside of the ship.

As the waves rolled the ship one way, the cannon slammed into the port side of the ship. When the ship rolled the other way, the cannon went with it and pounded the starboard side. Two crew members had already died trying to secure the battering ram the cannon had now become.

The ship was in peril. If the sea did not sink it, the cannon surely would. Oblivious to his own safety, the gunnery officer lowered himself below to confront the danger. As the huge cannon sped by him, he nimbly grabbed a trailing line and secured it to the hull. As the gun strained against its new harness, the officer grabbed a second line and tied it fast.

The beast had now been tamed.

When the storm abated, the ship's captain ordered the crew to assemble themselves topside. With great ceremony and solemnity, the captain pinned his country's highest medal on the gunnery officer's chest.

> "I am bestowing this medal upon you for bravery second to none. You have saved the ship and our lives with it. We are forever in your debt. Now hang him!"

It was true that the officer's quick thinking and nimble feet averted near disaster for everyone. For that, he was given a medal.

It was also true that he left the cannon unsecured when the tempest hit the ship. For his negligence and dereliction of duty, he was held responsible and hanged.

Hanging an employee who honestly deserves nothing better will certainly let other employees know how you feel about a loose cannon careening around your business.

If it is their job to tie down the cannon, those remaining employees will certainly see that they do the job properly. They will also recognize that there are no second chances for controlling risk that can send your ship to the bottom of the sea.

Honeycutt owned a graphics design firm that serviced large

corporations. His spectacular work earned his firm the respect of his competitors and the loyalty of his customers.

Mayberry was the account executive servicing the firm's largest client, a manufacturer of computer hardware. The client liked his friendly style, his low-pressure approach to sales, and the personal attention he directed toward their account.

Mayberry figured he had a career position with Honeycutt's firm. He probably did, too, until the day that Honeycutt learned just how much personal attention Mayberry had to offer:

"Mayberry! Do you have any time at the end of your day today?"

"It would have to be quick, Honeycutt. I have an afternoon appointment at Sterling Peripherals, Inc., and I'm not sure when I'll finish."

"I'd like to talk to you now for a few minutes if you have the time."

"Well, I'm real busy right now and the rest of this week looks booked up. We can try to get together some time later next week. If I didn't take the success of my client relationships so personally, I could spend more of my time in the office instead of out in the field. I want them to know that I'm available for them before they need me . . . ."

"Mayberry, sit down and stop your jawing. You have a problem and I'm going to solve it."

"Huh?"

"Tom Sterling just called me and said you've been harassing his receptionist."

"What? That's ridiculous!"

"Why would a busy man take twenty minutes out of his day to talk to me about a discussion his receptionist had with him in his office this morning?"

"I don't believe I'm hearing this! You're going to believe a receptionist's word before you believe mine?"

"I'm just asking for an explanation, Mayberry. I don't know who to believe."

"Uh, it wasn't anything like you think."

"Why don't you tell me what it was like? Then I'll know what to think."

"About a week ago, I asked her if she'd like to go out and get a few drinks after work one day. So we went out last night and stopped by a couple of bars. I took her home. Basically, that was it."

"Did she look OK when you dropped her off?"

"What do you mean?"

"Except for the effect of a few drinks, did she look the way she did when you picked her up earlier in the evening?"

"Oh . . . sure! Maybe she looked a bit unsteady on her feet, but that could have been from the drinking."

"Anything else?"

"What's there to tell? We had a few drinks and that was it."

"Mayberry, at the time this occurred, did you ever think about our firm policy specifically prohibiting social contact, casual banter, or other personal relationships with our clients and their employees?"

"Honeycutt, it was the receptionist. It was not like she was a department head or anything important . . ."

"Let me stop you right there, Mayberry. Everyone has a right to work in a harassment-free environment. My company policy tells you how I personally feel about that right. When Tom Sterling told me that his receptionist, who doesn't drink, was physically beaten by you, it made me sick."

"Honeycutt, you need me. Don't do this . . . ."

"Mayberry, the receptionist was his niece. You're fired effective right now. You need to get help. You are also going to need a very good defense attorney. Now get out of this building before I call the police."

The loose cannon in your operations may be more difficult to identify, but the punishment should be the same. You simply cannot allow risk of this sort to roll about in your business.

Risks like these persist for a single reason. The owners of some businesses never really understand that all risk control efforts start at the top.

MAKE IT YOUR JOB

LESSON

RISK CONTROL IS YOUR JOB
WHEN YOU OWN THE BUSINESS.

Too many entrepreneurs are not willing to accept the responsibility for adjusting risk in their own business. One reason is that adjusting risk is an exceptionally difficult job for the new business owner.

The initial focus of any entrepreneurial activity is usually on building a business. An entrepreneur takes one asset, buys a second, then acquires a third. Hopefully, when you manage these assets, they will produce income and increase your equity.

Unfortunately, most entrepreneurs never change their initial focus even after their business grows. They simply continue to accumulate business assets and do not manage them.

How can you identify this kind of behavior in your business operations?

You install a telephone system of thirty-two lines where you previously had three lines. Where you had two computers, you now have a network of sixteen that still need to be set up so they can talk to each other. You replace a single photocopy machine with one for each department. Each of your salespeople has a cellular telephone and an expense account with his own name embossed on a green plastic card.

Few, if any of these assets, produce income sufficient to pay for themselves.

Where does this stop? Sometimes it never does. That is why so many businesses fail. Failed business owners never really understand about responsible management.

Herbert Teasley had visions of owning a national real estate firm with a franchised office in each of the top 300 cities in the United States. A clear vision of the future can make business great, but by itself, it cannot make a great business.

"Teasley, this looks like a twenty-year business plan that you have prepared for me to review. Why not start with something more modest?"

"Mark, I don't have a lot of time. I'm sixty-two years old and this may be my last chance at these kinds of numbers."

"Herbert, you could just buy some General Motors stock. You'd receive a quarterly report with roughly the same magnitude of numbers you have in your business plan."

"Yes, but I wouldn't own the company . . . ."

"But you would own 100 shares of General Motors stock with a respectable quarterly dividend and considerably less risk than what I see in your proposal."

"It's not the same. I've got a profitable real estate office and I want to leverage that profitability a few hundred times over. This is the way to do it."

"I'm not so sure. What makes you think you can take the conditions that are specific to this particular marketplace and get the same results in Boise, Idaho?"

"Mark, I believe in myself. If you believe, you can achieve!"

(Cough.) "Herbert, what specifically did you want me to do today?"

"Revise my estate plan. I want my prospective franchisees to share in all of this new wealth."

"We can revise anything, Herbert. Before I do, take a moment and convince me this is more than an exercise . . . ."

"Here, take a look at this."

"It's a signed lease agreement . . . ."

"For my new world headquarters. It's a ten-year lease for 20,000 square feet of Class A commercial office space."

"That's a real investment, Herbert. It's also nearly ten times the square footage of your current offices. You're going to need a warehouse of desks just to occupy the space. At a monthly rental of $22,500, you may not need to worry about any estate planning."

"Lighten up, Mark. What can I do to show you I'm serious?"

"You can show me some revenue, Herbert. You currently spend about $3,500 per month on your existing office space. That monthly rent is one reason why you are profitable. Your annual profit will go away after only four months at the new proposed monthly rental amount."

"The revenue will be there, Mark. I just need to prepare and file the franchise offering documents. My budget provides for an initial franchise fee of $50,000 and franchise royalties of 5 percent of gross sales. All it takes is five profitable franchisees for me to cover the rent. I intend to have 300 franchisees."

"So when do we celebrate the approval of your first franchisee?"

"My attorney said it would take a minimum of sixty days to draft the franchise documents. After that, we can start selling."

"Herbert, you may have inadvertently omitted a few steps. Regulatory approval processes for individual states vary, but could take an additional 60 to 120 days. You must receive that regulatory approval before you begin to sell franchises in a particular state. Many of those states require that you submit audited corporate financial statements for the last two years with your application for approval. If we started audit work tomorrow, the earliest you could have your statements would be in forty-five days."

"So what are you saying?"

"I'm saying that you are probably six months away at my earliest estimate from selling these individual franchises. You also need a sales force and substantial advertising budget if you expect to penetrate any market this year."

"I don't know if I can wait that long. My cash flow may not permit it."

"Herbert, I don't know if you have any choice."

Entrepreneurs like Teasley never fully consider that there can be excess risk for which a business will never be compensated. When you fail to accept the responsibility for making timely risk adjustments, you have essentially passed a corporate death sentence on your business. What is worse, you have accepted the sentence.

Some entrepreneurs recognize the value in controlling risk and accept the job as their responsibility. The difficulty occurs when their employees arrive at a different consensus on the definition of responsibility.

HOLD THEM RESPONSIBLE

LESSON

THERE ARE NO DEGREES OF RESPONSIBILITY.
YOU ARE EITHER RESPONSIBLE
OR YOU ARE OUT OF BUSINESS.

His boss hired Fegley to manage the trading operations of a small registered securities firm. Fegley had the authority to establish overnight positions in certain stocks and options traded on those stocks. With this authority came the responsibility to review his daily trading reports to determine that the positions met specific risk control requirements.

In easy-to-understand language, Fegley's employment contract specified the amount of money he would receive if he met certain performance criteria. The contract also provided Fegley with a handsome incentive if he exceeded these criteria. The contract further specified how penalties would be assessed against Fegley for violating the contract's risk control parameters.

One morning Fegley failed to review his trading reports from the preceding day. That failure was a violation of his contract's first risk control parameter.

It may have been the morning traffic jam that threw off Fegley's schedule. Traffic snarls, however, are normal and customary events in any metropolitan area. If you accept traffic as a valid reason to excuse risk control today, tomorrow's reason is certain to stretch further your patience and the limits of credibility.

The report that Fegley did not review omitted a purchase of 5,000 shares of stock. During the day, the stock dropped $3. Fegley traded throughout the day as if he had not made this 5,000-share stock purchase. The company lost $15,000. His employer confronted Fegley with the loss one day later.

After twenty minutes of dodging, Fegley agreed he was responsible for the loss. The penalty that his employer assessed was $15,000, the amount of the loss.

"You mean I have to pay it?"

"You bet, Fegley!"

"But this is ridiculous! It was an oversight on my part, but it was an isolated event!"

"Perhaps, but you agreed that you were responsible."

"Yes, but just because I am responsible doesn't mean the loss should be charged to my account!"

"Fegley, then what did you mean when you agreed to accept responsibility?"

"I meant that I was the one responsible for the loss. I didn't mean that I should have to pay for the loss."

"Who, then, should pay for the loss, Fegley? A $15,000 loss is significant."

"Well, I agree that a $15,000 loss is significant, but the company has the equity to absorb the loss."

"Why would the company want to absorb a loss for which you agreed you were responsible and for which your employment contract says you are responsible?"

Fegley was never really certain in his own mind what responsibility meant. That uncertainty did not stop Fegley from leaving the meeting with a $15,000 lesson about risk control.

It took a year of semimonthly payroll deductions, but his employer made sure that Fegley paid for the lesson.

Sometimes it is difficult for owners to accept responsibility for risk even when they are paid to do so. When you clearly no longer care about assuming responsibility for the risk in your business, you have become a candidate for bankruptcy.

BANKRUPTCY, THE ULTIMATE RISK ADJUSTMENT

24

- Here's How One Business Did It.
- Postpetition Behavior Is Different.
- An Accountant Takes Exception.

If you do not reduce unnecessary risk in your business, your creditors will do it for you by forcing your business into bankruptcy. The first time this occurs, it will shake you beyond belief.

It is not a vote of creditor confidence when your creditors force you to file a bankruptcy petition.

Creditors believe that a court-approved plan will afford them a greater chance of getting paid than whatever arrangement you have offered them. The court will prohibit you from adding further risk to what has now become a creditor's investment in your business.

Sometimes business risk has become so unreasonable that creditors will insist on a straight liquidation of your company's assets. That occurs under the Chapter 7 provision of the bankruptcy code. Effectively, all of their bets on you are off, and you are simply out of business.

I am amazed at the reluctance of some business owners to accept these verdicts; they vigorously contest the consensus of their creditors. The energy spent in fighting to keep alive what is now an outrageously high-risk business can sometimes be remarkable.

There is no doubt that your attention would have been better spent in your business before risk control took flight. It may also have been better spent in a new business where risk and return elements are more evenly matched.

Bankruptcy is an act that is borne out of desperation. When your business risks move against you in a big way, you can either hope for a reprieve, or you can do something about it. Filing a bankruptcy petition allows you to accomplish both.

HERE'S HOW ONE BUSINESS DID IT

LESSON

FILING A BANKRUPTCY PETITION IS ONE WAY TO CONTROL RISK WHEN YOUR BUSINESS IS SPINNING OUT OF CONTROL.

Morgan was a bankruptcy candidate long before he filed his petition with the court.

His first set of financial statements came three years after he started his business. His second set came six months later. Morgan never had anything that remotely resembled an accounting system.

One view of Morgan's office would have been enough for vendors to terminate their business relationships with him. Month-old correspondence lay unopened on his desk. Invoices were scattered around the facility. It was impossible for Morgan to identify the amounts he owed to his creditors.

Suppliers exacerbated the problem when they started calling for payments. Morgan relied on them to provide outstanding balance amounts. Morgan mailed checks only to those suppliers who had called at least twice for payments that were long overdue. Since unpaid suppliers willingly provided third and fourth copies of detailed account balance statements, Morgan's office looked like a dead letter repository.

Morgan extended a generous amount of credit to customers. He also paid little attention to collecting past-due amounts. Customers paid Morgan only when it was convenient for them to do so. As a result, Morgan's bank accounts suffered massive amounts of cash flow deprivation.

Morgan also issued disbursement checks even though he knew he did not have sufficient funds to cover them. Returned check charges assessed by the bank amounted to over $700 per month.

Over a six-year period, Morgan accumulated a deficit balance in equity that exceeded $200,000. That meant Morgan had been consistent at losing money. His creditors financed this deficit and called repeatedly for amounts that they were due. As a result, Morgan spent more time ducking his creditors and crying poverty to them than he did running his business.

Even a steam shovel could not have dug a deeper hole.

The consensus of his advisors was to stop this nonsense and get on with managing his business.

How do you manage your way out of a hole that you have dug for your business? You do it by filing a bankruptcy petition.

It took six months of urging for me to convince Morgan that his pride had no place in delaying what was now inevitable. Bankruptcy was the next step.

But reality can be intrusive. Morgan believed what he wanted to believe. He heard what he wanted to hear. The fantasy of running a business was intoxicating. It clearly affected his ability to make even simple business decisions. Morgan's reluctance to realistically assess his current operations nearly destroyed his business.

There were other emotional factors that made Morgan reluctant to file a bankruptcy petition.

Morgan sired his business. That founding spirit produced a strong emotional bond between Morgan and his business. Pride of ownership, parenthood, and the Great American Dream were all part of the feelings. It was irritating to have creditors tell him how to raise his offspring. It was devastating to realize he was incapable of doing it.

In that bleak moment before the financial death of his business, Morgan recognized that risk in his business was spinning out of control. He was also smart enough to ask me to do something about it.

I accompanied Morgan to an attorney's office. Under protection of the courts and a Chapter 11 petition, Morgan started to reduce his business risk.

The bankruptcy petition was a blessing. When the court ordered the creditors to stop barking, Morgan gained some valuable time. With that reprieve, he also gained a new perspective.

Once a ship is no longer sinking and has stopped taking on water, it is easy to understand why you must plug the holes in the hull.

Without interruption from creditors, Morgan reorganized his entrepreneurial life. He started with his accounting system. In sixty days he had a reliable reporting system that reported on his operating losses two days into the following month.

He put customers under rigid credit controls by reducing excessive credit limits. He denied credit to customers where the privilege had been abused. As you may expect, the amount of overdue accounts dropped dramatically.

Morgan believed at one time that the only way to solve his financial problems was to grow out of them. Now, he pursued with vigor the option of shrinking out of them. Where his business once broke even on $75,000 of monthly revenue, he now needed only $45,000. Over the next few months, Morgan's business began to show a profit.

The bankruptcy laws worked in Morgan's favor. Less than one year after filing his bankruptcy petition, Morgan was out from under the supervision of the courts. His company was lean, profitable, and a great example of what can come from adversity.

It is truly remarkable what entrepreneurs can do at the edge of the abyss.

The stupidity of the largest creditor did not hurt the process either. Morgan disclosed on his bankruptcy petition outstanding state excise tax liabilities and related penalties of over $157,000. When the state presented its claim to the court, it listed only $11,400 of unpaid taxes. No state employee bothered to verify the claim amount against the liability disclosed on the petition. The court accepted the state's claim and closed the case.

Morgan's company received an instant windfall of $145,600 when the court forgave all other state tax obligations.

Luck does play its part, for better or for worse.

POSTPETITION BEHAVIOR IS DIFFERENT

LESSON

CUSTOMERS WHO FILE FOR BANKRUPTCY
CAN STILL BE GOOD CASH-PAYING CUSTOMERS.

If you are fortunate, your past behavior has never returned to haunt you. That will change the moment a customer of yours files a bankruptcy petition. When that occurs, your equity is locked in and you are locked out.

What does that mean? Just like the news that makes headlines, it is nothing good.

You now have what is known as a prepetition claim. A prepetition claim means that a judge will decide how and when to pay any of your bills that this customer incurred before the date of his bankruptcy petition. There is hardly a better way to ruin a day.

There is little you can do as a creditor to change the prepetition facts. After all, unless you are an attorney contemplating the quickest way to work your way through a client's retainer, no one in his right mind would ever waste time arguing about facts!

There are a few things you can do, however, to avoid a repeat performance.

Take the time to redefine your relationship with your customer. If it has not already occurred to you, you now have a prepetition relationship and a postpetition relationship. The courts and the lawyers will define what remains from your prepetition relationship. You will define your postpetition relationship.

That postpetition relationship need not be tainted.

Your casual attitude toward running the credit part of your business is the first behavioral pattern you will change. To any customer who has filed a bankruptcy petition, you offer simple postpetition credit terms: none! Cash before shipping and cash on delivery are the only acceptable payment methods.

You will amaze yourself at how easy it is for companies to pay your bills with cash in a postpetition relationship. You would think some of these companies owned a Treasury Department printing press!

I can understand the reluctance you may have in establishing a postpetition relationship. This is particularly true where the customer owes you a large prepetition balance.

It is unfair for you to blame the customer for your mistake in extending credit to his business. You are now a little bit smarter, a little bit poorer, but at least you are still in business.

When you can make a cash sale to any customer that will increase your equity, do it! That includes sales to customers who have filed bankruptcy petitions.

AN ACCOUNTANT TAKES EXCEPTION

LESSON

IF YOU ARE NOT AN ATTORNEY,
DISENGAGE WHENEVER PAYMENT
OF YOUR PROFESSIONAL FEES
IS CONTINGENT UPON COURT APPROVAL.

If you are an accountant, you may wish to take exception to establishing any postpetition relationship. I can appreciate why.

It is not for the reason that a client's bankruptcy filing is a poor reflection on your record. On the contrary, every wartime admiral has had a ship or two of his sent to the bottom. That does not make the admiral incompetent.

It is also not for the reason that you no longer wish to affiliate with a mismanaged operation. You should be the first to know that there is no such thing as a perfectly run business.

The reason you may object to postpetition involvement is that the court must now approve your professional fees before you receive them. It is no small reason to be concerned.

You probably earn more than a federal court bankruptcy judge. He is aware of this. As a result, he invariably applies a "haircut" to the bills you have submitted for court approval.

That means that in the name of fiduciary responsibility, he will reduce your bill by 20 percent without blinking an eye.

Bankruptcy attorneys are aware of another dilemma. In many bankruptcy cases, there are a limited amount of funds available to pay prepetition debts and postpetition legal and accounting fees.

It is a bankruptcy attorney's job to see that his professional fees are always paid before yours. If the availability of cash is ever in doubt, bankruptcy attorneys will move to protect their own interests.

"This is Cremshaw, Malinshack, Gladstone, and Sliggarty. I am holding a call for Frank Boyd."

"You got him! Say, if you guys don't stop admitting new partners to your business, your name is going to be 100 feet long! What can I do for you?"

"Mr. Boyd, I've received a detailed summary of your time charges for Slako Fisheries. Quite frankly, I am amazed."

"Yeah, I know what you mean. That business was in a shambles. The records were in such poor shape and the accounting department at Slako was so unhelpful that I even amazed myself . . . ."

"That's not what I meant, Mr. Boyd."

"Oh? Oh yeah! I couldn't believe that we managed to make sense out of two years of records filling ten shopping bags in time to meet your courtroom appearances . . . ."

"Mr. Boyd, let me get to the point. Thank God I am sitting down. I am looking at a bill from your office for $8,475. All you did was compile my client's financial statements for the last two years."

"That's all?"

"In good conscience, Mr. Boyd, I can't submit these bills to the court for its approval."

"What's bothering you?"

"Mr. Boyd, all you had to do was take a few numbers from the client's bank statements, twirl a pencil around their receipts and disbursements records, and give me financial statements for two years."

"And?"

"And now I've got a bill for $8,475!"

"You should pay it!"

"Mr. Boyd. You need to review your billing again before I submit it for court approval."

"What do I need to review?"

"I might suggest that you look at your time charges to be absolutely certain the billing is only for Slako Fisheries and not the rest of your clients."

"The billing is correct."

"Mr. Boyd, I am going to send the bills back to you so you can change what needs to be changed."

"You can keep my bills and pay them. Nothing needs to be changed! They stand as they were issued."

"I'm sorry you feel that way, Mr. Boyd. I'm afraid we're going to be adversaries the next time you see us in court. We're going to recommend to the judge that your professional fees be disallowed in full."

As an accountant, you certainly have your hands full of postpetition conflicts. If the petitioner's financial statements that you prepared and presented to the court are wrong, someone will sue you. Even if your billing is prompt, it may take four to six months to schedule a hearing for compensation approval. When your billing finally gets approved, there may not be sufficient funds to pay it.

With all of these conditions, it is unusually difficult to build equity in a postpetition environment that condones legal sharpshooting.

What then is your best course? The moment a business client files a bankruptcy petition, disengage!

Once you have witnessed the results of bankruptcy, you will understand why it is the ultimate risk adjustment. Your feelings about risk control will also never be the same.

You will certainly have a new awareness of the consequences of poor or incomplete risk analysis. You will also discover that your newly found feelings about risk control will temper your enthusiasm for sudden change.

Unfortunately, risk control will not eliminate all of your losses. On your way to making any business your best investment, some losses will be inevitable. When these losses occur, you must learn to live with them.

25

LIVING WITH YOUR LOSSES

- ➤ Learn to Accept the Losses.
- ➤ I Get Sacked.
- ➤ When Do You Stop?
- ➤ Control Your Equity Burn Rate.
- ➤ Terminate Your Business.

You will not always win in business. While it is difficult for risk-averse individuals to accept even reasonable business risk, it is considerably more difficult for most entrepreneurs to accept their business losses.

LEARN TO ACCEPT THE LOSSES

LESSON

YOU CAN HAVE YOUR SHARE OF LOSSES
AND STILL BE A SUCCESSFUL ENTREPRENEUR.

Nobody likes a loser.

You have had it rammed into you by no one less formidable than Vince Lombardi that "Winning isn't everything. It's the only thing!" So have 260 million other Americans.

As a result, few of you remember the runner-up in Super Bowl XII, the silver medalist in the discus in the 1968 Olympiad in Mexico City, or the defeated candidate in the 1984 presidential election.

The dilemma is not what losing means to you, but what it means to someone else.

When you launch a new product that fails, no one remembers that you have the largest soft drink distribution network in the world. They just remember that you tried to convince an old world there was a new Coke and you blew it.

When you design a car that consumers ridicule, what does it matter that you are the most profitable auto maker in the world? No one cares that your business is the one that has kept your parents out of the house and on the road for the last seventy-eight years. When they look, consumers only see an Edsel parked in your corporate driveway.

What others might think has created a fixation on the consequences of losing. It has fostered complacency, decision making by consensus, risk averseness, and internal reprisal.

Taking a public stance means being locked into your decision. The consequence of an incorrect decision is no less adverse than losing your promotability or your job along with your capital.

Losses are inevitable. Some investments, no matter what you do, no matter how hard you try, no matter what risk adjustments you make, just never work out. On your own way, you must learn to tip your hat to them and move on.

Letting go is not always easy, especially when you know you are right. You must remember that you cannot control all variables that affect risk. Chance and random events still influence the outcome on every business investment.

I GET SACKED

LESSON

SOME LOSSES WILL OCCUR WHEN YOU LEAST EXPECT THEM AND CAN DO NOTHING TO CHANGE THE RESULT.

Barry called me for some tax consultation. He also wanted to meet and discuss his personal financial affairs with a CPA who had no vested interest in the outcome beyond the welfare of his client.

The first few meetings were uneventful. However, they did give me a historical perspective of Barry's preference for risk.

Barry had a nice history of increasing earnings. His personal consumption habits required much of those earnings, but Barry still had a large remaining discretionary income. Barry wanted to invest it in four different private placement memoranda that he flipped to me across the conference table.

"Barry, are you serious?"

"Sure, why wouldn't I be? These guys are customers of mine. Besides, one of them is like a godfather to my children. With the exception of the oil well, these are all local investments. How could I possibly lose?"

"Where do you want me to start?"

"What do you mean?"

"Let me get a red magic marker. Do you mind if I circle a few things in these proposals?"

"No, that is what I want you to do, Mark. If there is anything in any of these proposals that you believe is not in my best interest, then I want to know about it going into these deals."

"What is your timing on this? Can I have a few days to read these?"

"Sure. Why don't we do lunch two days from today and you can tell me if you think these will be good investments."

"Barry, I don't do lunch. I work through it. But I'll be happy to meet you Thursday morning and at least show you the risks that I have identified in these proposals. Once you know the risks, then you can make the determination if these meet your investment criteria."

Two days later, I handed Barry the four private placement memoranda.

"So what do you think, Mark?"

"I have to tell you, Barry, this is a first for me. It usually takes me ten years to use up a single magic marker unless I forget to put the cap back on. I went through two of those big, thumb-sized magic markers on these proposals. The proposals sure are something else . . . ."

"Should we do them?"

"Barry, you have to be kidding! I would run as far away from these deals as I could. They are entirely one-sided and written only for the benefit of the promoter."

"If you were going to pick three out of the four to put your money in, which three would it be?"

"I'm not sure we're on the same page, Barry. Surely you don't believe that the concept of fairness was an inadvertent omission in all four documents! If you do any of these deals, you are likely to lose your entire investment before the ink on your signature line dries."

I must have been unconvincing because Barry tuned in the deal makers and tuned me out. One of the real estate promoters put it to Barry this way:

"Barry, sometimes you listen to your banker. Sometimes you listen to your accountant. There are even some times you should listen to your insurance agent. Then thank them for their time, ignore their advice, and just do what you need to do. If I followed everything these advisors told me, I would never have done one deal!"

With that convincing endorsement, Barry mortgaged himself silly to pay for a $200,000 investment in two real estate partnerships. He purchased an entire stamp collection for $40,000. A few months later, he also bought a working interest in an oil and gas well for $20,000 from the same promoter.

There was only so much I could do. I argued vigorously with Barry against his making these investments. I warned him against rolling from one deal into another with the same promoter. I cautioned him to wait for some tangible, verifiable economic return. A cash distribution or even a simple financial statement from any one of these deals would have been a good starting point.

Unfortunately, you cannot expect a thief to tell you that he is stealing your money.

And you cannot convince a victim he is going to be victimized until it actually happens. By then, it is too late.

In the next three months, Barry watched his investments collapse.

The $200,000 of capital for the real estate deals were diverted to the personal gain of the general partners. None of the investment ever reached the partnerships.

The $40,000 stamp collection was an exercise in peddling future valuations. Recently struck commemorative stamps with a combined face value of $1,000 were projected to be worth $40,000 in another sixty years. The investment was purchased at that future value!

The $20,000 working interest in the oil and gas deal was entirely fictitious. The only tangible item in that project was the letterhead on which nonsensical monthly operating reports were written.

In an interview on his way to federal court, one of the promoters had no sympathy or remorse:

> "Hey! Barry knew he was gambling! It's like Las Vegas and craps. When you place your bet, roll the dice, and lose, you don't ask for your money back!"

In the middle of these events, I advised Barry to do what any good football team does when it wants to protect its quarterback:

> "Control the line of scrimmage."

And that is exactly what he did. Barry lined up each investment, looked at the risks, and either adjusted them at fair market value prices or walked away from the investment.

It was a punishing exercise for Barry. Never before had he lost such a large sum of money in such a short period of time and had to live with the consequences.

His wife was furious and rightly so. Barry did not consult her before making any of his investment decisions. She had visions of her family being evicted from their home into the street.

Barry met this adversity as an All-Pro nosetackle would meet a runningback. He was awesome. His wife welcomed the pursuit. I am sure those who wronged him feared the change, for Barry went after them with a vengeance.

A federal court convicted the real estate promoter. There was no recovery of any of the initial investment.

The stamp appraisal firm saw a ten-minute videotape specially prepared for them. In repetitive, six-second clips, it showed Barry ripping off the helmet, and nearly the head, of a 300-pound offensive lineman. They promptly repurchased the stamp sheets for $40,000.

The oil and gas deal was history. At Barry's income level, at least the tax loss was worth nearly $8,000.

The impact of these losses took five years of Barry's life and enough legal fees to start a private law practice. The change also enveloped me, for his wife never forgave my inability to control her husband's destiny. Like Rome at the hands of the Visigoths, I was summarily sacked.

It was a hard loss for me to accept. Barry's interests were always in front of my own. I walked around for days wondering what I did wrong.

I discovered that I did nothing wrong. Any investment, no matter how good or how well hedged, can always run away from you in areas you cannot control. You will have your share of days where, despite your best efforts, it seems you just cannot buy sushi in San Francisco. All you can do is walk outside for a breath of fresh air, shake your head, and show up for work tomorrow.

WHEN DO YOU STOP?

LESSON

IT IS TIME TO STOP TAKING RISKS
WHEN YOU ARE ADDICTED TO THEM
AND YOU DO NOT LIKE THE RESULTS.

One of the sad facts of cigarette smoking is that it is easier to light up a cigarette than to put one out. The mechanics are comfortable, the motion is familiar, and the process is natural.

It is also easier for an entrepreneur to keep making investments and increasing business risk than it is to quit. It is this reluctance to put out the cigarette for good that leads to an early financial death. Entrepreneurs hooked on risk will also agree.

There are chess players who can play forty simultaneous games, remember every move, and never lose a board. The explanation for their success is nothing fancy. A world-class player simply lives in a different world.

There are very few entrepreneurs who can make forty simultaneous investments, control relevant risk, and never lose a dollar. The explanation is obvious. Most entrepreneurs live in the same world you do.

Unlike a world-class chess player, who stands to lose little more than his pride and, of course, his title, an entrepreneur stands to lose more than his equity on his bad investments. He also faces the prospect of accepting an inefficient return on his other investments simply because he is overextended.

It is impossible for anyone short of genius to manage effectively the risk of such a diverse portfolio. The relevant risks that you fail to monitor are probably far more numerous than those you can identify. By way of result, they are potentially far more damaging.

When risk is no longer manageable, you stop investing.

Risk may be unmanageable for a number of reasons. You may not have the authority to manage the risk. You may have the authority, but you may not have the knowledge. You may have the knowledge, but there is so much risk that controlling it is a lopsided effort. It is like trying to coach your high school basketball team to a win against the Boston Celtics.

When the outcome is that hopeless, enough is enough.

CONTROL YOUR EQUITY BURN RATE

LESSON

IT IS TIME TO MOVE ON WHEN YOUR BUSINESS BURNS MORE EQUITY THAN IT BUILDS.

There is not any one point at which you recognize your investment is a poor one and walk away from it. That point is different for each individual. Walking away is made even more difficult because individuals new to building equity have a tendency to cling tightly to their first investments.

The attachment is an emotional one. First investments take a disproportionate amount of time and emotional nail-biting. It seems fine to stay with these investments until you receive some return, even if it takes ten years longer than expected.

What these individuals fail to recognize is that first investments seldom produce any equity because risk-return relationships have not been properly analyzed.

Letting the business go the first time can be difficult. Some entrepreneurs consider it no different from selling your first-born child. Selling your child is an act that only a heartless person would consider.

It is not the selling of our children, however, about which we are talking. We are talking about the iterative process of building equity for our children, which is an entirely legitimate and responsible act.

You must learn to recognize when enough is enough for you. That occurs when the time and capital you have invested are totally out of proportion to the expected return.

Alton started a small cabinet shop because he enjoyed working with his hands. There was also a strong demand in the marketplace for custom kitchen cabinets.

Alton received $95,000 from his grandparents. He used that money to buy precision machines for his custom cabinet business. He rented a 5,000-square-foot shop in which to put the machines and hired six hourly employees to work them. Alton placed some advertising in the local magazines and started to look for business.

Customers, for a variety of reasons, were slow in coming. Everyone who saw Alton's work agreed that the finished product was a piece of art. However, only a few of them could afford to pay the average $18,000 price tag for his custom kitchen cabinets.

At even that rich price, Alton lost money on each installation. You explain that phenomenon by calling it a labor of love. Alton never cut corners. The amount of hours that went into each installation was staggering. So were Alton's net operating losses.

The first year of his operations, Alton lost $70,000. In the second year he lost an additional $165,000. The only way Alton could keep his business running without sufficient revenue was to advance additional amounts from his personal funds.

It was difficult for anyone to convince Alton his equity burn rate was bleeding him to death. Alton was surrounded by his grandparent's money, several million dollars worth. Losing equity in his business was unfortunate, but it was not a lifestyle-threatening event.

What forced Alton to pay attention to his financial hemorrhaging was the $130,000 he lost in the first three months of his third and final year of operations. At that rate, he stood to burn $390,000 of equity in the current year. Alton had finally reached his point where enough was enough.

You do not need to wait that long.

TERMINATE YOUR BUSINESS

LESSON

CLOSE THE BUSINESS WHEN YOU CANNOT STOP THE LOSSES.

In a business that is losing money, it is a good idea for you to convert what remains of your equity to cash before it all goes away. If you wait too long to close down an unprofitable business operation, there may be no equity left.

There is no point in panicking if you have lost your shirt in your business. People panic when they face choices. You really do not have many choices when you have lost everything in your business. All you can do is have a good cry. Remember, you did have a chance to do something about your business and the risks in it before things started going badly.

"Close it before you lose everything" is easy for someone to tell you. In practice it can sometimes be difficult to do.

The difficulty entrepreneurs face in closing a losing business operation rests on their attempt to predict what the marketplace will do.

"Sherwin. I hope you came here today to tell me you are going to close your downtown restaurant . . . ."

"Well, yes. I've wrestled with my conscience about that decision for the last few weeks. Let me tell you, it hasn't been any fun. I think I've accepted that closing it is a good idea. We've never made a profit since the day we opened four years ago."

"You also had time working against you, Sherwin. Your restaurant doesn't have a breakfast menu, and nobody stays downtown for dinner. You needed to turn your tables three times during lunch just to pay for the food and to meet payroll. When do we officially celebrate?"

"I think we can do that in August."

"August? That's six months from now!"

"I know. Believe me, I know. I called my franchisor yesterday. His advice is a bit different from yours. He pointed out that there are a few other buildings in the area that should be leased up in the next four to six months. He says I should focus on getting some of that lunch business."

"Sherwin, continuing to own that restaurant is like owning an hourglass with a very big hole in the middle. The sand in that hourglass, just like your working capital, goes ripping through that hole! You're losing $25,000 per month in that location. That is going to be a very big number six months from now . . . ."

Tunnel vision is fine when your business is your best investment. When you are losing equity, tunnel vision is not particularly helpful. What you really need to do is to stop the losses.

Living with your losses does not mean you must spend your future with them. It means that you have learned something valuable from an experience you could have done without. There will be many experiences in your entrepreneurial lifetime. Clearly, they will make you smarter.

It is certainly easier to understand the lessons from these experiences when they affect a single business that happens to be yours. The presence of multiple businesses only seems to cushion these lessons.

Cushioning is not particularly desirable because it can leave you with no lesson at all. You will certainly need the lesson the day you start betting in size.

26

BETTING IN SIZE

- ➤ Install an Accounting System That Works.
- ➤ Keep Payroll a Variable Expense.
- ➤ Shrink the Remaining Tasks.
- ➤ Examine Your Advertising Expenses.
- ➤ Look at Other Expenses Too.

There is a class of entrepreneurs who need to be saved from themselves. These entrepreneurs have a fixation on size.

These people consume themselves with sales growth, future expansion plans, new branch locations, and additional business acquisitions. For these individuals, high annual sales, more employees, and broader corporate activities all translate to a feeling of entrepreneurial success.

Unfortunately for them, this feeling of success seldom translates to business wealth. There are several reasons why it does not.

Rapid business growth always occurs at a cost. The cost may be a loosely managed business, forgone profit, or both. It can be an overwhelming task to manage a business for growth and for profit. Some professional advisors insist that it is an impossible task.

The managerial style required to obtain an ever-increasing stream of revenue is usually different from the style required to build wealth. Entrepreneurs who focus on growth to the exclusion of other areas frequently look no further than a monthly sales report for confirmation of their progress. Intentionally or not, growth-oriented entrepreneurs have shown an inclination to ignore nearly every control function that may slow or impede that growth.

As a result, they are free-spending and rarely manage their businesses efficiently.

You cannot justify that fact by explaining that you are expanding the overhead of existing operations in the hope of increasing future revenues. You cannot change that fact when starting a second business. That business will surely divert attention and capital from your first business.

Betting in size can be hazardous to your wealth. Some entrepreneurs who do not know their costs or understand their risks will insist that they have the qualifications to bet in size. Their behavior is no different from a gambler who increases his betting activity in a very big way to cover his previous losses.

Most entrepreneurs gamble when they bet in size. When you gamble, you cannot influence risk. If you cannot spend the time to be certain that your first business functions efficiently, risk will flourish and all of your business operations will suffer.

Owners who do not properly manage their businesses will almost certainly increase the risk under their entrepreneurial umbrella. These businesses will also assimilate the character of their owner. If you have a chronic problem managing risk, that problem will surface in each of your businesses. Losses will no longer confine themselves to a single business, but will now affect them all.

To put it bluntly, if you cannot hit a home run off your kid sister, what makes you think you are ready for a bigger game? The failure to answer responsibly that question has led many entrepreneurs and their businesses to financial ruin.

If you are still adamant about betting in size, there are a few things you can do to increase your chances of success.

INSTALL AN ACCOUNTING SYSTEM THAT WORKS

LESSON

POOR FINANCIAL DATA ARE AT THE ROOT OF ALL BUSINESS FAILURES.

Nandor ran a chain of tan and fitness centers in the Midwest. In his first three years of operations, Nandor sold nearly 6,000 lifetime memberships at premium prices before competitor discounting and state fitness center regulations ruined membership premiums.

Nandor asked me to meet him at his office after his partner's attorney insisted on receiving a meaningful financial statement.

"Well, Mark, how is it going so far? Have you found everything you need?"

"I'm not sure, Nandor. It looks to me that in the last three years, you've had a problem installing your accounting system."

"What makes you say that?"

"I can't find your current records, but I have seen the remnants of seven different accounting systems around the floor of your conference room."

"Oh, sorry about our filing system. I'm working on getting that organized."

"Nandor, without a reliable accounting system, how do you know if your locations are profitable?"

"There seems to be enough cash flow to cover our expenses . . . ."

"Could there be any other explanation for that?"

"Well, our sales must be doing nicely."

"Nandor, how do you know for sure?"

"Believe me, if we had problems, I'd be hearing about them from the managers!"

"Here, I think you may want to look these over."

"What's this you're giving me?"

"These are all the invoices I found in unopened envelopes in your conference room. The total amount is $177,605."

"I was just getting around to opening my mail. That does seem like an unusually large number, though!"

"Nandor, most of these invoices are over six months old. Wouldn't it be a good idea to pay some of them?"

"Well, yes, but our cash flow isn't that good. I think it will improve when our members see the new equipment we just ordered. I'm replacing all the old exercise bikes with a completely new line of equipment."

"How are you planning to pay for that new equipment?"

"That was one question I thought we could discuss after you had a chance to look at our records. Do you know any investors who may be interested? "

Nandor knew the exercise business. Unfortunately, Eskimos knew more about the game of waterpolo than Nandor knew about the profitablity of his operations. The term "meaningful financial statements" was entirely an academic concept to him.

In some fitness centers, cash payments received from monthly membership dues follow a circuitous route. Sometimes, those cash payments never reach the bank. Many of Nandor's cash receipts never reached the bank. He diverted the receipts to support a consumption pattern that was a marketing company's dream.

Nandor wore the most prestigious watches, drove the newest luxury cars, and always flew first class on his monthly business trips to the shore. His tan looked great, his gold chains did too, and his home could have been the feature residence on the cover of *Estates* magazine.

The profitability of Nandor's facilities deteriorated despite the purchase of new exercise equipment. New member enrollment declined and current members just stopped coming. As a result of his failure to make payroll tax deposits, the Internal Revenue Service arrived in his parking lot with a moving van. They seized the new equipment, loaded it in the van, and left members peering through the front windows of an empty club.

Nandor had not learned the first lesson about managing risk. If you do not know your costs or understand your risks, you cannot make your business your best investment. Until you have a real accounting system, you cannot possibly know your costs. Expanding your business or starting a second one before you know those costs will likely result in a failed business.

Once you have installed an accounting system that works, you will at least know your costs. The trick is knowing what to do about them.

KEEP PAYROLL A VARIABLE EXPENSE

LESSON

VARIABLE EXPENSES CUSHION BUSINESS RISK.

It is almost axiomatic that when revenues of a business increase, so do expenses. You would expect that to occur. One additional dollar of revenue will always have some fractional related expense that produces that revenue dollar. Those incremental expenses could be wages, materials, or any other normal and customary business expenses.

Incremental expenses that vary with revenue are known as variable expenses.

Seasonal businesses learn early on that the trick to working with expenses is to keep them variable. These businesses can survive large seasonal decreases in revenue simply because of the reliable and time-tested decrease in expense that also occurs.

Every entrepreneur has a strong incentive to learn which expenses are variable. The financial health of the business often depends on it. Once you develop the ability to identify variable expenses, expense control is almost a natural event.

The vast array of unprofitable businesses is silent testimony to the failure of many entrepreneurs to identify their variable expenses and to keep them variable! The challenge with variable expenses is that they have a nasty habit of turning into fixed expenses. Fixed expenses do not cushion business risk.

In an effort to increase gross revenues, keeping variable expenses variable is usually trodden under foot. It is an easy thing to do.

"Smedes! Did anyone you know die? You look so glum!"

"The bottom has fallen out of our gross revenues for the month of February, and so far, March isn't shaping up much better. I'm beginning to wonder if I made the right decision of moving to a larger facility for our catering operations."

"Well, if you want my opinion, I don't think you had any choice about the larger facility. Your old location wasn't wired for the electrical load. I still can't believe you didn't burn the place down. Besides, you simply didn't have the room to work. Your kitchen and prep areas were practically on top of each other. You literally didn't have the cooking space for another sweet potato cake."

"When you put it that way, I know you're right. We needed the larger space. But I sure do miss our $35,000 monthly break-even point at that old location. At least at that level, we covered all of our expenses. The numbers you gave us last week seem to point to a break-even at this new location of about $62,000. Ugh! With such a high break-even point, we are going to get clobbered when our seasonal business falls off. What can we do?"

"Look, you know your food costs and the catering business, Smedes, so I'm not going to make any recommendations there because you've already considered them. Besides, those costs have stayed in the 33 to 35 percent range for each month this past year. Whatever you are losing isn't through your food costs."

"What's next?"

"You tell me. What's your next largest expense?"

"I guess I'd have to say labor . . . ."

"So let's start there. What's your monthly payroll in dollars?"

"Well, it seems to be fixed at about $23,000 per month for the last couple of months."

"Okay. Let's take a moment and look at your payroll as a percentage of gross revenues. Nine months ago, your payroll dollars were about 27 or 28 percent of gross revenue. The last six months, they seem to be hovering around 35 or 36 percent of gross revenue. Take a look at this chart and see if you can remember what happened last September that caused your payroll percentage to increase to this higher level."

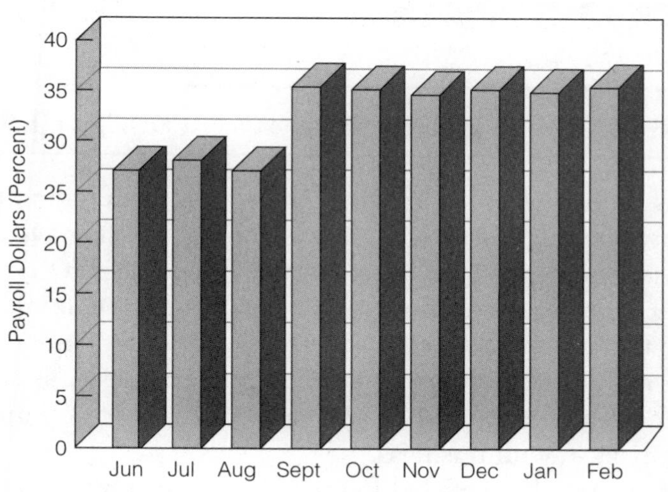

"Hmmm. Oh, that's an easy one. When we moved into the larger facility, we hired two additional middle-level managers for supervisory purposes and a salesperson for our corporate party business. We pay each manager $2,100 per month and each salesperson $1,800 per month."

"Are all three people salaried?"

"You bet! They wouldn't have it any other way."

"Well, Smedes, I think you've found a big part of your problem. In your operations, payroll should be a variable cost. That way, if the revenue isn't there, neither is the payroll expense. Payroll was a variable expense until you hired those additional people as salaried employees six months ago. You're treating their wages as a fixed cost, which has been a large part of the reason for the higher break-even point. You need to keep your payroll expenses variable."

"How can I do that?"

"Put on your owner's hat and convince these three new hires that they should be paid as percent of the additional sales dollars they produce."

"But what if they don't want the risk of a variable paycheck?"

"Then let them go . . . ."

That is exactly what Smedes did the following Monday morning. That day, he also lowered his monthly break-even point by nearly $14,000.

Keeping payroll a variable cost will usually provide you with the single largest reduction in your monthly break-even point. It is always an effort to make the adjustment, but you can hardly argue with the results.

Yet you are only half-finished with the job. When you reduce the absolute amount of payroll dollars, you must also consider reducing the work. It is a logical step in cushioning business risk.

SHRINK THE REMAINING TASKS

LESSON

REDUCE THE WORK WHEN YOU REDUCE THE STAFF.

There is nothing more horrifying in business than failing to meet a payroll. How do you tell a group of loyal employees who have given you their best that you cannot pay them? However you decide to rationalize, it is a humbling experience. You must explain to individuals who may not understand the first thing about business risk that you do not either.

It is always a good rule to be paid for your business risk. It is also a good rule to make a profit. When you cannot do either, you must adjust some of the risks in your business.

Entrepreneurs who have bet in size frequently solve the problem of failing to meet payroll by firing in size. That usually means prompt and massive layoffs.

It does not matter whether you call it restructuring, downsizing, or rightsizing. Whenever you reduce the number of your employees, you must also reduce the number of tasks. Otherwise, your remaining employees will leave too. The ones who do not leave will be so unfairly matched with the work that you will have a better chance building wealth by buying lottery tickets. Marlene discovered the truth to this statement in the months that followed a 50 percent reduction of her office staff.

"Marlene! Where is everyone this brisk winter morning? I know it snowed again last night, but the roads aren't that bad."

"We had a few more fatalities. Two more people in the accounting department handed in their resignations late yesterday."

"Did they give you any reason?"

"Sure! Ever since we had that staff cutback, they have had to do the same amount of work with half the staff. They've been taking work home at night. They've been working here on weekends for the last nine weeks. They're tired of the pace . . . ."

"They're exhausted. No wonder they quit!"

"I really don't know how I am going to replace them."

"Maybe you don't need to. What work were they doing?"

"I'm not sure."

"Well, their workstations aren't sacred anymore. Someone has already confiscated their staplers. Let's see what's left in these cabinets."

(Twenty minutes later.)

"What is all of this stuff?"

(Flips through the files.) "It looks like at least two dozen different variance reports for your business. Gee, this one looks interesting: 'Updated Comparative Summary of Historical Gross Margins by Product.' "

"Let me see that one." (Mouth opens in disbelief.) "This stuff is over twelve months old! Since our restructuring began, we have stopped carrying half of these products."

"Here's another good one: "Back Order Stock Status Report—Piedmont Store."

"The Piedmont store was closed three months ago. Why is anyone working on a report for a store that no longer exists?"

"Good question, Marlene. I think what we have seen is only the beginning . . . ."

It sure was. Two hours later, we finished clearing the filing cabinets in both workstations. Most of the work done by the recently departed employees was a result of habit. The reports Marlene examined were simply not essential to her restructured business. She eliminated nearly all of the tasks and the requirement for these two staff positions.

You can, too, if you take the time to look.

However, it is not always an easy job to determine which work or which employees are essential to your core business. This is particularly true if the position in doubt is occupied by an advertising director.

EXAMINE YOUR ADVERTISING EXPENSES

LESSON

IT DOESN'T TAKE AN ADVERTISING GENIUS TO SPEND 19 PERCENT OF GROSS REVENUES ON ADVERTISING AND GET GREAT RESULTS.

There is a common phenomenon that occurs in most entrepreneurial companies whose revenues have increased as a result of an advertising program. That phenomenon is the coronation of the advertising director.

The advertising director in smaller entrepreneurial operations is usually an employee who is smart enough to avoid the risk of working for himself and quick enough to claim the vacant position and title for his own. He is also crafty enough to claim responsibility for 100 percent of any revenue and net profit increase your business has the good fortune to enjoy.

Never mind that your engineers have redesigned your product so that it is the best in the industry. Never mind that your new and improved distribution system now allows you to deliver your product three days after the customer orders it when it used to take three weeks. Never mind that your vice president of finance has renegotiated all of your credit lines at the lowest interest rates you have seen in the last twenty years. If you have an advertising director on payroll, that individual may do far more than take all of the credit for your company's prosperity. He may also believe he is entitled to it!

The problem with permitting an advertising director to think this way is the potential effect it will have on your operating budget. This is particularly true when the advertising director is not accountable to anyone.

The common sense of many business owners has been known to take a sabbatical under the hypnotic patter of an advertising director asking to increase his advertising budget.

"Mort, did you get one of my advertising summary reports?"
"Not yet, Lenny. What did we do last month?"
"Take a look at this! $2.2 million in sales. How do you like those numbers?"
"Wow! I wish every month could be like that."

"I'm telling you, Mort, it can. All we have to do is advertise! Ever since I convinced you to increase your advertising budget from 6 percent of sales to 19 percent, our revenue has gone bonkers! It's all the warehouse can do to fill the orders."

"I think you've done a great job, Lenny. I remember only a few years ago when we could only dream about those kinds of sales figures."

"And those numbers will get even bigger, Mort, if we can increase my advertising budget by a few more percentage points. Just think how great it would be to do $3 million per month in sales."

"Lenny, you're going to give me a heart condition! I'd love the revenue, but with our advertising budget at 19 percent, we're already spending $418,000 per month on advertising. That's a big number. I remember when our monthly revenues used to be less than that! Can't we ratchet it down so we spend half of that and start to bank some of what we save?"

"Mort, we can't afford to decrease a penny of our advertising budget! We're getting a deal on everything we buy. Did you see how that guy from the *Tribune* looked when he left my office? He was practically crying! I really beat him up on his prices. I told him to keep his rate card out of this office if he wanted to keep our business . . . ."

"Lenny, don't get me wrong. I know you're buying advertising for us at good prices. I'm just wondering if you're buying too much. How do we know we can't do just as well by spending $100,000 less each month?"

"Mort! I know how our customers think! I'm telling you that you need to be in their faces each time they pick up a newspaper, turn on the radio, or watch a TV commercial. Once you cut your exposure back, even for a month, your customers are going to forget you even existed!"

"Well, we obviously don't want that, Lenny. But isn't there some way we can control this advertising number so we can save a few thousand dollars?"

"Not if you want the revenue . . . ."

Mort wanted the revenue and Lenny wanted his advertising budget, but for two entirely different reasons.

Mort knew there were some inefficiencies in his expense ratios. He also knew that the cushion provided by additional revenue covered a great deal of operating sins. The size of his advertising expense budget was one of those operating sins. Mort figured that as long as the cash flow was available to pay for those operating sins, it really wouldn't matter if the advertising expense ratio was out of line. Mort could learn to live with the advertising budget as long as Lenny continued getting the great results.

Lenny walked away from the meeting with Mort, feeling relieved for the moment. The advertising business was every bit as stressful as he knew it would be. Just as he had to fight with Mort for every nickel of the advertising budget, he also had to battle for every penny of his $85,000 a year salary. The salary was hardly worth the stress and it was not enough for Lenny.

What did make the job worth the stress was the $1,500 per lunch meeting fee that account representatives paid Lenny every Friday. Just like his elected congressman, Lenny reasoned there was only so much time in his day. If your business was advertising and you wanted to talk about how Lenny should spend his advertising budget, you paid him for the time.

The risks in bigger businesses are not fundamentally different from their smaller entrepreneurial counterparts. It is only the size of the risk and the impact of the mistake that make them distinctive. That absolute size is the reason why you need to scrutinize every single expense.

LOOK AT OTHER EXPENSES TOO

LESSON

BE SURE TO KEEP YOUR GOOD CUSTOMERS WHEN YOU DECREASE YOUR EXPENSES.

Reducing the absolute size of normal and customary business expenses can be a great way to reduce the risk in your business. Although the "meat cleaver" approach to expense reduction can be messy and has a tendency to produce unanticipated and unpredictable results, it usually works.

The reductions, however, must be sensible. When you start reducing expenses that affect the quality of product purchased by your customers, an unintended result will be the loss of your customers.

Andy owned a chain of six franchised restaurants with annual gross revenues of $4.5 million. The chain's consolidated pretax profit was $38,000. That net profit was less than 1 percent of gross revenues! Andy's restaurants were not his best investments for a variety of reasons.

Andy located each restaurant in a free-standing building on the grounds of a large shopping center. Andy leased each of his facilities on a percentage rent basis. Every lease agreement with a percentage rent feature starts with a high fixed monthly rent. As revenues increase, rent is recomputed using the percentage specified in the lease agreement. The lease agreement said that Andy must pay the larger of the two figures. Those lease agreements effectively made Andy's landlords his uninvited partners on each additional dollar of revenue the restaurants produced.

Employee turnover in the restaurant business is a fact of life. Few employees who start their careers by washing pots, dishes, and glassware want to be doing the same kind of work six months later. A restaurant operation can still be profitable as long as the employee turnover rate is not excessive.

Restaurant employees work six months on the average before quitting their job. That average length of employment is equivalent to an employee turnover rate of 200 percent. Andy's average annual employee turnover rate was nearly 400 percent. Andy's percentage was approximately twice the industry average. It also meant that each of Andy's 187 employees worked about three months before leaving his business.

Rent and payroll had a heavy impact on Andy's income statement; so did his utility costs. Andy had the option to bargain for more economical gas cooking facilities during his initial lease negotiations, but declined to do so. As a result, four of his locations had expensive-to-operate, poorly designed, electric cooking facilities that operated fifteen hours a day.

One restaurant was losing $10,000 per month. Three of his locations were just breaking even. The lease on another, his flagship location, was up for renewal and the landlord wanted to take back 50 percent of the net leasable space.

After eight years of building restaurant revenues, Andy recognized that expense control was the immediate key to his corporate survival. Andy focused on his single largest cost element: the price of food. Andy's expense-reduction program came from the mouths of his customers. Hotel food and beverage directors call it *portion control*.

In Andy's portion-control program, he did not change his menu prices. Instead, he downsized the glasses, plates, and hamburgers. He sliced bread thinner. He discarded ice cream spades in favor of a three-quarter-ounce scoop. He even halved the bananas in the banana splits!

Table servers who had listened to Andy's "No Extra Pickles" speech declined customer special requests with impunity.

> "Good afternoon! May I take your order?"
>
> "I'll have your club sandwich and a cup of coffee."
>
> "How do you drink your coffee?"
>
> "I usually pick up the cup in my right hand and bring it to my lips. If it's hot, I drink it very slowly."
>
> "Excuse me, please?"
>
> "I'm just kidding. Black coffee is fine. Say, would you mind giving me an extra pickle? I just love your pickles and club sandwiches!"
>
> "Oh, I'm sorry, but we don't have any extra pickles . . . ."
>
> "No extra pickles? You're kidding me! You mean to tell me that there's no way I can get a second pickle?"
>
> "Well, I guess you could order a second club sandwich. That way, you'd have a pickle for each sandwich . . . ."

Where their stomachs are concerned, customers are not stupid. Andy's regular customers started looking for other lunchtime options.

As his restaurant business declined further, so did Andy's interest in it. In the months that followed, Andy ignored his core business.

When Andy finally made meaningful risk adjustments, they were serious and costly. Andy closed three of his locations. The landlord at Andy's most profitable location took back 50 percent of the space. Andy was left with a shell of a business that could not support his administrative overhead. He closed his corporate offices and moved the records to storage closets at his three remaining restaurants.

The risk that reducing certain expenses will also reduce customer revenue was one that Andy had not even considered. Andy will now agree that it is far less expensive to keep an existing customer than to find a new one.

Competence in the area of controlling business risk can come at too high a price and will almost certainly come too late if you insist on learning exclusively through your mistakes. That is true even if you are a quick learner.

You may be better off looking to other professionals for skills to supplement the ones you do not already have. Working with professionals can be the answer to many of your business problems. It can also be an eye-opening experience!

PART SEVEN

Working with Professionals

WORKING WITH PROFESSIONALS • LIVING WITH CONTRACTS AND DOCUMENTS • THE TAXMAN COMETH

27 WORKING WITH PROFESSIONALS

- ➤ Self-Taught Brain Surgeons.
- ➤ Establish the Boundaries.
- ➤ Get a Written Fee Estimate.
- ➤ Engagements Are Not Forever.
- ➤ Who Coaches the Coach?

When you need a job done for which you have the skills but do not have the time, you need an employee. When you need a job done for which you have the time but do not have the skills, you need a professional.

A professional is anyone who has skills that you do not and consistently gets the job done.

Professionals may or may not be entrepreneurs, but they are masters of one or more skills. It is their expertise in a narrow field that makes professionals useful to you.

The measure of a professional is not just the size of the bill he delivers. It is whether he delivers on time what you and he agreed he should deliver at the price on which you agreed.

Some professionals will insist on a thorough understanding of your requirements before making any decision to work with you. They want to determine if the proposed scope of your engagement is within their technical ability.

There are other professionals who will work with you knowing they cannot deliver. All these professionals want to know is how you will pay their bill.

One type of professional wants to see you make your business your best investment. The other type of professional has no interest in any business but his own.

Despite the risk of hiring one kind of professional when you need the other, there are more reasons to use professionals in your business than there are reasons to avoid them.

The option of using professionals makes you efficient. That means you can pay attention to your core business instead of developing a nodding acquaintance of limited utility in a narrow field.

Even though you may be capable of developing a specialized expertise given enough time, it may not be practical or desirable. Your business and your customers will certainly not wait for you to meet minimum proficiency standards in an area that requires an immediate answer.

An unprofitable business is the more likely result of insisting you can do everything by yourself.

SELF-TAUGHT BRAIN SURGEONS

LESSON

SELF-TAUGHT BRAIN SURGERY IS EXPENSIVE
EVEN FOR THOSE INDIVIDUALS WHO CAN AFFORD
TO PAY FOR THEIR MISTAKES.

There are more than a few entrepreneurs who have convinced themselves they have read everything on the subject of brain surgery. Self-taught brain surgeons ignore their own limitations and the availability of professionals.

You can readily recognize self-taught brain surgeons by the bloody mess they have made of their business.

There are severe limitations to self-taught brain surgery. It is one matter to demonstrate that you know how to hold the proper end of a scalpel. It is entirely another matter to use that scalpel without harming your patient.

Macklin was a self-taught brain surgeon who owned a coffee business. He got there by starting a restaurant. When Mack's coffee sales exceeded his food sales for the seventh consecutive month, Mack closed the restaurant and opened a facility to roast, package, and sell his coffee.

Mack's first production facility was in a downtown basement room. The space was affordable and it was cheaper to pay the on-street parking tickets than it was to rent private parking stalls.

In the center of the room was a coffee roaster the size of a two-story furnace.

"Mack! Am I ever glad I'm not your landlord! What on Earth is that machine sticking through your basement ceiling?"

"It's our new commercial coffee roaster from Denmark."

"It looks more like a two-story stainless steel house."

"It sure is a big one. We can roast 600 pounds of coffee an hour in that machine."

"How much coffee do you sell?"

"Well, it varies. I'd say about 2,000 to 3,000 pounds a month. Say, 100 pounds a day."

"So, running your roaster for an hour a week gives you all the roasted beans you need for the week?"

"That's right."

"What's that piece of equipment over there?"

"That is our vac-u-pack machine. We used to shovel coffee into packages and twist-tie them. Whatever the stores didn't sell in two weeks would be returned to us. That vac-u-pack machine now takes all the air out of our packages. That extends the freshness and shelf life of our packaged product from two weeks to two years."

"How does it work?"

"Let me show you. You put the beans in this eight-ounce bag, put it over here, press the pedal, and presto! You have just locked in freshness! Here, catch . . . ."

The throw was a poor one and I missed the catch. I picked the package up off the floor.

"This is a great looking package. I like the design work. How many of these can you fill in an hour?"

"If we have someone operating the machine who knows what he's doing, we can do between three and four packages a minute."

"About 100 pounds an hour?"

"I never thought of it that way before, but that's about right."

"So, running your vac-u-pack for an hour a day seals all the eight-ounce packages you can sell in a month?"

"Yes."

"Mack, what happens when your volume increases?"

"We'll fill the orders. We've got the capacity . . . ."

"Just like that?"

"Sure! We don't need to buy any more equipment. We planned for future growth by buying the best and the largest capacity equipment we could afford."

"And you put it in a 1,500-square-foot basement . . . ."

"So?"

"Mack, you're busting out of this place. At your current level of production, you're already stepping on each other's feet, not to mention the coffee beans that you spill on the floor. When you have it turned on, the roaster makes it so hot down here that you could sell facials as another business!"

Mack was in a process-oriented business that required a production line, production standards, and time and motion studies. Mack had never read the *Handbook of Industrial Engineering* and had his own ideas about the way coffee beans should be roasted, ground, and packaged. When Mack moved to a larger facility, he took his production problems with him.

"Mack, if I didn't know any better, I'd think we were on the inside of a 7,000-square-foot Pachinko game."

"What do you mean?"

"Your raw materials get delivered in 100-pound bags over there. You move them across the plant to the roaster and then halfway back to the grinder. After the beans are ground, you move them in garbage cans to your vac-u-pack machine. When everything's done, you store the finished product back by the roaster."

"I already know what you're going to say. Getting at the finished goods inventory is not any problem. We just back our delivery trucks through the plant and load them up."

"Mack, a four-cylinder car running on three pistons is more efficient than this layout! Why didn't you retain an industrial engineer with experience in facility layout and production scheduling?"

"We couldn't afford one."

Affordability is a lame excuse for a bad decision. It is expensive when you must live with the consequences of a job that has never been done right.

Getting the job done properly is just one more reason why you may wish to work with a professional.

Once you make a decision to work with a professional, take time to establish some boundaries.

ESTABLISH THE BOUNDARIES

LESSON

MANAGE YOUR PROFESSIONAL ADVISOR
WITH WRITTEN BOUNDARIES.

Professionals are experts in their fields. They do not need you to tell them how to do their jobs. They do need you, however, to tell them which job to do.

That is why it is important to discuss the scope of any job in advance. Scoping the job establishes boundaries. Boundaries make the job easier to manage and the result easier to measure.

Boundaries also avoid unpleasant surprises. Where you thought you engaged an architect to redesign your office lobby, you now have a fifteen-pound set of blueprints for a twenty-acre regional office business center.

An engagement without boundaries is clearly reflected in the shock value of the bill you are asked to pay.

Any professional worth his billing rate will insist on a boundary discussion. Most professionals will take the time to draft an engagement letter. In it, a professional will restate your boundaries as he believes he heard them from you. When a professional has not drafted an engagement letter, it is a bad sign for several reasons.

Engaging a professional without a letter of understanding signed by both you and he suggests that there is no understanding. Any understanding that may exist is certainly open to interpretation. If a professional cannot articulate the scope of your work, then he probably cannot accomplish the work.

The absence of an engagement letter does not make your professional advisor any less qualified in his own specialty. It simply demonstrates that he is unconcerned about limiting the amount of fees he will charge you.

It is a simple problem to overcome. Draft your own engagement letter and have your professional advisor sign it.

Include a starting date and a completion date. If a completion date is critical to you, put a penalty clause of $500 per day for each day that is overrun. Outline as clearly as possible the work that you need done. If it is a long-term project with many phases, briefly outline the scope of each phase.

Always state under what circumstances the engagement will end. If all goes well, the engagement will terminate with the completion of the job. That is not always the case.

State how you determine the amount of the professional fee and how you will pay it. It is not unusual to pay an advance retainer when you engage any professional. This retainer shows you are serious about starting the job promptly. Paying a retainer also gets a professional's immediate attention. Subsequent progress payments by you are also fine as long as the job is on schedule.

Never, never, never pay for the full amount of a job in advance of its completion.

GET A WRITTEN FEE ESTIMATE

LESSON

REQUIRE YOUR PROFESSIONAL ADVISOR
TO PUT HIS FEE ESTIMATE IN WRITING.

Do not embarrass yourself at a later date by avoiding the fee discussion today. Ask how you will be billed and at what rate. Make sure you agree with the answer.

The professional fees you pay will usually have some correlation to the scope and the complexity of the work. When you cannot receive a clear answer about the cost of an engagement, do not retain the professional. You have either done a poor job in establishing the boundaries of the work or you are being positioned to be milked for whatever you are worth.

Never proceed with an unwritten fee schedule once you have established the scope of the work.

One law firm agreed to complete some standard legal work for a customer. The law firm quoted a $2,800 fee estimate. The actual bill was over $14,000.

Without a written fee schedule to which he could point, the customer was in a dilemma. He faced a bill so outrageous he could not pay it. He also faced a deadline that he could not miss. The compromise was still $10,000 over the initial fee estimate.

Another customer agreed to pay for all out-of-pocket expenses including telephone calls made on his behalf by his marketing advisor. After a brief afternoon call, the advisor forgot to clear the line on his cellular phone. That kept the phone "on the air" and the cellular time charges still running. The line finally disconnected when the cellular phone's nickel cadmium battery exhausted its charge eight hours later. The marketing advisor invoiced the customer $360 for that one local telephone call.

You do not need to look too hard for bargain-priced professionals. You will find them everywhere.

The damage these professionals inflict beyond their bill is sometimes difficult to see, but it is there. These professionals are a bargain for one reason. The marketplace has valued their advice at substandard rates! That should tell you something about their advice.

When you engage one of these professionals and he fails to deliver, you have more than yourself to blame. You must also engage and pay a second professional. That adds financial injury to insult.

Cheap professional help is always expensive. Competent professional help may be your least expensive alternative.

You may believe that it would be easier for you to use professionals if the profit and loss impact of paying their related fees was not so immediate. If that is your view, it is incorrect.

A professional's contribution to your equity should far exceed its cost.

An experienced professional with whom you have developed a satisfactory relationship is a nondepreciable asset to your business.

The fees that you pay to that professional are a long-term investment in your business. The benefit that results from good professional advice will stay with your business for years into the future. So will the resulting wealth that accumulates.

That is why it is better for you to use professionals when you first need them instead of deferring the decision to a later year.

Besides, you will not pay this professional forever.

ENGAGEMENTS ARE NOT FOREVER

LESSON

A PROFESSIONAL ADVISOR CAN EITHER DIE A NATURAL DEATH AT THE END OF AN ENGAGEMENT OR BE FIRED BY YOU BEFORE THAT TIME.

A professional is finished when he completes the job for which he was hired. He is also finished when he is unable to complete the job.

When you retain professionals, you expect them to deliver results. You are paying professional fees in exchange for this expectation. That does not mean to suggest that you should expect the impossible from each engagement. After all, there are limits to what any professional can do for you and for your business.

When professionals do not deliver what they have agreed to deliver or when they demonstrate they are unprofessional, give them their walking papers.

A defect is a defect, whether it is a service or a product. You would not dream of paying for telephone service that kept disconnecting every two minutes. Ma Bell would not expect you to!

Nevertheless, I am amazed at the number of entrepreneurs who continue to retain and pay unprofessional and ineffective advisors.

Hank had a pension plan for his business. Each year, an actuary estimated Hank's annual pension plan contribution. The actuary also prepared a report that Hank needed to file with his pension plan's annual tax return. Professional fees for this work were about $900 a year.

"Norbert, do you have the contribution estimate for me so I can make my defined benefit pension plan contribution this year?"

"Oh, Hank! I got your letter last week and was just getting ready to call you. When do you need this information?"

"My tax year ends in six weeks. Sometime between now and then is fine. Maybe a little sooner than later just in case I need to get some money together."

"Great! I'll be calling you in a couple of days."

Five weeks later:

"Norbert, you never got back to me! I need to know my pension plan contribution amounts by Friday. That's my year end!"

"Oh, Hank. I was just getting ready to call you. A part broke on my computer about a month ago and I've had to order a replacement for it."

"Norbert, I'm sorry to hear about your computer, but I need this information in three days. Can't you borrow some other computer and load your program?"

"Say, that's an idea! But I still need the amount of your expected salary for the year to do the computation."

"Norbert, I gave that to you over six weeks ago in my letter!"

"Oh that's right. I seem to recall seeing that information. Say, would you mind giving it to me again? I've looked all over the place, but I can't seem to find your file."

The last day of the tax year:

"Norbert, it's four o'clock. Do you have the numbers I need?"

"Oh, Hank! I was just getting ready to call you. I had a late lunch and a meeting right after that. I've got your number."

"Great! What is it?"

"$2,000."

"$2,000?!"

"That's the number . . . ."

"How did you figure that, Norbert?"

"Well, I know it's around here someplace, but I never did find your file. I just remembered though, that the maximum amount you can put into your individual retirement account is $2,000, regardless of your earnings."

"Norbert, my pension plan isn't an individual retirement account . . . ."

"It isn't?"

Competence for any professional is the rule, not the exception. At the first sign of its absence, get rid of your advisor.

WHO COACHES THE COACH?

LESSON

A COACH CAN SEE THE POTENTIAL
AND THE LIMIT OF YOUR TALENT
FAR MORE CLEARLY THAN YOU CAN.

There is yet another reason to seek out professionals. Even a coach needs coaching.

If you have employees building your equity, you are busy coaching them. The moment you stop coaching or the moment your coaching becomes ineffective, a finely tuned machine grinds to a halt. How can you run your business, plan for your future, motivate your employees, and still build equity?

Your coach will tell you how.

Not every entrepreneur has the kind of business record he would agree to make public. A coach will tell you how to improve your record and how to reallocate your limited resources. He will also tell you how to improve your coaching. If you listen to him, your coach will limit your losses and counsel you through them.

There are also a few times that a coach will bring you gently back to Earth.

"Lindey, it's six o'clock Saturday morning! Why do you look like a bunch of hooligans roughed you up and left you by my front door?"

"Mark, bill me your weekend rates for this meeting. I've got some terrible news! I just got canned by the Spitler account!"

"No kidding?"

"Do I look like I'm joking?"

"Lindey, you look awful!"

"Actually, I look much better than I feel. I found out last night and just drove around in shock. I've been parked in your driveway since three o'clock this morning waiting for you to get your paper."

"Hey, come on in! The kids are still asleep. Let's go out back and talk this over."

And we did. Spitler Chemicals had written a nasty note. No wonder Lindey felt lost. In a three-page blast, Spitler suggested that Lindey take a long walk off a short pier.

"Lindey, that's some piece of fan mail!"

"There goes my business."

"Why do you say that?"

"Are you kidding me? Spitler is 75 percent of my gross billings. I might as well just close my office. Are you any good at preparing resumes?"

"Slow down Lindey. Either you have an imagination that has run to the moon or I'm just not reading this right."

"Huh?"

"Spitler doesn't say anything about disengaging. He sounds upset and has given you a 19-point list of things you have not done that bother him, but I don't see where it says you're out of business."

"What?"

"Lindey, when was the last time you met with Spitler?"

"I talked to him over the phone two months ago. The account executive that I have servicing him talks to him just about every week."

"Spitler is 75 percent of your revenues and you haven't talked to him for two months?"

"No . . . ."

"That's the problem! He thinks you don't care!"

"But we've had great results with the program we set up for him!"

"The results of the program are not his complaints. This guy is screaming for personal attention. Why haven't you called him?"

"I'm beginning to see what you mean."

"Look, the kids are up. Let's eat some breakfast and figure out what you're going to say to Spitler today, OK?"

"Yeah. Thanks coach . . . ."

A coach's coach needs more than a knowledge of your business. Your coach needs a feeling for you, the holes you can dig for yourself, and the greatness you can achieve. When you have been properly coached, you will run your business like any other athletic team with state championship potential.

Qualified professionals have the capability of reducing your business risk. You will discover that using them is a cost-effective way to add task-specific skills that are otherwise absent from your management team.

Another way to reduce that risk without reducing your return is through the use of well-drafted contracts and documents. All you need is a lawyer.

28

LIVING WITH CONTRACTS AND DOCUMENTS

- Remember Who Wrote the Document.
- Watch Those Inadvertent Omissions.
- Here Is a Worthless Agreement.
- Sign Your Copy.
- Prepare for Your Deposition.

God took the time to write the Ten Commandments. He gave them to Moses, who read them, then promptly broke them into little pieces. God then gave Moses a second set of Ten Commandments. Only Moses and God will ever know what was in that first draft.

Clerics will tell us that the Law is without interpretation. It is a contract between Man and Divinity, written by God. Attorneys would thoroughly enjoy being paid a fee to argue either side of the previous statements.

How much contract law can you write on two stone tablets?

One problem that entrepreneurs face that Moses did not is that God is usually unavailable when you need to draft a document.

Thomas Jefferson would have been a good second choice, but he put down his quill in 1826.

Major law firms are out of the question. Anything less than a $10,000 retainer will only buy you a paralegal and a Styrofoam cup of coffee.

The choice left for most entrepreneurs is the sole practitioner or small-practice law office. These alternatives are usually affordable. They are not bad alternatives when you need to draft an agreement or review a document. Just be sure your attorney does the job properly.

REMEMBER WHO WROTE THE DOCUMENT

LESSON

READ EVERY WORD IN A CONTRACT BEFORE YOU SIGN IT.

Reading contracts has never been exciting work, especially for a non-attorney. The contracts look to be 80 percent longer than you might require.

Notwithstanding the foregoing, you may also need *Black's Law Dictionary* just to understand the terminology. In any case, the length of a document is always sufficient to justify the legal fees.

The days of doing business on a handshake were left behind the moment God gave Moses those stone tablets. The Ten Commandments were etched in stone for the reason that most people can no longer be trusted to keep their verbal agreements.

That comparison is not lost on entrepreneurs. Entrepreneurs build equity, in many instances, on margins so fine that there is just no room to absorb any loss through agreement disputes.

That is why I read every document that anyone asks me to sign.

An attorney will draft a contract to protect the interests of the party who pays for the work. Therefore, when I receive any contract, I read every word in it.

One party to the contract has taken time to have counsel state in a formal manner his understanding of an agreement. I want to be sure that it is also my understanding of the agreement.

If the contract provides for penalties if I fail to perform under the agreement, I want the other party to pay penalties if he fails to perform. If I am in breach of the contract and I am responsible for damages, then I want the other party to be at risk for an equal amount of damages if he is in breach of the contract provisions.

If the document does not reflect my sense of fairness, then I take the liberty of rewriting it. If the document does not represent my understanding of the agreement, then I also rewrite it.

If exhibits accompany the contract, then I read the exhibits. If the exhibits are incorrect, then I provide my own exhibits. If an attorney will compile the exhibits at a later date, then I will sign the contract at a later date.

If a specific name identifies one party to the agreement, then I make certain that name is consistent throughout the contract. If the signature of the party is different from the party described in the contract, then I will not sign the contract until an attorney makes the correction.

If no one has taken the time to draft a contract, then I prepare the first draft. An attorney will finesse the finer points of the document for me at a later time.

I know that an advantage goes to the side who drafts any contract. An advantage also goes to the party who is the last to sign the contract.

You should never expect an attorney who does not represent your interests to advise you of the contents of any legal document. After all, the attorney is being paid by the other party to the contract.

Most attorneys will stop at nothing to be certain that the interests of their cash-paying clients prevail over yours. I do not mean to suggest that this behavior is unexpected, unwarranted, or unethical. The legal profession, however, has been known to have its fair share of bad apples.

A story I recently heard confirms the widespread extent of the divergence of a few legal practitioners from any known set of ethical standards.

A pope and an attorney died. They appeared before St. Peter at the Gates of Heaven. St. Peter reviewed their qualifications, admitted them both, and assigned a few angels to handle their orientation program.

A few days later, the pope ran into St. Peter.

"Excuse me, St. Peter. May I speak with you for a minute?"

"Sure! What is on your mind?"

"Well, I don't exactly know how to say this. I like being here. The studio apartment you gave me has a heavenly view and the food is out of this world . . . ."

"Is something wrong?"

"Forgive me for appearing ungrateful, St. Peter, but do you remember that attorney who arrived the same day I did?"

"Boy, do I ever!"

"Well, I noticed that he has a whole suite of rooms, a fully stocked liquor cabinet, room service, three cable TVs, and a choir of angels that sing just for him . . . ."

"And?"

"St. Peter, I was a pope! He was just an attorney! Perhaps there was some confusion when we were admitted and the room assignments were reversed . . . ."

"Heck, there wasn't any confusion. We have dozens of popes up here. We've only got one attorney!"

There is no point in avoiding attorneys just because good ones can sometimes be hard to find. There are times when you will require their talents and will suffer great risks without their counsel.

Unfortunately, you should not expect even an attorney who represents your interests to do his job perfectly.

WATCH THOSE INADVERTENT OMISSIONS

LESSON

MAKE SURE YOUR RIGHTS UNDER ANY AGREEMENT ARE JUST AS STRONG AS THE RIGHTS OF THE OTHER PARTY TO THE AGREEMENT.

Wadlow sold a business for $17 million. The buyer's attorney drafted a forty-seven-page contract. When the proper exhibits were attached, the document was over two inches thick. Wadlow's attorney made no substantive changes to the document. Three months and $107,000 of legal fees later, his attorney put the deal to bed.

Putting a deal to bed can be like putting a two-year-old child down for the night. The amount of maneuvering can be incredible. You may also find your patience pushed to new limits. Even after the deal and the child are both in bed, neither one needs a good reason to fall out of it.

The buyer requested that a retainage of $250,000 be kept in escrow for a six-month period following the sale. The buyer designed the retainage to cover good faith disputes that might arise between him and Wadlow after the sale date. Wadlow agreed with the request.

Six months after closing, the buyer claimed the full amount of the retainage. The buyer argued that an unusual amount of activity had occurred in the company during the thirty-day period prior to closing. That activity allegedly depleted working capital.

More specifically, the buyer argued that the collection efforts directed at past-due accounts receivables were outside the normal course of business. Those efforts entitled the buyer to claim the full amount of the retainage.

I do not understand why collecting past-due receivables is outside the normal course of any business. Nevertheless, the new owners and their paid legal representative persisted in their efforts to claim the retainage.

Wadlow's reaction was to file a counterclaim for a similar amount detailing other claims against the buyer. Wadlow had a long list of equally valid claims.

Unfortunately, Wadlow's legal representative goofed. While reviewing the preliminary documents, Wadlow's attorney failed to provide a provision that would have permitted Wadlow to present these counterclaims.

Wadlow had two remaining alternatives.

He could fight a full-blown legal battle with depositions, preliminary hearings, examinations, cross-examinations, continuances, and a respectable stack of legal bills. Financing the legal profession was not Wadlow's idea of building wealth.

Wadlow could also submit the whole disagreement to binding arbitration. Wadlow's risks under arbitration were the same risks as the buyer's. Each stood to gain a little and perhaps to lose a lot.

They made their final agreement outside arbitration but not without considerable table pounding. The buyer kept $85,000 of the retainage and returned $165,000 to Wadlow. Wadlow agrees that he could have done without this $85,000 lesson.

It is not enough for a legal document to list your rights under a specific agreement. The other party to the agreement must also acknowledge that those rights are part of the agreement. Without that acknowledgment, you have a worthless agreement.

HERE IS A WORTHLESS AGREEMENT

LESSON

DO NOT WASTE TIME WITH AGREEMENTS IF YOU PERMIT NONSENSICAL REVISIONS TO THEM.

There are risks in using agreements, even if they have been properly drafted to protect your interests. One of those risks is the risk of modification. If the other party to an agreement modifies the agreement, signs it, and you fail to note the modification, you may have a worthless agreement.

A local advertising agency wanted to run some radio advertising schedules for a client. The station that they selected required the agency to sign a broadcast contract for $11,250.

If you have ever seen a broadcast contract, you will note that on the back of an 8$^{1}/_{2}$ x 11-inch piece of paper, a twenty-page contract has been photographically reproduced.

The contract is written in print that can only be read with a magnifying glass and in language that only an attorney can understand. The contract specifies payment terms, penalties, and other bad things that can happen if you ever default on the contract.

The agency modified the contract, then signed the front of the document.

The production department made the commercials. The traffic department scheduled the commercials. The payroll department computed the commission and paid the salesperson. The radio station ran the commercials. The accounts receivable department issued the invoice.

Six months later, the agency still had not paid a dime of their invoice.

After summoning the courage to sue the agency, the station received a fundamental lesson in contract law. Much to the embarrassment of the station manager, the station's legal representative pointed out that a statement had been added on the front of the document. In bold lettering and in language that most fifth-graders can read, it said:

"Back of contract does not apply because I have not read it."

That was the end of the collection efforts.

SIGN YOUR COPY

LESSON

SIGN LEGAL DOCUMENTS WHEN THEY SAY WHAT YOU WANT THEM TO SAY.

Lawton wanted a new employment agreement as a general manager with an annual salary of $105,000. The company owners agreed to Lawton's request and signed the employment agreement with him.

Lawton also wanted a second agreement. In that agreement, he would receive a bonus if the company was ever sold. Lawton drafted a preliminary document. The company's legal firm revised the document and then delivered it in draft form to Lawton for his review and comment.

Lawton did not think much of the document. If the company was sold, he would only receive a bonus equal to his annual compensation at the time of the sale. Lawton believed he should be entitled to a bonus twice the size of the amount offered by the owners of the company. As a result, he would not agree to sign the bonus agreement as it was written. The company would not change the document. Lawton effectively tabled the matter.

Two years later, the company agreed to sell its operations at a considerable profit. Lawton remembered the unsigned draft document and moved to establish his rights to a bonus. He signed the draft copy of the bonus agreement and delivered it to the owners.

The owners had reservations about honoring a proposal that was in draft form and had never been finalized. Lawton's signature was the only one on the document.

In the face of their indecision, Lawton hired an attorney to block the sale three days before it was scheduled to close.

The sellers, who employed Lawton, wanted to close the deal but not under Lawton's blackmail economics.

The buyer, and Lawton's future employer, also wanted to close the deal but was prevented from doing so by Lawton's lawsuit.

Lawton wanted a bonus but also wanted to keep his job.

Lawton could have continued to block the sale at the expense of considerable legal fees. That would have stopped the seller from converting his business wealth to cash. If the delaying tactic was effective, it might have made the buyer go away. As a consequence of his own actions, Lawton would then not receive any bonus!

There was also a good chance that Lawton would lose his job if a sale did not occur. He had worn his welcome thin when he filed his first lawsuit against his employer.

If Lawton filed a second wrongful discharge suit, it would be lengthy, costly, and have an unpredictable outcome.

The buyer contacted Lawton the night before the sale was scheduled to close and gave him an ultimatum: Drop the lawsuit or there would be no deal.

Lawton had a looming sense of disaster. He also had a fully mortgaged home and no personal savings. With these prominent risks in mind, Lawton folded the lawsuit. The deal closed, and the buyer renewed Lawton's employment agreement.

Lawton learned that blocking the transfer of risk from a seller to a buyer is an act that is not without its own risk. It is like standing in the middle of an expressway trying to stop traffic. Drivers will ogle you and drivers will curse you, but they will never stop until you step into their path. Unless there is a return commensurate with that risk, you are far better off just staying in your car.

Other points are not as obvious, but they are equally important.

The law was written to benefit those who can find competent legal advisors. A competent legal advisor can usually make the law do whatever his client wants the law to do.

That is why you should sign any legal document that you have requested and that has been properly prepared by your legal advisor. An unsigned legal document is hardly worth the paper on which it has been written.

There is also a time and a place for you to have a legal advisor represent your interests. That time is when no amateur representative will do. You have just been subpoenaed to appear at a deposition.

PREPARE FOR YOUR DEPOSITION

LESSON

YOU CAN ONLY LOSE A CASE IN A DEPOSITION.

You cannot avoid being deposed. It is a fact of business life, however unpleasant. You cannot avoid it even if you manage your business at the highest level of moral and ethical standards. Suppose there is a contract dispute because one of your suppliers or customers does not share your sense of responsibility and fair play. When a contract involves a large dollar amount and the dispute cannot be resolved through sensible discussion, you may be deposed.

The way your stomach behaves will tell you if you should worry.

A deposition is an exercise in legal maneuvering. You will be astonished at the level of foolishness involved. It is also the judicial system's way of permitting each party in a dispute to have an opportunity to obtain all of the relevant facts.

The deposing attorney is not your friend. He will make note of your dress and demeanor. He has only one job. That job is to identify any possible inconsistency in your testimony or claim. If you are inconsistent about little things, it may be the result of a memory lapse. It may also be because you lie about little things. If you lie about little things, the deposing attorney will assume that you also lie about big things.

Whatever you do, tell the truth. Answer questions to the best of your ability, but do not offer any information that is not specifically requested. If you are asked, "Do you know the time?"the answer is "Yes." Do not answer, "Yes. It's three o'clock."

Never bring anything with you into the deposition. Your briefcase, your address book, your wallet or purse, and any relevant documents should all stay at home.

Be prepared to stay a while. The more inexperienced the deposing attorney, the longer the deposition. If the deposing attorney begins by reading his questions to you, call your spouse during the next break. You may be home late for dinner.

A deposition is not the place to argue your case. Do not be tempted to make any legal points in your testimony. Legal points should be made in court by your attorney. You can only lose a case in a deposition.

A court reporter will transcribe your testimony. She may also record it. She will look at you so intensely throughout your testimony that you will wonder if a horn has finally sprouted from your head. Do not be alarmed. It is the court reporter's way of being sure that no spoken word is inadvertently excluded from the record. I have seen some court reporters who are so well trained that they do not even appear to blink.

You have no obligation to study for your deposition, although your attorney may suggest that some review of the relevant facts may be useful. Your attorney may recommend that for every hour in a deposition, you should invest an equal hour of preparation.

Some recall of the facts is useful. Otherwise, later memory lapses may not be believable. This is especially true if you intend to remember a key fact or two at a later time to strengthen your case.

You also have no obligation to remember events, dates, and conversations. If you cannot remember, say so. The following truthful responses are all acceptable:

"I don't remember at this time."

"I can't recall at this time."

"I don't understand."

"Yes."

"No."

"I don't know."

History is a function of those who write it. The deposing attorney knows this and will frequently try to recapture your testimony with a remark such as: "So, Ms. Rendlemen, what you have said is this . . . ." Take the time to correct the statement and enter your version of history into the record: "No, what I said before is more accurate . . . ."

You should bring an attorney to your deposition even if you must pay for his professional time. Your attorney will protect you from leading questions and other badgering techniques specifically designed to hammer at the integrity of your testimony. Your attorney will also object to intimidating tactics and other procedural issues that you cannot possibly anticipate.

Peter Hampton was a residential building contractor who arrived for his deposition at the federal courthouse promptly at 9:00 A.M.

"Mr. Hampton, I'm Lisa Thornhill from the law offices of Thornhill, Atwood, and MacCorkle. We are here to take your testimony with respect to the case that has been filed. You have been sworn in. Would you please state your name for the record?"

"My name is Peter Hampton."

"Are you being represented by counsel?"

"No." (BIG Mistake.)

"Has anyone coached you for this deposition?"

"What do you mean by 'coached'?"

"Have you been instructed how to respond to questions in your deposition?"

"No."

"Have you ever been deposed before?"
"Yes."
"When did that occur?"
"About fifteen years ago."
"Where did that occur?"
"I was living in Cleveland at the time, so it would have occurred there."
"Could you describe for the record the matter as you recall it?"
"It was such a long time ago. I simply don't recall why I was deposed. I seem to remember that the deposition lasted fifteen minutes and my typed testimony may have been only the equivalent of one or two pages."
"Was that deposition relating to any contract dispute?"
"I simply don't recall at this time. You must of course realize that since that time there have been four summer Olympics. Three presidents also served their full terms in the White House. As I previously stated, it occurred a long time ago."
"Would it be fair to say that you were deposed for a construction matter?"
"I don't believe I was in construction at the time. I just don't have any recollection of why I was deposed . . . ."

As a practical matter, depositions are private records without any index. If you do not volunteer a previous transcript, opposing counsel has neither the resources, ingenuity, nor time to locate the old transcripts.

Opposing counsel may not like the answers you provide them. Some will interject "Well, I will have to just start my questioning again until you may have reason to recall."

Take your time and then tell them, "I'm prepared to spend this entire week answering your questions truthfully and to the best of my ability. I hope that's acceptable to you." If you know their departure schedule involves taking a 4:30 P.M. flight out of town, your remark can be unnerving.

Avoid sarcasm. It simply does not read well in the record.

"Where do you work, sir?"
"Where I work depends on what I am asked to do."
"Would you describe that for me, please?"
"I am a general contractor who builds residential housing for different customers."
"Can you tell me where that would be?"
"All of my work is in this county."
"Would it be fair to say that all of your work is in Deerfield County?"
"That would be correct."
"Sir, can you tell me your experience in the construction industry?"
"I build four to seven custom homes a year. I have been doing that for approximately the last ten years."
"Would it be fair to say that you first started building in 1984?"
"I would have started in this business somewhere in the mid-1980s."
"Could you be more specific?"
"As I previously stated, I don't recall the specific date, but it was

approximately ten years ago. My license, however, is a matter of public record. You could consult the contractor's licensing division at the state office and find the exact date."

"Would it be fair to say that you started building in 1983?"

"I don't recall the specific date at this time. However, it would have been after I received my contractor's license."

"Could you tell me when that would have been?"

"It could have been in 1984 or 1985. It may have been in 1986, but I seem to recall receiving my license in the early spring."

"So it would be fair to say that you received your license in the middle of a job you started at the beginning of that year."

"Yes . . .(pause) . . .No! In Deerfield County, it would be illegal to represent yourself as a general contractor without having the proper license approval. I don't specifically recall saying that I had a job in progress at that time. Why did you say I started a job in the beginning of that year?"

"Sir, I am simply trying to help you recall when you were licensed."

"I would like to disagree with your previous statement. I believe you were asking me to agree that I was working as an unlicensed contractor. That statement of yours couldn't have been further from the truth . . . ."

You can short-circuit the previous line of questioning by knowing an exact date, insisting you don't know, or insisting on an approximate time, that is, the early 1980s. Your deposition is not the time to be a know it all.

Start to score your deposition. Give yourself one point for answers you know and two points for answers you don't know. The more answers you do not know, the higher score you receive.

(Three hours into the deposition. Don't let the boredom quotient get to you.)

"Mr. Hampton. When you build a house, are your customers satisfied with it?"

"They are, in practically every case."

"Would you explain for the record what you mean by that?"

"At the end of every job, the homeowner and I will do a walk-through and make a list of items they believe should be completed prior to closing on the house. Those items may require some touch-up painting, attaching towel bars in the bathroom, painting the tops of a few closet doors, cleaning up miscellaneous construction debris, etcetera."

"Sir, can you specifically recall any job where you had an unusually long list of unfinished items?"

"No, I can't think of any one specific job."

"Can you generally recall any job where you had an unusually long list of unfinished items?"

"Generally, there is always a list of miscellaneous items that need to be completed on every job. It is the normal and customary course of business in my industry. In order to get the customer to close, we usually complete all reasonable requests."

"So it would be fair to say that on all of your jobs, there is unfinished work that the customer must identify and ask you to complete?"

"I wouldn't refer to it as unfinished work. The whole job is unfinished until the customer is satisfied with our work and agrees to close on the residence. I want each of my customers to be satisfied. Satisfied customers are a great source of referrals. I make it my job to be sure that the customer is happy and wants to move into their new home."

"Would you agree with the statement that all of your jobs are unfinished until the customer is happy?"

(Pause.) "I don't understand your question. Would you please repeat it again?"

"Sir, I am simply asking if all of your customers are satisfied when you finish the work."

"Generally, yes."

"Is there a specific case that comes to mind where any customer was not satisfied?"

"Not specifically. However, every few years, there is always some project that requires more than the usual amount of attention."

"Could you describe for the record that kind of project?"

"Sure. I'll start a job knowing that the customer has agreed to a specific design and a specific contract price. A few weeks into the job, the customer starts changing the design. Some of those changes may involve structural considerations. It is our normal and customary practice to have the architect, if one was used, and the customer sign a work change order. The architect essentially approves any structural changes and the customer approves the additional cost. Some customers are surprised when they finally see the total bill at the end of the job for all of their work change orders."

"Could you explain what you mean by 'surprised'?"

"Yes. There is usually a direct correlation between the number of work change orders and a higher contract price for the residence. When work change orders involve structural changes, the additional costs can increase the residence price by 15 to 20 percent."

"Would you then agree that it would be fair to say that your residential construction contracts are underpriced by 15 to 20 percent?"

"What did you say?"

"Sir, let me say that in another way. Are your jobs underpriced?"

"Absolutely not! I price my jobs according to an initial set of plans selected and approved by the customer. If a customer wants changes made to those plans after I start construction, then I do my best to accommodate those changes. It is my normal and customary practice to have a customer pay for the changes that they request."

"Let's go off the record. It is now 1:00 P.M. Let's break an hour for lunch and return to this room at 2:00 P.M."

(Pete Hampton goes outside, buys lunch, checks for his messages, returns a few telephone calls, and appears at the room where the deposition takes place at 2:00 P.M.)

"Let's go back on the record. Mr. Hampton, do you understand that you are still under oath from the morning session?"

"Yes, I do."

"Did you speak about this matter to anyone during the lunch break?"

"Which matter is that?"

"The matter related to why you are being deposed today."

"I made a few telephone calls during the lunch break."

"To whom did you place those telephone calls?"

"I called my office and confirmed that a new set of plans that we were expecting had been delivered today. I also called my landscaping subcontractor and asked her that she deliver an additional truckload of mulch to a job site that required it."

"Did you speak to anyone regarding your testimony in this deposition?"

"Not specifically, no."

"Did you speak to anyone in general?"

"I called my partner whom you deposed yesterday and told her that she was right. You do ask a lot of questions."

"Did you discuss anything else?"

"Nothing that I can recall at this time . . . ."

"Sir, do you specifically recall any conversations with a customer named Bates?"

"I have had many conversations with Mr. Bates. He was one of those customers who requested a new work change order practically every day."

"Do you specifically recall any of your conversations with him?"

"Not specifically, no. I have at least a hundred conversations a day with different subcontractors. Then I go home to be with my wife and children. In the evening, I have what appears to be an additional series of conversations with family members, usually with two or three individuals at a time. I know I had many conversations with Mr. Bates because his job was one that just never seemed to end. However, I don't specifically recall any of those conversations with him at this time . . . ."

"Do you generally recall any of your conversations with him?"

"In general, yes. We discussed nearly every aspect of the residential construction job I did for him."

"What were some of those aspects, in general?"

"I seem to recall between 60 and 80 work change orders, so we could have talked about all of them. However, his job was completed nearly three years ago. I just don't recall any of those work change orders."

"Then, as you sit here now, you cannot recall any of those work change orders?"

"Yes, that's correct. His job wasn't the only job I had in the last three years. They all start to appear to be the same after a while. However, if you could provide me with some information that I could look at, that information may refresh my memory . . . ."

The opposing counsel probably expects to prove their case through documents. These documents may have been provided by their client. The documents may have also been provided by you in response to opposing counsel's request for all of your records. During the deposition, you will see only those documents they want you to see.

"Sir, may I ask you to look at this exhibit which we will enter into the record as PH6? Do you recall seeing this exhibit before?"

"It appears to be an illegible copy of a work change order request for the Bates residential contract."

"Is that your signature at the bottom of the page?"

"That is difficult to say. It looks like my signature but I couldn't say for certain. In any event, it appears to be a photocopy of something that resembles my signature."

"Then it would be fair to say that it is a photocopy of your signature?"

"It would be difficult for me to identify with certainty, but it looks similar to my signature."

"Sir, then as you sit here now, you are unable to identify the signature at the bottom of the work change order as your signature."

"That would be fair to say at this time."

"Let me direct your attention to the description on this work change order. The change provides for a six-foot fence approximately 460 feet in length along the rear and adjacent sides of the property. Is that how you would read this work change order?"

"Kindly permit me a moment to read this document." (Pause. Reads the document.) "You are only partially correct. The document also states that the fence would be constructed along a perimeter area that was already identified, staked, and started by the homeowner with yellow markers at 20-foot intervals."

"Then it would be fair to say that you asked Mr. Bates to mark the tentative location of his fence?"

"No, that would not be fair to say. As I sit here now, I specifically recall that Mr. Bates marked the location where he wanted his fence. He also started construction on the fence but later asked me to complete his work. He also specifically instructed me to be absolutely certain we constructed the fence where he placed the yellow markers. If those markers were placed incorrectly, then the error was his alone."

"Sir, I am not asking you to draw a conclusion with respect to your answer. Please limit your response to simply answering the question. Did you know the fence which you constructed was not on Mr. Bates's property?"

"I didn't begin construction of the fence. Mr. Bates did. I simply finished the construction of the fence after he started it. I assumed he had properly marked the location."

"Then would it be fair to say that you do whatever work a customer requests as long as he agrees to pay you for that work?"

"No."

"Would you please explain for the record what you mean by your answer?"

"For the record, the word 'No' means NO."

"Could you describe the steps that you took in constructing his perimeter fence?"

"As I previously stated, Mr. Bates marked the location for his fence and started constructing it. He dug the holes for the entire perimeter. He also set the posts for the fence along the rear and the left side of his property as you face the front of the house. When he determined that he did not have the time to complete the job, he asked me to complete it. I prepared the work change order and he signed off on it."

"Did you consult with anyone on this specific work change order?"

"I seem to recall discussing the matter with Mr. Bates. It appears I must have, since the work change order is on my letterhead and has his signature on it, approving the additional cost."

"My question, sir, was, did you consult with any other individual about the incorrectly sited fence other than Mr. Bates?"

"I had no way of knowing the fence was improperly sited at the time. Mr. Bates sited it on the lot and did most of the initial work on it. I also cannot recall discussing the matter of his fence with any other individual. I simply completed the work that he started."

"Would you explain for the record how you site a house on a specific lot?"

"Yes. A surveyor marks the corner boundaries of the property and we build the house as it is sited on the plans. There was no fence included on the initial set of plans."

"Then you would agree that it is your usual practice to identify the corner boundaries of the property before you begin your construction work?"

"Yes."

"I have no further questions."

The deposition is over and you have survived. It is now time to go home and relax. You have done your job. Let your legal representative now argue the facts on your behalf. Do not worry yourself with your testimony. You will have a chance to do a better job next time. It is adequate that you have answered questions truthfully and to the best of your recollection.

Nevertheless, you may intend to offer testimony at a later date as a party to this trial. Take the time to anticipate further areas of inquiry and be prepared to address them.

Your deposition is an experience you could have done without. But it was a necessary experience to endure so that justice could be served. Remember, you want justice to be served. After all, you and your legal representative are the good guys!

It is unfortunate that running your business successfully may require knowing a few attorneys. You may even need to establish a professional relationship with one or two of them. If for no other reason, an attorney on your side can deflect the attacks of other legal predators.

But there is considerably more to business success than hiring a legal gunslinger to fight your battles. In fact, the more you understand about building equity, the fewer legal battles you may need to fight. When you can run a business without paying legal retainers as a customary business expense, you can be confident that you are on your way to accumulating wealth.

The confidence you have now developed will stay with you as long as you manage your core business. It will help you deal with banks, employees, customers, and all kinds of business risk. But there is a limit to everything. If you are like most entrepreneurs, that feeling of confidence will evaporate the day the taxman knocks on your door.

29

THE TAXMAN COMETH

- ➤ Here's to the Special Interest Groups.
- ➤ Resolve Your Old Tax Matters.
- ➤ File an Offer in Compromise.
- ➤ File by the Due Date.
- ➤ Use Certified Mail.
- ➤ Find a CPA Who Will Work for You.
- ➤ Prepare for Your Tax Audit.

The U. S. income tax system is like the mythical Medusa to some entrepreneurs. It is fearsome, its power is seemingly without limit, and one look from a hostile auditor is enough to turn to stone the feet of most recession-tested entrepreneurs.

To others, the system is an overwhelming mass of myriad confusing and conflicting rules and regulations. To these individuals, the burden of calculating a tax liability and filing the related return is no less demanding than planning a winter assault on the Grand Tetons.

To an additional combative few, the system is a challenge that they must meet and win. To these individuals, the tax laws and speed limits are simply posted to encourage voluntary compliance. It is the combination of their personal preference for risk, prior case law, and their business's requirement for operating capital that determines their degree of compliance with these laws on any given day.

Just as it is futile to study the weather, there is little point in entrepreneurs studying the intricacies of a set of tax laws that are arbitrary, selectively enforced, and will probably change tomorrow. Unless you make a business of dispensing tax advice, you are probably better off just carrying your CPA's toll-free number.

Nevertheless, there is some value in knowing why the U. S. Tax Code, like tomorrow's weather report, continues to be rewritten.

HERE'S TO THE SPECIAL INTEREST GROUPS

LESSON

TAX LAWS ARE VOTED UPON BY THE SAME CONGRESSIONAL REPRESENTATIVES WHO VOTED FOR THEIR OWN PAY INCREASES AND WHO WANT TO BE REELECTED BY THEIR CONSTITUENTS.

Campaign contributions and votes.

Those four words explain why each new Congress eagerly competes with the one that preceded it to leave its unique signature on a package of tax reform laws. Those words are also the reason why few matters are more complex or confounding for entrepreneurs than the U. S. income tax system.

The U. S. Tax Code is a collection of tax reforms voted on by Congress and signed into law by the president. The regulations are the Internal Revenue Service's interpretation of those tax reforms. The Internal Revenue Service (IRS) is the collection arm of the free world's largest distribution system.

According to this complex set of rules and regulations, the IRS collects wealth from entrepreneurs and others who risk investment capital. Your congressional representatives then redistribute that wealth in a manner designed, they hope, to ensure their reelection.

If you have any doubt, ask to see one of Ross Perot's charts. Mr. Perot was the unsuccessful independent party candidate in the 1992 presidential election. He was noted for his home-style television political advertisements, his no-nonsense attitude toward government, and his charts on federal spending.

His charts showed that only 2 percent of the national budget pays for law enforcement and general government. Thirty-two percent of your taxes pay for social security, Medicare, and other retirement benefits. Twenty-four percent of your taxes pay for national defense, veterans benefits, and foreign affairs. Fourteen percent of your taxes pay for social programs such as unemployment compensation, assisted housing, social services, food stamps, and other related programs. An additional 14 percent pays for job training programs, agricultural programs, transportation programs, student loan programs, and general science programs. A final 14 percent pays for the net interest on the national debt.

It is no wonder why many individuals for whom these programs were intended want absolutely nothing to do with business risk or any income-producing activity. Congress has provided these individuals with everything they need for a comfortable lifestyle. The recipients of these benefits are simply not required to put any capital at risk in order to receive these benefits.

As sure as an inner-city public restroom will lose its fixtures, Congress will continue to find new ways to spend your tax dollars. You have every right to be concerned. Write your congressional representative to vent your frustrations; then get back to your business.

The largely incomprehensible U. S. Tax Code should be no barricade to your business aspirations. There are tax practitioners who know how to maneuver throughout the relevant sections of the code far better than you know how to drive a car across town. These practitioners, for a modest professional fee, will grapple with the tax risks in any transaction you have the creativity to contemplate.

What follows are a few simple lessons that will help you control some of the tax risks in your business. Before you get started in any new business, however, you need to conclude all previous unresolved tax matters.

RESOLVE YOUR OLD TAX MATTERS

LESSON

DO NOT START YOUR BUSINESS UNTIL YOU HAVE RESOLVED WITH FINALITY ALL PAST TAX MATTERS.

Bernie and Joann bought a sign manufacturing shop in Orlando, Florida, six weeks before they moved from Honolulu, Hawaii. Both believed the time was right for a change and that a family move to a new area would be the tonic for their financial problems. The day they departed Honolulu, they left behind them the records to a failed cosmetics business. They also left their bank with the keys to a house that was encumbered with so much debt that it should have been sitting at the bottom of the marina instead of adjacent to it.

"So Bernie, how do you like Orlando?"

"Great, Mark! What a relief to leave the islands and all those headaches we had the last few years. It just seemed as if nothing worked for us there. You know the cycle. All we ever did was work to pay our mortgages and other bills. All we ever wanted was a little confirmation that somehow, we were getting ahead . . . ."

"I know! And asking for that was like asking to see the tooth fairy. It was a request that just couldn't be taken seriously. Say, what did you ever decide to do about your 1993 tax liability?"

"Not much. We know that we owe a bundle. With the move to Orlando and this new business, we simply don't have the cash to pay the tax. We figured we'd just keep filing extension requests until business picked up or we somehow found the cash."

"Bernie! Filing an extension request doesn't give you any extra time to pay your tax. It simply gives you extra time to file your return if you have already paid your tax liability."

"But I thought we could get the additional time just by putting down zeros in the blank spaces on the extension request. Then we'd just file the regular return when we had the money and pay the tax at that time. One of the guys I used to fish with says it worked for him."

"Hmmm. Do you remember what he said his tax liability was?"

"He was unemployed for most of that year, so I guess he didn't have much of a tax liability."

"Well, that explains it! Even if he received a few thousand dollars in unemployment benefits, he probably wouldn't have a tax liability. That's an entirely different pattern of facts than yours."

"What's different?"

"Well, for one, you sold a home a few years back for over a million dollars and you didn't meet the gain deferral provisions of Internal Revenue Code Section 1034. By my estimate, you have a federal tax liability on the order of $83,000 and a state tax liability around $17,000."

"But I just don't have the cash to pay! What cash we haven't put into this new business, we lost in our old one."

"Bernie, by the time you get around to filing the returns, those tax liabilities plus the accrued late filing penalties, late payment penalties, and interest are going to make those amounts into very big numbers. In your current financial condition, about the only way you have any hope of settling those amounts is by compromising your tax liability with the IRS."

"Can we do that and still keep our business?"

"Hard to say. Right now, your chances are about the same as winning in a coin flip . . . ."

The prospect of losing their entire investment in a new business just to settle old outstanding personal tax liabilities was heartbreaking. That prospect and the active pursuit of creditors left unpaid from the first business stopped all forward entrepreneurial momentum. In a few months, it also forced Bernie and Joann to walk away from their second business in as many years.

Bernie and Joann could have avoided the tragedy of a second failed business if they had first settled the matter of their unpaid 1993 income taxes before buying the new business. An Offer in Compromise would have allowed them to do just that.

FILE AN OFFER IN COMPROMISE

LESSON

OFFER TO COMPROMISE YOUR TAX LIABILITY WHEN THERE IS NO REALISTIC POSSIBILITY FOR YOU TO PAY IT.

An Offer in Compromise is a procedure that allows financially insolvent taxpayers to compromise their tax liabilities for a fraction of the assessed liability. It is a process that is as involved as it is thorough.

Yes, the process is thorough. From the start of filing your application to its acceptance by the IRS, two years may pass. The IRS will analyze, examine, and interview you so many times that you will begin to wonder if you are the only taxpayer on this good planet. Your CPA and the Internal Revenue Service will each have several thick files on your application filled with months of related correspondence. The exact amount of your outstanding tax liability, the details of your net worth, and other once private information will now be a matter of public record. You will still have a few financial secrets, but only the ones that start when you conclude this process.

Why suffer the indignity of an Offer in Compromise at all?

For some entrepreneurs, there is no choice. The cumulative effect of years of noncompliance with tax laws has dug a hole from which even a bankruptcy petition is no escape. A bankruptcy petition may clear all nontax liabilities from your entrepreneurial balance sheet. However, there are only two ways for taxpayers to clear federal tax liabilities: Either pay the liabilities or offer to compromise them. It is almost always true that compromising a tax liability is a much better alternative than paying it.

Filing an Offer in Compromise also makes good business sense for entrepreneurs who still have the determination to start a new business despite their federal tax misfortunes. It is a fact that unpaid federal tax liabilities can allow the Internal Revenue Service to remain a creditor of yours even after the day you die. There is simply no point in starting a new business in the shadow of a creditor who believes that it should receive both the income from your business and the business that produces the income!

If you have marginal current earnings, no personal savings, a negative net worth, and an unpaid federal tax liability that is out of this world, you are an ideal candidate for an Offer in Compromise. Few entrepreneurs were better qualified for this doubtful distinction than Carolyn.

Carolyn worked as a broker for her husband's real estate business and then for that firm's competitor after she and her husband divorced. The recession of 1991 punished many real estate businesses and Carolyn's commission income nearly disappeared. Even though she survived this economic crisis, her ex-husband's business did not and was forced to close.

Carolyn's amicable relationship with her ex-husband ended a few months later when she received a certified letter from the Internal Revenue Service asking her to pay for amounts assessed against the two of them stemming from prior tax years and ending as far back as 1983.

"So, Carolyn, any luck in finding your ex?"

"Not one bit! It's like he fell off the face of the Earth. Even the private investigator I hired has run out of leads to follow. And now, I've got the IRS ringing my doorbell."

"Don't look so sad, Carolyn. I've heard rumors that the Publisher's Clearinghouse van has been seen driving through your neighborhood. Maybe they have a $10 million winner's notice to deliver to you."

"And the day they deliver it, I'm going to need every penny of it to settle this federal tax liability. I can't believe the size of these numbers. How am I ever going to get out of this mess?"

"Well, if tomorrow goes by without you receiving a winner's notice, we should probably talk about submitting an Offer in Compromise to the IRS."

"What good will that do?"

"In your current condition, quite a bit, actually. This notice that you have given me asks you to pay the sum of $147,835. If we prepare the Offer in Compromise properly, and if the Internal Revenue Service accepts the proposal, we can make most of the $147,835 go away."

"What do we need to get started?"

"A signed power of attorney and all of your bank statements for the last twelve months . . . ."

There is no assurance that an Offer in Compromise will always resolve your current tax dilemma to your complete satisfaction. At the time your offer is under consideration, you must be up to date with your current year's withholding requirements. That will give you less money to spend. You must also have a sensible personal budget with no extravagant or excessive consumption patterns.

Do you have a twenty-two-foot custom bass boat that you own without a nickel of debt? Your enjoyment on that boat is going to be history the day the Internal Revenue Service sells it to cover the noncompromised portion of your federal tax liability.

What about the title to that new four-wheel-drive that you gave your wife as a ten-year anniversary present? She will probably have to use a clunker at least five years old to transport the kids to school and to their music lessons. The music lessons may also have to go.

Your compromise agreement may require you to pay a percentage of your future earnings for the next five years to cover any of the compromised tax liability. If Uncle Steve dies during that time and leaves you with a large insurance settlement, do not waste time thinking on how you plan to spend it. The Internal Revenue Service will probably apply those insurance proceeds to your compromised tax liability too.

This restructuring of your personal assets may appear excessively harsh. However, just remember that you did enjoy some of these funds that you should have used to pay your prior year's tax liabilities. It is a little late to hope for any spasm of kindness from the IRS.

Erratic personal tax compliance habits always have the potential to increase your business risk. You increase that business risk when you fail to file a tax return by its due date and pay the correct amount of tax. Your risk in this area will increase in direct proportion to the number of tax returns you do not file and the size of the tax liabilities you do not pay.

Sometimes you have no choice but to employ the part-time services of a full-time tax practitioner to resolve these risks. There are other times you can control these risks by simply modifying your behavior.

FILE BY THE DUE DATE

LESSON

THE THREE-YEAR STATUTE OF LIMITATIONS NEVER STARTS TO RUN IF YOU NEVER FILE YOUR RETURN.

Filing a tax return by its due date and paying the tax is the single most cost-effective way to control tax risk in any business. There are a number of reasons why this is true.

There is a limited amount of time codified by law that the Internal Revenue Service can examine the information you report on your tax returns. That amount of time is generally three years from the *later* of the due date of the return or the date that you actually file the return.

You can more readily visualize the time limit as a door to your business affairs through which any uninvited guests can pass. Those uninvited guests also carry with them a considerable amount of grief potential. These guests can disallow deductions, reclassify income, assess penalties, and charge you interest on all of the above. They will take your time and attention away from your core business and bring the wrong kind of excitement to your life.

There is something else you must consider when you file your tax return by the due date. You must really mean it when you sign your return below the fine print that reads:

> "Under penalties of perjury, I declare that I have examined this return, including accompanying schedules and statements, and to the best of my knowledge and belief, it is true, correct, and complete."

If you have filed an honest tax return, that statute of limitation's door will close three years later. The day that door closes, the tax risk for that year for your business also goes away. Unfortunately, the Internal Revenue Service may still believe it has the right to open that door unless you are capable of proving that you filed a timely tax return.

USE CERTIFIED MAIL

LESSON

EASE YOUR BURDEN OF PROOF BY FILING YOUR FEDERAL RETURN CERTIFIED MAIL, RETURN RECEIPT REQUESTED.

The second most cost-effective way to control tax risk in any business is to mail your annual tax returns by way of certified mail, return receipt requested. Many courts consider a return receipt to be sufficient, competent, evidential matter. The receipt is also your proof beyond any reasonable doubt that you *mailed* the return before the expiration of a particular due date. This is true even if the U. S. Postal Service does not *deliver* the return until several days later.

Unfortunately, some taxpayers still persist in mailing empty envelopes return receipt requested to their regional Internal Revenue Service centers. You can prove beyond a reasonable doubt that there was a tax return in your envelope when you print the certified receipt number at the top of your return. It is also a good idea to print that number on a second page in the body of the supporting schedules attached to your return before you mail it. Any copy of your return that the IRS later recalls from its records will have this reference on it. This receipt number on the Internal Revenue Service copy of your return is your proof that you actually put a tax return in the envelope.

Always use the U. S. Postal Service to mail your returns. Do not use a private delivery service. The tax courts have not yet accepted the delivery manifests of Federal Express, United Parcel Service, DHL, and other private carriers as competent evidential matter for proof of *mailing* a tax return by its related due date.

Once you have modified your personal tax compliance behavior, there is one more step you need to take to control the tax risk in your business.

FIND A CPA WHO WILL WORK FOR YOU

LESSON

A COMPETENT CPA IS A MUST FOR UNDERSTANDING RELEVANT TAX LAW CHANGES.

You now know that Congress continually rewrites tax laws to benefit the changing demographics of the contributing and voting constituency. This unique design parameter increases the degree of difficulty of the U. S. Tax Code. It is also the reason you will need a knowledgeable tax professional when you consider the tax consequences of any important business decision. A Saturday afternoon clambake and tax question session with Cousin Bill is simply no longer a safe or a reliable alternative.

Why not?

It is true that Cousin Bill works as a corporation accountant. It is also true that he prepares tax returns as a side business. But Cousin Bill has only recently learned the 1992 tax law changes and it is now 1996. Since this line of work for him is part-time, Cousin Bill has been spending only enough time to learn about the tax law changes to avoid committing malpractice on a regular basis.

No matter how good you feel about your cousins, be truthful and logical about the tax consultation you require. Logic is one road to entrepreneurial success. Feelings are one road to personal success. Reverse them, and disaster is guaranteed.

There is very little that you need to know about tax law changes that you cannot discover by consulting with a full-time professional in the tax business. You are far better off in consulting with a tax professional several times a year regarding specific business matters as the need arises than in trying to learn the tax law yourself. As an entrepreneur, you do not have the time to develop anything more than a nodding acquaintance with a set of regulations that are arbitrary and will surely change one year from now.

There are three requirements you should look for in finding the right CPA for your business:

1. Your CPA must be a tax expert.
2. Your CPA must understand the concept of business risk.
3. Your CPA must be accessible.

All of the tax expertise in the world is of no use to you if it takes four days and half a dozen unreturned messages to reach your accountant. All of your accountant's time in the world is of no benefit to you if your accountant does not understand the first thing about managing business risk. A gambler's feel for risk and a willingness to talk to you are of little value if your CPA does not specialize in taxation.

There are other inquiries you can make about your CPA's business that may affect your decision to use this professional as your tax advisor.

A library of tax research material is a standard accounting office decoration. It can be impressive to look at and it makes your accountant look smart. However, researching the answer to three or four tax questions using a thirty-volume loose-leaf service is like using a pitchfork to find a needle in a haystack. You may eventually find the needle, but the task can be time-consuming and will almost certainly be expensive. However, given enough time to do the research and an unlimited amount of client funds, the tax research conclusions will probably be correct.

If your accountant has not already switched to a CD-ROM tax research data base, you should encourage him to do so.

CD-ROM technology permits instantaneous access to relevant tax material. You can store an entire tax library on a single compact disc. CD-ROM technology will allow your accountant to research several complex tax questions in the time it used to take to research a single tax question on a loose-leaf service.

The benefit to you should be obvious. You will receive more thorough answers to your questions for the same amount of professional fees. The benefit to your CPA should also be obvious. He will retain you as a satisfied client for another year.

There is another quality you should hope to find in your tax professional. Some professionals will exercise their initiative and will advise you of relevant changes in the tax law that will affect your business. This initiative and the related bill you receive for it are a sign that your advisor cares about your business and has taken the time to identify potential tax traps long before you put your foot in them.

It is an initiative you should encourage. That initiative gives you the answers to tax questions you may not have had the time to ask. Indeed, you may not have known how to ask these questions. But as long as you own your business, taxes will be a part of it and you will directly benefit from having a CPA involved.

It is a good idea to establish a relationship today that will be in place when you require assistance at a later date. You will certainly need this professional's help the day you get audited.

PREPARE FOR YOUR TAX AUDIT

LESSON

IT IS THE MISSION OF THE INTERNAL REVENUE SERVICE TO ENSURE THAT YOU PAY THE CORRECT AMOUNT OF TAX—NOT ONE DOLLAR MORE THAN THE LAW REQUIRES YOU TO PAY AND NOT ONE DOLLAR LESS.

It is inevitable that one day the Internal Revenue Service will audit you. When that day occurs, it need not be the end of the world. That is, of course, unless, like Joyce, you decide to represent yourself.

"Uh, Mark, if you're not busy, can I talk to you for a few minutes?"

"Sure, Joyce. It's April 6 and I have all the time in the world for you. What's on your mind?"

"I was wondering . . . do you . . . represent . . . people . . . in IRS audits?"

"You bet! People, corporations, tax matter partners, trustees, you name it."

"I sort of have a problem that I may need some professional help resolving."

"Well, as long as it's not a medical problem and I'm licensed for it, I'll give it a go. What kind of office audit invitation did you receive?"

"A five-pager! They wanted me to bring in for examination all my books and records, bank statements, contracts, lease agreements, loan documents, and a whole specification list of other information."

"Hey, with a request like that, maybe they'll bring the coffee and doughnuts! When do we have to be there?"

"Well, actually this was a few months ago. I've had three meetings so far. The first one lasted two hours. I just basically showed them everything I brought in. They asked if it would be OK for me to leave the records with them. I figured that since this had to do with 1991, I probably wouldn't need the material unless you needed to look at something . . . ."

(Silence.) "What went on at the other two meetings?"

"The second meeting was real friendly too. Just before we got started at 8:00 A.M., my auditor asked if it would be OK to have two other auditors sit in with us. You know, so they could get some experience. I didn't mind. They were nice and seemed to go out of their way to make me feel comfortable talking about my business. They offered me some coffee, and before I knew it, the whole morning was gone."

(Hopes for a miracle.) "And the third meeting?"

"That was a few weeks ago. It was just me and the first auditor by ourselves. All I basically did was answer some more questions about the business and that was it. He said he was going to write up the report for my signature and send it to me."

"So how did everything go?"

"Well, that's what I can't figure out. All of them seemed so satisfied with the answers I gave them about my business that I figured I would just have to sign off on his report, you know, as a procedural thing and that the audit would be over. Instead, I get this thiry-two page letter of proposed adjustments that simply floor me! They're saying I was grossly negligent, intentionally disregarded the rules and regulations, and want me to pay an additional $23,378 in taxes, penalties, and interest!"

"That's some damage! Did you enjoy the coffee?"

"Huh?"

"Um, what I mean is, why are you coming to me now instead of when you first received the letter?"

"I thought I could handle it myself."

That kind of thinking, unfortunately, will usually buy you a fairly expensive set of proposed audit adjustments. Unless you are a tax professional or file a 1040 short form, you really have no business hanging around a federal tax office. Deciding to represent yourself at an audit conference is about as smart as taking a late evening walk through an industrial graveyard. You are just asking to have your head handed to you and there are any number of people who will graciously oblige your wishes. The result is never a pretty sight.

If you have taken the time to prepare your tax return, I have no doubt that you are familiar with every item on it. You may even have receipts and canceled checks for most of your deductions. That is a great starting point because your first line of defense in an audit is having complete and accurate records. It is also no more than a starting point.

What you do not have is an appreciation for the line of questions that pass as normal conversation in a tax audit conference.

"So, Betty, how did you get into horseback riding?"

"Well, as a child, I was always around horses and took riding lessons for years. I've always enjoyed equestrian activity. That's why four years ago, I started Bent Creek Riding Stables."

"How do you find the time to do that and your regular job too?"

"Well, my regular job is a normal Monday through Friday activity. I really hate the work that I do there. It's so boring! The riding stables take up most of my weekend, but it's not a big deal because I really enjoy the activity. It gets me outside and essentially allows me to do what I really want to do."

"With all the teaching you provide, do you ever get the time to ride yourself?"

"Oh, sure. There are usually a few breaks between lessons. If my weekends go like I hope they do, I'd spend at least an hour or two a day riding myself. You know, there's a great amount of personal satisfaction for me since I started running the stables. I can't tell you how much more I've enjoyed myself since I started this activity. . . ."

The auditor noted the fact that Betty already had a full-time job that she did not enjoy. The auditor also listened while Betty talked about how much personal enjoyment she received from her riding activities. The auditor determined that taxpayers who do not enjoy their jobs usually have hobbies. The auditor concluded that the personal enjoyment that Betty received from her riding stables signified that it must have been a hobby! Hobby losses, Betty discovered, are not deductible.

There are a host of other complex issues that an auditor can raise during any examination. Betty lost her audit because she did not have the experience to identify these potential audit issues on her particular return. Identifying those issues would have allowed her to anticipate the line of questioning that she may have encountered. As a result of her failure to identify the relevant line of questioning, she was unable to prepare in advance an adequate defense of her disallowed deductions.

If federal income taxation is not your core business, you simply do not have the experience to move the discussion of these complex audit issues to any successful conclusion. The moment you receive an audit report, contact your CPA. That is one reason why you have a professional tax advisor. You will certainly need this tax professional's assistance the day you think about leaving your business.

PART EIGHT

Leaving Your Business

30

SELLING OUT

- There Is a Time to Say Good-bye.
- Determining Value.
- Some Valuations Are Misleading.
- Start with a Rough-Cut Valuation.
- For Sale by Owner.
- You Cannot Miss with This Shot.

Periodically converting equity to cash is a delicate part of making any business your best investment.

I know there are owners who insist they would never sell their business. Their reaction, in part, is understandable. Few of us would agree to sell our preadolescent children at any price!

Building a business is a parenting experience with no joy or crises left excluded.

Over the years, you developed an emotional bond with your business. Selling an investment that you birthed, nurtured through childhood, guided through adolescence, and shared adulthood with can be a soul-wrenching experience.

If you are like most entrepreneurs, you also look to your business for your main source of identity. You have a comfortable office, a desk, a credenza, and a door that closes. You have a corporate athletic club membership and a private telephone line for your special customers. Your business cards even say you are president.

You have been telling bankers for the last fifteen years that you know what you are doing. They may finally agree with you.

You have bloodied yourself through entrepreneurial firefights and have prospered. What, then, do you become when you sell the business and the fighting is over?

The fear is that you will become something of a man without a country.

You are being too hard on yourself. It is imprudent to think that a business or an ownership interest in one will always be yours. It is also unfair to think that you are nothing without these. There is a time to say good-bye. There are also compelling reasons: the reduction of risk and the lost opportunity of other investments.

Converting equity to cash is the final step in every business cycle. It is also a logical step.

Risk, your banker, and you have shared the same mattress since infancy. You have adjusted to each other's sleeping patterns and through your worst nightmares have managed to stay on the bed. That is an accomplishment.

The three of you, however, have grown larger than the bed. Risk is getting a little bolder, your banker is snoring, and you have to get up at four in the morning. If you want a good night's sleep, it is time to move on.

THERE IS A TIME TO SAY GOOD-BYE

LESSON

YOU WILL WASTE MUCH OF THE EFFORT THAT WENT INTO BUILDING YOUR BUSINESS IF YOU DO NOT UNDERSTAND WHAT IS INVOLVED IN SELLING IT.

There are several circumstances under which you would consider selling. Two of them are notable.

You have made your business your best investment. You have fully funded your retirement plan and you have a strong portfolio of investments. The economy is strong and so is your business.

Continuing to operate this business as you have in the past might be like betting all of your previous winnings in a poker game. There is a significant amount of downside exposure. Even great poker players lose.

There is another reason. Even a winning entrepreneur gets tired.

It is not so much a factor that the entrepreneur has lost his edge. It is more of a change in drive forces. The winning entrepreneur has met success in many investments over a long period of time. He has done so well in making his business his best investment that building equity is no longer the most consuming thing in life.

He would like to smell the roses, reaffirm his marriage, be a father to his children or his grandchildren, and travel. Perhaps he would like to meet a new challenge in another industry without the risk of an open, unexpired investment in his old business.

There are certainly many other reasons that might motivate you to sell. Whatever your reason may be, whenever you make that decision to sell, you must understand how to value your business.

DETERMINING VALUE

LESSON

THE MOST PRECISE MEASURE OF THE VALUE OF YOUR BUSINESS IS THE AMOUNT OF CASH THAT A BUYER WILL PAY FOR IT.313

In any sale situation, a buyer, who is under no obligation to buy, and you, who are under no compulsion to sell, will argue about the worth of your business. Presumably, both the buyer and you have a reasonable knowledge of all the relevant facts.

If your business is a going concern and you have emphasized building equity, the business has a readily marketable value.

Discard all the formulas you have heard that have anything to do with gross revenues in determining a business value. Gross revenues are only an indication to an interested buyer that you have a sustainable customer base. The buyer's accountant will never use gross revenues to support any proposed acquisition price!

How do you approach the problem of valuing your business? Wenton did it like this:

"Wenton! What brings you to my office?"

"I've been thinking about selling the business."

"I've heard that before. Do you want me to talk you out of it again?"

"No, not really. This time I'm really tired of the grind. It's something I've thought about for a while. I could be interested in selling if a buyer paid the right price. What I thought we could do was figure out what the business was worth."

"How accurate does the value have to be?"

"Pretty accurate."

"When do you need the number?"

"Say, in two weeks."

"OK, Wenton. I'll draft an engagement letter outlining your request, our responsibilities, and our fee arrangement."

"Can you give me an idea of what it might cost?"

"Since you want an accurate value, Wenton, but are only giving me two weeks to do the work, it might be anywhere from $7,000 to $10,000."

(Gulp!) "I don't need it that accurate!"

"I thought you might feel that way, Wenton. Did you remember to bring the information I requested?"

"You mean my business tax returns for the last four years?"

"That's right."

"They're in my briefcase in the trunk of my car."

"It's your choice, Wenton. I can either spend two weeks on this project or you and I can knock out a rough-cut value in the next hour."

"Don't go anywhere. I'll get my briefcase!"

Selling a business is an art. Valuing a business is a science. Do not be fooled by anyone who might tell you differently.

There are some very good reasons to pay for a comprehensive business valuation. Some of these reasons include estate valuation purposes, an Internal Revenue Service audit, minority shareholder transfers, or acquisition financing. If your reasons are not as good as these, it makes no sense to pay for precision that you do not require.

The day you sell your business, the cash that a prospective buyer pays for it is the ultimate determination of value. Any other proposed value prior to closing a sale is just a theoretical number useful only for discussion purposes.

SOME VALUATIONS ARE MISLEADING

LESSON

VALUATION REPORTS PAID FOR BY THE SELLER ARE AN INDICATION OF WHAT THE SELLER THINKS HIS BUSINESS IS WORTH. THAT VALUE IS PROBABLY NOT THE REAL VALUE OF THE BUSINESS.

The cash received by the seller of any business is one measure of an artist's skill. If it is a large amount of cash, the seller is the better artist. If it is a low amount of cash, the buyer has the better artistic skills.

It is perfectly acceptable to pay for art if you can hang it on your wall and enjoy it. I have yet to see a business valuation that has been framed, mounted, and illuminated. Conventional artwork is a far less expensive alternative. Most business valuation reports are simply too heavy for normal display. The boilerplate in many of them is enough to start your own recycling center!

Most valuation reports for entrepreneurial businesses are disappointing. The errors in analysis and the related concluding values do nothing to soften my anger at seeing poor professional work.

The appraiser's relative inexperience can be partly to blame. He is frequently a casually supervised, young master of nothing. He is a self-proclaimed artist working with scientific equipment, producing results he does not understand.

He is accorded the same responsibility as a judge, but offers his verdict before any settlement between buyer and seller has been reached. Is it any wonder his theoretical value for your business is different from yours?

For all of his prodding, the seller is no less guilty. In the course of talking to the appraiser, the seller may disclose his own valuation estimate. That estimate may influence significantly the appraiser's value. That is why you must never provide an appraiser with your estimate of value before they issue their valuation report.

There is a reason that the seller's comments about the value of his business may have a considerable amount of influence in the final valuation report. The appraiser has a significant vested interest in his work. He wants to be paid for it!

It is far easier to be paid if the valuation report is noncontroversial. It is a controversial report if it is the subject of subsequent litigation or if it does not permit the seller to support his asking price.

It is also easier to be paid if the weight of the report is greater than the weight of the seller's favorite publication.

That is an easy requirement to meet if the seller is largely illiterate or is a reader of the typical weekly business tabloid.

That presents a unique problem if the seller enjoys spending a cozy evening with *Webster's Unabridged New International Dictionary*.

There are many methods than can be used to value a business. Comparative business sales are a readily recognized valuation method. For that reason, many business appraisers will include comparative business sales in their valuation reports even if the sales they include are not comparative.

There is no uniform requirement of publicly recording sales of privately owned businesses. That makes it difficult to find the kind of comparables that are so readily available in real estate property sales.

The nonpublic nature of most privately held small businesses also makes any comparative analysis a difficult task at best. There is no Small Business Securities and Exchange Commission that insists on minimum disclosure guidelines.

That is why some business valuation professionals insist on including whatever business sales are known to them. It makes them look thorough. It can also make them look ridiculous.

In noncritical moments, you can ignore the nonsensical inclusion of noncomparable business properties. The inclusion is difficult to forgive when an appraiser derives an improper value from it. The insult is complete when the appraisal firm asks you to pay for the valuation.

START WITH A ROUGH-CUT VALUATION

LESSON

A ROUGH-CUT VALUATION WILL GIVE YOU AN ESTIMATE OF THE VALUE OF YOUR BUSINESS.

If your business is privately held and you wish to sell it, you can do a rough-cut valuation.

A rough-cut valuation is a tentative and preliminary valuation. A bank will not accept the results of this valuation for primary loan documentation support. The Internal Revenue Service will probably object to any value derived from a rough-cut valuation if it has an opportunity to do so.

A rough-cut valuation will tell you if you have a business that might be worth selling. It will also provide you with a possible starting point in identifying a reasonable asking price for your business. That is all it will tell you!

"Wenton, you're back!"

"I would have returned sooner, but I forgot what floor your offices were on. I went back down and looked at the lobby directory!"

"That's what I like about you Wenton. If you don't know the answer, you always know where to go to look for one! Are these all of your tax returns?"

"Yes."

"Were there any amended returns filed?"

"What do you mean by that?"

"Were there any corrections made to these original returns? If you made any corrections, your accountant would have amended the original filing."

"There weren't any amended returns."

"Were there any audits of these returns?"

"No, but I did get a refund check last year for an overpayment of taxes I made for the business."

"What was the refund amount?"

"Three hundred forty-eight dollars."

"Not a big deal, Wenton. I see that your accountant checked the accrual accounting method box on your tax return. That tells me I don't need to make a lot of adjustments to these numbers. Let's pull a few of the numbers from your returns."

	This Year	Last Year	Two Years Ago	Three Years Ago
Taxable Income	42,000	30,000	62,000	74,000
Owner's Excess Salary	80,000	75,000	70,000	70,000
Pension Plan	75,000	73,000	15,000	0
Adjusted Income	199,100	179,500	150,100	147,000

"What are you doing?"

"Just figuring out what you really made the last four years, Wenton. I'm adding your business taxable income, your excess salary, and your pension plan contribution."

"What about adding back interest, taxes, and depreciation too?"

"Wenton, this is a rough-cut valuation. If you want to ride in a Cadillac, you're going to have to pay for one. Besides, let's not pretend we have more precision than we really do. You still made a lot of money."

"Actually, I made a little more."

"Oh? What do you mean?"

"I bought some things for my home and charged it off to cost of sales."

"Wenton, how much is some?"

"Oh, about $9,000 of items a year."

"For each of four years?"

"Yes. I never told my accountant that. Now that I'm confessing, I should probably add an additional $14,000 per year to that number."

"What for?"

"Trips, vacations, and personal entertainment I deducted through the business. I also paid for my daughter's wedding through the business, but I charged that off over two years."

"Wenton, are you telling me that your average adjusted income is an additional $23,000 higher?"

"Actually, a bit higher."

"What don't I know?"

"I've had problems getting good cashiers for the business so I've had to work the registers myself. If I were to guess, I probably forgot to ring up $12,000 a year in sales."

"That's $1,000 per month!"

"That's about right."

"Wenton, how do you propose to explain all of this to an interested buyer?"

"Pretty much the same way I explained it to you. After all, I want the highest price I can get. If 'coming clean' will do that for me, why not?"

"I can think of two reasons why that might not work, Wenton. Once you admit an indiscretion of this magnitude to any buyer, you will have stirred his considerable interest in your accounting records. Just about as much interest as you might receive at a chicken farm if you knocked over a bucket of worms. You'll be lucky if you ever get out of the disclosure phase of negotiations!"

"What's the other reason?"

"How do you know your prospective buyer isn't an Internal Revenue Service informant?"

You never really know until it is far too late. If there is considerable hidden value in the portion of your business that is not evident from your tax returns, you have two immediate choices. Either amend your business tax returns to reflect that value or forget those other items in the valuation discussions.

Whatever you choose, you will have to live with the consequences.

When you amend your returns, you will pay professional fees, additional taxes, penalties, and interest. Amending your returns may also bring an unwarranted amount of attention to other areas of those returns.

Deleting these items from a valuation discussion is also expensive.

Either way, persuading a buyer to pay for revenue you inadvertently failed to disclose on your tax returns is not without risk. If you insist that the revenue is there, you have perjured yourself with the Internal Revenue Service. If you do not insist, you can kiss the net liquidating value of the related income stream good-bye.

Some sellers will ascribe a value to their business that simply cannot be recomputed using conventional valuation methods. It is also not possible to move the sellers from a high and seemingly arbitrary sales price. Only the inexperienced will fail to recognize that there is a previously unreported income stream that the owner will not disclose but for which he insists on being compensated.

There is a cost to that alternative too. The sales price may be so high relative to any available numerical support that the owner may never sell the business.

"OK, Mark. For discussion purposes, let's use your 'adjusted-income' figures. What do they tell us?"

"Your business is worth something!"

"Heck. I know that! I think I could get $200,000 for my business without a lot of work."

"I would buy it from you today at that price, Wenton."

"You would?"

"Sure! Your business is worth that adjusted-income figure multiplied by some factor. The $200,000 figure of yours essentially uses a multiplier of one. That means if I bought your business today for $200,000, I might expect to have my investment returned to me in a year. That's a great deal for me!"

"How much more do you think I can get?"

"That's hard to say. It depends a lot on the buyer. If he bought your business and managed it himself, he might pay a higher price. Your adjusted income figure has also been growing. I would say your multiple should be between two and three times your average adjusted income. That would put a sales price somewhere between $340,000 and $505,000, before any marketability discount."

"Why the range?"

The multiple any buyer will use on the adjusted-income amount will depend on a number of criteria.

The selection criteria will include the rate of return the buyer is looking to receive, his perceived risk of the seller's business, and the relative maturity of the seller's industry. It will also include some factor for the shade of truth that he thinks the seller is telling.

Shareholders make this determination all of the time when they buy and sell publicly held stocks.

A multiple is also a function of expected earnings and interest rates in the marketplace. These multiples reflect the market's expectation of the good things and the bad things that could happen to a company.

Anyone can buy or sell a publicly traded investment because other public investors, specialists, and market makers provide them with a high degree of liquidity. As a result, sellers can convert their investments to cash at market-driven prices simply by picking up a phone and calling a broker.

It is this liquidity issue, or the lack of it, that limits a privately held company's ability to command a high multiple.

It takes a considerable amount of work to sell an illiquid business. You cannot call someone on the telephone and tell him to convert your investment to cash.

Further, transaction costs (sales fees, business valuation reports, audited financial statements, legal fees, etc.) are significantly greater than what you would pay for a discount stockbroker to execute a trade. Those costs are usually reflected in the form of a marketability discount from any calculated value that can approach 15 to 30 percent.

"That gives me an idea of the value of my business!"

"We're not done yet, Wenton. We haven't discussed your working capital."

"What's that?"

"Think of it as the degree of difficulty you have had every month in paying your bills."

"I never have any problems paying my bills. Except for my daughter's wedding. That's why I had to charge it over two years."

"Then you probably have positive working capital."

"What does it say on the tax returns?"

"I'm checking that, Wenton. I am adding what you have available to pay your current bills. That includes cash, accounts receivable, inventory, and prepaid items. From that total, I'm subtracting your current bills. Those are your accounts payable, accrued liabilities, and current portion of long-term debt."

"How did I do?"

"You passed, Wenton. Your business is alive and your working capital is healthy!"

"What do you mean?"

"You have a positive working capital of about $80,000. Whoever buys your business should also be willing to pay you for that."

No entrepreneur will ever confirm that he has sufficient working capital, irrespective of its amount. A large amount of positive working capital could be a sign that you have managed your business effectively. It could also be a sign that you have overcapitalized your business. It definitely is a sign that you have more equity in your business than what the business requires to pay its current debts.

When you sell your business, you are entitled to be paid for working capital that you leave in it.

"There's still more, Wenton. Did you bring that schedule of fixed assets I asked you to?"

"Yes, but I'll tell you something about that! My accountant charged me $4,600 to prepare this computerized fixed-asset report!"

"How many assets are there on the report?"

"Four hundred twenty-five."

"Do you want to be paid for them when you sell your business?"

"Of course I do!"

"Then you'd better have a current listing of them to show a prospective buyer. It will be too late for you to think about putting this list together one week before you close a sale. What are these assets worth today?"

"You mean what they would cost if I bought them today?"

"No, Wenton! I mean as they sit today, mostly used but probably functional, what are they worth?"

"I'd say about $100,000."

"Are they fully paid for?"

"I said I didn't have any problems with my bills . . . ."

"OK. Just one other question. Are they all used in the business?"

"What do you mean?"

"There's no way to ask this delicately, Wenton. Are any of these assets furnishing a vacation house, a daughter's home, or a home office that I don't know about?"

"Heck no! I'm not that aggressive!"

"Then that's about another $100,000 that you should expect to receive in sale proceeds."

Lack of fixed-asset documentation can be a deal breaker in a business sale.

How will a buyer ever know what assets are being transferred to him? The records of course, must agree with what is physically in your business. That is why you must periodically reconcile them. If you do not, a disgruntled buyer may sue you for selling him a listed asset that does not exist!

If the dollar value of the assets is material in relation to the sales price, a fixed-asset appraisal is mandatory.

Flexible, self-determined fixed-asset values are no longer an option. The Internal Revenue Service has put down a hobnailed boot on arbitrary fixed-asset allocations.

There is another point of courtesy. The remaining income-producing life of the assets should be long enough to pay off any related long-term debt. When it is not, you are asking a buyer to assume a risk without compensation. Informed buyers will look at you as if you are out of your mind.

Of course, it never hurts to ask.

"We're done, Wenton. Whoever buys your business should pay about $100,000 for your fixed assets and about $80,000 for your working capital. If a 15 percent marketability discount were applied to the previous valuation range we computed, a buyer would also consider paying approximately $290,000 to $430,000 for your adjusted-income amounts."

"Great! Now that I know how to do it, I'll do the figuring myself the next time!"

That, unfortunately, is where selling a business bogs down. It is true that you can press the buttons on a calculator as well as any other professional. All that means is that you know how to press buttons.

There are dozens of other relevant issues that will affect the price you will receive in a sale. The difference can be greater than 50 percent. You may have the qualifications to deal with one or two of those additional issues. You do not have the competence or the time to deal with them all.

It is when you sell a business that artistic skills show their value. Some artists will be comfortable making the most from whatever medium is available. Others are great at making something from nothing. Whatever an artist does for you, it is worth every penny that it costs.

If you are in doubt of an artist's real worth, try painting the ceiling of the Sistine Chapel by yourself.

FOR SALE BY OWNER

LESSON

UNLESS YOU ARE THE WORLD'S GREATEST SALESPERSON, NEVER TRY TO SELL A BUSINESS BY YOURSELF.

FSBOs (fizzbos) are one way to sell real property without the help of an artist. Brokers will tell you that it will take more time if you do it yourself. They will also say that your market exposure to possible interested buyers will be nowhere as great. Both of these statements are true.

Nevertheless, you will clean the house Saturday night, stick your "Open House" sign in the ground on Sunday morning, and hope for the best. At the worst, you will miss seeing a few football games and taking your afternoon nap.

That is what makes most FSBO options impractical for your own business. No potential buyers will talk to you on the weekend, when you have the time. They are out looking at real estate or watching football games!

The inquiries you do receive will come at the worst possible moments. Those moments are when you have no time to consider the requests.

You must prepare this week's payroll, process today's customer orders, and smooth out the bugs in your new billing system.

Unfortunately, your secretary is sick, your bookkeeper is on vacation, and your children are waiting for their ride home from school.

When you make the time to answer any inquiries you may receive, you ignore what is most important to you: your business. But even despite your apparent qualifications to sell your business by yourself, there is another reason to assign the task to a professional.

Selling a business involves a far larger set of risks than the ones you took to build it. They are also different kinds of risk without the customary elements with which you have grown familiar.

Further, they are risks that you absolutely must control. Your future retirement capital may be at stake. Your future risk capital certainly is at stake. When you are ready to sell your business, you need the leadership that a professional can offer. This professional has one job: to identify risks that you have never even imagined while converting your business investment to cash.

Harris knows something about FSBOs. He built a seafood wholesale business that grossed approximately $2 million a year.

Harris met with a competitor of his to discuss the competitor's interest in buying Harris's business. The negotiations moved far too fast for Harris to follow.

One day Harris had his own office and cold storage facilities. A day later, his competitor had agreed to manage them. His competitor merged all of the data files for the two entities. All of the cash went into one account. The bankruptcy court is still trying to determine who owned what.

It is not clear that Harris ever sold his business to his competitor, although that was his intent. It is not clear what amount, if any, his competitor paid for it.

The only document evidencing any agreement was a single sheet of paper prepared by Harris on his home computer. Attorneys for both parties are still arguing the substance of that document.

The document listed no acquisition price, no terms, and identified none of the items that were transferred. Yet both parties signed the document and the word "sale" appeared throughout.

One point is clear. The pre-FSBO business Harris had no longer exists.

YOU CANNOT MISS WITH THIS SHOT

LESSON

A ONE-SHOT TAKEOUT SOLVES ALL VALUATION DISPUTES.

A one-shot takeout is the most effective way to avoid a valuation dispute with your co-owner.

Harry Callaghan, everyone's favorite detective, knows this. That is why he carries a .44 Magnum. One well-aimed shot will stop all arguments, every time.

Wyatt Earp also knew this. That is why he carried a Buntline Special. He was never out of pistol range in a gunfight.

The superpower countries also recognize this. There is no reason to threaten mutual assured destruction with a 10-kiloton nuclear warhead when you can drop a 50-megaton warhead with the same amount of navigational effort.

The ominous tone in a one-shot takeout should not be lost on you. When one partner wants to sell his interest in a business and the other does not, you have all the ingredients of a chainsaw massacre.

Valuation is always an issue. Conventional buy-sell agreements may require averaging the results of three appraisals. No entrepreneur on the topside of his grave would ever agree to pay professional fees for two valuations more than he needed.

Averaging valuation results, at its best, will find a middle point between extremes. If the average is unreasonably low, the seller will be unhappy. If it is unreasonably high, the buyer will object.

Each party will then hire its own team of lawyers and accountants to argue or justify the unfairness of the arrangement. If you have ever had any difficulty with the concept of depletion, you will recognize it the moment you pay the related professional fees.

There is a better way. That is the one-shot takeout.

"Rudy, I've been thinking about our business. Our arrangement as equal 50 percent shareholders has been great. It has let me and my husband pay for a wonderful home and put our kids through college. I think, however, that it is time for one of us to move on."

"Are you buying or selling, Gloria?"

"Buying!"

That is the start of a one-shot takeout. It is a friendly Dodge City shoot-out. Gloria, the buyer, has one shot at buying Rudy's interest. There are no protracted negotiations, appraisals, or second shots. If Gloria misses on her first shot, she catches Rudy's bullet and loses.

"What are you proposing to pay for my 50 percent interest, Gloria?"

"Two hundred thousand dollars, cash."

Unlike a running gun battle, Rudy has three business days to consider the offer. If he accepts, he is out of the business and has $200,000 in his pocket. If he does not accept, he must buy Gloria's 50 percent interest for the same amount. That is how you solve all shareholder valuation disputes.

There are few individuals better qualified to argue the net liquidating value of a business than its current owners. They know its daily pulse rate and are seldom misled by an appraisal of comparables. There are no comparables for most small businesses. Each business is unique, with its own strengths and risks.

There is only one shot for each shareholder in a one-shot takeout. The first shareholder to pull the trigger will do whatever is necessary to arrive at a fair valuation.

Rudy thought Gloria arrived at a low valuation. As a result, Gloria lost her interest in the business.

"Gloria, I've thought about your offer and I am not a seller at $200,000. I am exercising my right to buy out your 50 percent interest for the same amount, under the same terms. We can close this deal on Friday. It's been great doing business with you!"

That is all there is to it. Gloria took her best shot and missed. In a one-shot takeout, those are the breaks. A bit more liquid now, Gloria is nevertheless out of business.

The consequences of no longer owning a business are still livable as long as you know how to retire without risk.

31

RETIRE WITHOUT RISK

- ➤ The Hammer Will Fall.
- ➤ You Can't Get There from Here.
- ➤ Social Security Doesn't Do It.
- ➤ Pay Yourself First.
- ➤ You Are Worth the Investment.

There is a point when you may be forced to accept risk when you are least prepared to do so. That is the day you retire. The day you retire, you will face an entirely new risk.

Retirement risk is the risk of surviving your wealth. It is a risk of becoming a ward of the state. It is the risk of depending on your children to learn a lesson that you never did.

Retirement risk can be a difficult concept for anyone to understand for a number of reasons.

Retirement involves the concept of disengaging. It is an orderly withdrawal from business risk. Retirement risk can be difficult to assess. You have focused far more entrepreneurial attention on business risk than on risk after business.

Disengaging from business risk involves considerable planning if you want to retire without risk. Some last-minute Individual Retirement Account contributions and inquiries to your local Social Security office will just not do it.

Time no longer works for you the way it once did. Where you once had thirty-five years to cushion retirement risk, you may now have considerably less. There may hardly be enough time for one or two good business cycles.

Retiring without risk involves far more than a theoretical demonstration of building equity. The day that you retire, you can no longer dream about building wealth. You either have it or you do not.

THE HAMMER WILL FALL

LESSON

PLAN YOUR RETIREMENT TODAY
WHILE TIME IS ON YOUR SIDE.

If you are under thirty, I can understand your lack of urgency in confronting a risk that is another thirty years in the future. It is like waiting to be hit by a hammer in the year 2025. When the hammer falls, you will worry about moving your thumb at that time. Whatever you do today seems a bit premature and certainly overreacting.

In the case of the hammer, that may be true. In the case of retirement risk, it is not. The longer that a retirement fund can grow at a tax-free rate, the less retirement risk there is for you. That is why your business needs a retirement plan.

Having a business without a retirement plan is nothing short of gross financial negligence.

The objection that many people have toward retirement planning is the remoteness of retirement risk. The further away you are from retirement, the more remote the retirement risk. That remoteness is a thirty-year-old entrepreneur's problem.

"Mark! Do I really need to set up a retirement plan this year?"

"Why do you ask, Bert?"

"I can think of so many other things that I could do instead with the money. I've always wanted to own a Porsche, and I've had my eye on a Rolex for several months now."

"What do those items have to do with your business?"

"Well, nothing, but I'd like to have them!"

"Bert, you certainly have the money for them, but those are not income producing assets! I think you need to distinguish between what you want and what you need."

"What do you mean?"

"You might want a Porsche but may only need a Chevy Sprint. You might want a Rolex but may only need a Timex. Get the idea?"

"That sounds like total deprivation!"

"Hardly, Bert. That still gives you a car and a watch! What is left will be sufficient to fund your retirement plan."

"But I'm not going to retire for another thirty-five years!"

"I know. When you do retire, though, you can do it in style! But you have to plan for it today, not when you're fifty-five."

"Look. Why don't we agree to talk about retirement planning next year? The dealer I talked to about the Porsche said he would throw in a cellular phone and some mud flaps for free!"

"Bert, you're not listening. I think you are going to face a big risk in thirty years. If I'm wrong about that risk and you have done as I recommended, you lose nothing. Your business receives a deduction for your retirement contributions and the money is still yours. Further, it grows tax-free until you pull it out when you retire. If you're wrong about retirement risk, and you don't do as I've recommended, you retire on a park bench!"

"You mean I get a business deduction for my retirement plan contribution?"

"That's the way the law reads today, Bert!"

"Oh! That's a whole different story! Why didn't you say so in the first place?"

Young entrepreneurs like Bert are usually consumption-oriented. High-tech toys and other paraphernalia help satisfy their cravings and polish their images.

Their retirement plans frequently suffer as a result of these expensive nonincome-producing habits.

YOU CAN'T GET THERE FROM HERE

LESSON

SOME PREMATURE WITHDRAWAL PENALTIES
THAT APPLY TO RETIREMENT FUNDS
ARE THERE FOR YOUR PROTECTION.

It is hard to believe, but for each entrepreneur who has a retirement plan, there are many who do not. There is a universal objection to setting up any retirement plan. Once you make your retirement contributions, the contributed funds become largely inaccessible.

"Mark, I was talking to my brother-in-law and he said I should come to you. He said I'm paying too much in taxes."

"What are you paying, Horace?"

"About $35,000 a year in federal and state taxes."

"He's right! You are paying too much in taxes."

"What can I do?"

"You could stop working, Horace. Without income, your tax problem would go away."

"Believe it or not, that sounds appealing. I can't wait for retirement. I've only got twelve years left!"

"Why don't you set up a retirement plan, Horace? You're self-employed, have a nice income, and are the right age for making the maximum contributions available. That could save you about $12,000 per year in taxes."

"Sounds like a great idea! What do I have to do?"

"Fill out some forms and then fund your plan with your initial contribution."

"I can do that. What's the contribution amount?"

"I can't be certain, Horace, but I think it will be around $30,000."

"That high?"

"That's what you'd need to put in to save $12,000 of taxes."

"When could I withdraw this money?"

"Virtually any time you wish. Unfortunately, if you take it out before you retire, you're going to get socked with some penalties and taxes. That wouldn't be a problem if you leave it in there until you are sixty-five years old."

"You mean I wouldn't be able to use that money until I'm sixty-five?"

"No, Horace! You could direct the funds to just about any prudent investment. The only restrictions on these funds are that they must stay in your retirement plan until you retire. That's only twelve years from now!"

"But what if I would like to get at it earlier?"

"Not without penalties, Horace!"

"I've got to think about that one."

Horace's difficulty with funding his plan is the potential inaccessibility of the money he contributes. Once he has made a contribution to his retirement plan, that amount is no longer available for discretionary spending.

If there is one area of justice in the U. S. Tax Code, it is the onerous penalties that accompany premature retirement fund withdrawals. These penalties protect you from yourself. If you never pay them, the penalties have worked.

The simple threat of paying these penalties has reduced your retirement risk.

The penalties are only a threat. You will pay them only if you steal from your future. As the pension provisions of the tax law are currently written, there is no punishment if there is no crime!

SOCIAL SECURITY DOESN'T DO IT

LESSON

YOUR CONGRESSIONAL REPRESENTATIVE WILL DO NOTHING ABOUT THE GREATEST FINANCIAL DEBACLE OF ALL TIME.

There are several compelling reasons to begin funding your retirement plan today. One of those reasons is that Social Security cannot do it alone. At its best, Social Security will only supplement your retirement. The federal government is the first to tell you that it is a base on which to build.

Social Security is no more than a base.

Social Security as a retirement fund is also the world's greatest con. There are great disappointments with this federally mandated program.

One of these disappointments is that the amounts withheld from your paycheck are not yours. They do not go into a personal savings account or into a restricted fund that will accumulate for your benefit.

It is a surprise when most entrepreneurs discover how Social Security really works.

"I don't think I need a retirement plan. I've been paying in all of that Social Security the last twenty years. I've got a great retirement fund built up!"

"Not exactly. What you've paid in Social Security is not really yours."

"Don't be ridiculous! Who do you think took the self-employment risk to earn that money?"

"You did, I suspect . . . ."

"Who do you think made the estimated tax payments?"

"You again . . . ."

"Since I earned it and I paid it, it looks to me like I've guaranteed myself a retirement benefit!"

"Well, that's where your good common sense and Social Security part company."

"What do you mean?"

"Look, you've been self-employed for the last twenty years. Remember all the times you took the Tulsa to Denver shuttle?"

"Yes . . . ."

"Where do you think all those senior citizens in Denver were traveling wearing their cameras and aloha shirts?"

"Hawaii?"

"Right! You've been working to pay for their retirement . . . ."

"No! They paid Social Security too."

"That's true. They paid in to the Social Security system about $8,000 each over the course of their entire income-producing lives. They now get paid more than that amount in a single year! According to the actuarial tables, they'll continue to receive that benefit for the next seventeen years. Essentially, your current contributions are paying for their beachside hotel rooms . . . ."

"That's like getting something for nothing!"

"I know."

"But that's not fair!"

"I know. I would tell you to write your congressman, but this is one issue he won't touch . . . ."

Even suggesting sensible revisions to the Social Security Act has adverse political consequences. Retired citizens represent a formidable, growing political constituency. A politician who would propose to stop stealing from entrepreneurs and giving to retired, risk-averse voters would lose any reelection race.

What you pay in Social Security withholding today goes into a pipeline. At the end of that pipeline, someone receives a benefit who has paid in far less than you. That is the first injustice.

Congressional representatives then try to divert the flow of overfunded retirement benefits to pay for budget deficits, savings and loan bailouts, mismanaged housing projects, and other federal demonstrations of fiscal irresponsibility. That is the second injustice.

Federal officials will tell you in a hushed tone that the Social Security system is a pact between generations. You are responsible for your parent's retirement and your children are responsible for yours.

These officials stop just this side of suggesting that none of you will learn how to balance a budget or how to make your business your best investment in an average lifetime that will span twenty presidential elections.

Let them speak for themselves.

As an entrepreneur, it is also difficult for me to accept the fact that without my consent, someone has negotiated a long-term, binding financial agreement on my behalf.

That agreement is Social Security. Congressional representatives continue to insist that the program is in my best interests. I am not so sure.

In the simple case where I retire widowed at age sixty-five with four adult children and die shortly thereafter, my estate will receive none of the economic benefit of my lifetime contributions! If I have paid the maximum amount in Social Security taxes during my income-producing life, at my death, this amount would be worth considerably greater than $1 million. It is a staggering sum to give away.

If you want any retirement wealth to pass to family members, you need another plan.

PAY YOURSELF FIRST

LESSON

WRITE A CHECK TO YOUR RETIREMENT ACCOUNT THE FIRST BUSINESS DAY OF EVERY YEAR.

There is a way to be certain you will retire without risk. Pay yourself first! It is so easy to remember but so difficult to do.

You developed your current bill-paying habits from a combination of astute operational budgeting and a desire for a good credit rating.

Your landlord is happy, the banks are happy, the phone company is happy, and so are your employees. Your business has a great credit rating. The cash from your business has always been adequate to pay your bills. However, it has never been sufficient to pay your bills and fund a retirementplan.

It is an easy problem to fix. Make your retirement plan the first creditor you will pay. The first check that you write every year should be to this plan. It should also be the single largest check that you write.

If you are short of cash to cover the check, then borrow the cash. You will discover that all of your other expenses will adjust themselves to make room for this disbursement. If you later find that your business has only broken even at the end of the year, it has not been a complete disaster. Remember, you paid yourself first!

What amount is an appropriate contribution to your retirement plan? Make the largest contribution that the law will allow. It should not be less than 25 percent of your salary. Some retirement plans will permit you to contribute a far greater amount. Do it!

When you have learned to pay yourself first, you have all the ingredients of making your business your best investment.

YOU ARE WORTH THE INVESTMENT

LESSON

THERE IS NO BETTER INVESTMENT THAN YOUR BUSINESS AND ITS FULLY FUNDED PENSION PLAN.

The math begins to look quite sporty after only a few years of making large contributions to your retirement plan. It does not take an insightful entrepreneur to see that his retirement plan can be worth far more than his business.

That is not to suggest that your business efforts have been wasted. Do not forget that the contributions to your retirement plan came from your business.

In order to build equity in your retirement plan, you must first succeed in building equity in your business. That is the starting point in retiring without risk.

If your business is worth $500,000 after thirty years of entrepreneurial risk, that is an accomplishment.

Contributing $10,000 a year to a retirement plan over that period of time is also an accomplishment. If your retirement plan earned interest at 8 percent, it would be worth over $1.1 million. If it earned interest at 10 percent, it would be worth over $1.6 million.

It is the combination of a salable business and a fully funded retirement plan that makes your business your best investment.

There is no more magic to making your business your best investment. The steps are simple ones:

1. Start a business within your abilities where customers will pay for value.
2. Set up a retirement plan.
3. Manage your business by controlling risk.
4. Contribute the maximum amount to your retirement plan.
5. Repeat steps 3 and 4 until satisfied with your investment results.
6. Convert the residual value of your business to cash by selling it.

There is no specific period of time that you must follow these steps. I have seen great investment results for some entrepreneurs achieved in less than five years. I have also seen many situations where fifty years of self-employment risk have not been enough time.

Each of you will move toward your goals and objectives at a different pace. As long as you are satisfied, that is fine. Entrepreneurs have always been their own toughest customers.

32

ONE FINAL POINT

➤ A Bird in the Bush.

There is little left for you to know about running a business after reading this book.

To be sure, changing market conditions and tax laws will always require localized adjustments of these equity-building principles. The principles themselves, however, should guide you reassuringly from your first investment to your best investment.

There is, of course, one slight catch. That involves getting off the seat of your pants and doing it.

A BIRD IN THE BUSH

LESSON

START TODAY. YOU ARE WORTH THE INVESTMENT.

Two young men were climbing a mountain to talk to the wise man who lived there. On their climb, they found a bird that had snagged itself in some branches and had broken its wings.

When they got to the top of the mountain, one of the young men told the other:

> "We'll see if this man is truly a wise man. I'll hold the bird behind my back and ask him if I have a live bird in my hand. If he tells me 'No,' I'll show him the live bird. If he tells me 'Yes,' I'll wring its neck and show him a dead bird."

They found the wise man and stood in front of him. Holding the bird behind his back, the young man asked his question:

> "Wise man, is the bird I am holding in my hand alive or dead?"

The wise man paused for a moment and then answered:

"Son, whether that bird lives or dies is up to you."

The decision to make your business your best investment has always been yours.

When are you going to get started?

SUMMARY OF LESSONS

You are no longer the same individual who started reading this book. You are smarter, you are focused, and you now know a thing or two about business risk. That knowledge puts you ahead of the curve. It also puts you in front of your competition. Congratulations are in order. You have taken a solid first step toward making your business your best investment.

There are other steps you must also take.

Managing any business has always been a full-time job. It is a job made easier once you develop the skills to recognize business risk.

Learning how to recognize business risk no longer has to be an expensive or dicey process for you. Read these lessons every week and absorb them. In time, they will become part of your entrepreneurial profile. That profile is the same one you see in successful entrepreneurs with years of relevant business experience.

They have made it. Now it is your turn.

1

SOME BASIC REQUIREMENTS FOR ENTREPRENEURS

There is no such thing
as wealth without risk.

Do not waste your time starting a business
unless you are totally committed to it.

Stamina will help to carry you
over the rough spots in any business.

The growth rate of your business
depends on your ability to sell.

Your best opportunity
begins the day you invest in yourself.

2

SOME BASIC CONCEPTS ABOUT BUILDING WEALTH

The real equity in any business
is often affected by your ability
to convert assets to cash.

❖

It is easier to run a business
when you control the risks in it.

❖

Stop paying risk premiums.
Start collecting them.

3

HOW TO ASSESS RISK

The biggest risk in any business can
be the way you personally feel about risk.

❖

Assessing business risk
involves finding a level of risk
for which you will be paid
as long as you own your business.

❖

Every customer has a sword in one hand
and a bag of gold in the other.
When you have properly assessed
customer risk, you will get the bag of gold
without falling on the sword.

❖

Assessing market risk is a matter
of paying attention to what is
happening outside of your business.

❖

You can reduce your exposure to
dependency risk simply by recognizing it.

4
EXCESSIVE RISK

No two individuals feel the same way about business risk.

❖

You can change your tolerance for risk.

5
REASONABLE RISK

You can control business risk.

❖

It is easier to control risk if you think ahead.

❖

Do not wait for a big loss before you get serious about controlling risk.

6
FALSE STARTS ARE INEVITABLE

Do not expect to be paid a risk premium when you have no business risk.

❖

Limit your scope of service with any single customer.

❖

Do not work full time for customers who will only pay you quarter-time prices.

❖

Do not expect to be paid professional rates for an undeveloped expertise.

7
LOOKING FOR OPPORTUNITY

Paralysis can occur when you
mistakenly believe
you are the victim
of other people's choices.

❖

There is no opportunity to build we
with reasonable risks by
acquiring nonincome-producing
assets at fair market value prices.

❖

An opportunity
with a guaranteed return
is not always a low-risk opportunity.

❖

Look for your first opportunity
in a business you know something about.

8
DO YOU REALLY NEED A PARTNER?

If you have the talent
and all of the capital
you may not need a partner.

❖

Some look at customers and say,
this is my market. Others
look at the market and say,
those are my customers.

❖

Your partners must share
similar work ethics.

Keep your money partners informed
about their investment risks.

Insist that your return
in any partnership
be proportional to your risk.

Never accept a minority ownership interest
where you have no voting rights.

A 50 percent ownership interest
is no guarantee that your other partner
will ever consider you an equal.

When a partnership
has met its business objectives,
terminate the partnership.

9

THE CHALLENGE WITH BANKS

Banks will agree to share
your business risk for a fee.

Do not sit down with a loan officer
until you have practiced
talking about yourself.

It is easier to borrow money when you
can demonstrate you do not need it.

The ease of borrowing money
increases in direct proportion to the
number of qualified loan guarantors.

Your loan proposal must look serious
if you want to borrow serious money.

Draw a picture of the assets
that are not on your balance sheet.

Banks will try to secure their loans
so they do not need to worry
about the risks in your business.

A large retirement account balance
reveals that you have been serious
about building wealth.

Banks are reluctant
to finance their competitors.

Do not be casual
about accepting the terms
offered in an equity credit line.

A financial data base
will level the playing field.

BUYING IN

Every business owner
will one day have a reason
to sell the business.

Do not rush to close the deal
when you buy a mismanaged business.

When you buy a business,
pay only for what is there today.
The future of that business
and whatever value is hidden there
already belongs to you.

A seller may be entitled to receive a
premium when he has sold the business
but has kept the risk.

It is easier to teach the
consequence of poor risk control
two hundred feet above the ground.

Fair market value
is the most you should pay
for any business.

If you cannot negotiate an advantage
in a proposed business acquisition,
you should either hire the seller
or walk away from the acquisition.

11

CREATING VALUE FOR YOUR CUSTOMERS

Customers will pay for value
only when they see it.

The value of a service
is directly related to the level of relief
the customer receives.

When you increase your rate of return,
you also increase your business wealth.

Value billing is a great way
to increase your rate of return.

Value can be judged
through the eyes of the customer.

You cannot recognize value
when you know nothing about it.

Let your customers pick
two of the three service components
that are valuable to them.

12
THE OPPORTUNITIES WITH CUSTOMERS

Not every individual
who requires your services
deserves to be your customer.

Say good-bye
to your Level III customers.

A quality product
offered at a fair price makes
it easy to cross-sell any customer.

Obtain the customer's permission
before you solve his problem.

Any proposal by a service provider
must start by correctly identifying
the customer's pain.

Customers will gladly agree to your solution
if it makes their pain go away.

A broad mix of customers
reduces your exposure to business risk.

Place your shots
at new Level II customers.

13
THE CHALLENGES WITH CUSTOMERS

Large customers
lose much of their leverage
when you diversify your customer base.

Require all small customers
to be cash-paying customers.

Do not extend credit
unless you are prepared
to bill all customers promptly.

Be firm about getting paid.
You can go to the beach for free.
Why should you work for free?

Examine a customer's credit report
before you extend serious business credit.

Stay away from customers
with litigious histories.

Professional customers
will pick your pockets.

14
THE OPPORTUNITIES WITH EMPLOYEES

Good employees drive their positions.

The head is the most important part
of any employee.

Every hive must
have its share of worker bees.

Every dollar has an emotional value.

Handcuffs made from gold
do not require any key.

Employees are partner material
when they consistently overperform
and begin thinking like an owner.

15
THE CHALLENGE WITH EMPLOYEES

Be sure that you are qualified to coach
before you hire any employees.

List only relevant job requirements
when you advertise for employees.

No one has the right to eat your profits.

When you hire employees,
tell them how and when they will be
evaluated for merit increases.

Firing an employee
is usually the end result
of a poor hiring decision.

When you fire an employee,
give him your complete attention
until he is out the door.

An employee who you discharge
for misconduct is not entitled
to receive unemployment benefits.

16

HOW TO AVOID SHOOTING YOURSELF IN THE FOOT

Keep your business relationship separate
from all other relationships.

Eliminate entertainment as a normal
and customary business expense.

A customer who buys you lunch
has just established the value of your time.

Decline all employee advance requests.

Never cosign a loan unless you
put the entire loan amount into your
business and you control the business.

Never guarantee a loan for an
income-producing asset beyond your
proportional interest in the asset.

You cannot solve a problem
by throwing money at it.

17
YOUR TIME IS MONEY

Customers will learn to value your time
only when you do too.

You can easily create wealth
when you turn off your TV set.

Customers will pay you more for comfort
than any other technical skill.

Your appointment will see you sooner
if you stay on your feet.

Do not agree to any sales demonstration
that you have not personally requested.

Manage your time
with the word "No"
and your To Do list.

Your employees will have time to do their
jobs when they stop attending meetings.

18
TIME DECAY

Bad time decay
is the consequence
of many minor mistakes.

Time works for you
when you know your costs
and understand your risks.

Waiting for your business to build
wealth can sometimes be the
most difficult thing to do.

Pay attention to your business.

Time usually works against you
in an unfamiliar business.

19
CAPITAL INVESTMENTS

Every business
requires an equity investment.

The only reason to buy an asset
is for the income it produces.

Insist on fast paybacks
for all asset acquisitions.

Analyze the profit contribution of
each asset before you buy it.

Equipment leasing offers a
variety of ways to make
poor capital investments.

You always pay for the
flexibility in the lease.

Unlike well-managed businesses,
there is an overabundance of office space.

You do not need a daytime office
to have a full-time business.

20

COMPUTERIZING YOUR BUSINESS

There is more to
automating your accounting
system than buying a computer.

Technical support contracts
will increase the cost of your system.

"Sounds like a hardware problem" is
really technical support's way of letting
you know they are in over their heads.

You cannot automate an accounting
system that has no internal controls.

A request for proposal offers
some assurance that the system you buy
will actually meet your specifications.

21

SOME FINER POINTS OF RUNNING YOUR BUSINESS

Your integrity will make you a leader.

Take the credit when you
have been worth the risk.

Do not overreact to changes
in the performance of your business.

❖

There is more to building your equity than the element of finance. Balance the other elements of equity growth with an annual plan.

22
RISK ADJUSTMENTS

Make the adjustment if it helps you sleep better at night and is less expensive than your future losses.

❖

It may be less expensive to pay for the adjustment than to pay for the continual exposure to risk.

❖

The marketplace will tell you at what price to make your risk adjustment.

❖

All risk adjustments require time to work.

❖

Do not spend your time and effort adjusting for every minor risk.

23
NOW HANG HIM!

The consequence of ignoring business risk should be a hanging offense.

❖

Risk control is your job
when you own the business.

There are no degrees of responsibility.
You are either responsible
or you are out of business.

24

BANKRUPTCY, THE ULTIMATE RISK ADJUSTMENT

Filing a bankruptcy petition
is one way to control risk when your
business is spinning out of control.

Customers who file for bankruptcy
can still be good cash-paying customers.

If you are not an attorney, disengage
whenever payment of your professional
fees is contingent upon court approval.

25

LIVING WITH YOUR LOSSES

You can have your share of losses
and still be a successful entrepreneur.

Some losses will occur when
you least expect them and can do
nothing to change the result.

It is time to stop taking risks
when you are addicted to them
and you do not like the results.

It is time to move on when
your business burns more
equity than it builds.

❖

Close the business
when you cannot stop the losses.

26
BETTING IN SIZE

Poor financial data is at
the root of all business failures.

❖

Variable expenses cushion business risk.

❖

Reduce the work
when you reduce the staff.

❖

It doesn't take an advertising genius
to spend 19 percent of gross revenues
on advertising and get great results.

❖

Be sure to keep your good customers
when you decrease your expenses.

27
WORKING WITH PROFESSIONALS

Self-taught brain surgery is
expensive even for those individuals
who can afford to pay for their mistakes.

❖

Manage your professional advisor
with written boundaries.

❖

Require your professional advisor to put his fee estimate in writing.

A professional advisor can either die a natural death at the end of an engagement or be fired by you before that time.

A coach can see the potential and the limit of your talent far more clearly than you can.

28
LIVING WITH CONTRACTS AND DOCUMENTS

Read every word in a contract before you sign it.

Make sure your rights under any agreement are just as strong as the rights of the other party to the agreement.

Do not waste time with agreements if you permit nonsensical revisions to them.

Sign legal documents when they say what you want them to say.

You can only lose a case in a deposition.

29
THE TAXMAN COMETH

Tax laws are voted upon by the same congressional representatives who voted for their own pay increases and who want to be reelected by their constituents.

Do not start your business until you have resolved with finality all past tax matters.

Offer to compromise your tax liability when there is no realistic possibility for you to pay it.

The three-year statute of limitations never starts to run if you never file your return.

Ease your burden of proof by filing your federal return certified mail, return receipt requested.

A competent CPA is a must for understanding relevant tax law changes.

It is the mission of the Internal Revenue Service to ensure that you pay the correct amount of tax—not one dollar more than the law requires you to pay and not one dollar less.

30

SELLING OUT

You will waste much of the effort that went into building your business if you do not understand what is involved in selling it.

The most precise measure of the value of your business is the amount of cash that a buyer will pay for it.

Valuation reports paid for by the seller are an indication of what the seller thinks his business is worth. That value is probably not the real value of the business.

A rough-cut valuation will give you an estimate of the value of your business.

Unless you are the world's greatest salesperson, never try to sell a business by yourself.

A one-shot takeout solves all valuation disputes.

31

RETIRE WITHOUT RISK

Plan your retirement today while time is on your side.

Some premature withdrawal penalties
that apply to retirement funds
are there for your protection.

Your congressional representative
will do nothing about the greatest
financial debacle of all time.

Write a check to your retirement
account the first business
day of every year.

There is no better investment
than your business and its
fully funded pension plan.

32
ONE FINAL POINT

Start today.
You are worth the investment.

REVIEW QUESTIONS

1. The ability to sell is a nonessential skill for self-employed entrepreneurs.

2. Equity is the value of your business after the assets in it have been converted to cash and everything has been repaid.

3. Academic credentials and letters of reference are the most important parts of any employee.

4. When a customer is fully sold on your services, cross-selling is almost a matter of simply asking for the work.

5. As long as you own 50 percent of the business, your partner will always consider you an equal.

6. Assessing market risk is a matter of paying attention to what is happening inside your business.

7. A forward motion premium is an incremental value that a buyer may decide to pay for a business that knows where it is going.

8. Entrepreneurs who have successfully controlled customer risk are those who have extended additional credit in order to keep a nonpaying customer solvent.

9. Customers always mean what they say.

10. You can be assured that any employee salary discussion you hold behind closed doors will be kept in strict confidence.

11. Any risk for which you are not paid is excess risk.

12. Logic is one road to entrepreneurial success. Feelings are one road to personal success. Reverse them, and disaster is guaranteed.

13. Risk adjustments always work even if the marketplace no longer functions reliably.

14. The marketplace will always pay you risk premiums even when you have no business risk.

15. Rebalancing your risk-and-return relationships is usually more expensive than continuing to pay for unfavorable variances.

16. Customers will pay your professional rates as long as you let them know you are starting a new business.

17. When you pay a bonus to an employee who has not earned it, the recipient will usually consider that payment part of his nonnegotiable, nonreducible base compensation.

18. Once you develop the ability to identify variable expenses, expense control is almost a natural event.

19. An Offer in Compromise is a tool that entrepreneurs normally use to negotiate better financing terms and conditions from their banks.

20. Your partners will always recognize the direct relationship between their work and your business results.

21. Most accounting systems in entrepreneurial operations are notable for their strong internal control features.

22. Unpaid federal tax liabilities from your old business venture cannot affect the operations of your new business.

23. It is a good idea to let your money partners know about all of the problems facing their investment in you.

24. Value billing permits you to receive a rate of return for your work that is commensurate with the value to a customer.

25. In order to be extraordinary in the eyes of your customer, you must have at least one graduate degree and three professional certifications.

26. Becoming a partner can be an opportunity to lose your friends, incinerate your savings, forfeit your self-esteem, and forever put to rest your misplaced belief in your good business judgment.

27. Never accept a minority ownership interest where you have no voting rights.

28. The outcome in legal battles is always predictable and can be a reliable substitute for good judgment.

29. The best way to make an affordable risk adjustment is to make the adjustment contingent on some arbitrary price.

30. When a partnership has achieved its business objectives and further synergistic results are no longer possible, it may be time to terminate the partnership.

31. Cosigning a bank loan for a family member is a great way to keep a family together.

32. You have every reason to expect an optimistic settlement after a customer files for bankruptcy protection.

33. Planning will dispel every uncertainty in your business.

34. As long as you know your business, any bank loan officer will be sympathetic to your loan request.

35. Any attorney who does not represent your interests is still obligated to advise you of the contents of any legal document.

36. All banks recognize your retirement contributions as an alternative form of owner compensation.

37. There is always a second or third chance to control any business risk.

38. Professional fees usually have some correlation to the scope and complexity of the work.

39. The access to capital markets is largely a relational matter.

40. Time, just like any other business asset, must enter and exit the conversion process before it has any value.

41. When the buyer of a business can keep the seller at risk, the seller may also be entitled to receive some of the future returns of the business.

42. Entrepreneurial businesses are generally known for the speed at which an equity investment in them can be converted to cash.

43. You can charge for value even if you are the only one who recognizes it as long as you are a member in good standing with the National Organization for Value Added Services.

44. Capital budgeting is a systematic and rational method of planning for fixed-asset purchases and retirement.

45. You can reduce your exposure to dependency risk simply by taking the time to identify your dependencies.

46. When employees feel the price they have paid for job security is too high, they ask for a raise.

47. The profit in technical support services is one reason why software vendors price accounting software packages so inexpensively.

48. If you leave reason behind in any value billing arrangement, customers may also wonder if you are worth the premium.

49. You can control all the variables that affect the risk in any business investment.

50. Building equity in your business is easier once you know how to stop giving away your goods and services.

51. Every individual who requires your service deserves to be your customer.

52. Making your business your best investment is a task that is far easier done without the additional burden of Level III customers.

53. Excessive risk is just too darn much risk, whether you are paid for it or not.

54. A deposing attorney that is nice to you wants to be your friend.

55. Balancing your customers may involve prospecting for new Level II customers.

56. A partnership is a financial marriage of entrepreneurial objectives.

57. Level III customers will bring numerous profitable service opportunities to your business.

58. The full benefit of any value billing arrangement comes from retaining the eternal loyalty of the customer.

59. Customers belong to the firm that first acquires them.

60. It is always financially prudent to build revenues at the expense of declining operating margins.

61. Billing promptly for your goods or services is an optional step in the process of converting assets to cash.

62. It is a simple matter to sustain value billing even where goods or services are generically available.

63. Customers with memory lapses are federally protected by the Customer Disabilities Act of 1994.

64. A professional customer is knowledgeable in using your inexperience to build wealth in his core business.

65. Employees with the ability to drive their positions usually offer you strengths you can use immediately in your business.

66. Although the meat cleaver approach to expense reduction can be messy and has a tendency to produce unanticipated results and unpredictable results, it usually works.

67. Road Warriors are motivated by fixed salaries, routine schedules, and an annual cost of living adjustment.

68. When employees begin to think of the incentives you offer as entitlements, you need to think of a few additional incentives to satisfy them.

69. Selling a business involves the same magnitude of risks as the ones you took to build the business.

70. You cannot have a successful business without having a business partner who shares your work and the related business risk.

71. It is an easier task to make your business your best investment when you combine your business and personal relationships.

72. One difficulty in establishing value effectively in a service business is that individual customers and clients pay your bills, not the marketplace.

73. The element that you exclude from risk assessment may be the one that will damage you the most.

74. Business lunches are a great way to teach customers how to value your professional time.

75. It is prudent to personally guarantee a $100,000 loan for a business as long as you receive at least 25 percent of the profits in the business.

76. A cash call is a provision that allows a prompt method of solving problems to any business partnership that is having operating difficulties.

77. Changing market conditions and tax laws will always require localized adjustments of equity-building principles.

78. You can increase your rate of return when customers readily recognize the value in the service you provide.

79. Successful entrepreneurs are good at creating on paper a series of cash inflows to support any proposed capital asset acquisition.

80. A lease with a high residual value is a conservative way to finance new business equipment.

81. The biggest risk in any business can be the way you personally feel about risk.

82. When a technical support specialist tells you that it sounds like a hardware problem, you should immediately contact the vendor who sold you the computer.

83. Business forecasts occasionally need to be met not only for the good of the business, but for the satisfaction of the lender.

84. An entrepreneur who lacks integrity generally has a rudderless sense of fairness and responsibility.

85. Building equity means accumulating the greatest amount of financial assets in the shortest amount of time to the exclusion of any other factors that may affect your life.

86. You have failed in your initial assessment of business risk when you later make a risk-reducing adjustment.

87. When you clearly no longer care about assuming responsibility for the risk in your business, you may be a candidate for bankruptcy.

88. It is a vote of creditor confidence when your creditors force you to file a bankruptcy petition.

89. Tunnel vision is not particularly helpful when you are losing equity.

90. The true measure of a professional advisor is the number of academic degrees and professional designations listed after his name.

91. Boundaries make a job easier to manage and the result easier to measure.

92. Banks make great investments for their shareholders and diversify their lending risk to entrepreneurial businesses by securing independent sources of repayment.

93. A deposition is a good place to make the legal points for your case.

94. It is the mission of the Internal Revenue Service to assess and collect as much tax as they possibly can.

95. It is a time-tested rule that a service business usually sells for 1.3 times gross revenues.

96. Valuation reports paid by the seller are usually a reliable indicator of the true value of the business.

97. Disengaging from business risk can involve some considerable planning if you want to retire without risk.

98. The Social Security funds withheld from your paycheck are remitted to an account that will accumulate a retirement benefit that is specifically earmarked for your benefit.

99. The strength of any legal document is directly proportional to the professional fees that you paid to have it prepared.

100. Building equity in any business involves identifying opportunities with real value and putting capital at risk.

INDEX

D

N

O

P

Q

R

S

T

U

V

W

Y